With Them were Ten Thousand and More

ORATORIO SOCIETY

Of Salt Lake City

Empress Theatre

THE MESSIAH

January 1, 1915

With Them were Ten Thousand and More

The Authorized History of The Oratorio Society of Utah

Marcus Sidney Smith

Published
Through the Generosity of
Edith S. Anderson

Actaeon Books

In fond memory of
Dr. Howard T. Anderson
whose enthusiasm and guidance
awakened and nurtured
my interest in
oratorio

Published in the United States of America
ACTAEON BOOKS
P. O. BOX 520068
SALT LAKE CITY, UTAH 84152-0068

Printed in the United States of America
PUBLISHER'S PRESS
Salt Lake City, Utah

Library of Congress Catalog Card Number 88–82639
ISBN 0-9621403-0-9

The cover of the first Salt Lake Oratoril Society Messiah program reproduced on page ii is by courtesy of the University of Utah Library Special Collections Department and the Arthur Freber manuscript collection

Contents

In a great auditorium sat the choirs and the ministers of all the churches. **With them were 10,000 and more**—*men and women from every part of the city. They knew no sect, no religious distinction, they had no thought of material affairs.*

It was Sunday evening near Christmas. One people had assembled to lift one voice to one God—to pour out their souls in informal worship. Handel's Messiah *was being sung.*

Outside, the trees bowed reverently, burdened under white mantles. The moon covered all with a halo of light. Peace pervaded the air—such peace as one feels in the mountains or on the sea.

Then rose the great chorus singing "Glory to God in the highest, peace on earth, good will toward men."

Squire Coop, *Deseret Evening News* 16 December 1916

Preface

In undertaking to write the history of the Oratorio Society of Utah it soon became apparent that the most obvious and fundamental questions could not be answered, perhaps not even properly asked, without first surveying the pioneer musical activity from which the Society developed. Were Salt Lake music a subject on which a comprehensive body of literature already existed, this would have been easily done, a short summary abstracted, and a suggestion or two added as to what additional works the interested reader might consult. But relatively little has been written about the musical history of Salt Lake City. Many of the early organizations and musicians are all but lost to memory. Especially obscure is the wonderful diversity of backgrounds, interests, and hopes that were shared among the pioneer musicians, the multiplicity of faiths they represented, and the important contributions these dedicated men and women, Mormon and non-Mormon alike, made to the welfare of the greater community.

Without reference to these early musicians, their organizations, and the dreams their struggles were meant to fulfill, it is not possible to understand why the Oratorio Society should ever have come into existence. For this reason what may seem a disproportionately large part of the present work has been given over to an introductory section on the almost seventy years of Salt Lake musical activity that preceded the Society's founding. And in the case of symphonic music, because of the important part it played, the introduction intrudes into the Society's early decades. It is by no means an exhaustive account of Pioneer music, to which volumes could be devoted, but it is, I believe, accurate and fair if somewhat thinly drawn.

It is based on records gleaned primarily from the *Deseret News*, *Salt Lake Daily Herald*, *The Salt Lake Tribune*, Church of Jesus Christ of Latter-day Saints (LDS) Archives Journal History, collections held by the Manuscript Section of the Special Collections Department in the University of Utah library and by the Utah State Historical Society, and from the precious few books and articles that treat the subject.

The story of the Oratorio Society itself rests on similarly obtained information—including that from several private collections. From this research I soon learned that considerable myth had developed concerning the early days of the Society. This was myth in which I, along with many others, had come to believe, so that I had not only to dig out the available facts, but to give up a good many preconceptions along the way.

The reader can scarcely overlook the strained feelings that occasionally arose between the Society and some other organizations and individuals. There is nothing that has come to my attention, however, that would indicate this ever involved more than the natural competitiveness of musicians striving for recognition in a highly prized field of endeavor. Certainly the LDS Church, one of the major influences in all aspects of Utah life and culture, could scarcely have taken a more charitable attitude toward the Society than the one evidenced in granting it use of the Salt Lake Tabernacle. As much as any other single element, it was the use of this world famous building that helped elevate the Society to the prominent place it now enjoys among American choral organizations, and for this the Society remains ever appreciative.

Because of the many thousands of persons who have been involved with the Oratorio Society, it is anticipated that many readers will wish to verify the participation of relatives, close friends, or even their own participation. To accommodate them, three appendices have been included which list names in what is hoped will prove a convenient manner. Concerning two of these, however, a few words are warranted. Due to frequent periods for which no records are available, that portion of Appendix B which lists chorus officers and functionaries is necessarily incomplete. This is also true of the second part of Appendix C, the long list of chorus members, where there has been the additional problem of avoiding duplicate entries. This has been made difficult by the long period of time the chorus has been in existence, the haphazard way in which early records were kept, and the fact that chorus members have not always been consistent in the way they listed their names, thus confronting the author with the problem, by way of example, of deciding if C. H. Jones, C. Henry Jones, Charles H. Jones, and Charles Henry Jones—all of which might be given on various chorus lists—represent one person or, perhaps, several. In practice, duplicates have been removed and where variations have given the appearance of belonging to one person, they have been reduced to a common denominator—for example, C. H. Jones. In some instances, however, long periods separating one form from another, or simultaneous entries, have led to the conclusion that two or more persons must have shared variations on the same name, and in such cases all are listed.

A word concerning two of the newspapers frequently quoted in these pages also seems advisable. Though both the *Deseret News* and the *Salt Lake Herald* went through numerous name changes (which are reflected in the notes), for the sake of uniformity they are referred to in the following text either by these, their simplest names, or by the shortened forms of the *News* and the *Herald.*

There were many times during the preparation of this book when I feared that if the natural brevity of the human life span did not prevent my finishing, microfilm-induced blindness would. Finally though, I have finished my work, such as it is, and I hope that those who have participated in the Society, those who have enjoyed its music over the years, and those who are just plain interested in the historical development of the Society and of Salt Lake music in general, will derive from it some pleasure and benefit. Nothing could please me more.

There are a number of people without whose help and advice this book would have been much more difficult, if not impossible, to write. Foremost among them are the late Dr. Howard T. Anderson and his widow, Mrs. Edith S. Anderson. The former, throughout his life-long association with the Oratorio Society, made a habit of collecting all manner of Society memorabilia, including minutes of board meetings, financial reports, letters to and from the important soloists who appeared with the Society, and much more. Following Dr. Anderson's death, Mrs. Anderson, who now serves on the Society Board, continued the doctor's habit of saving documents, clippings, and mementos. Much of this material had recently been donated to the University of Utah Library Special Collections Department, and whether by Mrs. Anderson or by the wonderfully cooperative library staff, all of it was made available for my use. Also, from her own collection and elsewhere, it was Mrs. Anderson who supplied, or arranged for, many of the photographs contained in this volume—a considerable task for which she has my heartfelt thanks. And not the least of Mrs. Anderson's contributions has been the encouragement and the generous financial support she has given this project, so that it is no exaggeration to say that without her, this book could never have been written.

Another important contributor has been John Marlowe Nielson, the Society's recently retired music director, who made available his own collection of Society memorabilia covering his twenty-five years with the Society. Likewise, the scrapbooks of Society chorus member Jeanne Wignall Ames have proven very helpful for the period from 1945 through the early 1960s.

Others who have been helpful include the staffs of the Church of Jesus Christ of Latter-day Saints Historical and Genealogical Libraries and Archives, the Utah State Historical Society, University of Utah Archives, and the University of Utah Vice-president's Office; Daniel Luckenbill, assistant to the archivist at the University of California at Los Angeles (UCLA); and Carol Reid Briggs, manuscript librarian and archivist of the William Andrews Clark Memorial Library on the UCLA campus. I also wish to thank Society President Richard G. Horak, Society Vice-president for Productions and former Society contralto soloist, Annette Richardson Dinwoodey, Chorus Secretary Helen Wilcox, former Production Manager M. A. (Denny) Bird, and the families of John W. Summerhays, Royal W. Daynes, and Squire Coop, all of whom have made material available; and especially, all the Society chorus members and Board members who responded to questionnaires. In addition, I thank *The Salt Lake Tribune*, *Deseret News*, *Ogden Standard-Examiner*, and the *Provo*

Daily Herald for permission to quote from their respective publications; and the University of Utah Library Special Collections Department for permission to quote from documents in their files.

Very special thanks is due four persons. Dr. James H. Wolfe cheerfully read the manuscript while it was still in its formative stages, parts of it more than once, and his keen intellect and sound judgment were responsible for many important suggestions. S. Paul Smith did likewise, and his sensitivity to artistic and literary considerations has proven invaluable. More recently the manuscript was read by two long-time Society members whose suggestions and insights have also proven extremely helpful. These were Mrs. Dinwoodey, who has already been mentioned as a contributor of valuable information, and Justice J. Allan Crockett, director emeritus of the Board.

Final editing was by Tom Zeidler, whose experience and skill saved the finished book from any number of blunders and grotesqueries.

University of Utah Library Special Collections

George Careless conducted Utah's first Oratorio Society, the nondenominational Handel and Haydn Society, in the first Mountain West rendition of *Messiah* on June 3, 1875, in the Salt Lake Theater.

PART ONE

The Origins of Salt Lake Music

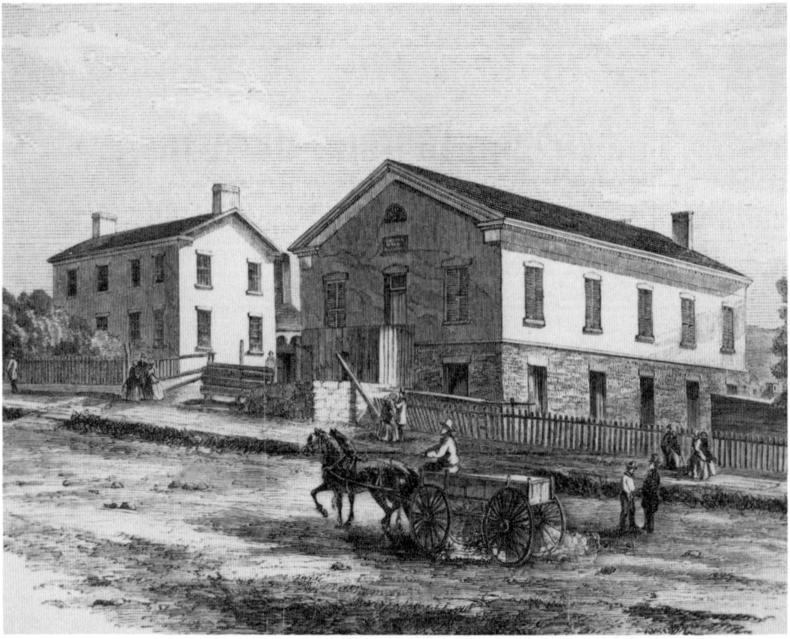

Utah State Historical Society

Social Hall (building in forground) was home to the most important Salt Lake City musical, dramatic, and social events from the time of its opening in 1852 until the construction of the Salt Lake Theater in 1862. This engraving of the venerable old building appeared in *Harpers Weekly* of December 4, 1858.

CHAPTER ONE

The First Musicians

From its founding during 1914 and the early weeks of 1915 through the time of this writing in 1988, the Oratorio Society of Utah has presented four renditions of Beethoven's *Christ on the Mount of Olives*, nine of Mendelssohn's *Elijah,* twelve of Haydn's *The Creation*, and seventy-two of Handel's immortal *Messiah.* One of the oldest active oratorio societies in the western United States, it is also the oldest continuously active independent major musical organization in Salt Lake City. Only the Church of Jesus Christ of Latter-day Saints (LDS) sponsored Mormon Tabernacle Choir is older, and of all Utah musical organizations, only the Tabernacle Choir, the Utah Symphony, and the Oratorio Society are of sufficiently far reaching fame to warrant inclusion in the internationally prestigious *Encyclopaedia Britannica.*

Formerly known as the Salt Lake Oratorio Society (its name was changed in 1975), it is the natural and perhaps the inevitable outgrowth of the musical tradition that preceded it. Its roots lie deep in the development of pioneer music. Its founders, Mormon and non-Mormon alike, drew their inspiration and their ambition from the most exalted of pioneer aspirations.

The elements of Salt Lake City's musical culture, like its settlers, were gathered from such far away places as Kirtland, Ohio; Nauvoo, Illinois; from the Mormon Church's London mission; Germany; and even from Australia, where Joseph Ridges constructed the first great church organ ever to be played in the valley of the Great Salt Lake. In 1846, when continuing persecution made the Mormon exodus from Illinois inevitable, the first party to strike westward toward Nebraska included in its midst Captain William Pitt's Nauvoo Brass Band. This organization, reputed to have been converted to the faith en masse in England, declined, it is said, to accompany the Mormon Battalion to the Mexican war in California, choosing instead "to march with the camp of the Tabernacle" on its quest for a new Zion. Colonel Thomas Kane, one of the early chroniclers of LDS Church activities, told of its members that "they had led the farewell service in the Nauvoo Temple. Their office now was to guide the monster choruses and Sunday hymns; and like the trumpets of silver made of a whole piece, 'for the calling of the assembly, and for the journeying of the camps,' to knoll the people into church. Some of their wind instruments," he wrote, "were uncommonly full and pure toned, and in that clear dry air could be heard to a great distance. It had the strangest effect in the world, to listen to their sweet music winding over the uninhabited country; something in the style of a Moravian death tune blown at day-break, but altogether unique. It might be when you were hunting a ford over the great Platte," he recalled, "the dreariest of all wild rivers, perplexed among the far reaching sand bars and curlew shallows of its shifting bed;—the wind rising would bring you the first faint thought of a melody; and as you listened, borne down upon the gust that swept past you a cloud of the dry sifted sands, you recognized it—perhaps a home-loved theme of Henry Proch or Mendelssohn. Mendelssohn Bartholdy, away there in the Indian marches."[1]

The Mormon vanguard arrived in Salt Lake Valley during July 1847 and within days had marked out the site of present day Temple Square, heart of the new Mormon refuge. On it was built the first Bowery, a simple structure of poles roofed over with branches and brush, and it was here, on August 22, 1847, shaded from the desert sun, that the first Salt Lake general conference of the LDS Church was held and the forerunner of the Mormon Tabernacle Choir made its debut singing "The Spirit of God Like a Fire is Burning" and "From All that Dwell Below the Skies." It was here also that the band gave the valley's first concerts when precious moments could be spared from the herculean task of creating a new settlement.

Devout as they were, the early Mormons shared none of the Puritan's distaste for amusements and entertainments. They were avid dancers, lovers of music, and, after the devotions of their church itself, their greatest passion may have been the theater. In 1850, only three years after the Mormons entered the valley, the Nauvoo Brass Band, several of whose members were also enthusiastic actors, associated themselves with the newly organized Musical and Dramatic Company.

In the meantime a second Bowery had been constructed on the Temple block and it was here that the new theater company presented most of its work. Orchestra members for these early productions were almost all original members of the Nauvoo Band. Captain Pitt, a violinist and a flutist, continued as band master; Jacob F. Hutchinson played violin and clarinet; and James Smithies, future leader of the Tabernacle Choir, was cellist. Other members were David Smith and George Wardle (given by some sources as Warde) and these were joined, when they were not acting upon the stage, by John Kay, R. T. Burton, William Clayton and Horace K. Whitney.

In addition to musical accompaniment for dramatic productions, several Bowery concerts were given during 1850. In June of that year Salt Lake's pioneer newspaper, the weekly *Deseret News*, reported that "One thousand people...attended the concert last Saturday evening; and...all were not only satisfied but highly gratified,—and will be ready for more at a proper time."[2] Other programs billed as "Grand Concerts" were held in July, September, and November, and though it is probably unwise to over emphasize the quality or sophistication of the music, these concerts clearly indicate a lively interest during the earliest and most difficult years of settlement.

At about this same time an amusement house was built at Warm Springs on the northern outskirts of the young city. It was the home of Salt Lake's first string dance orchestra, consisting of Hopkins C. Pender, Jese Earl, and Jacob F. Hutchinson, and the scene of several important early social events.

Another important musical figure of this earliest period was Dominico Ballo. The exact date of his arrival in the valley is uncertain, but he arrived in time to form his own organization, Ballo's Band, and to lead it at a military ball given at Warm Springs by LDS Church President Brigham Young during December 1851. An Italian, he was a graduate of the Milan Conservatory of Music, and in this country he had been a successful clarinetist with New York orchestras and a bandmaster at West Point. In addition to his Salt Lake band, he organized a church orchestra for LDS functions and founded and operated Ballo's Music Hall, for several years one of the city's popular places of entertainment.

The building of the adobe Social Hall during 1852 was another important event in Salt Lake's earliest cultural and social development. Its auditorium measured forty by sixty feet and seated, depending on how tightly they were crowded in, between three and four hundred persons. The stage measured twenty by forty feet and the basement contained two dressing rooms and a banquet hall. With the Social Hall's opening the Musical and Dramatic Company was reorganized as the Deseret Dramatic Association with a greatly enlarged membership, including as honorary members President Young and other dignitaries of the LDS Church. Ballo's Band became the Social Hall theater orchestra and until the Salt Lake Theater was built in 1862, this small building remained the center of Salt Lake drama, dance, and music.

By 1855 the first of early Salt Lake's many musical societies was founded and the event subsequently announced in a letter published in both the *Deseret News* and the *Millennial Star*, an LDS publication printed in England:

> I have the pleasure to inform you that a Society by the [name of the Deseret Philharmonic Society] has been organized in the city, consisting already of upwards of fifty members, whose object is, the cultivation of all kinds of Vocal and Instrumental Music.
>
> By the counsel of President Brigham Young, br. James Smithies, the respected leader of the Tabernacle Choir is appointed President of the society, and conductor of the music. He will be assisted by br. John M. Jones as leader of the instrumental department.
>
> It is needless for me to expatiate on the advantages of such an organization, confined as it is to no band or party, but intended to combine the musical talent of the city, and to promote the love and study of harmony throughout the territory.
>
> I wish through you to inform our brethren and sisters preparing to come from Europe and the eastern states and who feel an interest in the objects of our society, as to what kind of music we are most in want of, so that it may be a little guide to them in their selection, which they can either donate or loan to the society on their arrival here.
>
> We are much in want of Oratorios of Handel, Haydn, Mendelssohn, &c.; the Masses of Mozart, Haydn, Beethoven &c., and new works of

merit; the whole with full orchestral accompaniment in separate parts, and as much as possible with singing copies in separate parts. We also want the best Overtures, Symphonies, and Dancing Music for a full orchestra; together with Quartets, Trios, Duets, Solos, Glees, Songs, &c.[3]

Among the society's activities were an address on the nature of music delivered by its secretary, Jonathan Grimshaw, before the Polysophical Society (another early organization formed with the encouragement of LDS Church leaders) and reprinted in the *Deseret News* of May 16, 1855. One of the more ambitious events, however, and one that inaugurated the city's career as the hub and driving force of territory-wide musical activity, was a tour undertaken by members of the society and others during August 1855, and subsequently recounted in another Grimshaw letter to the *Deseret News*. The following excerpts give a vivid insight into the esteem in which early Mormon leaders held music and musical activity, and into both the hardships and the simple pleasures of early pioneer life:

With the permission of President Brigham Young, a concert band was organized early this month, whose object was to visit the northern settlements of this Territory, giving concerts of vocal, brass, and orchestral music in the various school houses and boweries. The company consisted of John M. Jones, leader; Jonathan Grimshaw, clerk; Myron Brewer, treasurer, chaplain, and general spokesman; Philip Margetts, Henry Margetts, George Wardle, Joshua Midgley, Henry W. Baker, (who joined us at Bingham's Fort [later renamed Lynne]) and Alfred B. Lambson, teamster and doorkeeper; all but the teamster being members of the Nauvoo Brass Band.

We started on the morning of Monday the 13th Inst., and staid for the night at sister Baker's, Bingham's Fort, having made our business known as much as possible on our way, intending to perform on our return. We had a recommendation from Bishop Hunter to the Bishops of the north of this city.

On Tuesday the 14th Inst., we arrived at Box Elder [now Brigham City], and were kindly received and entertained by President Lorenzo Snow, and Bishop Pierce. These gentlemen advised us to postpone our concert until the next evening, and they would take steps that evening and the next day to circulate the news. Accordingly, on Wednesday evening we had the school room pretty well crowded, and I am happy to say, the people were much interested with the performance, and all expressed themselves as being highly gratified. This remark applies equally to the whole of the concerts we gave on the trip.

I am sorry to say, that just previous to our arrival at Box Elder, the grasshoppers had made a terrible descent on the corn and late crops, and had done incalculable damage. The wheat crop was all cut, and the people busy hauling it to their stacks; some had suffered severely, not so much from the grasshoppers, as from the extreme drouth, while on some of the wet bottom lands the crops had turned out first rate, averaging 45 bushels to the acre.— A large band of Indians from the neighborhood of Fort Hall, under the pretence of gleaning, are committing great depredations on the wheat still in the fields.

On Thursday, the 16th Inst., we proceeded to Willow Creek [now Willard], where sister Hubbard, in the absence of the bishop, her husband, did her best to make us comfortable, and was very anxious we should stay and give a concert that evening. Three of the resident brethren therefore kindly formed themselves into a committee, and went round to obtain subscribers, making arrangements for the concert to come off in the Bowery. Towards evening we were extremely gladdened by the arrival of Elder Parley P. Pratt, en route for this city. We immediately presented him with tickets, for which he thanked us in Spanish.— He honored us by opening the concert with a few remarks and prayer, and we had a good time, the concert being numerously attended. Bishop Hubbard was busy most of the day hauling wheat, in consequence of one of his hands being sick; but was released towards evening, and presided over the assembly. He has raised about a thousand bushels of wheat this season, and his brethren generally have done well, although they would have done better but for the scarcity of water. Bro. Zondal [probably a misspelling of Zundal] and others exerted themselves to entertain us to the best of their ability.

On Friday the 17th, we arrived at Ogden Hole [now known as Ogden Valley, in the vicinity of Eden], and were hospitably and nobly entertained by Bishop Thomas Dunn, and his brother Crandell Dunn. We gave a concert in the school house in the evening to a very respectable and somewhat numerous audience. This is a fine and prosperous settlement, although their wheat crops this year are considerably below the average.

On Saturday the 18th, we [returned] to Bingham's Fort, but owing to a thunder storm in the evening, and the indifference of the bishop, who is unquestionably a good man, but somewhat in years, we had a very poor turnout to the concert.

The letter continues with descriptions of the group's visits to Ogden City, Kay's Ward (since renamed Kaysville), and to Farmington, where the extremely poor harvest and resulting low spirits made a concert impossible. It concludes, finally, with the observation that although this was "the first experiment of the kind in the Territory, we consider it on the whole to be successful, and in improving the taste of the people for fine music, highly beneficial. At least it was so expressed by the various presidents and bishops on the route."[4]

Other personalities left a significant mark on this earliest period of pioneer music. Among them was Mrs. Sarah A. Cooke, who came to Salt Lake from England in 1852. In 1854 she began classes in sight singing and soon after, under the patronage of Brigham Young, presented *Flora's Festival* (a juvenile operetta by John Hill Hewitt) in Social Hall with Mrs. Luna Young as May Queen. Later still, after the arrival of the Ridges organ (see below), she was noted for her skill on that instrument. She was also an actress, both at Social Hall and the Salt Lake Theater; but her principal and lasting contribution was as a teacher of music and an instiller of enthusiastic appreciation for that "divine art," as music was often called by Salt Lakers.

David O. Calder, a Scotsman, came to Salt Lake the year following Mrs. Cooke's arrival. By late 1853 he had established a singing school in what Edward W. Tullidge, in his 1886 *History of Salt Lake City*, referred to as "Across Jordan." In addition to his musical ability, his clerical skill was early recognized and he spent several years as a clerk in President Young's office. By 1861, under Young's patronage, he had also established singing classes for several hundred students, which he instructed in the Curwen Tonic Sol-fa method, an English form of musical notation popular in the nineteenth century.

From these students he organized the Deseret Musical Association. Its purpose was to practice "the higher classes of anthems, choruses and glees,"[5] and it gave successful concerts well into the 1860s. At one point he transcribed Bellini's *La Sonnambula* into Curwen Tonic notation with the idea that the Deseret Musical Association could present it in concert. But a personal tragedy intervened. According to Tullidge, the sudden death of five of his children from diphtheria so undermined his own health that he was forced to resign; and deprived of his energetic guidance the musical association quickly succumbed to the dissolution and failure that were to bedevil nearly all pioneer musical organizations.[6]

The first Tabernacle on Temple Square, an adobe building on a stone foundation now commonly referred to as the old Tabernacle, was completed on the sight of the present Assembly Hall in 1851. It measured 126 by 64 feet and seated 2,500 persons. For several years thereafter the Tabernacle Choir was accompanied by the instrumental music of such organizations as Captain Pitt's Nauvoo Band and Ballo's Church Orchestra, but in 1857 Utah's first large organ arrived from half a world away.

Joseph Harris Ridges, an Englishman, had gone to Australia to hunt for gold and while there was converted to the Mormon faith.

Unsuccessful in his quest for riches, he settled in Sydney where he worked as a carpenter and in his spare time fulfilled a childhood ambition by building a church organ, reputedly the first such instrument ever built on that continent. At the urging of the Church, the organ was shipped to California on the schooner *Jenny Lind* and, accompanied by the Ridges Family, carried overland in mule-drawn wagons to the Salt Lake Valley. It was installed in the old Tabernacle and first played on October 11, 1857.

The first rude shock to the Mormons' emerging culture, a shock from which in some ways it would never recover, was the "invasion" of 1858. Initially the occupying force, known as Johnston's Army and led by Col. Albert Sydney Johnston, consisted of twenty-five hundred U.S. soldiers, plus civilian officials and the usual contingent of camp followers. Col. Johnston's orders from President Buchanan were to remove Brigham Young as territorial governor, to install in his place a new federal appointee, and to otherwise assert federal authority in the territory. Until this time the great bulk of non-Mormons passing through Salt Lake had been gold seekers bound for California and Nevada and the number of those who stayed on in the valley, as merchants or for whatever reason, was insignificant. But with Johnston's arrival and the construction of Camp Floyd southwest of the city, the Gentile, as Mormons referred to persons of other faiths, had conspicuously and permanently established his presence in the midst of the young Mormon dominion.

The first effect on Salt Lake music, while the invasion was still pending, was the disbanding of the Deseret Dramatic Association in the fall of 1857 so that its members could participate in what turned out to be the bloodless and largely futile "defense" of the territory. Later, with the establishment of a theater and the Military Dramatic Association at Camp Floyd, some of the actors defected to the government camp and throughout the remainder of the decade attempts to revive dramatic and musical activity in Salt Lake met with only limited success. But the most significant effect was the transformation of the valley from a cohesive Mormon culture ruled unequivocally by the LDS hierarchy to one that would ever after be forced to compromise in all its activities with the Gentile world both within and without its own borders.

A brief respite from outside interference began in 1861, when the increasing likelihood of civil war over the slavery question prompted the government to decommission Camp Floyd and to order the troops to more strategically located posts outside the territory. Rather than attempt to ship the huge stockpile of supplies it had accumulated there, the government decided instead to auction the entire camp and its contents, and millions of dollars worth of provisions and building materials were sold at prices that amounted to only pennies on the dollar.

These goods served as the stimulus for several new fortunes in the territory. One large share, purchased by Brigham Young, made possible construction of the famous old Salt Lake Theater—which was destined to be the principal center of Salt Lake musical and dramatic art for more than half a century. Excavation for the new structure was begun in July 1861. The first performances were given in March 1862, before audiences that often taxed the buildings seating capacity of fifteen hundred (by some sources put at twelve hundred).

Charles J. Thomas, a Mormon convert and a theater orchestra conductor from London, arrived in Salt Lake Valley just in time to be appointed the first director of the Salt Lake Theater Orchestra. It was an all-volunteer group that played without pay and included Captain Pitt and David Evans, first violins; William Clayton, Stephen Alley, and Ebeneezer Beesley, second violins; John Toone and George D. Watt, violas; Joshua H. Midgley and James Smithies, cellos; David O. Calder, bass; Horace K. Whitney and a Mr. Nines, flutes; Henry Sadler and Stephen Hale, clarinets; Mark Croxall, cornet; Charles Evans and Thomas McIntyre, French Horns; Charles Sansom, trombone; and John Wakeham, ophicleide (an early brass instrument with keys since replaced by the tuba).

At about the same time Thomas was also appointed director of the Tabernacle Choir. His predecessors in this post had been John Parry, appointed in 1849 (before the Choir had a tabernacle in which to sing); Stephen H. Goddard, who was appointed in 1854; and James Smithies, an original member of the Nauvoo Brass Band and instrumentalist in the Nauvoo Temple, who was probably appointed choirmaster in 1855.

Though Thomas's musical ability later proved limited, there can be no doubt that it represented a considerable step forward at the time he first arrived in the valley. In Edward Tullidge's opinion, "the Tabernacle Choir had never risen above the musical status of an ordinary choir of a country church; but under C. J. Thomas it soon became fairly metropolitan, and good anthem music was frequently performed on Sundays to the delight of the congregation, the majority of whom had come from the musical cities of Great Britain," and who, until Thomas's arrival, "had seldom heard in the Salt Lake Tabernacle those fine English anthems with which they were familiar."[7]

In scarcely fifteen years Salt Lake Valley had been transformed from what early visitors described as an empty and wild desert into a thriving young city capable of sustaining one of the few large theaters between the eastern seaboard and San Francisco, one with a theater orchestra under the direction of a London-trained conductor. It also boasted a tabernacle with a great church organ, an accomplished choir, several martial and brass bands, and dance orchestras. It was a slight beginning, perhaps, but one ripe with promise for a musical future equal to the agricultural miracle that was already making the desert bloom.

CHAPTER TWO

George and Lavinia Careless

From the completion of the Salt Lake Theater in 1862 until late in the nineteenth century, a relatively small number of strong personalities dominated the city's musical development. Of these one of the earliest and certainly one of the most influential was George Edward Percy Careless, an Englishman who emigrated to Utah in 1864.

He was born in London on September 24, 1839. On October 20, 1850, he was baptized into the LDS Church, and within two years of his conversion left his parents' home rather than submit to his father's demand, not that he abandon his new faith, but that he give up the study of music. A fortuitous apprenticeship with a shoemaker who recognized his exceptional talent enabled Careless to pursue his musical ambition while supporting himself, and in 1859 he entered London's Royal Academy of Music.

By 1862 he had begun a professional career in music which included, Tullidge tells us in his *History of Salt Lake City*, engagements with London orchestras conducted by "Sir Michael Costa, Sir Jules Benedict, Dr. Arnold, G. W. Martin, Wm. Ganze, Randegger, Barnard and other famous conductors in oratories [*sic*], operas, concerts, etc., with from thirty-five to four thousand performers, in Exeter Hall, Crystal Palace, Drury Lane Theatre, Italian Church and other places."[1] He also conducted a gentleman's orchestra of forty pieces and the London LDS Conference Choir in some of the principal London concert halls. It was due to his success in this latter connection, especially, that he was encouraged by Church elders to emigrate to Zion.

In Salt Lake he soon established himself as a prominent music teacher and during April 1865 he joined the Salt Lake Theater Orchestra. Shortly after, Ebeneezer Beesley was appointed conductor of the orchestra to succeed Charles J. Thomas, when Thomas was sent south to help settle the area around what is now St. George, Utah—and in October of the same year Careless succeeded Beesley.

According to Careless, one of his first acts as conductor was to reduce the size of the orchestra. This episode was recounted to *The Salt Lake Tribune* some sixty-odd years later, when the venerable musician was almost ninety years old, and not improbably the passage of time had obscured his memory on some of the finer details of his appointment. Certainly, his recollections contrast sharply with the high opinion in which Tullidge and other early commentators seem to have held the Theater ensemble. "Mr. Careless's description of the first Salt Lake Theater orchestra is as comic a picture as ever drawn by Charles Dickens," the Tribune reporter wrote.

Even today, as he tells the story, Mr. Careless, in his prim black suit and hat, stiffly starched shirt, gleaming white collar and necktie, rocks with laughter:

"You should have seen it. The leader had a beat rigid, up and down, up and down, like an automatic doll. There was a left-handed violinist who sawed away at his violin as if he would cut it in two. A clarinetist so nearsighted that he kept his nose almost against the music. And, oh, such a squawking. The first time I went to the theater I almost died. It was so different from what I had been accustomed to in London."

Mr. Careless said he rehearsed the orchestra diligently for a week, until at last, utterly worn out, he sought Manager H. B. Clawson.

"Brother Clawson, I want to cut the orchestra down to seven men. Seven of them can be made into an orchestra, and I want pay for them."

"I don't think President Young will like that, " replied Brother Clawson.

"I can't help it. I can't stand any more. If I can't have the men I want and pay for them by Saturday night, I'm going to quit."

"And do you know on Saturday night, we got word that the orchestra would be cut to seven men and they would all be paid. This was Utah's first professional orchestra."[2]

Besides Careless, remaining musicians and their usual instruments were David Evans, first violin; Ebeneezer Beesley, second violin; Joshua Midgley, cello; Mark Croxall, cornet; Horace K. Whitney, flute; and Orson Pratt, Jr., piano.

In 1865, at about the time Beesley was assuming Thomas's duties at the Theater, Robert Sands succeeded Thomas as Tabernacle Choir leader. Four years later, by 1869, Careless had definitely replaced Sands at the head of the Choir, but the exact transition is obscure. One account is related by George D. Pyper, who later became the first president of the Salt Lake Oratorio Society. Though Pyper was little more than a toddler in the mid-1860s, he later knew Careless personally and wrote while the pioneer musician was still living. He puts Careless in charge of the Choir in early 1865, when it still sang in the old Tabernacle, and recounts the following story of Careless's appointment:

> Only a few months after his arrival in the Valley, President Young sent for [Careless], and he was soon standing before the great Pioneer.
>
> A thrill went from the musician's head to foot as President Young said: "Brother George, I have a mission for you. I want you to be the Chief Musician of the Church. I want you to take the Tabernacle Choir and the Theatre Orchestra and lay a foundation for good music."
>
> "I will do the best I can with the material I can get," responded the surprised musician.
>
> "You will have to make that," said the President.[3]

It is clear, however, that Sands was leading the Choir as late as the October 1867 General Conference, the first held in the recently built "new Tabernacle" (as the world famous building presently standing on Temple Square was known for many years), and that he continued as director for some time after. Not improbably Careless's entry into the Choir was a gradual one, as to some extent it seems to have been with the Theater Orchestra, so that even in his own mind, in later years, he was not certain at just which point in time he had taken full charge.

During the years of Careless's tenure, both the Theater Orchestra and the Tabernacle Choir gained increasing prestige. Pyper credits Careless with having enlarged the Choir from forty voices to more than a hundred and the *Deseret News*, in reporting on the Spring 1870 General Conference, noted that "never before, we think, has the Tabernacle Choir been in such a state of efficiency."[4]

In 1868, at a time when the Overland stage was still the most comfortable means of traveling from points east to Salt Lake and beyond, Careless conducted the Theater Orchestra's accompaniments for the concerts of Parepa and Carl Rosa. She was one of the reigning divas of that era, he one of the highly acclaimed violinists, and George Pyper refers to their Salt Lake visit as "the first noteworthy musical event in the history of the Theater."[5]

Following the railroad's completion on May 31, 1869, and the relative comfort and speed of coast-to-coast transportation it initiated, Salt Lakers enjoyed a regular diet of music provided by traveling companies. Offenbach's *La Grande Duchess*, said to have been the first complete opera heard in the Mountain West, was given with Theater Orchestra accompaniment between May 31 and June 19, 1869, by the Howson Opera Burlesque and Comedy Troupe from Australia.

Though Careless remained in the service of the LDS Church as Tabernacle Choir leader until 1880, he left the Theater Orchestra in 1871. The musicians' intention of forming a union, and his own strongly held antiunion views are sometimes cited[6] as the reason for his resignation, and for the subsequent return of C. J. Thomas to that post. In all events, Careless was not long free of his Theater duties when he began demonstrating a talent for organizing independent musical productions.

Early in 1871 he directed a concert in the Seventh Ward[7] schoolhouse that, though by Careless's own later standards it would be considered lightweight, was a great hit with the public; and the News referred to it as "One of the greatest successes ever achieved in this city."[8] On March 7, 1871, he followed with a Salt Lake Theater concert that moved the same paper to "trust that this concert will give such an impetus to musical study and progress in our midst, that it will be speedily followed by the formation in Salt Lake City of a Philharmonic Society, in which study and practice will be systematically persevered in by the members."[9]

Later that month a meeting was held in City Hall for the purpose of creating the second Deseret Philharmonic Society (Smithies and Grimshaw's in 1855 having been the first), and by midyear this new organization was able to join the Tabernacle Choir in Fourth of July ceremonies with Careless conducting. The society incorporated a teaching department, headed by David O. Calder, society president, and Charles Smith, secretary, that advertised in late April 1871 that "The Society is now prepared to organize classes for tuition in vocal and instrumental music."[10]

Meanwhile, in late 1862, the military presence of the United States had been re-established with the founding of Camp Douglas east of Salt Lake City. Colonel Patrick Connor, commander of the post, took an actively hostile attitude toward the LDS Church and its religious, political, and economic domination of the territory, and this, with the steadily increasing non-Mormon population of prospectors and merchants, the Godbeite schism, and other apostasies of the 1860s and 1870s, worsened the already smoldering hostility that had persisted between Salt Lake Mormons and the Gentile minority since the days of Johnston's Army. On both sides inflammatory rhetoric not infrequently erupted into violence and the period was marred by numerous assaults and even murders.

It was during this time that Careless and Calder's Deseret Philharmonic Society was created, played out its short existence, and was supplanted by the more broadly based Salt Lake Choral Union, the first Salt Lake City musical organization to distance itself from LDS Church domination by actively and openly embracing the membership of both Gentile and Mormon elements. Early in 1873 *The Salt Lake Tribune*, at that time self-avowedly the publication of the Gentile community, announced the formation of the Choral Union with George E. Whiting as president; Orson Pratt, Jr., vice-president; Thomas Griggs, secretary; J. T. Cutting, treasurer; and an executive committee consisting of Mrs. Haydon, Mrs. Hamilton, and J. T. Lynch.[11] George Careless was persuaded to take the post of music director, Orson Pratt, Jr., that of accompanist, and by the following April the Union was able to present its first public performance in the Liberal Institute. Included in the program, besides several popular songs, an orchestral "overture," and a duet for violin and piano, were choruses from Auber's *Masaniello*, Bellini's *La Sonnambula*, Balfe's *Bohemian Girl*, and Rossini's *Moses in Egypt*; and arias from Flotow's *Martha*, Verdi's *I Lombardi*, and a selection from Donizetti's *Anna Bolena*.[12] Following this program the Union gave monthly programs in St. Mark's School (Episcopalian) throughout 1873 and into 1874, before ultimately dissipating its energy and following its predecessors into dissolution.

In 1875 the Salt Lake Handel and Haydn Society was organized by "the associated musical talent of the city to raise the standard of musical taste."[13] Once again it was Careless who was invited to conduct, and on January 9, 1875, the city's musicians and singers were "respectfully invited to be present at a meeting to be held at the Fourteenth Ward Assembly Rooms on Wednesday evening next, the 12th inst., at 7 o'clock, to take into consideration the desirability of giving a performance in Salt Lake City, of Handel's great oratorio *The Messiah*, by the associated musical talent of this city and vicinity, on some date to be hereafter decided upon, said performance to be solely for the furtherance of the divine art, (music) and not for the benefit of any institution or person."[14]

Rehearsals were held in St. Mark's School and on June 3, 1875, what is generally conceded to have been the first rendition of *Messiah* given between Chicago and the Pacific Coast was presented in the Salt Lake Theater. According to the *Salt Lake Herald*, the Theater had not in recent years "contained such a crowd of people as was assembled there last night on the occasion of the first performance in this city of Handel's sacred oratorio....Long before night, yesterday, every chair in the parquette, and parquette and dress circles, was taken, and still the purchase of tickets for standing room continued unabated. And what is more significant, is the fact that the audience was made up almost entirely of the best people of the town." In the *Herald*'s opinion it was "scarcely fair to criticize musically so great an achievement in our comparatively small musical community as the introduction of oratorio....but we can with confidence assert that the production last night of the *Messiah*—perhaps the finest of all the scriptural oratorios—gave promise of future excellence in our midst, which may compete in time with many of the performances of the oratorios east by societies that rank among the best."[15]

The ten soloists, who shared parts more traditionally sung by four, were Careless's wife, Lavinia, Mrs. William Haydon, Nellie Rooks, Miss E. Haydon, W. D. Williams, O. J. Hollister, W. D. Owen, R. Horn, John Black, and August Podlech. The pianist was Orson Pratt, Jr.; S. A. Kennicott was organist; Mark Croxall played the trumpet obbligato on his cornet; and the orchestra consisted of picked local musicians advertised as including the principal professional and amateur talent of the city. So successful was the performance that it was repeated the following Saturday, June 5, and a final performance, the last ever given by the Handel and Haydn Society under that name, was presented December 26 of the same year.

Tullidge, in his Salt Lake history, wrote that this first Messiah was most significant because it marked:

> the beginning of the musical culture...of a people with the genius and subject of the Messiah actually embodied in their whole history, running now through a fifty-six years' period. The Mormon Temple, if it survive, will as certainly bring the oratorio into its service as that its dispensation has brought in the "gathering" of modern "Israel from all nations." The work of George Careless and others like him, then, has only just begun. The very prophecies, in the history of the past of this peculiar community, proclaim with trumpet tongue that Salt Lake City in the coming time will be the city of America pre-eminent in the oratorio performances. The Gentile artists as well as the "musicians of Israel" will help to accomplish this grand musical result, for art is not sectarian, but universalian.
>
> Apropos of this latter remark may be noted particularly the fact that Professor Careless succeeded in combining the principal singers and instrumentalists in a "Handel and Haydn Society," for the performance of the Messiah, without the thought even occurring to the artists whether their fellows were Mormons or Gentiles. This of itself was a great musical triumph; and the fact that the Messiah was performed in Salt Lake City in 1875, in a style as it never was in any city west of Chicago, is most worthy of a page in our local history.[16]

Following *Messiah* the society changed its name to the Salt Lake Philharmonic Society and soon after presented a rendition of Dudley Buck's *Forty-sixth Psalm.* Careless remained as conductor until 1880, when other interests and, some say, a period of declining health prompted his resignation.

In 1879, while still leading the Philharmonic Society, Careless organized the Careless Orchestra, a body of musicians that seems to have numbered variously between fifteen and twenty members. On March 24, 1879, the orchestra made the first of its many appearances in a program that, though it included several songs and opera selections, was dominated by overtures, piano solos, duets, cornet pieces, and waltzes, and featured such composers as Liszt, Mendelssohn, Beethoven, von Suppé, and Verdi.[17]

During April of the same year the orchestra combined with the Philharmonic Society in a production of Gilbert and Sullivan's *H.M.S. Pinafore*, and continued the collaboration in September with a bill that included two acts of Flotow's *Martha* and a rendition of

Gilbert and Sullivan's *Trial by Jury*, with the two last-named works featuring a traveling artist, Amy Sherwin, in starring roles.

On March 6, 1880, the Careless Orchestra joined the eminent German violinist August Wilhelmj in the Salt Lake Theater. This signal honor came when the orchestra undertook to serenade Wilhelmj during a Salt Lake visit he made as part of a four-year world tour begun in 1878. The famous violinist was so pleased by the gesture, and impressed by the orchestra's ability, that he invited Careless and his men to join him on the Theater stage.

On April 4, 1880, the Careless Orchestra performed with the newly formed Home Dramatic Club in the club's first production, a play titled *A Poor Young Man*. This was followed on May 23, 1880, by a second appearance. Finally, these and subsequent joint efforts with the Dramatic Club proved so numerous and popular that by 1883 the orchestra had forfeited its independent existence, with the result that there was no further concertizing.

During June, 1879, David O. Calder, with LDS Church encouragement, organized Zion's Musical Society. This ill-starred society, conducted by Charles J. Thomas, presented one lightly regarded rendition of Gilbert and Sullivan's *The Sorcerer* in the Salt Lake Theater during March and April 1880. Then, according to Pyper, it "collapsed of its own weight,"[18] though a *Herald* article notes that the society lost $350 worth of music in a 1883 Council House fire.[19]

Meanwhile, the Salt Lake Philharmonic Society, unwilling to disband simply because it had lost Careless as its conductor, began searching for a new director. According to Tullidge, letters were written to the New England Conservatory of Music and ultimately, on the recommendation of a Mr. Tourjee of that institution, a non-Mormon Englishman named Thomas Radcliffe was engaged.[20]

An accomplished pianist, organist, and orchestra leader, Radcliffe arrived in Salt Lake during April 1880 and on May 10, 1881, having trained both the Philharmonic Society chorus and an orchestra specially organized for the occasion, he presented Salt Lake's first rendition of Haydn's *Creation* in the Salt Lake Theater. Soloists were Mrs. F. B. Hamilton, Emma White, O. J. Hollister, R. Gorlinski, J. Carlisle and W. D. Williams. Unhappily, weather and indifference, the latter perhaps reflecting the absence of the charismatic Careless, conspired to rob the performance of the large audience that had been hoped for, and the *Herald* seems to have drawn the appropriate conclusion. "Prof. Radcliffe," it observed, "must have labored very hard to get up so difficult a production in such a creditable manner, and marked praise is to be bestowed on all sides. It is a serious question, however, whether, under the circumstances, it is wisdom to attempt the production of such heavy works. Good judgment, it seems," the *Herald* critic concluded, "would, for the present, commend lighter selections as the more fitting to the times and conditions."[21]

Discouraged by this experience, the Philharmonic Society soon disbanded. In the process, however, the city gained one of its most able musicians. Professor Radcliffe was appointed organist of the First Congregational Church soon after his Salt Lake arrival and it was not long before he had established himself as the city's foremost musician on that instrument. In addition, he was recognized as a talented teacher and his music students soon became numerous enough to assure him a comfortable living.

By October 1883, Careless was once again feeling the urge to found a musical organization and on the twenty-sixth of that month hosted a meeting in the music store he then operated jointly with Mark Croxall, the well-known cornetist and band leader. This meeting led to establishment of the first Salt Lake Choral Society with Careless as music director. John S. Barnes was chairman and Pyper was treasurer. Meetings and rehearsals were held throughout the winter and on June 2, 1884, the society gave its only concert, a two-part program that included popular numbers and instrumental solos in the first part, followed by a rendition of John Stainer's cantata, *The Daughter of Jairus*, in the second. Soloists for this Salt Lake Theater performance were Pyper, Lavinia Careless, Edith Clawson, Mrs. L. Cummings, Thomas Crawford, L. L. Van Praag, James Dunbar, Horace G. Whitney, John D. Spencer, M. H. McCallister, and John S. Barnes.

By the beginning of 1885 the need was once again felt for an independent orchestral organization such as the Careless Orchestra had been before its absorption into the Home Dramatic Club. In response, the *Herald* editorialized for a joining of Salt Lake Theater Orchestra members with those of the Walker Opera House, which had been opened in 1882 by the pioneer banking and mining family of the same name. Surprisingly, within a few days of this writing the *Herald* was able to report that thirty-one musicians drawn from the two theaters, which usually represented hostile camps wary of any mutual enterprise, had committed themselves to a new organization under the baton, once again, of George Careless. The orchestra grew over the next few weeks to thirty-five members and was soon known as the Careless Mammoth (or sometimes Leviathan) Orchestra. Rehearsals began in mid February and a single concert was given in the Salt Lake Theater on March 25, 1885, by what was advertised as the largest home-talent orchestra ever to have performed in the territory. In addition to the usual songs and operatic selections, the program included three overtures, among them the *William Tell* and one written by W. C. Clive especially for the occasion titled "Evening Thoughts." There were also violin and piano concertos, both by Mendelssohn; a cello solo; piano duet; and a short piece composed by Careless himself.[22]

After the Salt Lake Philharmonic Society's 1879 rendition of *H.M.S. Pinafore*, the popularity of home-talent operetta increased rapidly. By the mid-1880s a number of home opera companies, both adult and juvenile, had made their appearance in LDS ward meeting halls and the Salt Lake Theater. Having pioneered the field with the Philharmonic, Careless was not to be left far behind. During the late summer of 1885 he formed the Careless Opera Company for the purpose of presenting Gilbert and Sullivan's new work, *The Mikado*. Besides Careless as music director, the company included John D. Spencer as business manager and D. S. Spencer as secretary and treasurer.

Mikado was first presented on November 2, 1885, and though this initial performance was criticized rather severely in some circles, subsequent performances were considered so much improved that it played a total of fourteen times before closing on March 13, 1886. Other productions of the Careless Opera Company were Gilbert and Sullivan's *Pirates of Penzance*, performed several times between February 22 and March 12, 1886; a revival of *H.M.S. Pinafore* the following September; and a November 1887 production, in cooperation with local dramatic talent, of *Ben Israel*, a play written by Edward W. Tullidge, author of the Salt Lake City history frequently quoted in these pages. Tullidge's drama had first played in New York City in March 1876, then followed later that month with a Salt Lake Theater production. Shortly after, it was done in London; but the musical parts, in which the Careless Opera participated, were written specifically for the 1887 version by Careless himself.

Following the demise of Calder's Zion's Musical Society in the early 1880s, elements within the LDS Church retained the hope of establishing another church-oriented musical society and in late 1886 Careless was called upon to found Zion's Choral Union. As was the case with most Salt Lake choral organizations to this time, especially those encouraged by the Church, the purpose of the Choral Union was as much educational as artistic, and the hope in this instance was that the quality of ward choirs would be enhanced by their member's experience in the Union chorus. According to a *Salt Lake Herald* article, the Choral Union was to be "devoted to the study of classic music and oratorio" and a chorus of three to five hundred voices was optimistically predicted.[23]

After a winter of study and rehearsal, the Choral Union gave its first and only public performance, a rendition of Handel's *Belshazzar*, in the new Tabernacle on June 7, 1887. The chorus approached four hundred voices and a picked orchestra of thirty pieces was gathered for the occasion. Soloists were Pyper, John D. Spencer, Heber S. Goddard, Moroni J. Thomas, Harry Gardner, Edith Knowlton, Lizzie and Agnes Thomas, Edith Dinwoodey, Mrs. C. E. Silverwood, Chrissie Lawson, Louie Poulton, and Vilate Young.

The performance was favorably reviewed and a paid audience estimated at seven thousand persons, besides exceeding the ushers' capacity to seat them, assured the financial success of the venture. The *Herald*, commenting on the huge crowd, described a problem that for years to come would from time to time plague Tabernacle entertainments:

> The drawback of last evening was in the confusion—it might almost be said riot—which took place over the reserved seats. All the downstairs portion except the few back rows, with the east end of the gallery, had been reserved and sold at 50 cents. The coupons handed holders of tickets bore the name of the section and the number of the row. As each row holds seventeen to twenty people, it will be seen that such a crowd as that which surged in at the doors last evening would swamp a regular army of ushers, even if it had been provided. There were only fifteen, as it was, and the crowd tossed them derisively aside, overwhelmed them and took seats where it listed. The most inextricable confusion arose. People who had checks for certain rows arrived to find those rows groaning under the crush

of a half a dozen more people than had been allotted to them. As a consequence there was growling, demands for [refunds], and a final stampede upstairs as the only way of getting seats at all. Thus a vast portion of the 50 centers were in 25 cent seats, and probably vice versa.[24]

Notwithstanding the Choral Union's success, which far outweighed the difficulty it encountered in handling the audience, interest declined rapidly following *Belshazzar* and though there was much scolding in the newspapers, by mid-1888 the Union had ceased to exist. Except for some relatively minor involvements, *Belshazzar* also marked the end of the twenty-three-year career of George Careless as conductor, choir director, and organizer of Salt Lake musical organizations, though he continued as an important musical educator throughout the remainder of a very long life.

No account of George Careless, or of early Salt Lake music, would be complete without special mention of his talented wife, Lavinia. Born as Lavinia Triplet on the island of Jersey on December 2, 1846, she was destined to become Salt Lake's first lady of pioneer song. In 1901, sixteen years after her death, the *Deseret News* paid her the tribute of noting that "It is not too much to say that she towers above any other singer the state has ever known, and it may well be doubted whether we shall know her equal again."[25]

At the age of eleven Lavinia was singing in London and by the time she was fifteen she was singing with the London LDS Conference Choir where George Careless, her future husband, was director. In 1863 she emigrated to Salt Lake City with her family. A year later, when Careless came to Salt Lake at the urging of Church elders, she began studying with him, and in 1865 made her Utah debut at the Salt Lake Theater singing to his violin accompaniment. Early in 1866 they were married and from then until her death in 1885, her career paralleled his. She was the principal soprano of the Tabernacle Choir, the featured vocalist of the Handel and Haydn Society *Messiah*, frequent vocalist with the Careless Orchestra, principal soloist of Careless's Salt Lake Choral Society, and a favorite of President Young himself. In his *History of Salt Lake City*, Edward W. Tullidge wrote of her that "she is worthy of more than fame. She possessed one of the best English voices of her generation; and had she traveled as a star," he wrote, "she would undoubtedly have won a world-wide name, for not only was her voice of the purest quality, but her singing was burdened with soul and her exquisite delivery intense with feeling, which, in oratorio, rose to the exalted pitch of epic song."[26]

It would be difficult to exaggerate the importance of the Carelesses to the little world of Salt Lake City music. At the Salt Lake Theater George created and conducted the City's first professional orchestra. With Lavinia at his side and taking an important role in the production, he conducted the Mountain West's first oratorio society in the first rendition of Handel's immortal *Messiah* between Chicago and San Francisco. He organized and conducted the first significant concert orchestra in the territory and directed the first opera, albeit light opera, given by home talent. He brought the Tabernacle Choir to new heights of artistic accomplishment. Most important of all, in a time of dangerous strife, he pioneered in disclosing the great healing potential of the "divine art," its ability to bring Mormon and non-Mormon together in a single organization for a single purpose—the creation of beautiful music. So comprehensive had the musical interests of George and Lavinia been that little was left for those who followed, except to build on the work they had begun.

University of Utah Library Special Collections

Utah State Historical Society

Top: Salt Lake City's first paid orchestra played at the Salt Lake Theater beginning in about 1865. Its members (L-R) were Joshua Midgely, cello; Ebenezer Beesley, second violin; David Evans, first violin; George Careless (also with violin), conductor; Mark Croxall, cornet; Horace K. Whitney, usually identified as a flutist; and Orson Pratt, Jr., piano.

Left: Pioneer musician and educator David O. Calder founded the Deseret Musical Association in the early 1860s with a membership drawn mostly from his music classes.

CHAPTER THREE

Evan Stephens, Choirs, and Operas

The most prominent heir to the choral and light opera traditions established by George Careless was a young Welsh immigrant, Evan Stephens. He was born in Carmarthenshire, South Wales, on June 28, 1854, and emigrated to Utah Territory with his parents, converts to the LDS Church, in 1866. The family settled in Willard, north of Ogden, and it was there that young Stephens developed his interest in music as a member of the ward choir. He later studied with Joseph J. Daynes, the first Salt Lake Tabernacle organist; with George Careless; and with Ebeneezer Beesley.

By 1883, under the auspices of the LDS Church Deseret Sunday School Union, he was conducting children's singing classes in Salt Lake City, and during March of that year he presented the first of his many Salt Lake concerts featuring choruses drawn from among his students—concerts which, in later years, sometimes boasted choruses numbering in the thousands of voices.

During the 1885–86 academic year he studied at the New England Conservatory of Music, following which he resumed his work in Salt Lake City. He also took a new position at the University of Deseret (now the University of Utah), where he was put in charge of music instruction for the Normal School—as departments of education were then generally known. The scope of his teaching, both privately and at the university, increased dramatically during this period, and his adult classes, particularly, led him into Salt Lake opera productions. These performances, with key soloists drawn from among the community's more experienced artists, functioned as the culminating exercises for his students, whom he first presented during June 1888 in a Salt Lake Theater production of Balfe's comic opera, *The Bohemian Girl.* This work was revived for a New Year's Day 1889 presentation, and was then followed in March and April by a rendition of Donizetti's *The Daughter of the Regiment.* During May and again in October 1889 Flotow's *Martha* was given in the Theater. Solo artists, many of whom had sung with the Careless company, included John D. Spencer, Heber S. Goddard, J. T. White, George D. Pyper, Lizzie Thomas, and Edith Clawson.

Besides the work already discussed, Stephens was the principal force behind formation of the second Salt Lake Choral Society, an organization that, like the Salt Lake Choral Union, the Handel and Haydn Society of 1875, and its successor, the Salt Lake Philharmonic Society, was a self-avowedly nondenominational organization in which both Mormon and Gentile music lovers could meet on an equal footing. So well was this ideal realized that in 1891 *The Salt Lake Tribune* was moved to observe, with perhaps a touch of irony, that "Both Mormon and Gentile elements in the Society are so united that it would puzzle many of the members at first to say who is, or who is not a saint."[1]

The genesis of Stephen's Salt Lake Choral Society lies in two events of 1889. The first was the Johnstown, Pennsylvania, flood and the Flood Relief Concert it occasioned in the new Tabernacle. For this concert, one of many relief efforts undertaken across the United States, Stephens organized a chorus of three hundred voices. The following October many of these same singers formed the nucleus of a four hundred voice chorus he organized for a Tabernacle concert by the "Great Gilmore" and his Gilmore Band, which was one of the preeminently popular U. S. musical attraction of that era. Following the concert newspaper editorials called for preserving Stephens' Gilmore chorus, considered by many to be the finest ever heard in Salt Lake, as a permanent organization; and during a series of meetings in November the new Salt Lake Choral Society was founded. Stephens was elected music director. Thomas Radcliffe, the last music director of the Philharmonic Society, became accompanist.

The LDS Church generously granted use of the Assembly Hall for rehearsals and the Tabernacle for performances; and on May 30 and 31, 1890, and June 5 and 6, 1891, the Choral Society gave ambitious spring music festivals. Each year's effort consisted of a matinee and two evening concerts, and they proved as popular as any musical event yet held in the city. The programs were of relatively light and well-known pieces, solos by local artists and imported talent, excerpts from opera and oratorio, and Radcliffe solos on the great Tabernacle organ. The impression given by *The Salt Lake Tribune* is that the concluding concert of the 1890 festival was more than usually laden with unfamiliar and classical music. It included the "Priest's March" from Mendelssohn's *Althalie* and two arias from *Elijah*, selections from Rossini's *Stabat Mater*, Verdi selections from *La Traviata* and *Ernani*, a polonaise with chorus by Glinka, a clarinet solo, and a solo organ performance by Radcliffe.[2]

During November 1891 the society combined forces with the Tabernacle Choir to provide a six-hundred-voice chorus for a second Gilmore Festival, and on October 22, 1892, it gave a Tabernacle concert that in the press was noted chiefly for Radcliffe's fine solo organ work.

From the time of the Choral Society's founding there had been frequent calls for it to undertake complete oratorios and on December 26, 1892, it fulfilled this request with a Tabernacle rendition of *The Light of Asia*, a cantata with music by Dudley Buck and libretto from a poem by Edwin Arnold that is based on the life of Buddha. The chorus of 250 voices was joined by an orchestra specially organized and trained by the prominent Salt Lake violinist and orchestra leader, Willard Erastus Weihe. Soloists were Pyper, Anna Colborn Plummer, and Alfred H. Peabody, who with Pyper eventually played an important role in the early history of the Oratorio Society.

The following spring, on May 27, 1893, the society gave its second and final oratorio with a rendition of Haydn's *Creation* in the Salt Lake Theater—its first appearance outside the Tabernacle. Soloists were Jennie Winston, Anna Colborn Plummer, Mrs. John Greene, Bert Havens and Horace Ensign. *The Creation* drew an audience that barely filled half the theater and this decline in interest in the society was not merely on the part of the public. The chorus was rapidly losing its singers, and the winter of 1893-94 saw the final two society concerts, both of which were presented in the hall of the First Congregational Church. On December 5, 1893, "An Evening with the Italian Masters" was given that featured excerpts from the operas of Verdi, Rossini, and Donizetti. On March 8, 1894, the society concluded its concert career with "A Night with the German Masters."

At a meeting held in Coalter and Snelgrove's Hall on March 19, 1894, the society received and accepted Stephens' letter of resignation as music director. As his reason for quitting he cited the diminishing interest of singers with the accompanying diminution of the society chorus and the loss of its commitment to grandeur of scale—a significant matter to a man whose taste ran to choruses of five hundred or more. He also noted the disappointing lack of public interest resulting in small audiences and insurmountable financial difficulties, and perhaps most importantly of all, the impossibility of competing with an organization, such as the Tabernacle Choir, "that may be heard every week free of charge, [overshadowing] smaller organizations who depend on public performances for support." Finally, he expressed the hope that the experience of the Salt Lake Choral Society would one day "give rise to something higher and nobler—an organization whose support will come from within itself, the outgrowth of a deep love for master works, and the public will be put in a position of begging for admission to the feast, rather than being appealed to to come."[3]

In truth, it was in no small measure due to the work of Stephens himself that the Tabernacle Choir achieved such stature and popularity that other Salt Lake organizations found themselves unable to compete; and because of this, in fact, his complaint about the dwindling Choral Society chorus might be seen as somewhat disingenuous.

Initially, Stephens' success with the Salt Lake Choral Society so outshone the smaller and less versatile LDS Church organization, in the words of Charles Jeffrey Calman in his history of the Choir, that "in all the excitement, no one was paying any attention to the Salt Lake Tabernacle Choir. This was clearly an unacceptable state of affairs," Calman relates, and "to reestablish the Choir as the leading musical organization of Salt Lake City, the church leaders turned to the man who had created—and could best solve—their dilemma."[4]

Stephens' appointment as Tabernacle Choir director came late in 1890, four years before he quit the Choral Society. No sooner had he succeeded the retiring director, Ebeneezer Beesley, than characteristically of his fondness for enormous choruses he began enlarging the Choir until it finally approached six hundred voices, a number that almost certainly included many Choral Society singers.

During the ensuing months, in addition to weekly recitals, the Choir formed the nucleus for a number of Tabernacle concerts. Then in September 1893 a contingent of 250 Tabernacle Choir members competed at a Chicago World's Fair Eisteddfod where they astounded many observers of the American music scene by winning second prize for large mixed choruses—a triumph that firmly established the Choir's national reputation and its domination of Salt Lake choral music.

In such an atmosphere, in the face of such competition, and undermined from within by Stephen's compromised loyalty, it is remarkable that the Choral Society lasted as long as it did.

Following the Choral Society's collapse, the Choir appeared frequently as an adjunct to Tabernacle Concerts by such nationally and internationally prominent artists as Mademoiselle Charlotte Maconda, John Philip Sousa, Lillian Norton (Nordica), Paderewski, and Dame Nellie Melba; and throughout his twenty-six years as director, until his retirement in 1916, Stephens promoted his Choir with the same relentless energy and enthusiasm he had brought to his every enterprise. In 1896 he took the Choir on a tour of Northern California and later that same year attended an Eisteddfod in Denver where the Choir, though not participating in the competition, gave a series of highly regarded concerts.

In 1903 the Choir returned to California. In 1909 it toured Idaho, Washington, and Oregon. In 1911 it attended the American Land and Irrigation Exposition in New York City where it appeared several times daily at Madison Square Garden for more than a week, then twice at the Hippodrome, after which it traveled to Washington, D.C., for a White House performance before President and Mrs. William H. Taft and their guests.

Besides Careless and Stephens, there were other important musicians active in Salt Lake opera during the 1880s and 1890s. H. S. Krouse, a New York City native who arrived in Salt Lake in 1881, became not only a popular orchestral conductor, pianist, and music teacher, but one of the city's most energetic early organizers and conductors in the comic opera field. During February 1885, several months before the Careless Opera Company was formed, he conducted a Salt Lake Theater rendition of Gilbert and Sullivan's *Patience* that traveled to Ogden, Brigham City, and Logan during March, then returned for two final Theater performances in April. The following December he conducted another Salt Lake Theater Gilbert and Sullivan opera, *Iolanthe*, that was repeated during 1886. In May 1889 he directed *Maritana*, a popular opera by the Irish composer, W. V. Wallace; then in December 1891, he followed with a Theater rendition of von Suppé's *Fatinitza* that traveled to Ogden on New Year's Day, 1892. During February, 1894, he conducted *The Crimson Scarf* in the Eighteenth Ward as a charity benefit for the poor. It then traveled to the outlying towns of Lehi and Bountiful and finally, because of its popularity, was brought back for a Salt Lake Theater performance early in March. He concluded his home opera career in the Theater during May 1895 with three performances of *Priscilla, or Pilgrim's Proxy* for which George E. Lask of San Francisco's Tivoli Theater was engaged as stage director.

Many of the same singers who starred with the Careless and Stephens Opera Companies were also prominent in Krouse productions. Among them were Pyper, Edith Clawson, Heber S. Goddard, and Willard Squires. Others were Chrissie Lawson, Robert Gorlinski, and E. Haviland, Jr.

During November 1896, more than a year after Krouse's *Crimson Scarf*, an ad hoc (or perhaps periodic) company referred to in the newspapers as the Ladies' Aid Society Opera Company, gave a Salt Lake Theater rendition of *Pirates of Penzance* as an Aid Society fund-raiser. It was directed by Alfred H. Peabody and proved so successful that it was repeated in December with the use of the Theater donated by manager Charles S. Burton, after which it was taken to Ogden for a final performance. So popular was this opera that *The Salt Lake Tribune*, in its enthusiastic reviews, urged formation of a permanent new home-opera company, an idea that was heartily seconded by many in the community.

Almost simultaneously with this resurgent enthusiasm, three Salt Lake musicians announced their intention of forming a new choral society. They were Willard Weihe (mentioned above in connection with the *Light of Asia* orchestra), who had been conductor of the Salt Lake Theater Orchestra since succeeding Charles J. Thomas in 1885; J. J. (John Jasper) McClellan, a young Utah organist and conductor who had only recently graduated from the University of Michigan Conservatory of Music and who was destined to become the Salt Lake Tabernacle's first nationally prominent organist; and Heber S. Goddard, the promising young baritone who had made a name for himself with both the Stephens and Krouse opera companies, and who had sung one of the leading roles in the recent Ladies' Aid Society rendition of *Pirates of Penzance.* Over the next several weeks the newspapers continued to dwell on the hazards awaiting new Salt Lake choral organizations while emphasizing the need for home opera; and whether heeding the papers or because of some inner process of its own, the new choral society scheme ultimately evolved into the Salt Lake Opera Company, one of the young city's most successful musical ventures.

By early 1897 organization was complete. On the governing board Weihe and Goddard were joined by Horace G. Whitney and John D. Spencer. Whitney was named manager, Weihe music director, and McClellan, though not a member of the board, was designated accompanist.

The Opera's first production was of Edmond Audran's *The Mascot*, initially given four performances during February 1897 with a chorus of thirty-six voices picked from the Tabernacle Choir, the Orpheus Club male chorus, and the Harmony Club. The Opera starred Louise Savage as Bettina, Spencer as Prince Lorenzo, and Goddard as Jover Pippo. Among the other principals were two, Della Daynes (later Hills) and Fred C. Graham, who would eventually take solo roles in Oratorio Society renditions.

During the six years it was most active the Salt Lake Opera Company gave a total of twelve light operas. By present day standards this may not seem impressive, but it does not begin to indicate the full scope of the company's work. Virtually all of these works were repeated, many of them over a period of several years, so that during the season one home-talent production or another was almost always playing. Robert Planquette's *The Chimes of Normandy* is but one example: after its initial engagement during November 1897 it was revived in January 1898, then in January, November and December of 1899 and April of 1902. In addition, almost every production enjoyed a successful road trip to Ogden, Logan, and Brigham City in the north, and to Provo and frequently other points in the south.

Besides *Chimes of Normandy* and *The Mascot*, the company's repertoire included Gilbert and Sullivan's *Patience*; Stahl's *Said Pasha*; Strauss's *The Queen's Lace Handkerchief*; Victor Herbert's *Madeleine*; De Koven's *The Mandarin*; von Suppé's *Fatinitza* and *A Trip to Africa*; Strange and Edwards' *The Wedding Day* and *The Jolly Musketeer*; and Flotow's *Martha*.

Most of Salt Lake's prominent soloists appeared at one time or another with the Salt Lake Opera Company. Spencer and Goddard were in practically every performance and other important leading roles were taken by Graham, Pyper, Alfred Best, and Robert C. Easton, the last of whom also experienced considerable success beyond Utah's borders.

Among female soloists, there were several who went on to considerable professional success. Blanche Aldrach played with stock companies in Seattle and Chicago, Sally Fisher sang with traveling companies in the east, Arvilla Clark was credited by the *Deseret News* with having been the first Utah singer to appear in European grand opera,[5] and the prominence attained by Emma Lucy Gates in her grand opera career, both in Europe and America, is all but legendary among Utah music lovers.

But despite the success of the Salt Lake Opera, by 1902 it was becoming clear that it would suffer the fate common to most early Salt Lake music organizations. The strong personalities that had created and sustained it were drawn into other pursuits, and as usual there proved no one both willing and capable of continuing the organization. In 1900 Weihe left the company, and the departures, first of Blanche Aldrach, then Sally Fisher, seriously depleted the solo ranks. By May 1902, with Goddard and Arvilla Clark having announced their intention of leaving for extended periods of musical study in Europe, the newspapers began predicting the company's imminent demise.

Finally, a rendition of *The Jolly Musketeer* in May and June 1902 proved to be the last that would be made by the original company, though in later years a few of its members were occasionally called together to participate in "revival" performances under the old name. These began in September 1906 when Pyper, Spencer, Graham, and Emma Lucy Gates formed the nucleus of a Salt Lake Opera Company revival in a performance of *The Wedding Day*. In September 1908 Julian Edwards' *The Girl and the Governor* was performed and then, in December 1909 a benefit performance of De Koven's *The Serenade* was given in the Salt Lake Theater for "the old folks of Zion." In March 1911 De Koven's *Robin Hood* was given by a Salt Lake Opera revival that once again included Spencer and Graham, both members of the original *Mascot* cast. Finally, beginning on March 7, 1912, both the company and its name were laid permanently to rest with repeat performances of *Robin Hood* that were given on four successive nights in celebration of the fiftieth anniversary of the Salt Lake Theater's 1862 completion.

University of Utah Library Special Collections

This 1888 rendition of Balfe's *The Bohemian Girl*, given by a chorus of Evan Stephens' voice students and Salt Lake City soloists in the Salt Lake Theater, was one of the important events in the early development of the city's musical life. Principals were Nellie Druce Pugsley, Arline; Bessie Dean, the Gypsy Queen; Robert C. Easton, Thaddeus; John D. Spencer, Devilshoof; Heber S. Goddard, Count Arnheim; and J. T. White, Florestan.

CHAPTER FOUR

Early Symphonic Music

In addition to the public enthusiasm for bands and dance orchestras, there was a continual yearning in early Salt Lake for the more sophisticated music of Europe and the expanded and more accomplished orchestras that could render it. The first small steps toward providing such music were taken by the Social Hall Orchestra, then the Salt Lake Theater Orchestra, and later yet by the instrumental organizations that came under the baton of George Careless.

In the years following the Careless Orchestra's absorption into the Home Dramatic Club there were regular calls in the city's newspapers for a real home-talent symphony. The likelihood of any such idea resulting in a permanent orchestra was seriously diminished, however, by the antagonism that existed between the managements of the Mormon-owned Salt Lake Theater and that of the new Walker Opera House, the entertainment and cultural flagship of the non-LDS community. Each theater, in the scramble for patrons and prestige, discouraged its orchestra members' participation in outside musical activities, especially those involving musicians from the other theater. In 1884 the *Salt Lake Herald*, commenting on the brief and unusual cooperation among musicians resulting in the picked orchestra that accompanied Careless's Salt Lake Choral Society *Daughter of Jairus*, opined that "it would be more gratifying still if we could record that all branches of the musical body had forgotten their disagreements, jealousies and disputes, and united in one grand endeavor to further their art before the public."[1]

The following year, with the financial and artistic success of the short-lived Careless Mammoth Orchestra as a hopeful model, the same paper lamented that "once or twice in every season when amusements from the outside seem to languish, there comes to us with renewed force the thought of how many excellent musicians we have in Salt Lake, and how rigidly and clannishly they seem determined that they will unite in nothing that may give the public pleasure." And it was a public, the *Herald* felt certain, that would flock to hear them if only "the skilled musicians of the Opera and the Theatre [would] realize that there is money in their uniting, drawing in what talent there may be outside of both, and forming a perfect orchestra."[2]

By 1888 an attempt was actually underway to form a symphonic ensemble, with the *Deseret News* announcing that "the Salt Lake Symphony Orchestra is the name under which a majority of the orchestral musicians of this city have organized themselves, with the intention of producing some of the works of the great composers."[3]

It was not until approximately two years later, however, after the Walker Opera House was destroyed by fire on July 3, 1890, that regular rehearsals are known to have begun. By early August of that year twenty-five musicians had already been gathered under the joint direction of H. S. Krouse and a young Norwegian musician named Anton Pedersen.

Pedersen's musical career began at Skien, where he was an assistant organist and a member of the symphony orchestra. Later he moved to Christiana (now Oslo), where he played under the batons of Edvard Grieg and Johan Svendsen. He came to Utah in 1874 not, as was usual, for the attractions of the LDS Church, but for those of his young sweetheart, who had recently emigrated to Utah with her parents. The couple were married and he soon became one of Salt Lake City's most respected musical talents.

Throughout the remainder of 1890 and all of 1891 the orchestra met with Pedersen for frequent rehearsals. Works studied included Beethoven symphonies, Strauss waltzes, Mozart's *Magic Flute* and *Natchlanger* overtures, Schubert's *Unfinished* Symphony, and music from *The Merry Wives of Windsor.*

Finally, on April 4, 1892, the orchestra, by then consisting of thirty-two (some sources say thirty-six) musicians, appeared in joint

Tabernacle concert with a Tabernacle Choir chorus of six hundred voices. Six weeks later, on May 17, 1892, the orchestra gave what is generally considered to have been Utah's first home-talent symphonic concert. This Salt Lake Theater program included Schubert's *Unfinished* Symphony and two movements of Beethoven's First Symphony. In addition, there were lighter selections, mostly instrumental solos, from Kéler-Béla, Hubert Leonard, Pohle (probably David), a vocal solo from Gounod's *Faust*, selections from an obscure work identified as Moses' *Nanon*, and several songs.[4]

The next morning the *Herald*, in addition to its enthusiastic assessment of the orchestra's artistic merits, reported that the concert was well enough attended that it must have netted on the order of two hundred dollars. But even if this were true, it amounted to less than six dollars for each musician, including compensation for nearly two years' rehearsals. And that it was an excessively sanguine estimate is indicated by a subsequent *Tribune* article quoting what the paper called a "well posted and prominent local musician." According to this mysterious personage, "the audience was a creditable one for the programme as announced was classical, and there was no attraction advertised which would catch anyone not more or less interested in music. At the same time," he noted, "although making a splendid showing in numbers the audience was not as remarkable for the people who were there as for those who were not. It is always so," he lamented. "The ones who are avowedly interested in music and who should be counted upon on any such occasion are the very ones who stay away." And more directly confronting the issue of finances and the orchestra's chances of surviving as a permanent organization, he said, "Well, that depends on the public to a large extent....If the public realized the significance of the recent concert, future ones would be better patronized."[5]

Later that spring the Symphony provided music for University of Utah graduation ceremonies and its final official act seems to have been to supply fifteen musicians for a Memorial Day concert at Garfield Beach on the banks of the Great Salt Lake. Thereafter, having had the dubious distinction of being the first organization to demonstrate the difficultly of sustaining symphonic music in Salt Lake City, it ceased to exist.

Following the Pedersen Symphony, picked orchestras were from time to time organized for special events and there were still the regularly recurring calls for a permanent symphony orchestra, voiced both by prominent members of the musical fraternity and by the newspapers. An event significant for the further development of the city's musical establishment occurred in 1894, when the new Grand Theater was opened with Weihe leaving the Salt Lake Theater to conduct its orchestra. At about the same time an amusement house, previously known as Wonderland, was remodeled and renamed the Lyceum Theater with Carl Zehnter conducting its small orchestra.

These theaters were but the forerunners of several that would open during the early years of the coming century, swelling employment opportunities for musicians, encouraging the study of music, and generally increasing the level of musical activity and competence throughout the city. In 1900, in this atmosphere of waxing musical enthusiasm, George D. Pyper, who had by this time become manager of the Salt Lake Theater, offered free use of the Theater to anyone who would organize a symphonic orchestra, and during January 1902, while Pyper's offer languished, a Chicago Symphony Orchestra performance in the Salt Lake Tabernacle renewed the music public's interest in the possibility of a home-talent symphony. Finally, the return of one of the city's most remarkable young musicians, Arthur Shepherd, proved to be the last essential ingredient needed to bring the new orchestra into existence.

A native of Paris, Idaho, Shepherd first entered the New England Conservatory in 1892, while but twelve years of age. Following his graduation in 1897 he established himself as a teacher of piano and harmony in Salt Lake City. This was followed by another period of study at the Conservatory, and upon his second return from Boston, in mid-March 1902, he was appointed conductor of the Salt Lake Theater Orchestra. Shortly thereafter, with the Theater management agreeing (many would say recklessly so) to underwrite expenses, including musicians' salaries, organization of the new Salt Lake Symphony Orchestra was begun.

Recruitment of musicians and rehearsals continued throughout the spring and summer and with approximately thirty pieces the orchestra's first public performance was given in the Theater on November 24, 1902. The program, in addition to the operatic selections invariably demanded by Salt Lake audiences of that period, included the first movement of Schubert's *Unfinished* Symphony, the *Merry Wives of Windsor* overture, two *Norwegian Dances* by Edvard Grieg, pieces by Westerhout and Boccherini, and a composition for harp designated as "Caprice, Concert Mazurka," that was played by its composer, an itinerant musician named Setaro who was at that time traveling through Salt Lake with the Royal Italian Band.[6]

The concert was pronounced an artistic success, but the financial result was much less auspicious. Regretting the small attendance, the *News* commented that it was "pleasant to note that the Theater management and Mr. Shepherd do not propose to accept the recent financial verdict on the Symphony Orchestra as final, but that they already have their coats off vigorously at work on a second concert." The *News* writer explained that "to give a high class concert like that of last week will cost at any time not less than $500, and it is to solve the question of how to bring this amount into the box office for each concert that Messrs. Pyper and Shepherd will have to deal."[7]

The orchestra's second concert was given in the Theater on January 28, 1903, with at least forty musicians and, according to one review, possibly as many as fifty, but with the same disappointing financial results as before, and this second failure prompted the Salt Lake Theater to withdraw its underwriting. As a result, the 1903–04 season was suspended altogether.

By the fall of 1904 Salt Lake music patrons, responding to a plea from the orchestra, had pledged enough money to allow the resumption of concerts. The first was an October 20 appearance in conjunction with Emma Lucy Gates. It was her first major Salt Lake engagement since a 1902 role in the Salt Lake Opera Company's *Jolly Musketeer*. A large audience attended and this, with the ongoing subscription drive that was by then reported to have earned more than two thousand dollars, allowed four more concerts to be given during the following winter and spring. These came on December 5, January 16, March 20, and April 19.

At the beginning of the 1905–06 season a new problem was encountered. Reminiscent of the Walker House and Salt Lake Theater attitudes of the 1880s, managers became reluctant to release their musicians for Symphony rehearsals and performances. Because there was no other time when the entire orchestra could be present, rehearsals had to be scheduled for Sunday afternoons and a concert was announced for early December. But this concert was cancelled when members of the Orpheus Club, whose participation had been counted upon, refused to rehearse on the Sabbath, and it was not until the 1906–07 season, when theater managers adopted a more cooperative attitude, that activity resumed with Friday afternoon concerts on October 12, December 14, and February 1.

Shepherd conducted the Symphony through the 1907–08 season, with concerts on November 1, December 13, and February 9, following which he left the city to accept a position on the faculty of his alma mater, the New England Conservatory of Music. He was succeeded as conductor by J. J. McClellan, the young pianist and organist mentioned above in connection with the Salt Lake Opera Company. Under McClellan's leadership the orchestra gave concerts on November 29, 1908; January 17 and April 18, 1909; January 16, April 3, and December 29, 1910; and February 21 and April 6, 1911.

Beginning with Shepherd's final concert in 1908, notwithstanding the previous difficulty with trying to schedule Sabbath-day rehearsals, the radical step was taken of moving the performance itself from Friday afternoon to Sunday. This change was made possible by abandoning the Salt Lake Theater which, as a policy first established by Brigham Young, would not allow paid performances on Sundays. In part it probably also reflected the inevitable consequences of the city's increasing commercial activity, including the business of entertainment, and the effect this had of gradually eroding the public's resistance to previously unacceptable practices. Shepherd's farewell, an evening concert, was given at the old Orpheum (130–32 South State Street)[8] and the following five McClellan concerts played on Sunday afternoons in the Colonial Theater (Third South between State and Main). Late in 1910 the orchestra returned to the Salt Lake Theater in mid-week concerts and concluded its career at the Salt Lake Tabernacle in a Thursday concert that was assisted by the Tabernacle Choir and the Orpheus Club with Alexander Heinemann, a German *lieder* singer of international reputation, as the featured guest artist.

Thereafter, citing continuing financial difficulties, unacceptable union demands, and a renewed reluctance on the part of theater managers to release their musicians for concerts, the Salt Lake Symphony was dissolved. During the nine years since its organization it had given twenty regular concerts and one special concert with Emma Lucy Gates. Among the composers whose works were presented were Beethoven, Mozart, Wagner, Schubert, Liszt, Tchaikovsky, Grieg, Strauss, Mendelssohn, Chopin, Puccini, Verdi, Humperdinck, Massenet, Weber, MacDowell, Benoit, Nicolai, and Luigini.

Though the public must have regretted the Symphony's dissolution, it seems to have been the musicians who were most reluctant to do without it. Almost the moment the Symphony ceased to exist, a movement began to replace it with a new organization, the Salt Lake Philharmonic Orchestra.

Among leading figures in the formation of this new ensemble were Anton Pedersen, already mentioned as conductor of the first Salt Lake Symphony Orchestra in the early 1890s, and his son, Arthur Pedersen Freber. The disparity in names between father and son resulted from Anton's having been compelled to adopt his stepfather's name while Arthur, with his father's encouragement, subsequently reverted to the original family name of Freber.

Young Arthur was something of a child prodigy. His first public violin solos were played in the Salt Lake Tabernacle when he was but four years old, and while still scarcely more than a teenager he graduated from the New England Conservatory of Music and secured a position with the New York Philharmonic Orchestra. The elder Pedersen, since the demise of the first Salt Lake Symphony, had organized several popular bands and orchestras. He was also the instructor of music at All Hallows College (a Catholic high school for boys founded by Bishop Lawrence Scanlan in 1886) where he conducted both the band and orchestra.

Arthur spent the summer of 1911 with his family in Salt Lake and in September, not improbably because of his father's less than robust health, he obtained a leave of absence from the New York Philharmonic. During the ensuing winter, as it became clear that the Salt Lake Symphony would not be revived, he joined in discussions with Alfred Rordame (violist), Clarence J. Hawkins (clarinetist), W. J. Flashman (flutist), and Alfred Press (violist) that led to the formation, in May 1912, of the new orchestra with Charles L. Berry as president and general manager. Pedersen, though at first he declined, ultimately accepted appointment as conductor and Arthur, choosing to remain in Salt Lake after the expiration of his leave from the New York Philharmonic, accepted the post of concertmaster.

The primary interest of the Salt Lake Philharmonic appears to have been with the cultivation and enjoyment of its members, rather than with public performances. Regular rehearsals continued throughout 1912 and into early 1913 without a single public appearance and with the only breaks in its work coming during summer vacation of

1912, and again late that year when Pedersen's health prevented his working for several weeks.

Finally, in March 1913, Latter-day Saints University[9] students were invited to a Philharmonic rehearsal. The first public performance was scheduled for Sunday, April 6, at the Empress Theater (on Main Street between First South and South Temple) with an orchestra of forty-five pieces. Charles Shepherd, a brother of Salt Lake Symphony founder Arthur Shepherd and one of the Philharmonic's future conductors, was the piano soloist in a program that included, besides Grieg's Piano Concerto in A Minor, Schubert's *Unfinished* Symphony; Wagner's Prelude to *Lohengrin* and Overture to *Tannhäuser*; and Hallén's Rhapsody in F Major.[10]

Conducting the orchestra in public recital proved more than Pedersen's fragile health could bear. Following the performance he suffered a severe physical collapse and five weeks later, on May 21, died without having left his bed. *Musical America*, a national magazine published in New York City, noted his death and credited him with having been the father of military bands and orchestras in Salt Lake and (in a reference to the 1892 Salt Lake Symphony) founder of the city's first true symphonic orchestra.[11]

The next autumn, when the Salt Lake Philharmonic resumed activities, Arthur was elected to succeed his father as conductor. Under his direction the orchestra gave concerts on December 14, 1913, and April 5, 1914, in the Empress Theater. The following season's Salt Lake concerts fell on December 13, 1914, and April 4, 1915. During November 1914 he attempted to resign, but the orchestra prevailed on him to reconsider. He continued as conductor through three more seasons, with concerts on December 12, 1915; February 20, April 9 and December 10, 1916; and concluded his tenure as Philharmonic conductor with concerts on March 4 and April 22, 1917. Five years later, in 1922, he rejoined the Philharmonic as concertmaster, a position that he retained until the orchestra ended its career in 1925.

Under Freber's baton the Philharmonic established two interesting new firsts. On March 19, 1915, he conducted the orchestra in Provo's Columbia Theater, marking the first time that a Salt Lake based home-talent symphonic orchestra had appeared outside the city. In its next concert, on April 4, and after four successive appearances at the Empress, he conducted the Philharmonic in its first appearance in the Salt Lake Theater. It was a Sunday concert for which tickets were sold and as such it ended an era that had begun with Brigham Young's personal prohibition against the Theater's being used for such activities on the Sabbath.

Freber was succeeded as conductor of the Philharmonic by Charles Shepherd, the aforementioned younger brother of Salt Lake Symphony founder Arthur Shepherd. Due to World War I, however, and the induction or enlistment of many of the musicians (including its new conductor), there was a three-year hiatus in the Philharmonic's regular concerts—though the orchestra participated in two programs in early 1918. The first was a Tabernacle Choir concert on February 22, and the second was as orchestral accompaniment to a Tabernacle Choir rendition of *Elijah* on April 5.

Postwar activity began with January 25, March 28, and May 16, 1920, concerts in the Salt Lake Theater. In 1921 no concerts were given, but they resumed in 1922 with appearances on February 26 and April 16 at Wilkes Theater (later the Promised Valley Playhouse on State Street south of First South). On February 26, 1923, a special afternoon youth concert was given in the Salt Lake Tabernacle. That evening there was a regular concert at the Orpheum, following which the orchestra returned to the Tabernacle for its final 1923 concert on April 12. In 1924 the Philharmonic changed its name to the Salt Lake Symphony Orchestra and its final five concerts were given in the Tabernacle on February 4, April 7, and May 26, 1924; and in the Salt Lake Theater on February 24 and April 21, 1925.

After a period of two years in which there were no professional home-talent concerts, symphonic music was revived by yet another of the Shepherd brothers, Albert. Under the name of the Salt Lake Orchestral Society a single concert was given on May 18, 1927. Thereafter the combined effects of sound movies, phonograph records, radio, and the economic calamity of the 1930s so devastated theater orchestras and the other musical entertainments on which local players had depended for a livelihood, that it became impossible to sustain a professional orchestra. Consequently, and despite several heroic amateur and school efforts, the city was for most of a decade deprived of the caliber of professional music it had recently enjoyed and it was not until the Works Project Administration-sponsored Utah State Sinfonietta was established in the years immediately preceding World War II that a resident professional orchestra once again became a staple of the Salt Lake musical diet.

Utah State Historical Society

University of Utah Library Special Collections

University of Utah Library Special Collections

Top Left: Anton Pedersen, a native of Norway and orchestra conductor at Salt Lake City's elegant Walker Opera House, founded the first Salt Lake Symphony Orchestra in 1892 and in 1913 conducted the inaugural concert of the Salt Lake Philharmonic Orchestra.

Top Right: Arthur Shepherd, one of Utah's most brilliant musicians, founded the second Salt Lake Symphony in 1902. He was a graduate of the New England Conservatory of Music and later joined the faculty of that institution.

Left: J. J. McClellan, the first Salt Lake Tabernacle organist to gain national prominence, conducted the second Salt Lake Symphony during 1908–1911.

CHAPTER FIVE

A New Century

In 1890, when the city's population had reached almost forty-five thousand, *Polk's Salt Lake Directory* listed but twenty-six music teachers. That same year, following the destruction by fire of the Walker Opera House, the only remaining large amusement hall was the Salt Lake Theater with its small contingent of regularly employed musicians. Yet by 1914, when the population had scarcely more than doubled to one hundred thousand, there were listed sixteen theaters, opera houses, and movie emporiums in the city and five more in nearby Murray and Sandy.

Of those within the city's boundaries, seven are known to have had orchestras ranging in size from as small as four or five pieces to the seventeen and sometimes more members of the J. J. McClellan conducted American movie house orchestra, which was advertised as the largest permanent theater orchestra in the city. Even those theaters without orchestras often employed organists or pianists and occasionally other instrumentalists. In addition, there were a number of dance halls and pavilions with orchestras and bands, and band concerts continued to be an important part of every day musical life.

Equally remarkable, from 1910 through 1914 *Polk's* listed an average of more than 130 private music teachers, or an increase over the number in 1890 of about five hundred percent. In addition, almost every secondary and preparatory school in the city, as well as LDS University, Westminster College, and the University of Utah, added music programs or departments. There were also several independent music schools established, including the Salt Lake Musical College and the Utah Conservatory of Music. And in a parallel development, by the 1890s significant numbers of students were following the early lead of such musicians as McClellan, B. B. Young, Arthur Shepherd, and Willard Weihe by traveling east and even to Europe to expand upon the musical educations they had begun at home, thus broadening the taste, aspirations, and technical ability of the city's musical elite.

One of the events of the late nineteenth century that lent great encouragement to Salt Lake's musical establishment was the aforementioned success of Evan Stephens' Tabernacle Choir appearance at the 1893 Chicago World's Fair Eisteddfod. The Choir's fine showing gave Salt Lake musicians a strong dose of self-confidence and the effort that was made to include Gentile musicians in the enterprise went a long way toward healing the still festering rift between non-Mormon and Mormon segments of Salt Lake society. Anton Pedersen, the prominent non-LDS instrumentalist, conductor, and educator, joined the choir as pianist; and Thomas Radcliffe, George Careless's successor with the Philharmonic Society and long-time First Congregational Church organist, traveled to Chicago as a guest of the First Presidency of the LDS Church.

In 1895, and again in 1898, national Eisteddfods were held in the Salt Lake Tabernacle at which local musicians made noteworthy showings. Pedersen, particularly, enhanced his reputation as a bandmaster by winning successive gold medals.

Of the major choral efforts made during the first decades of the twentieth century, the first was the organization, in the fall and winter of 1906 and 1907, of the Spring Music Festival. As early as 1904 *The Salt Lake Tribune*, noting a successful Worcester, Massachusetts festival, chided local musicians for not organizing a festival of their own. Again in May 1906, the *Tribune* noted the celebration of Cincinnati's seventeenth annual music festival with a renewed suggestion that Salt Lake follow that Ohio city's lead.

The *Tribune*'s idea finally caught the imagination of Salt Lake musicians, and on October 14, 1906, the paper was able to announce that the organization of a festival to be held in the Tabernacle was already well advanced. The chorus was put under the direction of

Stephens, who enlisted the best voices from the Tabernacle Choir. A number of the city's other prominent musicians, among them respected non-Mormons, were also put in charge of recommending the names of potential chorus members and following a winter of preparation some five hundred LDS and Gentile singers participated in what was sometimes referred to as the combined Spring Festival and Tabernacle choruses, sometimes as the augmented Tabernacle Choir.[1] The Chicago Symphony Orchestra of fifty pieces was engaged for these April 8 and 9, 1907, performances, which opened with Coleridge-Taylor's cantata, *The Death of Minnehaha*, on Monday night; then followed with a matinee program composed of miscellaneous shorter works; and concluded that night with a performance of *Messiah*. For all three concerts the vocal soloists, as well as the instrumental musicians, were supplied by the Chicago Symphony.

For the next year's program a distinction was drawn between the Tabernacle Choir and the Festival Chorus. Rehearsals for the latter began in October under Stephens, with Peabody—who was then St. Mark's Cathedral organist and director of the Orpheus Club male chorus—as his assistant. Stephens' Tabernacle Choir, though continuing to participate, did so as a separate organization, and a Juvenile Chorus was also incorporated.

The Chicago Symphony, complete with vocal soloists, returned in 1908, and two evening and two matinee performances were given on April 1 and 2. *Hiawatha's Wedding Feast* by Samuel Coleridge-Taylor was performed on the first night, a rendition of Sir Arthur Sullivan's *The Golden Legend* on the second. The first afternoon program included a selection of lighter music, while the second matinee, billed as the artists' concert, featured what many felt was the highlight of the festival. Arthur Shepherd, who was at that time the young conductor of the Salt Lake Symphony Orchestra, mounted the podium to lead the Chicago Symphony in a rendition of his *Oriental* Orchestral Suite, Op. 5, for which he had been awarded the prestigious Paderewski Prize for the best recent work by an American composer.

The entire festival was such a success, both artistically and financially, that it was decided to give an encore performance of *The Wedding Feast* on April 6 for the benefit of those who had been unable to attend the four regular performances. The Tabernacle Choir, Festival Chorus, and Juvenile Chorus all participated and a corps of local soloists, recruited in the absence of the Chicago

Symphony and its vocal artists, included M. J. Brines, Edna Evans, and Horace S. Ensign.

During the coming autumn J. J. McClellan organized his Salt Lake Choral Society (the third organization to use that name) with the purpose of competing in a national Eisteddfod that was held in the Tabernacle that October. Following the Eisteddfod his new Choral Society gave Salt Lake City's first performances of *Elijah* in the Salt Lake Theater on January 27 and February 5, 1909. The chorus numbered two hundred voices and it was joined by the complete Salt Lake Symphony Orchestra. Soloists were Anna Colborn Plummer, Edna Evans, Edna Dwyer, Emma Ramsey Morris, Hazel Barnes, Fred C. Graham, Hugh W. Dougall, M. J. Brines, and Horace Ensign.

For the same October 1908 Eisteddfod the Salt Lake Male Chorus was organized by Squire Coop, the musician who would later found the Salt Lake Oratorio Society—or the Oratorio Society of Utah, as it has been known since 1975. After taking first prize at the Eisteddfod, his Male Chorus joined forces with the Salt Lake Festival Chorus and the Schubert Male Quartet for an ambitious program at the Colonial Theater, where Coop was then orchestra leader. The featured work was Max Bruch's *Fair Ellen.* Others were a rendition of "Steersman, Leave the Watch" from Wagner's *The Flying Dutchman,* and several instrumental numbers played by a Colonial Theater Orchestra that had been especially enlarged to thirty pieces. Vocalists for *Fair Ellen* were Edna Evans and Horace Ensign.

Following these events, Evan Stephens was elevated to the position of general director for the 1909 Spring Festival while Professor Coop, fresh from the success of his Colonial Theater program, was appointed director of the Festival Chorus. To complete the festival, McClellan's Salt Lake Choral Society and the Salt Lake Ladies' Chorus, also directed by McClellan, were both included as independent organizations, along with return engagements by Stephens' Tabernacle Choir and the Chicago Symphony Orchestra.

Unfortunately, misunderstandings and contract disputes seriously marred the third Festival. On the night of May 10 the combined Festival and Salt Lake Male Choruses performed selections from *Cavalleria Rusticana* and a complete rendition of *Fair Ellen*; but a scheduled rendition of Gounod's *Gallia* by the Salt Lake Choral Society had to be rescheduled for the following night when the Chicago Symphony soloists, saying they had not been informed the piece would be done, were unprepared to participate. Compounding this difficulty, the first evening's concert and the single matinee, a largely orchestral concert given on the second day of the festival, were so poorly attended that the Symphony feared it could not be paid; and when it asked for assurances, festival organizers could offer none the orchestra found adequate.

Negotiations continued throughout that afternoon, but no way was found to meet what had by then become the orchestra's ultimatum that it must be paid before it would play. As a result, the final evening's performance was given with neither an orchestra nor vocal soloists, necessitating that the Choral Society's *Gallia* and the featured highlight of the festival, a Tabernacle Choir rendition of Ludwig Spohr's *The Last Judgment*, be significantly abbreviated.

Poor receipts and the dispute with the Chicago Symphony Orchestra had an understandably chilling effect on the Spring Festival organization and in 1910 no festival was attempted. In 1911, however, the idea was revived and the Russian Symphony Orchestra of New York engaged for May 22 and 23. Initially it was planned to have the Tabernacle Choir perform Buck's *Light of Asia* and the Festival Chorus join the Russian Orchestra's vocal soloists in a rendition of Verdi's *La Traviata.* However, at a time when other activities had begun to monopolize Salt Lake musicians, this proved overly ambitious. In the end, a program almost exclusively of orchestral works and opera selections featuring the Russian Orchestra's vocalists and with only limited participation by the Tabernacle Choir was provided for one matinee and two evening performances.

Meanwhile, the Festival Chorus had disappeared entirely and with its loss had gone much of the sense of community participation. A halfhearted attempt was made to present a festival in 1913 with the aid of the St. Paul Symphony Orchestra. But when this organization cancelled, the entire effort collapsed.

An ambitious new choral organization of this period was the University of Utah Musical Society which, despite its name, incorporated many singers from outside the University community. In fact it was to this organization that the mantle of LDS Church-independent choral work had passed even before the collapse of the Spring Festival. Organized by Professor Coop during February and March 1911, it gave Salt Lake's first rendition of Beethoven's *Christ on the Mount of Olives* in the Salt Lake Theater on April 21, 1911, with a chorus of seventy-five voices and an orchestra of forty pieces. The three soloists, picked from among the best available Salt Lake talent, were Mrs. A. S. Peters, M. J. Brines, and Fred Smith, the last named of whom was a future Oratorio Society soloist.

In 1912 The University Musical Society followed *Mount of Olives* with Salt Lake's first truly successful home-talent rendition of Haydn's *The Creation.* It was given with a chorus of one hundred voices in the Salt Lake Theater on April 22 and 24, then taken to Ogden on May 17, and finally repeated on May 26 in an open air performance on the University of Utah campus. Soloists were M. J. Brines, Fred Smith, and Margaret Tout Browning of Ogden, another future Oratorio Society soloist.

In 1913 two oratorios were undertaken. On May 23 Handel's *Messiah* opened in the Salt Lake Theater with a chorus numbering 150 voices and forty members of the Salt Lake Philharmonic Orchestra. Margaret Tout Browning returned for a second consecutive Musical Society appearance. She was joined by contralto Edna Cohn, who would also later appear with the Oratorio Society. Male soloists were tenor Alfred Best and bass Anthony C. Lund, who was then head of the Brigham Young University Music Department. The performance was repeated May 24 in Ogden, then brought back to Salt Lake on May 25 for two final appearances. That morning it was performed "for the enjoyment and edification of the prisoners" within the walls of the Utah State Penitentiary (on the grounds of what is now Sugar House Park), and in the evening its final performance was given in the Empress Theater.

Following *Messiah*, on July 10, 1913, a second Musical Society rendition of *The Creation* was given as part of the entertainment for a National Education Association convention then being held at the University of Utah. The featured artist of a special cast enlarged to five members was once again Mrs. Browning. Joining her were Margaret Summerhays, John T. Hand, Horace Ensign, and Melvin Peterson. Arthur Freber conducted thirty-eight members of the Salt Lake Philharmonic Orchestra and Professor Coop made his last appearance conducting the Musical Society chorus before leaving the university faculty.

Professor Coop's successor as chairman of the department of music at the university, Thomas E. Giles, turned the Musical Society in a new direction. He had previously been with the Utah Conservatory of Music, where he collaborated with his conservatory colleagues, Willard Weihe and J. J. McClellan, in organizing and directing a rendition of *Cavalleria Rusticana* that was given on June 2 and 3, 1913. After joining the university he continued to indulge his preference for opera. On May 13–15, 1914, he led the Musical Society in its first opera, a rendition of *Pagliacci* that, like the Conservatory *Cavalleria*, was presented in the Salt Lake Theater.

A number of other noteworthy vocal and instrumental organizations were active from the 1890s through the years preceding the First World War. One of the most important and most enduring of these is one that has already been mentioned in connection with its cooperation with other groups—the Orpheus Club. Founded in early 1892, it was one of the longest lived of all Salt Lake musical organizations. Its first director, Alfred Peabody, remained in that post until 1911, when Anton Pedersen was elected to succeed him. Following Pedersen's death in 1913, Peabody was re-elected director and held the post until his own death during the influenza epidemic that followed World War I, when he in turn was succeeded by W. J. Curtis. Under the successive batons of Professor Coop, Frank W. Asper, Ferenz Steiner, Albert J. Southwick, and John Marlowe Nielson, the Orpheus Club was active well into the 1960s.

From the late 1890s through the first decade of the twentieth century the Harmonie Singing Society, a German vocal organization, was active. Others were the Imperial Quartet, Salt Lake Ladies' Choral Society, and the Salt Lake Opera Quartet. In 1914 the Montgomery Opera Company was formed to give operas in the Salt Lake Theater and the John T. Hand Opera Company performed opera excerpts at Lagoon, a resort north of Salt Lake City. In 1913 the new Grand Theater, after having been closed for several years, was reopened especially for the purpose of giving light opera and other musical entertainments. In addition, during the summer months, lake-side resorts such as Saltair, Garfield Beach, and Black Rock became centers of musical activity, as did such places as Wandamere (on the sight of what is now Nibley Park Golf Course), Liberty and Pioneer parks, and, during its brief existence, the original Salt Palace.

Important instrumental groups, in addition to such popular bands of the day as Held's Band, Mollerup's Band, the Utah State Band, and the Salt Lake Military Band, were Romania Hyde's String Quartet, which toured widely through Idaho, Nevada, and California; the Salt Lake Women's String Orchestra; Genevieve Malone Quintet; and the Schubert String Quartet. Probably the premier chamber group was the Salt Lake Quintet, made up of Arthur Freber and George Gronman, violins; Alfred Press, viola; Otto King, cello; and Professor Coop, piano. It gave a series of concerts in the First Congregational Church during the 1912–13 and 1913–14 seasons and was highly acclaimed critically.

The Hotel Utah maintained two orchestras, the Commercial Club featured orchestral music with frequent guest soloists in its dining room, and the Kenyon Hotel introduced a string quartet into its dining room as early as 1903. In addition there were a number of oddities, such as the Christian Endeavorer's Utah State Prison String Quartet (guitars and mandolins) in 1903 and the Utah State Prison Band organized for the convicts by L. P. Christensen in 1913. The latter gave a series of summer concerts on the lawn in front of the prison that drew regular comment from *The Salt Lake Tribune*. One of the more amusing episodes occurred earlier, in 1896, when Anton Pedersen conducted a rendition of *H.M.S. Pinafore* on a boat moored alongside Saltair resort. In rough weather the boat broke free and the entire cast was very nearly swept away on the waters of the Great Salt Lake.

Though there had been significant difficulties, small mishaps, and the infrequent absurdity, in less than three-quarters of a century Salt Lake Valley was transformed from what is often described as an inhospitable desert into a thriving city that was not only the spiritual center for members of the LDS faith wherever they might be scattered, but a rapidly developing regional center of culture and art, and especially of music. It was a transformation that had been achieved by Mormon and non-Mormon alike, by men and women who almost always worked shoulder to shoulder for the same high artistic ideals, and in doing so they had shown the larger community at least one way to peace and harmony, even during some of the young city's most trying moments. Notably, it was some among the LDS Church's most exalted pioneer musicians, George Careless and Evan Stephens especially, who had taken the first steps to embrace their non-Mormon colleagues.

In the years before the First World War, with these initial successes behind them, it seemed to many only a matter of a little more time before Salt Lake City, pursuing the promise of worldwide musical prominence Edward Tullidge had seen for it in his history of the early years of the city, would come into its own as a national, perhaps even a world center of musical accomplishment.

University of Utah Library Special Collections

The Salt Lake Opera Company's 1900 rendition of De Koven's *The Mandarin* starred (L-R from top) Lennie Savage as Jesso; Heber S. Goddard, Fantan; George D. Pyper, Hop Sing; Lottie Levy (center), Ling Lo; Sally Fisher, Fing Ling; and Fred C. Graham, Kwei Tso. Pyper later served as the Oratorio Society's first president and Graham sang the tenor role in the Society's 1918 *Messiah.*

University of Utah Library Special Collections

Utah State Historical Society

University of Utah Library Special Collections

Above: Margaret Summerhays sang one of the leading roles in Squire Coop's University of Utah Musical Society *Creation* in 1913.

Above Right: Lizzie Thomas Edwards was a frequent principal in Salt Lake operatic roles.

Right: Emma Lucy Gates, in addition to her early and stunning career in European grand opera, was a favorite recital and operetta star with Salt Lake audiences. With the Oratorio Society she eventually sang *Messiah* in 1926 and January 1935, and *The Creation* in 1928.

Facing Page: John D. Spencer, here costumed for an operatic role in the Salt Lake Theater, later joined the Oratorio Society Board of Directors for the period 1915–17.

Utah State Historical Society

University of Utah Library Special Collections

This 1879 performance of *H. M. S. Pinafore* was presented by the Salt Lake Philharmonic Society with George Careless conducting. The singers pictured above, all Salt Lakers, are B. B. Young, Emma White, and J. T. White.

PART TWO

The Squire Coop Era

University of Utah Library Special Collections

This outdoor rendition of *The Creation* was presented May 26, 1912, by Professor Squire Coop and the University of Utah Musical Society on the university campus. The chorus numbered one hundred voices, instrumental musicians were drawn from various theater orchestras, and the vocal soloists were M. J. Brines, Fred E. Smith, and Margaret Tout Browning.

CHAPTER SIX

Professor Squire Coop

Prior to 1915 Salt Lake City had no annual *Messiah.* Only four major home-talent renditions had been undertaken since the city was first settled in 1847. These were the two Handel and Haydn Society renditions, in June and December of 1875, the 1907 Spring Music Festival rendition in which Evan Stephens and the augmented Tabernacle Choir joined with the Chicago Symphony Orchestra and its soloists, and the four performances of Professor Squire Coop's University of Utah Musical Society rendition in 1913.

It was Professor Coop himself, as musician and educator, who inherited the small and tentative interest in oratorio that had first come into existence under the tutelage of George Careless, Thomas Radcliffe, Evan Stephens, and the other early molders of Salt Lake City's musical taste. Through his involvement in the Spring Music Festivals and his work with the University of Utah Musical Society, it was he who created the atmosphere in which an oratorio society could grow. Finally, that *Messiah* should be repeated, annually, relentlessly even, until it had become a tradition inseparable from the fabric of Salt Lake City life, was his special dream.

The Salt Lake Oratorio Society, now known as the Oratorio Society of Utah, is therefore the spiritual child of his talent, of his love of music and his untiring work, and especially of both the triumphs and the adversities of his life. "The love child of my mind" is how he sometimes referred to it, a choice of words suggesting both his estrangement from Mormon orthodoxy and the suggestion of impropriety that attended the Oratorio Society's inception and birth during the period from 1913 through the early weeks of 1915. Fortunately, for those who have come to cherish the Oratorio Society and its annual musical feasts, this "love child" was the beginning of the only major pre-World War I Salt Lake City musical organization, other than the LDS Church sponsored Mormon Tabernacle Choir, that remains in existence at the time of this writing in 1988.

Professor Coop came to Utah as a child, and the circumstances culminating in his arrival in the new Mormon Zion are not untypical of those leading to the immigration of many another English convert to the young LDS Church. His mother, Martha Hurst Coop, had joined the Mormon faith while still a girl and among early Mormon missionaries she was reputed to be little less than an angel for her help and hospitality to them as they labored in the English mission field. Eulogizing her upon her death in 1902, Bishop Beatie of Salt Lake's Seventeenth Ward, who had known her while a missionary in Leeds, referred to her as having been faithful as a mother "in doing all she could" for the brethren.[1]

While still in England she married William Coop, Jr., and together they had six daughters and three sons, the youngest of whom was Squire. LDS Church baptismal records show him to have been born at Leeds, in what is now West Yorkshire, on April 14, 1872, while present day Coop family tradition holds that he was born at nearby Belle Isle, the birthplace of his father, on April 17.

Leeds, at that time, was a manufacturing center. Since 1848 it had also been an important railroad junction, and the region was well known for its iron smelters and coal mines. Squire's father was the superintendent of one of these mines and it was there, on September 5, 1875, that he was severely injured in an explosion. Ten days later he died and the family was left with no choice but to support itself by what work the children could find in nearby mills; so it is little wonder that by early 1878, faced with the difficulty of their situation, and no doubt longing to share more closely in the fellowship of their mother's adopted church, that the entire family made the decision to emigrate to Utah.

Three of Squire's sisters were the first to make the trip, arriving in Salt Lake during October 1878. Squire and his mother arrived the following spring. Young Esquire, as his name appears in Church records, was baptized under the auspices of Salt Lake City's Seventeenth Ward, and shortly thereafter he and his mother moved to Ogden where the Coop name reappears on the roles of the Ogden Fourth Ward. The remaining sisters came in October 1879, and Albert Coop, one of Squire's two brothers, arrived with his wife and two children in 1883. But as was so often the case, the difficult migration was not without its toll. Raistrick, the third brother, left England during June 1881, but succumbed to the hardships of the journey before he could be reunited with his family.

Even in Utah life was not easy for the Coop family. For several years Squire's mother supported herself and her young son by cooking meals for prisoners in the Ogden City Jail, meals that Squire himself delivered daily with a horse and cart.

By the time he was eight years old Squire demonstrated a keen interest in music, and with the encouragement and considerable sacrifice of his family studied piano, musical theory, and composition. He first came to the attention of the Utah music world when Professor Evan Stephens, who was later to become director of the Salt Lake Tabernacle Choir, undertook the organization of a boy's chorus in Ogden. So impressed was he with Squire's beautiful voice and musical talent that he took him on as a private student in both voice and piano.

During those early years Coop also studied with L. D. Edmonds and Anton Pedersen. But for talented and ambitious youngsters of that time the lure of the cultured East was strong, and in 1891 Squire entered the New England Conservatory of Music in Boston, where he studied with Ferruccio Benvenuto Busoni, the Italian composer, conductor, and virtuoso pianist.

On his return to Ogden in 1892 he assumed the directorship of the Ogden Tabernacle Choir. At about the same time he was appointed supervisor of musical education in the Ogden public schools under Superintendent William Allison. In 1895 he organized and directed a chorus that competed in the first National Eisteddfod held in the Salt Lake Tabernacle. That same year he opened a studio in Ogden that incorporated the services of two well-known Salt Lake musicians, Willard Weihe and Heber Goddard, as instructors of violin and voice culture.

In 1898 he organized another Ogden Chorus, to compete in the Salt Lake Tabernacle's second National Eisteddfod. This time he won second place in his category and, according to some, should at least have shared in the first prize. By 1899 he was assisting Evan Stephens as accompanist and assistant director at Salt Lake Tabernacle Choir rehearsals and during December of that year completed his move south by establishing both his residence and his studio in Salt Lake.

In 1901, with the aid of a loan from his mother and an LDS Missionary Permit from Church President Joseph F. Smith, he again left Utah, this time for study in Berlin with the famous Polish pianist, Leopold Godowsky. These years abroad were a kind of pilgrimage for the handsome young Utah musician. He traveled to Bayreuth and through Italy and France. His growing musical sophistication could never blunt the tenderness of his spirit, so that during April 1901 the *Deseret News* was able to report that "in a program mailed from Milan, Italy, Squire Coop incloses...a little bunch of leaves taken from the casket that enclosed the remains of Verdi on the day of his funeral." And, the *News* responded, "the memento is greatly appreciated."[2]

Informed of his mother's illness in early 1902, Squire immediately left Germany with the intention of returning to the United States. Travel in those days was slow, however, and by the time he reached Liverpool, where he was booked for a return crossing of the Atlantic, he received word that she had already died. Following this news, instead of going back to Berlin, he spent most of the following year studying in Paris, where he met Carmen Lense, a French actress. They were married while still abroad and the ceremony was repeated in New York City on February 23, 1903, following which his new bride accompanied him home to Salt Lake City.

He established private studios in both Ogden and Salt Lake, where he gave instruction in voice and piano—both before and during his tenure at the University of Utah. Among his many students were Lester Hinchcliff, later director of the Ogden Tabernacle Choir; J. Spencer Cornwall, future Salt Lake Tabernacle Choir director; W. Jack Thomas, who would be prominent in organizational roles with both the Oratorio Society and the Salt Lake Tabernacle Choir; and Emma Lindsay who, as Mrs. W. Jack Thomas, would serve as both Salt Lake Tabernacle Choir and Oratorio Society secretary.

Prior to Coop's joining the University of Utah, music had long been included in the school's curriculum, though generally as part of the Normal Department. Both George Careless and Evan Stephens were connected with the institution, the former as early as 1869, the latter beginning in 1883 and continuing through the end of the century. Other early instructors were Harmel Pratt in 1869–70 and Henry Tuckett during 1885–88.

Beginning in 1888 steps were taken to establish the first full-fledged department of music with Stephens as instructor of vocal music; Orson Pratt, Jr., of piano and organ; Weihe for violin; and A. André for guitar, mandolin, and banjo. Later L. D. Edwards and Anton Pedersen joined the staff. At the close of the 1891–92 school year, however, the department was discontinued, as were several other innovations initiated by University President John R. Park. Only Stephens was retained as a part-time instructor with the Normal School, in which position he remained until 1900. In 1899 Valeria Brinton joined the faculty, ultimately becoming Normal School music supervisor. She was joined by J. J. McClellan in 1900 and he, in turn, was superseded by Alice E. Westervelt in 1902 and 1903, but aside from teaching the rudiments of music to future school teachers, little was done to organize and direct the kinds of musical activities usually associated with a university. According to Ralph V. Chamberlin in his history of the university, "music activities [outside the limited Normal Department curriculum] were dependent upon the initiative and leadership provided by the students themselves, factors which varied considerably from year to year."[3]

Following the 1892 dissolution of the first music department there were periodic suggestions that it might be reestablished and in the fall of 1904 *The Salt Lake Tribune* reported that "there has been considerable talk of late of a Salt Lake Conservatoire of music in connection with the University of Utah. Professor Evan Stephens is mentioned as the prospective director." Stephens, however, was reported as having "heard nothing but gossip on the streets."[4]

That same autumn Coop first joined the faculty as a part-time instructor and due largely to his efforts, the university administration finally began to move in the direction of reestablishing a formal department. During October, 1905, Coop delivered an address before the students and faculty of the institution. *The Salt Lake Tribune*, noting the event, commented that "determined and persistent effort to raise the music standard in the University is being made by Professor Squire Coop, head of the department of music in that school [*sic*]," who, it was reported, "has aroused the interest of the authorities of the University to the extent that the hours devoted to the course have been added to, and arrangements have been made whereby credit will be given for choral work and instrumental music as well as the sight-singing of the regular course." The *Tribune*'s article also included the following excerpts from Coop's address:

America needs music to redeem it from perversion by pelf. It is building high edifices and filling them with gold, but where are the monumental personalities of the past, the poets and the philosophers of the days of Webster, Emerson and Whitman.

Students' music is not Tweedle-dum, Tweedle-dee. It is not the sound of a trumpet or the voice of a singer; it is something nearer and farther than these. It is a great emotional quality. It is soul life.

Out of the 1600 students that have registered here, not more than one in eight or nine has learned any music or heard any talked about in these halls. The music section of the institution has been confined to a very limited course afforded normal students. The institution has not been able to do more than place a small sum of money at the disposal of the music department, which has meant a limited attention from the professors engaged and the consequent limited results....

Here should be an efficient choral organization capable of interpreting the masterpieces of oratorio and opera, and here should be a hundred players of instruments who could reveal to us the beauties of orchestral literature. Here should be heard the music of Beethoven, Mozart, of Wagner; and here the names of all the great music-makers should be known and the power of their music felt.

A great school of learning needs the spiritual and purifying force of music.

You that draw and paint need the pulsating musical development to make your pictures vibrate. You literary students need music in and through you, that you may feel the spirit of the poem. Reading needs the nuance play of subjectivity. And you engineers need something besides the calculative genius; you must have temperament in your work. Temperament gives enthusiasm, and enthusiasm prompts initiative, without which you will be a failure.[5]

By the 1908–09 school year the university catalogue listed a total of six music classes being taught by Coop; and by the spring of 1910, eighteen years after the first music department was discontinued, the decision was made by the administration to upgrade the program to the status of a department within the school of arts and sciences. The result was that on April 26, 1910, the Board of Regents sent a letter notifying Coop that he had been "appointed as Professor of Music in the University of Utah, for the year 1910–1911, at a salary of $2,000 per year with the understanding that you will work up music in all lines, including an orchestra, a chorus, and a students' band (providing for assistance in instruction at your own expense, if necessary) to the best of your ability under the circumstances; and with the further understanding and agreement that you will not undertake any outside work that will in any way interfere with your duties to the University."[6]

Not long after his appointment, Professor Coop undertook to centralize and coordinate the various student initiated musical activities and by early 1911 *The Salt Lake Tribune* was able to report that "plans for the consolidation of all the musical organizations of the University of Utah students into a single body are now making progress. At a meeting held Thursday under the direction of Professor Squire Coop..., Julian Thomas was named as temporary chairman and committees were appointed for the drafting of a constitution and by-laws for a permanent organization. It is planned," the paper reported, "to have this permanent musical body conduct all student musical activities under the direction of an executive board and be answerable to the general student body."[7]

This notice marked the beginning of the University of Utah Musical Society, which was destined to be one of the important Salt Lake musical organizations for several years to come, and the organization with which Professor Coop, in particular, would produce renditions of Beethoven's *Christ on the Mount of Olives*, Handel's *Messiah*, and Haydn's *The Creation* (see Chapter Five). During this period he also maintained a private studio in the Deseret National Bank Building (later at the Templeton Building), arranged frequent recitals for both his private and university students, and otherwise took a very active role in the day to day musical activities of the city. In the summer of 1911 he conducted an outdoor performance of *H.M.S. Pinafore* at Wandamere as a benefit for the Free Kindergarten and Neighborhood House Association. In 1912 he repeated with a rendition of *The Mikado* to aid the same cause; and that same year he served as president of the Music Section of the Utah Teachers' Association.

Along with Evan Stephens, who still directed the Salt Lake Tabernacle Choir, and with Tabernacle organist J. J. McClellan, Salt Lake Philharmonic Conductor Anton Pedersen, and a handful of others among his colleagues, Professor Coop was one of the select few who wore the mantle of leadership in Salt Lake music circles. In the spring of 1913, as his University Musical Society was making final preparations for its third spring oratorio in as many years, he seemed to have climbed very near the pinnacle of his profession—into as rarefied air, at least, as it was possible for one to climb who had dedicated his life and work to this out of the way corner of the world where the brave and energetic beginnings that had been made in music only served, for a man like himself, to emphasize how very much remained to be accomplished. If ever the course of a man's life seemed set and secure, it must have seemed so to Professor Coop.

Suddenly, however, the professor's world received a serious shock. On Tuesday, April 15, 1913, the *Deseret News* informed readers that Squire Coop would not be reappointed to his position as professor and head of the university music department. "Some speculation has been indulged in as to the reason for the decision of the Board of Regents not to re-appoint Professor Coop," the *News* reported, but "W. W. Riter, chairman of the Board of Regents, today declined to be quoted in reference to the matter."[8] The same day the *Tribune* reported in a story at the top center of page one that

this information, which leaked out yesterday, and which will come as a surprise to musical circles of the city and state, was confirmed last night both by Mr. Coop and by Dr. James [*sic*] T. Kingsbury, president of the university.

When questioned last night, President Kingsbury said: "I have no statement to make bearing on the case. I have always been a friend to Professor Coop."

"Is it not true that one or two members of the board of regents have taken the view that a change should be made?"

"That, I understand to be the case, but I have no statement to make."

"Do you know when a meeting will be held for the appointment of a successor to Mr. Coop?"

"I cannot say. Probably not more than two weeks."

"Can you suggest who might be his successor?"

"No, not at this time. There are several applications, but I cannot now give out their names."

Seen at his studio last night, Mr. Coop was buried in the study of Handel's *Messiah*, the great sacred oratorio upon which he is drilling the members of the University Musical Society for its presentation in May.

No amount of questioning could draw from Mr. Coop any statement other than confirmation of the report that his connection with the university would terminate at the end of the present school year.

Among the few who know of the decision of the board of regents not to employ Mr. Coop....No one could be found to question the high standard and faithfulness of his work, but it is said that since the closing about two years ago of an unhappy chapter in his domestic life influences have been working in opposition to him.[9]

The following Sunday the *Tribune* reported that "not in the last decade have musical circles of Salt Lake City been so deeply stirred as by the announced retirement [*sic*] of Squire Coop from the University of Utah chair of music. As befits the man, an artist who has admittedly ably and conscientiously performed his duties and carried an additional and self-imposed burden of extra work at heavy personal expense and with little voluntary assistance, Squire Coop maintains a dignified silence and refuses to discuss the case."[10]

The *Deseret News*, echoing the *Tribune*, reported that "the feature of the week in music circles has been the announcement from the university that Prof. Squire Coop will not be reengaged at the end of his four year's term," and adding that "no official explanation is forthcoming [for his discharge], and the professor himself has nothing to say."[11]

On the university campus a furor arose and two articles appeared in the April 21, 1913, issue of the student newspaper, *The Utah Chronicle*. The first of these reported that there had been a "very heated and indignant meeting of the Musical Society" resulting in a resolution that accused university officials of having "allowed suggestive reports against [Professor Coop's] personal character to be circulated" while declaring that they, the undersigned students, had "always found him an inspiring teacher and a man of the highest ideals and moral standing."[12]

The second article, an editorial page comment, noted that when Professor Coop came to the university, "there was no music department. He has created one that is a credit to the school. It has even been his aim to raise the musical standards not only in this school, but throughout the state." And, the paper emphasized, "he has always displayed the highest ideals and has done a great work in providing for this school a little of the artistic atmosphere in which we are so deficient." The article then concluded with the demand, never met, that "school officials make public some justifiable reason for the professor's discharge, in order that he may have a chance to exonerate himself, and that [the officials] may remove from themselves the imputation of rotten politics."[13]

The "suggestive reports" mentioned in the *Chronicle* article, and their insinuation of some undefined moral turpitude, as well as the influences in opposition to him suggested by the *Tribune*, may have had their basis in the professor's recent divorce and the circumstances leading to it, including his former wife's accusation, later refuted completely, of a romantic attachment between the professor and his wife's teenaged niece. Or there may have been the allegation of some recent indiscretion more directly involving his activities at the university.

In the absence of an explanation from either the school or the professor, or of any other evidence, it is impossible to say exactly why he was fired; but it is interesting to note that in the wake of similar university dismissals only two years later (1915), the suspicion was shared by not a few that the motivation was a desire to staff the faculty with the most orthodoxly devout members of the LDS Church as was possible, and such considerations conceivably affected Professor Coop's career.[14] Though he never officially left the LDS Church, was in the end buried with LDS rites, and all his life was ruled by a deep spirituality, it is clear that by the time of his termination from the university he had drifted far from active participation in Church activities—so much so that at least some among his acquaintances and associates considered him not to have been Mormon at all.

Whatever the reason for his dismissal, his colleagues, students, and friends were as one in their support of him, his work, and his manner of living, and the following tribute, published in *The Morning Examiner* in Ogden, is but one more instance of the support and concern he received:

> Ogden people are a good deal interested in the published statement that Squire Coop will leave the University of Utah at the close of the present school year. Ogden is interested because Squire Coop is really an Ogden man; but even more than that because he has here a very host of friends. They are appreciative of his merits as a musician and a teacher of music; and they value, in addition, the sterling character of the man, his loyalty to friends and to every social obligation.
>
> His service to the state has been of inestimable value. Whatever advancement has been made in the music department of the state university must be credited to Squire Coop. Of course he has had cordial support in his efforts, but that support never was unworthily provided, nor was any trust ever betrayed by him. He has rendered more of service to the people of Utah than they ever can pay him for; and the appreciation of music by the people of our state is better because of him.

Whatever his work may be in the future, Squire Coop will carry with him the sure knowledge that he is prized and appreciated and loved by his fellow citizens wherever he is known—and that those who know him best prize him most highly.[15]

As difficult as it must have been for him, Professor Coop nonetheless managed to complete the school year, including the planned May rendition of *Messiah* and a special July performance of *The Creation* given in conjunction with a National Education Association convention on the university campus, but his remarkable courage was not without its toll.

Losing a valued job must always be difficult. Losing it publicly, having one's character and worth debated in the press, must have been especially difficult for a man subsequent events show to have been of keen moral sensitivity and an uncommon devotion to public service. It is little wonder, then, his duties finally fulfilled, that he sought refuge in a trip abroad.

But, as the *Tribune* reported during September 1913, events had proven too much for him. "Intending to make a flying trip to Europe, [the professor] was unable to reach the other side of the water," the paper announced. "While in New York Mr. Coop suffered a nervous breakdown and for a time his condition was so serious that he was cared for in a hospital. Fearful of worrying his sisters, who are residents of Utah and Idaho, Mr. Coop did not inform even his closest friends of his condition, preferring to fight out alone the battle for restoration to health. Mr. Coop, when able to travel, came back unannounced," the paper reported, and was now convalescing at the Hermitage in Ogden Canyon.[16]

Courtesy of Elinor Coop Frost

Left: Squire Coop in the summer of 1893. It was at about this time that he began to direct the Ogden Tabernacle Choir and to supervise musical education in the Ogden public schools.

University of Utah Library Special Collections

Right: Evan Stephens, one of the best loved of all Salt Lake Tabernacle Choir directors, early recognized Squire Coop's talent and personally undertook his education in both voice and piano.

CHAPTER SEVEN

The Salt Lake Oratorio Society

Following the failure of his health in the late summer of 1913, Professor Coop's European trip was necessarily postponed until the following spring. In the meantime, as soon as he had sufficiently recovered his strength, he devoted himself to his private students and to his work with the Salt Lake Quintet. Also, in the autumn of 1913, he was appointed to succeed Frederick Midgley as conductor of the Salt Lake Theater Orchestra, a position he would retain so long as he remained in Salt Lake City.

During the ensuing winter and spring he was also involved in helping to found the Musical Arts Society, an organization of Salt Lake musicians and music lovers dedicated to promoting the growth of local musical culture by both underwriting Salt Lake appearances of nationally and internationally prominent artists and patronizing and otherwise encouraging the efforts of local musicians and musical organizations. In addition, throughout the winter and spring of 1913–14, the possibility of forming the Salt Lake Oratorio Society, the name by which the Oratorio Society of Utah would be known until 1975, was discussed among Professor Coop, his friends, associates, and former students.

In the late spring of 1914, accompanied by Lester Hinchcliff, one of his more talented students, the professor finally set out on his long delayed European excursion. Not long afterward, on May 17, and largely as a result of the professor's encouragement and support, notice was published in *The Salt Lake Tribune* of a meeting to be held that afternoon for all singers interested in forming an oratorio society. The *Tribune*, responding enthusiastically to the idea, was of the opinion that "a permanent oratorio society is worthy of every consideration. Why not," the paper suggested, "perpetuate the work that has found so auspicious a beginning in the productions [by the University of Utah Musical Society] of the last three seasons? Why not, using as incentive and foundation the artistic renditions of the *Mount of Olives*, *The Creation* and *The Messiah*, go on to permanency? Let us have *The Messiah* every Christmas until it becomes a tradition, and another of the big oratorios every spring."[1]

The initial meeting was held in the Commercial Club with Evans B. Houtz, a teacher at the Lafayette School and former member of the University Musical Society, presiding. A temporary board of directors was appointed to oversee creation of a permanent society with Houtz as president; Lillian Thomas, a teacher at Hawthorne School, as vice-president; and Kate Thomas, a University of Utah student, as secretary. Harold Goff, a former University of Utah elocution instructor, who was presently proprietor of the Goff Press Bureau; and David E. Smith, a University of Utah premedical student, were appointed directors. It was also at this meeting, even though he was absent from the city, that Professor Coop was made the Society's first musical director and that it was decided to present *Messiah* during the following Christmas season.

Next day *The Salt Lake Tribune* noted that actually "the society had its inception from a resolution that was adopted following the rendition of Haydn's *Creation* [presented by the University of Utah Musical Society and Professor Coop in 1913] at the time of the N.E.A. convention in this city. Immediately after that convention," the *Tribune* writer recalled, "those who participated in the oratorio resolved Salt Lake was in need of a permanent musical society that would give at least one and if possible two oratorios each year. The matter has been simmering ever since with a growing enthusiasm among those who were advocating the organization."[2] The *Salt Lake Herald* also attested to this version of the Society's origin, while at the same time more clearly emphasizing Professor Coop's role by pointing out that "to him much credit is due for the present movement;"[3]

and in fact, his absence from the city notwithstanding, the Society was for all practical purposes Professor Coop's personal creation.

During the summer and fall of 1914 the original organizational board was supplemented by a board of managers appointed to oversee the Society's first production and by mid November the *Tribune* was able to report that the board included "some of the most prominent patrons of musical art in the city."[4] Herbert Salinger, a musicians' agent and promoter, was appointed business manager. Kate Thomas, secretary of the original organizing committee, filled the same office on the enlarged board. Other members were Mrs. Hugo W. Druehl, wife of the treasurer of the Druehl and Franken drug store; Karl A. Scheid, the Salt Lake City Recorder; Agnes Dahlquist-Beckstrand, a Salt Lake pianist and music teacher; F. W. Reynolds, a University of Utah English instructor; Mrs. A. S. Peters, one of the soloists in the 1911 *Mount of Olives*; George C. Wise, a teacher of modern languages at the University of Utah; George D. Pyper, manager of the Salt Lake Theater; George Q. Morris, a prominent Utah business executive; Mrs. Torild Arnoldson, an active member of the American Music Society; Jane Sands, a teacher of voice culture; Spencer Clawson, Jr., one of Salt Lake's most prominent pianists and music teachers; Elbert D. Thomas, professor of political science; Alice Merrill Horne, a prominent Salt Lake promoter of the arts and a former Utah legislator; and Dr. William C. Ebough, a University of Utah chemistry professor. Others were Houtz, the president of the original organizing committee, and Daniel J. Lang.

By early September Professor Coop was again in Salt Lake and, in view of the onset of World War I, feeling lucky to have gotten out of Europe so easily as he had. Several Utahns traveling and studying in Germany and Austria (Romania Hyde prominent among them) were trapped by the onset of hostilities and their return home delayed for weeks, in some cases even months.

Upon Professor Coop's arrival two assistant directors were appointed to help with rehearsals. These were B. Cecil Gates, the director of music at Latter-day Saints High School and the brother of Emma Lucy Gates; and Alfred H. Peabody, the well-known choral director and organist. At about the same time an executive committee was named to oversee the actual incorporation of the Society. Kate Thomas was again appointed secretary, with Mrs. Druehl, Professor Coop, and Herbert Salinger also included. The new members were

Salt Lake lawyer Mathonihah Thomas, as chairman, and Mrs. A. J. Gorham.

Throughout the final weeks of 1914 interest in the Society, and especially its chorus, continued at such a high level that on November 22 the *Tribune* reported, with perhaps slight exaggeration, that "applications for membership are coming in so rapidly that it appears a process of selection will be required in order that only the very best voices may be used in the production."[5]

On November 29 the Oratorio Society met at the Consolidated Music Hall to elect permanent officers and trustees and to discuss bylaws and the articles of incorporation. Of those elected, most had already served on the temporary committees and boards. They included Pyper as president; Mrs. Gorham and Mrs. Druehl as first and second vice-presidents; Kate Thomas, secretary; Peabody, treasurer; and Dahlquist-Beckstrand, Morris, Salinger, and Mathonihah Thomas as directors.

The only officer of the permanent Board who had served on no previous Society committee was Dr. E. G. Gowans, the State Superintendent of Public Instruction, who was elected third vice-president. New trustees were the Reverend Ward W. Reese, Rector of St. Paul's Episcopal Church; Royal W. Daynes, manager of Consolidated Music Company; Horace Ensign, an assistant director of the Salt Lake Tabernacle Choir; and Mrs. Daniel Alexander who, with her husband, had long been a supporter of Salt Lake music.

On December 16 the names of 75 charter members were entered into the minutes of the Society (see Appendix C). Articles of incorporation were approved, the selection of the above named officers ratified for inclusion within the articles, and Mathonihah and Kate Thomas, as chairman and secretary of the executive committee, authorized to file the articles as required by state law. This was done on January 15, 1915, bringing into official existence "the Salt Lake Oratorio Society...for the purpose of presenting from time to time, oratorios, operas, and kindred and similar musical productions and to give concerts and to do all things proper to advance the musical interest of the community and to join with similar organizations in the production of oratorios, operas, concerts, recitals, and the like."[6]

In the tradition of the Handel and Haydn Society, the Philharmonic Society, and the various other nondenominational musical organizations that had struggled to survive in the city, the new Oratorio Society was from the beginning self-avowedly open to all interested persons. This was a policy that reflected not only Professor Coop's attitude, but that of most of the Society's members, many of whom had first discovered their enthusiasm for music in the tolerant atmosphere of Careless and early Stephens organizations, with the University Musical Society, or with the three prominent Gentiles—Pedersen, Radcliffe, and Peabody—who had always been willing to join forces with their LDS colleagues.

Another factor in this regard was an invitation extended to the Tabernacle Choir to represent Salt Lake City at a 1915 San Francisco Eisteddfod. Many in the city, objecting to the idea that the Choir could adequately represent so diverse a population as Salt Lake's, called for the combining of Tabernacle Choir singers with those of non-LDS organizations. When this suggestion went unheeded, the call was once again raised for a permanent community choral organization independent of LDS Church and Tabernacle Choir domination, and there can be little doubt that the Oratorio Society was in part the inheritor of this sentiment.

The choice of *Messiah* as the Society's first oratorio, and its retention these many years as its principal annual rendition, was both appropriate and inevitable. No other work of its kind has achieved the widespread acclaim accorded Handel's great masterpiece. Throughout the English-speaking world it is given Christmas and Easter renditions in the most prestigious halls and in the most humble country parish churches, and by the beginning of the present century thousands, perhaps tens of thousands, were participating in its multitudinous yearly performances.

Messiah made its Western Hemisphere debut, in abbreviated form, in 1770 at the Musick Room of the City Tavern in New York City. Parts of it were presented in Boston in 1773 and during 1786 two hundred thirty singers and fifty instrumentalists rendered the "Hallelujah" chorus in Philadelphia. Throughout the 1780s at least parts of it were sung in private services by the Moravians in Bethlehem, Pennsylvania, and in 1818 the Boston Handel and Haydn Society (founded in 1815) gave the first U. S. performance in which a substantial portion of the entire composition was used.

By 1859 *Messiah* had reached Chicago. It was given for the first time on the Pacific coast of the United States in an 1874 San Francisco rendition, and the first Mountain West performance was that of George Careless and the Salt Lake Handel and Haydn Society on June 3, 1875.

So long as Handel lived he continued to make revisions in the *Messiah* score. Many of these were of a temporary nature to accommodate whatever soloists he had available at any given time, others were probably intended to be of a more permanent nature. The effect of these changes, combined with the fact that no definitive text was published in his lifetime, was to insure that so long as *Messiah* is performed there will continue to be controversy over how it should be interpreted. Several important editions have gained popularity since Handel's death, the more recent ones being by Ebenezer Prout, J. M. Coopersmith, and Watkins Shaw.

Handel composed late in the baroque period and during his lifetime produced *Messiah* with modest-sized chorus and orchestra, and with instrumentation limited, of course, to that of the period. In subsequent years, however, the tendency was toward ever greater forces. In 1784 a performance was given in Westminster Abby, to commemorate Handel's birth in 1685, that included 257 singers plus soloists, and a corps of instrumentalists numbering 253 pieces. In 1859, for the commemorative of Handel's death, Michael Costa conducted twenty-seven hundred singers and four hundred instrumentalists before an audience of twenty-eight thousand in the Crystal Palace. During the years prior to World War I, more or less contemporaneously with developments leading to the founding of the Salt Lake Oratorio Society, Sir Thomas Beecham conducted choruses of four and five thousand voices in Crystal Palace *Messiah*s.

These large forces were partly a response to romanticism, in part they probably reflected an English proclivity to grandness of scale. In all events, the trend was infectious. In 1881 Leopold Damrosch, co-founder of the New York Oratorio Society and its first conductor, directed a chorus of two thousand voices in a New York City rendition of *Messiah*, and during the late nineteenth century one-thousand-voice renditions were not uncommon in Chicago.

Salt Lake Music circles were also influenced by this tendency. In the one *Messiah* rendition with which Evan Stephens was associated, he provided a chorus of five hundred voices and Professor Coop, perhaps having been infected by Stephens, longed throughout his life to present a Salt Lake *Messiah* with five hundred—or more. During most of the twentieth century, however, and especially post-World War II, the tendency has been toward choruses of much more modest size.

Not until 1947 was the complete score of *Messiah* performed in the United States. This rendition, given by the New York Oratorio Society, was based on the J. M. Coopersmith edition and lasted three and one-half hours. Most of the Salt Lake Society's early renditions, excepting the first Salt Lake Tabernacle rendition in 1917, were quite short, even by contemporary American standards. The 1915 program shows that only one-half of the numbers were used, including the overture and Pastoral Symphony. Other sources make clear that for many years a musical program of any sort lasting about one to one and one-half hours was considered the maximum Salt Lake audiences could endure gracefully. Through time, of course, the Salt Lake music lover's stamina has increased, along with the scope of Society renditions, so that by 1985 a rendition was given in excess of two hours and including more than two-thirds of the score.

Preparations for the Salt Lake Oratorio Society's first *Messiah* were begun in late September 1914, which was many weeks before the Society's existence was made official by the filing of articles of incorporation. As is still the case, the Society's chorus was the heart of the organization. Newspaper accounts put its size sometimes at 130, sometimes at 140 members. Even the larger number is small by comparison to later Society choruses, and particularly so when measured against the mammoth four, five, and six hundred voice choirs Evan Stephens was at that time conducting in the Tabernacle.

Unfortunately, no chorus list from the Society's first performance has come to light, but at the very least it would have included the Society's seventy-five charter members whose names were entered into the minutes of the Society. Among them were included twenty members who had been University of Utah students during the period when Professor Coop was conducting the University Musical Society. Two others were university professors whose names had already become linked with Professor Coop's work.

Of the sixteen officers, directors, and other persons involved in organizing the society who are not listed as charter members, it is certain that Peabody and Ensign sang with the first chorus, and it is not improbable that several more, perhaps that even all of them did likewise. In addition, it is known that the first chorus included A. G. Brain, Mamie (Summerhays) Rich, W. Jack Thomas, and Howard T. Anderson.

It was planned to give the Society's inaugural performance in the

Salt Lake Theater. This proved impossible, however, because the theater had already been so heavily booked, and as late as December 20, when it was announced that *Messiah* would be given at 4:30 P.M. on New Year's Day 1915, *The Salt Lake Tribune* reported that "the question of the auditorium for the production is not yet determined, but will be announced within a few days."[7]

Finding an auditorium on the announced date was critical. The day and hour of the performance, once set, could not be changed because of the arrangements which had necessarily been made far in advance with concertmaster Arthur Freber and the forty musicians comprising the *Messiah* orchestra. Almost all of them would have had theater engagements throughout the holidays, including both before and after *Messiah* on the day of the performance.

Finally, on December 27, Salt Lake papers announced that *Messiah* would definitely be given in Loew's Empress Theater at the previously announced time and place, and the *Deseret News*, observing that there was no hall available, except by sandwiching between the "three a day" vaudeville and movie performances at the Empress, concluded that it was "a feather in the cap of manager Cook that he allowed his handsome house to be used for the purpose on a holiday."[8]

As the hour of the performance approached the enthusiasm of Salt Lake music lovers exceeded the expectations of most veteran observers. The *Tribune*, reporting on what it called "a lively public zeal," announced that the Musical Arts Society members planned to "attend in a body and scores of them, some of whom are members of the Oratorio society, are looking forward to the occasion with confidence and high hope."[9]

Of the four soloists, Della Daynes Hills, the soprano, was the best known. Among female Utah vocalists of her era only the Tout sisters of Ogden (Margaret and Nannie) and Emma Lucy Gates herself could have commanded greater respect. Her singing career began in the early 1890s, when she appeared in such attractions as *Billie Taylor*, an operetta produced with the participation of George Careless at the Salt Lake Theater. Since then she had been a frequent soloist with the Salt Lake Opera Company, the Tabernacle Choir, and in recital. In 1913 she sang the part of Santuzza in the Utah Conservatory rendition of *Cavalleria Rusticana*, and for some time she had been a prominent member of the conservatory staff.

Edna Cohn, who earlier sang the alto role in Professor Coop's Musical Society *Messiah*, had studied in New York City and later with Alexander Heinemann in Berlin. She was a frequent Salt Lake recital soloist, and had recently sung selections from Saint-Saëns' *Samson and Delilah* with the Salt Lake Philharmonic Orchestra.

Bass Willard Andelin, originally of Provo, had spent several years in Europe, England, and New York City. He had been associated with the Lortzing Opera House, for two years he was the leading low bass at the Royal Opera in Hanover, and he had sung *Messiah* with the Belfast Philharmonic Society.

Only Coyle Crosby Tullar, the tenor soloist, was not a long-time Utah resident—though for some months he had been settled in Salt Lake where he was taking an active role in musical affairs. He had pursued a career in European opera for twenty years, and was said to have made oratorio appearances in many of the world's famous concert halls.

When at last the performance came, it was pronounced superior in every respect. The *Salt Lake Herald* reported that the "theater was crowded to the roof, with scarcely a seat left even in the balcony, and the attendance so far exceeded expectations there were not programs enough. From the musician's standpoint," it added, the performance "left little to desire," and it closed with the observation that Professor Coop had "produced something that will live as a musical moment in the history of the state."[10]

The *Tribune* opened its review with Professor Coop's own assessment. "The thing that impresses me most of all," he is reported to have said, "is the fact that we are coming to a realization of the immortality of the greatest work of Handel. Considering that this production was the maiden effort of the Salt Lake Oratorio society, I feel gratified and satisfied, particularly with the beautiful spirit of support and loyalty manifested alike by the public, members of the chorus and the orchestra." He added that "a production approaching more nearly to the ideal can be given in a larger auditorium and given free to the public if the plans of the society are realized."

After leading with Professor Coop's remarks, the *Tribune* followed with a review at least as enthusiastic as that of the *Herald*:

> It was but a few months ago that the Salt Lake Oratorio society, then in the formative stage, decided upon the rendition of The *Messiah* during the Christmas season. That the work was strenuous for requisite preparation no

one doubts; that it was effective and to an artistic standard never in its entirety surpassed here was the opinion of auditors, scores of whom took occasion to express their congratulations.

David Reese, noted among grand opera tenors, was among the first to compliment Director Coop with the statement that he had never heard anything finer than the work of the chorus.

That financial as well as artistic success marked the rendition is doubly a cause for congratulation for those who have labored unceasingly in the work....While the soloists for *The Messiah* are too well known to need more than mention, it was, after all, the work of the chorus of 140 voices and orchestra of forty that is mostly to be noted. Sympathy, assurance of knowledge and comprehension of much of the greatness of the work were evident in the interpretation of the magnificent setting to the immortal thought.

Honors were divided between [the soloists]....Mr. Tullar's style was eminently artistic, and Mrs. Hills rose to unanticipated heights in her aria, "Rejoice Greatly." Miss Cohn sang every selection as a true artist, but is deserving of special praise for the splendid rendition of "He Was Despised."

Mr. Andelin, a favorite from the time that he arose, was especially complimented for the beauty of the recitative "Behold, I Tell You a Mystery."

The trumpet solo [played on the cornet] by L. P. Christensen was up to the standard set, and the swelling chorus of "Worthy Is the Lamb," with its never to be forgotten "Amen" held the throng until the last harmonies died away.

Then there was a rush to the stage to extend congratulations to conductor, soloists and scores of well known musicians who played their part in the initial and successful production.[11]

By contrast to the *Tribune* and the *Herald*, the *Deseret News* seemed grudging in its praise. Following several prefatory paragraphs recalling the triumphant *Messiah* of George Careless some forty years before, it noted that for the Society's effort "the response of the public astonished everyone concerned. We have before us," the *News* critic wrote, "the *New York Sun* of a recent date, containing a letter from Walter Damrosch, making an appeal to the public for greater interest in oratorio performances and deploring the fact that *Dream of Gerontius*, recently given by the Oratorio Society of New York, attracted only a fair sized audience." In fact all oratorios, the *News* felt, "have of late years elicited only languid interest in the United States, so the Salt Lake projectors had little reason to expect that their enterprise would be rewarded by more than a fair-sized turnout; but every seat in the Empress yesterday was filled and that by an audience which followed the work with rapt attention, and one that told by its almost devotional interest and discriminating applause that it understood and appreciated the purpose of the work." In conclusion the paper hoped that Professor Coop would "double his chorus next time a work of such pretension is given."[12]

To the Oratorio Society one of the most pleasant aspects of the entire enterprise was the large audience that filled the Empress Theater, and the resulting profit that remained after all expenses were paid—which was, unfortunately, one of the few profits it has shown in its seventy-plus years. Even if newspaper critics here and there overlooked an empty seat, the audience must have been of a very respectable size to give the seventeen-hundred-seat auditorium the appearance of being full. Ticket prices ranged from twenty-five cents to only one dollar for the best box seats. Considering that a total of $706.75 was collected, plus the fact that 250 members of the Musical Arts Society attended on a subscription of only $102, it seems probable that the paid attendance was in the neighborhood of twelve or thirteen hundred, to which unpaid Society guests would be added.

Understandably, the Society was optimistic, and the *Tribune* wrote that the success of the whole enterprise "means much, for none made or planned to make a dollar of profit from it. But it spells the development of a musical taste that will assure the permanency of the organization's aim, two or more oratorios each year, with the opportunity of affording the public a hearing of at least one great production without cost."[13]

At the January 21 meeting of the trustees, Royal W. Daynes, chairman of a special executive committee, submitted a financial statement that showed total expenses of $641.60. It was an amount that today would no more than meet the travel expenses of one *Messiah* soloist, but it left the Society with a net profit of $77.65. The jubilant trustees, heartened by this success, immediately began preparation for their first presentation of Haydn's *The Creation*—an event which, unfortunately, circumstances would postpone for two years more.

Courtesy of Virginia Hills Rothman

University of Utah Library Special Collections

Della Daynes Hills (L), soprano soloist for the Society's first *Messiah* in 1915, had been a frequent soloist with both the Salt Lake Tabernacle Choir and the Salt Lake Opera Company; and at the Utah Conservatory of Music, where she was a prominent member of the staff, she had sung the role of Santuzza in a 1913 rendition of *Cavalleria Rusticana.* George D. Pyper (R), after serving as the Oratorio Society's first president (1915–21), remained on the Board of Directors until 1938. He was also manager of the Salt Lake Theater and a popular soloist with the Salt Lake Opera Company.

CHAPTER EIGHT

The Tabernacle Debut

Many of Salt Lake City's most important musical events were held on Temple Square. Since the 1880s the new Tabernacle, particularly, had at various times been the home of the Spring Music Festival, of Stephens' Salt Lake Choral Society, and of Careless's Choral Union. It had been the scene of such noteworthy musical events as the Johnstown flood relief concert, various Gilmore and Sousa band concerts, appearances by Patti, Nordica, Paderewski, Theodore Thomas, and a virtual army of other notables, and in 1895, 1898, and 1908 it was the site of three national Eisteddfods hosted by the city. But even the neighboring Assembly Hall, completed on the site of the old Tabernacle in 1881, was a beautiful auditorium, and many of the city's important musical events occurred there—not because they were artistically or culturally less important, but only because they could not be expected to draw the kind of audience necessary to fill the much larger Tabernacle.

It is not surprising, then, that following the success of the Society's first *Messiah* Professor Coop aspired to a Temple Square rendition. Early in 1915 the *Deseret News* reported that he would "endeavor to secure Assembly Hall next holiday season for the annual presentation of The Messiah, with a chorus of twice the size of the present one. In addition to the orchestra there will be the organ to help," the News observed, "so that the performance promises to be even more impressive and effective than the one given on New Year's Day."[1]

Unfortunately, this initial request resulted in nothing more than disappointment for the professor and the Society and finally, with a chorus little larger than that of the preceding year, the second *Messiah* was relegated to a Salt Lake Theater performance.

In the meantime, Professor Coop's health had continued to be a worry, both to himself and his friends. Not since his collapse in New York City, following the trying spring and summer of 1913, had he really felt strong, and during the winter and spring of 1915, as the Society was struggling futilely to organize a first rendition of Haydn's *Creation*, he began to fear another decline.

Once it had become clear there could be no 1915 *Creation*, he left Salt Lake for an extended California vacation. He went first to the San Francisco Exposition where he attended the widely acclaimed Saint-Saëns concert. But the bulk of his time was devoted to extensive tramps though the California countryside with the hope that fresh air and exercise would restore both his spirits and his strength.

Whatever benefit he may have received from his trip, however, it was not his own lack of strength and enthusiasm that threatened the Society's second *Messiah*, which was given on New Year's Day 1916. A malaise had afflicted the Board of Directors, and it was not until a meeting of October 28 that the professor was able to secure its cooperation. Even then, the agreement came only after his pledge to personally underwrite any financial loss that might be incurred, a request that seems strange in view of the previous year's financial success, but one that proved justified in the end.

Another problem was that of expanding the chorus. Throughout the early years of the Society its numbers fell short of Professor Coop's aspirations. In part this was due to the high standard he brought to the music, in part to the difficulty of the music itself. *Messiah* is not well sung by a less than thoroughly trained chorus, and the discipline and commitment this implies was no doubt daunting to many a would-be Society member. Late in 1915 the situation was made particularly difficult by an outbreak of influenza that incapacitated many an otherwise qualified participant. It was not the deadly strain that would sweep the world during the closing years of

World War I, but it did play havoc with the voice. Fortunately a contingent of Ogden singers, the first of many known to have come to the Society's aid during ensuing decades, saved the chorus from actually diminishing.[2]

Further difficulty was encountered in finding an alto soloist; and in this matter, also, the limitations of the Society's purse may have been aggravated by influenza reducing the available candidates. Not until the last moment were the services of Edna Lamb Williams secured. Previously a resident of Salt Lake City, she had since lived in the South and in California, and her fortuitous return to Utah came just in time to save the young Society from a difficult situation.

The remaining soloists were soprano Fay Loose Stiehl, tenor Farquhar Murray, and bass Willard Andelin. Stiehl, at one time of Provo, was reported by the *Tribune* to be "gifted with voice, musical talent and stage presence" and to have "the culture and training necessary to insure her interpretation of the part in a manner fitting to its dignity and beauty." Of Andelin, the paper wrote, it needed only a mention of his name "to assure the public that the work on his part will be well and artistically performed."[3]

Murray, who was then a resident of Denver, had at one time been leading tenor with the Moody-Manners Opera Company of England, and he boasted a wide experience in both opera and oratorio. It is interesting to note that he is the first of the Society's imported guest soloists and though this aroused nothing more than cordial interest in 1916, the practice of including outside soloists would later become so controversial as to threaten the Society's existence.

Murray's arrival from Denver was delayed until late New Year's Eve, necessitating an early morning rehearsal with both chorus and orchestra on the day of the performance, and the influenza continued to be a nagging annoyance. More chorus members were stricken and "The trumpet shall sound" had to be omitted because Andelin's voice was so weakened by the illness that he dared not attempt it.

Surprisingly, in the face of such adversity, the actual rendition was well received. The *News*, overcoming the reluctance it seemed to exhibit in its review of the year before, was almost lavish in its praise. "As a general thing," the paper felt, "soloists are given the most attention by critics, and chorus work is treated incidentally. But the oratorio chorus of Saturday afternoon calls for special prominence, and that, too, without slighting the principals." In a burst of enthusiasm, the paper declared that "it is doubtful if any equal number of local singers ever rendered the final chorus 'Worthy is the Lamb that was Slain,' with the spirit and technical accuracy of that oratorio chorus. Handel's oratorios are fairly peppered with floriture [*sic*], and in solo work its use is enough to inspire admiring awe for the singer among an audience. But in ensemble the difficulty of rendering such music with anything like technical correctness is augmented many fold. And as it happens, Handel in this particular chorus fairly outshone himself in that class of elaboration" without regard, the *News* writer felt, for the limitations inherent in any chorus.

"Yet," he marvelled, "this oratorio chorus not only threaded its way through this intricate musical tracery with accurate execution, but with a heartiness of enunciation and purity of tone that was most gratifying; it was a remarkable performance....It indicated careful, continuous training and intelligent conception of the task in hand. The audience was delighted, and the applause had nothing of the perfunctory about it. In fact, it must be observed that every number was applauded, and the applause was deserved." The soloists were also warmly praised and the paper felt that the orchestra, consisting of thirty-eight members of the Philharmonic, might almost have been "singled out as the star feature of the occasion....The 'Pastoral Symphony' was a dream of beauty, and too much praise can not be accredited the string section." The *News* critic was also impressed with "the devotional interest with which the rendition was followed," and the "most ultra British" way in which the audience rose for the "Hallelujah" chorus.

The only real disappointment of the afternoon was the relatively small audience, prompting the *News* to suggest that "If the society is 'out of pocket,' as is likely, it would be a most generous and timely thing for some of our well-to-do lovers of music to see that the deficit is made good.[4]

The *Salt Lake Herald*, in its review, put the attendance at one thousand, but even at this, most of the house must have taken the lowest priced seats. In a later article it too lamented the financial difficulties in which the performance left the Society, noting that "in the little city of Oberlin [Ohio], with a population of less than 5000, *The Messiah* was given in full by the Oberlin Musical Union and conservatory orchestra, a custom that has been observed there with few exceptions for fifty years." If Oberlin could do it, the *Herald* chided, "Why not in Salt Lake?"[5]

Expenses, the increase mainly reflecting larger fees for soloists, totaled $803.34. Murray's fee and expenses alone came to $141.95. At the outset of preparations the Society's bank account stood at $20.96. In a special account there were an additional $1.40, a $10.00 donation was received, and the ticket sales of $489.50 brought the Society's total cash assets to $521.86. This dismal showing left a deficit of $281.48, a sizeable sum in those days, and true to his word Professor Coop made good the shortfall from his own pocket.[6]

Understandably, as the time came to begin preparations for its January 1, 1917, *Messiah*, the Society was in great need of encouragement. Despite its best efforts during the preceding spring and summer, it had once again failed to promote a performance of Haydn's *Creation*, and in some circles the likelihood of the Society's continued existence was openly questioned. Finances, particularly, were a problem, as no way had been devised of improving on the difficult fiscal condition in which the Society found itself. So it was probably none too soon for its faltering morale when, late that year, the Society received what was undoubtedly the best news of its young career.

On December 4, 1916, George Q. Morris, one of the Society's founding board members (and, coincidentally, a well-connected bishop in the LDS Church), announced that the Church had at last granted Professor Coop's request to give his oratorio on the Temple grounds. But instead of using Assembly Hall, as Professor Coop had requested early in 1915, the Society was to have the Tabernacle itself, providing that two conditions could be met. First, the oratorio must be given as a community service; and second, satisfactory arrangements must be made with the Tabernacle Choir so as not to interfere with the Choir's regular program of rehearsals and performances. Anthony C. Lund, who a few months before had succeeded Evan Stephens as director of the Choir, attended the meeting and, after a brief consultation with his friend Professor Coop, announced that he and the Choir would cooperate with the Society in every way possible.

The Society immediately began efforts to enlist participation from the widest possible spectrum of organizations in the hope not only of a fine Tabernacle performance, but also of establishing

Messiah as an annual community project with an assured financial base. Letters were sent to chorus and other musical organizations, churches, elected officials of city and state government, civic groups, businessmen's organizations, and wherever else it was thought interest might be aroused. That the Society was successful in these efforts is evident from the attendance of the first general meeting on December 14, 1916. Church representation included bishops of both the local Catholic and Episcopalian dioceses, pastors of the Unitarian and Presbyterian churches, a representative of the Presiding Bishopric of the LDS Church, and presidents of several Stake and Relief Societies. Also present were the principal elected city and state officials or their representatives, representatives of fifteen women's organizations, many prominent business men, and the president of Westminster College.

At this meeting a Citizens' Committee was appointed that included Utah Governor William Spry; Salt lake Mayor W. Mont Ferry; Salt Lake Commercial Club President Fred C. Richmond; Rotary Club President George O. Relf; David A. Smith of the Presiding Bishopric of the LDS Church; Salt Lake Stake President Nephi L. Morris; Hugh J. and Sylvester Q. Cannon, respectively presidents of the Liberty and Pioneer Stakes; the Right Reverend Joshing S. Glass, bishop of the Catholic diocese of Salt Lake; Rev. Less Bowerman, president of the Ministerial Association; Rev. Elmer L. Goshen, pastor of the First Congregational Church; Rev. John Malik, pastor of the First Unitarian Church; John D. Spencer, who represented several of the city's leading businessmen; Horace G. Whitney, business manager of the Deseret News; Richard Young, an attorney and former commander of the Utah National Guard; Bryant S. Hinckley, general secretary of the Deseret Gymnasium; Mrs. Adolph Simon, wife of the treasurer of the Paris Millinery Co.; and George D. Pyper, George Q. Morris, Alfred H. Peabody, and Mrs. A. S. Peters, all of the Oratorio Society

An executive committee was also appointed with Karl A. Scheid, by then a Salt Lake City Commissioner, as committee chairman; and May Bell T. Davis, secretary of the Oratorio Society, as committee secretary. Other members were the Right Reverend Paul Jones, bishop of the Episcopal Diocese of Utah; Royal W. Daynes, a trustee of the Oratorio Society; Mrs. Ira D. Travis, president of the Ladies' Literary Club; Mrs. C. H. McMahon, representing the City Federation of Clubs; and Nephi L. Morris, who also served on the Citizens' Committee.

The coming event was by all measure the most important of the Society's early years, and perhaps the most important in its history to date. The *Herald* announced that its chorus "would be augmented by singers from many of the local choirs, including the Tabernacle Choirs of Salt Lake and Ogden, and will be supported by an orchestra of forty or more, with Arthur Pedersen Freber as concertmaster."[7] Initially it was hoped, particularly by Professor Coop, that *Messiah* could be presented without charge. But it proved a simpler task to enlist the gentry in committees than to separate them from sufficient cash to cover *Messiah* expenses. The instrumentalists also presented a problem. Union rules, which it seems could be neither suspended nor modified, forbade their donating their services, and ultimately the Society, bowing to these realities, charged fifty cents for the more desirable downstairs seats, twenty-five cents for the balcony; and the *News*, calling this a "nominal tax," commented that "it is thought this small price of admission will be adequate to cover all the outlay."[8]

Chicagoan Marjorie Dodge Warner, the 1917 soprano soloist, was a frequent enough visitor to Salt Lake that she was considered in some circles to have settled in Zion. In Chicago, meanwhile, she was considered one of that city's leading concert and oratorio soloists, and she had recently sung *Messiah* with the Philharmonic Society of Cleveland. During the coming years she would make a total of eleven Society appearances, the most by any soprano to the present time. The contralto, Florence Jepperson, was a Utah native who had developed a considerable reputation in the East. It was said of her that she had sung *Messiah* so many times, with so many organizations in the country's large cities, that she had the part memorized. Dr. William R. Worley, the tenor, had recently toured as a soloist with the Ogden Tabernacle Choir in California, where he had been praised for his excellent singing and musical ability. The baritone, Ray M. Russell, was a member of the University of Utah music department. He had previously resided in Denver, where he was also prominent in music circles as both teacher and performer.

This first Tabernacle *Messiah* program was by far the most ambitious the young Society had yet undertaken. The complete list of numbers included has been lost, but newspaper accounts make clear that it was more than double the length of the 1916 version. In its review the *News*, ever generous with advice, commented that in order "to maintain the popularity of so noble an endeavor, the managers should study one point—that is to somewhat shorten the program. While it is difficult to determine which parts of so fine a work should be cut, it is hard to hold an audience...and, after the two hour point was passed yesterday there was a long string of withdrawals which greatly impaired the effects of the closing numbers."[9]

Unfortunately, programs for neither the 1916 nor the 1917 *Messiah* are available, but it seems likely that the 1917 rendition was an expanded version of those of 1915 and 1918, when all or part of twenty-seven and twenty-five numbers respectively were given and a total of thirty numbers used in at least one or the other rendition. Probably it is not far off the mark, judging by the length of the program, to assume that most if not all thirty of these, and perhaps more, were included.

The community service motif rapidly captured the imagination of the public, successfully cutting across sectarian boundaries and serving to further entrench the idea of the Oratorio Society as an independent organization embracing all elements of Salt Lake society. This spirit was enhanced when, on Christmas Eve, local newspapers printed the following proclamation by the Salt Lake City Commission:

> Whereas, with a fine civic spirit and the high purpose of rekindling a love and appreciation for the great musical masterpieces of Christian people, the various clubs and churches of the city have arranged for a community service at the tabernacle the night of New Year's Day, at which Handel's famous oratorio, *The Messiah*, will be rendered; and
>
> Whereas, it is highly desirable that this, our city, should not pass heedlessly through the holiday season without an appropriate observance and expression, as a community, of the deep and sacred feeling that should and does underlie the generous impulse of these days of cheer and good will; and
>
> Whereas, it is manifest that the proposed community service at the tabernacle will afford a benefiting medium for such observance, and will in a very special sense, serve to express the united spiritual sentiments of the city on the occasion of this season of gladness; and
>
> Whereas, it is proper and needful that this body should lend its support to all undertakings that serve the civic welfare, regardless of the limitations of its official functions; now therefore,
>
> Be it resolved, that the board of commissioners of Salt Lake City does hereby extend its sincere indorsement to the committee having in hand the

community service plans and earnestly urge upon all citizens the value of their personal interest to the end that so high and worthy a project shall be crowned with the full measure of success it deserves.[10]

As New Year's Day approached enthusiasm was running high, and on the eve of the performance the *Tribune* reported that "the whole community stands behind the Salt Lake Oratorio Society in this undertaking of presenting the composition in a better manner than it has ever been able to do before;" adding that "from the reports of the various members of the committee in charge of the presentation of the oratorio and from the statement of Squire Coop, the musical director, [it is clear] that never before in the history of the mammoth building...will there have been such a large and enthusiastic audience as will assemble at 4:30 o'clock New Year's afternoon."[11]

Mayor Ferry opened the performance with a brief address in which he expressed his own and the entire city's thanks to the committees, chorus members, officials of the Society, and everyone else who had made the Tabernacle *Messiah* possible. He added that he trusted this demonstration of community interest in the great works of sacred music would be maintained and that the presentation of *Messiah* and other oratorios would become an annual community affair.

Judging by the reaction of the critics, little was left wanting by the performance. They praised the chorus as splendidly trained, male soloists as definitely high class, the orchestra as excellent, and the directing of Professor Coop as inspiring. "Dr. Worley sings with ease and good expression," the *Tribune* observed, and "Mr. Russell has a deep and rich voice, a pleasing stage presence and a knowledge of his part." The female soloists were equally well treated, with Mrs. Warner declared "an artistic delight from her first solo to the last," and Mrs. Jepperson cited for singing of a nature "that tends to arouse the religious emotions" and "a wealth of phrasing that evidences her feeling of the thought in the text and the music."

For the chorus the highest moment came when the audience, applauding enthusiastically for five full minutes, demanded a repeat of "For unto us a child is born." Later, when the "Hallelujah" chorus was reached, Professor Coop dramatically broke into the performance to ask if Professor Evan Stephens was in the audience. The grand old man of choral music was found, brought to the platform, and to the delight of the audience, invited to direct this most popular of Handel's choruses. The audience, the *Tribune* reported, "broke into a storm of applause" and Professor Stephens, "deeply affected, accepted the honor and handled the chorus with his well known musicianship."[12]

In this first Tabernacle rendition the society made no use of the famous organ. It was an omission that particularly annoyed the *Deseret News*, and probably the LDS Church as well, because the previous spring a reported sixty thousand dollars, a staggering amount in the dollars of that period, had been spent refurbishing and enlarging the beloved instrument, making it what the *Herald* called "the most costly as well as the best pipe organ in the world."[13] The *News*, in its review, suggested that "the fine orchestra assembled gave capable support, but to have an oratorio rendered...without the use of an organ of such renown as the Tabernacle instrument seemed somewhat incongruous, and was the occasion of comment."[14]

It is evident from his published remarks, however, that Professor Coop felt his chorus (still relatively small at 214 voices) would be overwhelmed by the enormous instrument, which prompted the *News* to comment that "Salt Lake's musical forces ought to be strong enough to bring together 400 or 500 voices. In that event it would have been possible to have the great organ added to the accompanying instruments."[15]

The Salt Lake Tribune estimated the *Messiah* audience at six thousand persons, the *Herald* at seven thousand. The *News*, however, reported that "there were not fewer than 4,000 people present, [and that] other published estimates were wild as usual."[16]

The matter of Tabernacle attendance has always presented something of an enigma. It is, by nature of having benches rather than individual seats, a very elastic auditorium. A few thousands can appear to have filled it even though, by squeezing everyone a little more tightly, an almost equal number more might be crowded in. Combine this with the sympathy or antipathy of individual reporters, and attendance estimates can vary quite radically. The Oratorio Society presently considers a full house to be about five thousand, but the Tabernacle audience attending the inauguration of Utah's first governor in 1896 was estimated at fifteen thousand, a number that must certainly have been exaggerated, no matter how tightly the audience was packed. Crowds on other occasions, including more than one Society *Messiah*, have been put at very nearly as large, and these too must have more closely reflected the enthusiasm of the writers than the actual size of the audience.

In the final tally *Messiah* receipts were $1,441.95. Had the entire house purchased fifty-cent tickets, this would indicate a paid attendance of nearly three thousand; and had all purchased twenty-five cent tickets, of well over five thousand. The real number must have been somewhere between, thus tending to vindicate the practiced eye of the *News* reporter, though to this number must be added a considerable attendance of church, state, and municipal dignitaries and a large contingent of the city's elderly and blind who attended as guests of the Society and the Community Service Committees. However many were in attendance, the Society was left, after paying all expenses, with a balance on hand of $761.53,[17] and its future, the future of annual *Messiah* renditions, and of all other Society ambitions and dreams, seemed for the moment assured.

So heartened were Professor Coop and his chorus by the large attendance, in fact, that important decisions were taken even before the adding up of receipts and expenses had begun. According to the *Tribune*, "Mr. Coop detained the members of the society for a few minutes after the oratorio had been given [and] placed before them a suggestion that *The Creation*...be given in the spring on the state capitol grounds. The idea was received with unanimous and enthusiastic approval and plans for the details of this production will be worked out at an early date."[18]

It was a proud moment for the Oratorio Society, and a portent of accomplishments yet to come. It was true enough, of course, that the Society's was not the first Salt Lake Tabernacle *Messiah*. Parts of it had been done by the Tabernacle Choir, and by other troupes of artists who had from time to time appeared there. In 1907 a more or less standard performance was given by the augmented Tabernacle Choir in combination with the Chicago Symphony Orchestra and the orchestra's regular soloists. But this rendition by the Society was the first that was exclusively home organized, promoted, and produced. The two-hundred-plus chorus members, forty instrumentalists, and the conductor were all Utah musicians depending upon the participation or sponsorship of no outside organization. Thus it was in itself a historical occasion, and it was, of course, the beginning of a traditional Christmas season Tabernacle *Messiah* that has lasted, at the time of this writing, for more than seventy years.

Utah State Historical Society

Utah State Historical Society

Top: The old Salt Lake Tabernacle was built in 1851.

Above: It was replaced by the present Tabernacle building (with oval roof) during 1864–67, and by 1881 its site was occupied by Assembly Hall (upper left). This 1889 photograph also shows the unfinished Salt Lake Temple (right).

CHAPTER NINE

The First Creation

In 1791, when Joseph Haydn attended a Handel festival in Westminster Abbey, he is said to have wept like a child during the "Hallelujah" chorus and to have cried out "There is the master of us all!" So impressed was he with the Handelian oratorio, not only with its music, but with its immense public appeal, that he resolved to make the genre his own; and in 1795, when he left England for the last time, he carried away with him *The Creation*, an English-language libretto that, according to at least some commentators, had originally been prepared for Handel himself.

The oratorio that resulted has ever since been one of the most popular in the repertoire. It was first performed in 1799 in Vienna and by 1819 had crossed the Atlantic, where a complete rendition was given in Boston. The San Francisco Handel and Haydn Society sang it with a chorus of 250 voices in 1862 and the first Salt Lake City performance was by Thomas Radcliffe and the Salt Lake Philharmonic Society in the Salt Lake Theater on May 10, 1881. A second rendition was given by Evan Stephens' Salt Lake Choral Society in 1893. Thereafter parts of it were from time to time performed, but nothing approaching a full rendition was again attempted until Professor Coop and the University Musical Society renditions of 1912 and 1913.

It was following the last of these Musical Society renditions, of course, that the earliest discussion concerning the possibility of founding the Salt Lake Oratorio Society took place; and as soon as the new Oratorio Society had successfully presented its first New Year's Day *Messiah* in 1915 it began laying plans for a spring *Creation*. It was a major topic at the first board meeting following *Messiah*, the minutes of which record that "Mr. Coop asked the committee to decide upon the time for the next production and what it should be. He stated that while he desired to give the *Messiah* every Christmas, at least until it was known thoroughly by the community, he also wished to give a new theme each year. For the coming Spring," the minutes note, "he preferred to repeat the *Creation*, inasmuch as the time is short and it would be a strain upon the singers [most of whom were evidently familiar with *Creation* from having sung it with the University Musical Society] to master new work. This idea was approved generally by the committee and it was decided that Mr. Coop should obtain the necessary copies of that Oratorio, and that it should be given Easter or in early May."[1]

Later events indicate that Professor Coop may have been more firmly committed to annual *Creation* performances than these remarks would indicate, and it is not improbable that he was at that moment catering more to the wishes of other board members than to his own plans when he suggested the possibility of a different spring oratorio each year. Certainly the Haydn oratorio was dear to him, and by mid 1917 he was publicly urging that performances of both *Messiah* and The *Creation* be given yearly.[2] But for the moment it made little difference, as *Creation* plans were destined to meet with failure in both 1915 and 1916.

In 1915 the chorus was gathered together and trained by Professor Coop, who announced at a February 21 board meeting that he and the chorus would be ready for an Easter performance. It was brought to the attention of the Board, however, that the Salt Lake Philharmonic Orchestra had also scheduled a performance for Easter. One consequence of this was that any musical event given on that day would be presented with a seriously diminished instrumental corps, as the best musicians would all be playing with the Philharmonic. But even more significant, an Easter rendition would put the Society in direct competition with the orchestra, a situation it would at all costs wish to avoid on the simple grounds of common artistic courtesy.[3]

A committee was appointed to choose an alternative date, but by early March it had become obvious that the spring entertainment scene was to be so crowded that a suitable hall at a suitable time would probably prove impossible to find. For a while it was hoped the Salt Lake Theater might be free on May 2, and tentative plans were made for that date. In the end, however, neither the Theater nor adequate soloists proved available and *Creation* plans were postponed indefinitely.

The financial difficulty resulting from the Society's 1916 *Messiah* had the effect of putting a *Creation* performance beyond the Society's means; but some hope was seen during late winter and early spring in the State of Utah's plans for an elaborate dedication ceremony for the newly completed State Capitol Building. Construction work was nearing completion and initially it was thought the ceremony would be held not later than early July. With this in mind the Society appointed a committee to investigate the possibility of including a publicly financed *Creation* as part of the planned festivities.

On March 21 the committee presented a written proposal to the Capitol Commission for what was described in the press as an elaborate and magnificent presentation of Haydn's master oratorio. It proposed a chorus of five hundred voices made up of the Society's one hundred fifty members and augmented by representatives of the finest Ogden, Provo, and Logan choruses. It also called for a special children's chorus of one thousand voices to sing "The heavens are telling," an orchestra of sixty pieces, and the state's finest soloists. This proposal was taken under advisement by the Capitol Commission, which indicated it would make a decision during its next weekly meeting.

At this next meeting the committee appeared in person and May Bell T. Davis, acting as spokesperson, presented the plan in detail before the Commissioners, who expressed themselves as grateful to the Society for its offer to donate the services of its members and to enlist the participation of additional organizations. But due to the crush of other business, further discussion of the matter was delayed until a special meeting the following Friday. In the meantime the Commission had also failed to set a date for the dedication ceremony and there were indications that at least some members favored postponing it until the following autumn when landscaping, exterior lighting of the grounds and building, and a special memorial to the Mormon Battalion would have been completed.

To the disappointment of the Society, the Friday meeting was devoted entirely to hearing presentations from electrical contractors, the letting of a contract for Capitol grounds lighting, and to other minutia of a technical nature, while the matter of the dedication was again continued to a later date.

In the end the Capitol dedication was set for the following October 9. In the meantime the Society's plan was rejected and the Tabernacle Choir, singing "The heavens are telling" from *The Creation* and "Utah We Love Thee," was scheduled as part of a program including vocal and instrumental music by several prominent Utah singers and musicians.[4]

Fate, however, frowned on even the Tabernacle Choir. For reasons which remain uncertain, the Choir failed to appear. The *Deseret News* reported only that the reading of a poem written by Herbert S. Auerbach had been "substituted for the singing of "Utah, I Love You" [*sic*] by the Tabernacle Choir, which was unable to attend the ceremonies."[5] The equally cryptic *Salt Lake Herald* reported that "the members of the Tabernacle Male Quartet were unable to be present and a poem by Herbert S. Auerbach was read by Prof. A. C. Lund."[6] *The Salt Lake Tribune*'s explanation was more detailed, though perhaps not more factual. Seating, it explained, had been placed in the rotunda to accommodate as many as possible of the expected visitors (estimates placed the number as high as ten thousand for the ceremonies and forty thousand for the day) and a platform from which the governor was to deliver his dedicatory address was placed on the landing of the great stairway at the west end of the executive floor. "It had been arranged to seat the Tabernacle Choir directly in front of the governor's stand," the *Tribune* reported, "but the crowd had filled the seats before the choir arrived, and for that reason the musical numbers on the programme by this organization were omitted."[7]

By the spring of 1917, due largely to the success of its recent Tabernacle debut, the Society's *Creation* plans commanded greater interest and cooperation. The community service motif that had been developed for *Messiah* was retained and the idea of the Capitol Building as an appropriate *Creation* site was also carried forward from the previous year's abortive effort. The *Deseret News* enthusiastically supported the Society's plans and endorsed the idea that as many as twenty-five thousand persons could be drawn to the performance if it was given with no charge, adding that of course "the expense will have to be borne by public subscription and with what could be spared from the treasury of the society."[8]

As usual, a priority item in 1917 was enlarging the chorus, which began weekly rehearsals in early February. It was also hoped to have five hundred or even a thousand guest singers join in the popular chorus, "The heavens are telling the glory of God." Approximately fifty letters were sent to choral directors and organizations and by the third week in March the *Tribune* was reporting that the Orpheus Club, First Methodist Church, St. Mark's Cathedral, Emmanual Baptist, and thirty-four ward choirs had pledged the participation of at least some of their singers.[9]

Professor Coop's ideal of presenting *Creation* without charge, as had been done by the University of Utah Musical Society in 1913, was pursued vigorously. Pleas were made for private donations, a petition was presented to the Salt Lake City commission asking that funds be appropriated for the purpose, and Professor Coop published a short article in the *Tribune*. "It is a matter of regret," he wrote, "that the endeavor to raise the standard of musical appreciation and understanding in Salt Lake should have gone so long without financial support. With the exception of a very limited assistance from educational institutions and churches, the burden of progress has fallen upon a few individuals, notably such as are not the beneficiaries of funds, institutional, parochial or state. The history of musical affairs in this city," he lamented, "reveals many instances of financial unreward for services rendered. It has been observed also that such music as is purveyed to the public and considered in the light of entertainment is rarely of a character that would add anything to the dignity of a city or distinguish it from commonplace regard. The kind of music that an intelligent and progressive community should cultivate has too few friends."[10]

He pointed out that by contrast Los Angeles had recently subscribed seventy-five thousand dollars for an opera production and that Minneapolis gave seventy thousand dollars annually for the support of a municipal orchestra. In the end, however, the city rejected the Society's petition and other donations were so meager that the Society's plans had to be modified to the extent of setting apart a choice selection of seats for those willing to pay the nominal fee of twenty-five cents, while only the more distant areas on the lawns were to be available to those who could not or would not pay.

An interesting sidelight to the 1917 *Creation* has to do with what was called the "Humanity Hymn." World War I had begun in Europe at the very time the Society was coming into existence and the idea of peace on earth and universal brotherhood embodied in the message of the Christian Messiah and echoed in Handel's oratorio had frequently been alluded to in connection with the Society's work—as an antidote to a war-maddened world. So it is not altogether surprising, despite growing indications the United States would soon become ensnared in European hostilities, or perhaps because of those indications, that Professor Coop proposed a contest for a humanity hymn to be performed as part of the *Creation* program. The decision was made in March, and though the United States entered the war on April 6, the idea was pursued. On April 22 the *Tribune* reported that "one of the features of [The Creation] will be the singing of a 'Humanity hymn,'...for the best stanzas of which the competition is now on. Quoting Professor Coop, the paper explained that "the best hymn expressive of universal brotherhood and fitting the accent and character of the music of 'Old Hundred' (which is virile and uplifting, not sentimental) will be sung by all present on this occasion. Will you not offer us a hymn from your pen or invite someone to do so whom you feel to be capable?"[11]

The Society received several entries, but it was almost immediately evident, with the nation by then actually at war, that some board members were uncomfortable with the idea. Despite misgivings, however, five finalists were chosen by the "Hymn" committee and on May 2, after they had all been sung to piano accompaniment, the following one by M. T. Moffat[12] was declared the winner.

Come lift a universal strain,
One mighty truth in one refrain;
Pledge we before one God above,
One creed for all, the creed of love.

Great nature leads the Holy song,
Symphony old as time is long;
Flag of all people, free unfurled,
One blended rainbow spans the world.

Father of love, accept our vow,
Sealed in thy sunlight here and now:
Break we our bonds and brothers be,
To live for all humanity.

The dispute over the propriety of singing it was far from settled, however, and at a meeting a few days later May Belle T. Davis, Society secretary, proposed that the "Hymn" be reconsidered on the grounds that a patriotic song would be more appropriate. When Mrs. Davis's motion failed to carry Professor Coop countered with a motion, which did carry, that both the "Hymn" and the patriotic song "America" be sung. In the end, however, this compromise was rejected in favor of a more martial stance.[13] The *News*, commenting on the matter, reported that "it was proposed to sing a universal brotherhood hymn, in the shape of an original poem and composition selected by competition. But as this was to be on the pacifist order, and this country is at war, Lieut. Edwin Guthrie, commanding the local naval recruiting station, sent Lieut. W. F. Fox, his assistant, to talk the matter over with Prof. Coop, with the result that the peace hymn scheme was given up, and 'America' will be sung instead."[14]

Originally, as plans were first being made, it was hoped *Creation* could be given during late April. This was changed to May 6 and then, partly in hopes of better weather and partly to accommodate Mrs. Warner, who was to return to the Society following the success of her *Messiah* role the preceding January, it was postponed until May 13.

For the performance the chorus, soloists, and an orchestra of fifty-five pieces were placed on the south steps of the Capitol Building. State, city, and ecclesiastical dignitaries and social leaders were seated under the colonnades above the chorus and the greater part of the audience spread over the walks, lawns, and groves of the newly landscaped grounds. It was a magnificent setting. From the eminence of Capitol Hill one saw the city stretching away to the south, on the west the Great Salt Lake with its expanse of blue water and islands, and on the east the mighty cup of the mountains with their imposing stone faces and snow-laced peaks.

Besides Mrs. Warner, the soloists were tenor John W. Summerhays and bass Fred E. Smith. Summerhays had studied in Europe for two years prior to 1914, and while there had made a number of successful opera appearances. Since returning to Salt Lake he had appeared with the Salt Lake Tabernacle Choir and in frequent recital, and he would soon become one of the principal soloists with the Emma Lucy Gates Grand Opera Company.

Smith, who had appeared with the Metropolitan Opera Company, was well known to Salt Lake music lovers for his solo roles in Professor Coop's Musical Society *Mount of Olives* and *Creation* in 1911 and 1912. He had also sung with the Salt Lake Symphony Orchestra and in local light opera productions, and in future years he would take a prominent role in the founding of the Utah Symphony, serving as the first president of the Symphony Association from 1940 until 1948.

Since the Tabernacle *Messiah* rendition in January, the Society's own chorus had swelled to almost three hundred voices, and there were enough guest singers from other organizations to bring the total to approximately four hundred for "The heavens are telling." This was far from the thousand voices the Society had hoped to present in that chorus, but it was the largest number of singers yet to appear under the Society baton, and the volume of sound it produced was impressive, at least for those among the estimated fifteen thousand in the audience lucky enough to be situated where they could hear it.

The *Deseret News* related the manner in which Capitol Building acoustics were tested. "George D. Pyper stood in front of the statehouse Thursday afternoon, and sang a few selections from a popular opera," it reported, while Professor Coop "stood several hundred feet away near the car tracks, and as he was able to hear every word Mr. Pyper sang, the acoustic question was considered settled. It was assumed," mistakenly as it turned out, "that the great structure would make an acceptable sounding board."[15]

Unfortunately, weather conditions on the day of the performance differed significantly from those on the day of the test. Though it was a bright and warm day, uncomfortably warm, some complained, there was a stiff breeze blowing up the Salt Lake Valley from the south. The effect of this was to send "the volume of the choruses back toward the building rather than down toward the assembled multitude," and to cause the "big volume of sound to be heard better at a distance farther back on the grounds, than by the nearer audience."[16] The result of these acoustical aberrations was that it would be several years, and not until after the availability of powerful electronic amplifiers, before the Society would again attempt a Capitol grounds oratorio.

Another problem more directly affected the Society's pocket book. As already noted, when the Society was unable to otherwise raise funds it decided to provide seats at twenty-five cents each in what was considered the choice area directly in front of the Capitol steps. For this purpose it arranged to barrow a large number of park benches from the city. At the very last moment, however, some unidentified person gave the order to paint all the city's benches, thus rendering them unusable. The sale of seats, consequently reduced to the meager number of chairs and benches the Society could borrow elsewhere, generated less than $150 while expenses topped $650. "The sale of 3000 seats at the price fixed," the *Tribune* reported, "would have paid all of the expenses of the production, still leaving the opportunity for thousands of others to enjoy the masterpiece without charge. That at least 3000 seats could and would have been sold is evident from the conditions that prevailed last Sunday, when hundreds of music lovers left the grounds because they were unable to secure the seats" while others "were compelled to wander around without opportunity for quiet and mingle with those who were attracted not for love of the great music, but from curiosity."[17]

Despite these and lesser difficulties, however, it was agreed that those lucky enough to hear it had enjoyed one of the young Society's finest efforts. "Mrs. Warner was specially effective in the aria 'With verdure clad,'" the *Herald* reported, "and also in the coloratura 'song of the birds' that distinguishes the fourth episode [*sic*] of the oratorio." And "Mr. Summerhays never sang better. He pitched his clear tenor voice resolutely against the south wind that made singing in the open air manifestly difficult for the soloists, and his delivery of recitatives and arias was charmingly suited to the text in every instance. His rendition of the aria, 'In native worth,' glorifying the creation of man, was a masterly effort." In conclusion the *Herald* reviewer felt that "the voices of the three soloists blended admirably in the several trios, interspersed through the oratorio. As heretofore, the oratorio chorus did itself proud in all requirements of voice and volume. It was emotionally devotional to yield to the sway of 'The heavens are telling the glory of God, the wonder of His work displays the firmament.' The closing chorus also was uplifting and a fitting climax to a great work given a notable performance in an extraordinary environment."[18]

Although only an hour and a quarter long,[19] this first *Creation* was a remarkable achievement. Unlike the University of Utah Musical Society renditions, it had the sponsorship of no established private or public interest. It was performed with virtually no charge. And it was given before one of the largest audiences yet gathered for an event of this kind, an audience drawn by a broadly based community organization with nothing more to offer than its cultivated artistry in presenting the sacred masterpieces.

Utah State Historical Society

The Utah State Capitol Building as it appeared in 1914. It was later the scene of the Oratorio Society's first rendition of Haydn's *The Creation*, which was given only a few months after the building's 1916 completion.

CHAPTER TEN

Judas Maccabaeus

During the autumn of 1917 Arthur Freber resigned his position at the head of the Salt Lake Philharmonic Orchestra and it is of at least passing interest that soon afterward the *Tribune* announced that he was to be succeeded by Professor Coop, whom the trustees had "elected conductor for the coming season."[1] Subsequent newspaper accounts make it clear that this action was taken without obtaining Professor Coop's prior consent; but that he gave serious consideration to the offer is indicated both by the fact that nearly two weeks elapsed before he formally declined it, and by the respectful tone of the letter in which ultimately he did decline.[2] Subsequently, Charles Shepherd was elected and he held rehearsals throughout the fall of 1917 and the early months of 1918. Because of the war, however, no official Philharmonic concerts were given until 1920, when both the war and the world-wide influenza epidemic had ended.

Shepherd's involvement with the Philharmonic would be of little consequence to the story of the Oratorio Society were it not that he was destined to play an important role as Society music director, and that the disruption in the affairs of the Philharmonic, including Shepherd's entry into the armed services, foreshadowed the wartime difficulties, triumphs, and disappointments the Society itself was to experience.

Already, as preparations began for the fourth *Messiah* on January 1, 1918, the war had become a disruptive reality for Utahns. A number of the Society's male chorus members, in the first flush of patriotic enthusiasm, volunteered for service. Others were later drafted, and the Society was forced to issue a call for new singers to replace them.

On November 5, 1917, local papers reported that the first American lives had been claimed by German troops. Before the end of the coming year thousands more, including hundreds of Utah sons, would add their names to the staggering list of dead, and as New Year's Day approached the *Tribune* noted that "in this time of world sorrow and strife it is indeed fitting that the universal need of 'good will toward men' should be emphasized, and there is no more effective means than through the music of the world's greatest oratorio, Handel's *Messiah*."[3]

Except for the declining numbers of available male singers, *Messiah* preparations went smoothly. The LDS Church continued to give the Society access to the Tabernacle, as it has generously done every year since. The chorus was maintained at its *Creation* level of approximately three hundred voices, a considerable increase over the first Tabernacle *Messiah* and enough to justify Professor Coop's using the great organ to accompany the "Hallelujah" chorus, though not for the other numbers with which it is nowadays regularly used. At the console was Edward P. Kimball, an assistant Tabernacle organist and a former student of J. J. McClellan. He also played for the January 1929 and December 1931 *Messiahs*.

Marjorie Warner and Florence Jepperson returned in the soprano and alto roles and Harold Dale Sauerer, an accomplished oratorio and recital bass, was brought from Chicago. The tenor role was to have been sung by David Reese, a former member of the Utah Conservatory of Music staff noted for his opera roles with the University of Utah Musical Society. Reese, however, was at the time starring with the Emma Lucy Gates Grand Opera Company in a rendition of *Romeo and Juliet.* Unfortunately, as the opera company schedule developed it came into conflict with that of the Society, and too late for program notes to reflect the change, Fred C. Graham was substituted. John D. Spencer, in a summary of Utah music prepared for the Daughters of the Utah Pioneers, suggests that Graham assumed the role with only two hours notice, a feat made possible by Professor

Coop's having previously trained him for it.[4] In all events, Graham was well known for his many starring roles with the old Salt Lake Opera Company, as well as his solo appearances with a variety of local church choirs and membership, through the years, in a half-dozen fine quartets.

Neither the military draft nor the change of leadership the Philharmonic was currently experiencing seem to have had much impact on the Society's ability to engage an orchestra. At forty-two pieces, with Freber as usual as concertmaster, it was, the *Deseret News* wrote, "a special feature and its beautiful execution of the famous 'Pastoral Symphony' had the true 'touch of infinite calm.'" In general, the *News* reported, the entire program was met with tempestuous applause.[5]

If the Society could complain of anything in 1918, it would have to be that their *Messiah* was too successful. Even the *News* put the attendance at between five and six thousand. "That the annual community service in Salt Lake by the Oratorio Society is no longer an experiment, but that it has taken its place as one of the city's institutions, was demonstrated by the outpouring at the Tabernacle yesterday," the *News* reported, adding that no such audience had been seen there in recent years and that it upset all expectations of the management. "In future there ought to be three places to take tickets instead of one," the paper's reviewer suggested, and "the force of attendants inside too, ought to be increased, for when the 1,000 35-cent seats in the north gallery were all occupied yesterday, people kept on arriving there while on the south side there were several rows vacant, whereupon the late comers simply 'walked over' the dividing line and occupied the 50-cent seats [actually, with the war tax, seats were thirty and fifty-five cents]. It is imperative," he lectured, "that a work like *The Messiah* should be rendered when the audience is in a proper mood and this could not be assured when the hands of the clock pointed to 7 o'clock or after. The lateness upset many dinner plans, to say nothing of the catching of trains by the suburbanites who are always strongly represented on these occasions."[6]

This was the kind of criticism and the kind of problem the Society was able to relish at this moment, when it at last felt it could rest a little on its hard won laurels; but no sooner was the second Tabernacle *Messiah* history than the Society was faced with a challenge from a new quarter. A *Deseret News* article early in 1918 gave notice to all who might wish to present oratorio in Salt Lake City, and to the Oratorio Society in particular, that the Salt Lake Tabernacle Choir was entering the field on an elaborate and permanent basis. "It has been often remarked," the *News* announced, "that a permanent body of fine singers like the Tabernacle Choir ought to render oratorios at regular intervals," adding that the Choir would "shortly be in a fair way to manage successfully in this line of work." A committee, it continued, had "recently waited on the First Presidency [of the LDS Church] with a proposition that the choir should branch out in this line of endeavor" with the result that it was now proposed "to begin with a presentation of *Elijah* in April next, and work on this great oratorio is to be started without delay."

The paper concluded by informing its readers that it was also "proposed to present one great oratorio annually—perhaps oftener later on—and that success will attend the effort is reasonably believed," since "a full symphony orchestra and the organ will be used for the instrumental parts."[7]

By the end of January *Elijah* rehearsals had begun, and soon after the *News* announced that "in view of the Tabernacle Choir's entering the oratorio field, plans of the Salt Lake [Oratorio] Society for the future are not likely to be decided upon until later, when the situation has been carefully considered."[8] Not unnaturally, the Society was discouraged by this turn of events and there must have been a reluctance to assume the expense of presenting *The Creation* or any other oratorio at a time when the potential audience, not to mention musicians and vocalists, might have to be shared out so thinly as to ruin both enterprises.

Toward the end of March the coming *Elijah* was being referred to as the "spring music festival." Vivian Gosnell, an English bass-baritone currently experiencing a vogue in the United States, was engaged as guest soloist. Seven local soloists were also slated, with a chorus of three hundred, an orchestra of forty-five pieces, and J. J. McClellan at the organ.[9]

On April 5, however, when the performance actually came, it was marred in several important ways. The *News* review indicates that despite the Choir's advantage in having seen the Society commit the same mistake a few months earlier, the evening started badly when there was difficulty dispensing tickets, collecting them, and seating the audience. Gosnell, his advance billing notwithstanding, proved a disappointment when his voice fell short of the "full power such an auditorium [as the Tabernacle] calls for," and the audience might be said to have lacked enthusiasm, "only lapsing into applause," the *News* reported, "after some particularly telling number." Another disappointment was the eleventh hour illness of soprano soloist Francesca Parkinson, which forced the omission of much of the oratorio's second part. The greatest disappointment of all, however, must have been the small attendance. The *News* reported expenses to have exceeded one thousand dollars and it is probable that the Choir, charging an admission comparable to that charged by the Society, made very little money on the venture.[10]

Meanwhile, the Oratorio Society maintained its silence and if its members took any pleasure in the Tabernacle Choir's difficulties, it was at the expense of having been denied their own spring oratorio in a year when their financial strength might otherwise have assured them of another success. Following *Elijah* the Society announced that it would hold an outing on Ensign Peak. At first it was hoped to make this a public affair with at least parts of *Creation* sung by the chorus. In later plans it was scaled back to the proportions of a Society picnic, though there is no record of any such event having finally taken place, and by late June the following notice appeared on the door of Professor Coop's studio in the Templeton Building:

Closed For The Period Of The War
Engaging In War Work
Squire Coop

When he closed his studio, Professor Coop went to New York where he worked as a song leader at Camp Upton on Long Island and on battleships anchored at nearby Naval installations. By autumn he had received a Red Cross appointment for service in Europe, and at the time the armistice was signed on November 11, 1918, he was temporarily engaged as a conductor with the YMCA while awaiting embarkation for France.

In the meantime, even before the war's end, the Oratorio Society voted to continue with preparations for the traditional New Year's Day *Messiah*. Late that summer Alfred H. Peabody, the Society's treasurer and assistant choral director, was appointed acting director;

and his extensive musical training and experience leave little doubt that he could himself have led the Society in a competent Tabernacle rendition, had not circumstances prevented it.

Influenza, or "the grippe" as it was frequently known in its less virulent manifestations, was no stranger to Salt Lake City. There had been serious outbreaks in the late nineteenth century and the reader will recall that the 1916 *Messiah* had been marred by its effects. There had been nothing, however, to compare with the world-wide influenza epidemic of 1918 and 1919. It began in the spring of 1918 in Europe, among the nations whose troops were engaged along the western front, and by early the following winter had spread world-wide.

Known frequently as the Spanish influenza (in Spain it was labeled French), it became so virulent in Salt Lake City that by mid autumn of 1918 the city cemetery had to augment its staff and buy additional equipment to handle the increased mortality. During much of October, November, and December schools were closed and all public gatherings, meetings, and other commerce not absolutely essential to the city's survival, banned—with violators subject to arrest and imprisonment. For at least part of this period the situation was so dire that only one mourner at a time was allowed to visit a chapel or mortuary. Under these circumstances, of course, all musical activity ceased—including *Messiah* rehearsals.

Only as Christmas neared did the epidemic abate sufficiently for the city to resume anything like its normal routine. On December 22 the *Tribune* reported that *Messiah* rehearsals had been planned for October, "but the influenza ban prevented and a public performance cannot be given...owing to the insufficient time for preparation." However, the *Tribune* explained, "the society has made tentative plans for a celebration on the afternoon of New Year's Day, and it is purposed that the chorus will assemble then and sing the great oratorio, and later have a social gathering with light refreshments in order that the anniversary may not pass unnoticed."[11]

By New Year's Day the idea of a social gathering had developed into a private performance at the Odeon dance hall (25 East North Temple), to which many of the Society's friends and supporters were invited. The only soloists of whom a record survives were soprano Margaret Summerhays and bass Walter Wallace, both of whom were Society chorus members and frequent soloists in Salt Lake musical entertainments. The performance, as the *News* noted, was well underway when Professor Coop "unexpectedly appeared, having come home entirely unannounced. He reached the Odeon about the middle of the performance, with John D. Spencer [one of the directors], who took him up to the front and 'introduced' him to the audience. The professor made a short speech indicating his pleasure on returning to Salt Lake and resuming his musical profession and was given a warm welcome." Peabody offered to surrender the baton to Professor Coop, "but the latter declined and took his place among the singers."[12]

During rehearsals for the private *Messiah* it had been hoped that later in the year the Society would be able to present a rendition as part of a ceremony commemorating the war's end. This hope was bolstered by the opening, in France, of the peace conference on January 18, 1919, which made the return of Utah servicemen and the scheduling of a Utah victory celebration seem imminent. Within the Society, however, there were those who felt an oratorio more appropriate to the celebration of a great military victory should be chosen, and combining forces with those who had always favored a more varied repertoire, they prevailed. Thus by February the chorus was rehearsing *The Children's Crusade*, a relatively recent work by the French composer Gabriel Piern é; but Professor Coop soon found the instrumentation so exacting that it was decided to look for something home-talent musicians would find less formidable. Ultimately, an abbreviated version of *Judas Maccabaeus* was chosen.[13]

Handel's "War and Peace oratorio," as *Maccabaeus* was sometimes referred to in the Salt Lake press, was considered particularly appropriate because of its martial origins and content and triumphant conclusion. In 1746 Frederick, Prince of Wales, commissioned Handel to write it with the intention of giving it in celebration of the Duke of Cumberland's recent victory over the *Young Pretender* at Culloden Moor in Scotland. The libretto chronicles exploits of the second century B.C. Jewish hero who defeated the Syrians and rededicated the temple at Jerusalem, a theme that particularly recommended itself to the present occasion.

By early March of 1919 rehearsals were well underway, and they continued regularly until the beginning of June while the Society waited anxiously for the promised celebration; but much as the dedication of the State Capitol Building had slipped away just when it seemed most near, so did the final peace treaty and the promised Utah Peace celebration recede ever farther into the future. Finally the *Tribune* announced that "as the peace conference in Paris has extended its work so far into the summer and a number of the Utah boys are still on the other side, it is not likely the expected state celebration of peace will soon take place. The Society has decided, therefore, to postpone the public rendition and to take a vacation, pending the course of events."[14]

While the Society had been perfecting its new oratorio, the Tabernacle Choir was also busy. On June 6, 1919, it presented its second annual spring oratorio, a rendition of Mendelssohn's *St. Paul.* By doing so the Choir reiterated its intention of competing with the Oratorio Society, and it could have been little comfort to the Society that *St. Paul* was probably less well attended than the previous year's *Elijah.* The *News* opined that "the merits of the performance justified a turnout three or four times as large,"[15] which would seem to indicate that the Tabernacle had been very lightly used for the occasion.

On June 28, 1919, the war with Germany was officially concluded by the signing of the treaty at Versailles. It was ratified by Germany on July 9 and soon after Utah's peace celebration, or victory celebration as many preferred to call it, was finally scheduled for October 8. Early in September the *News* printed a letter that Professor Coop had sent to all Society members:

Dear Friends:

Our society has been greatly honored. We have been invited by a committee, appointed by the governor of the state, to render the oratorio Judas Maccabaeus on the occasion of the state's memorial to those who served in the recent war. These number over 25,000, over 500 of whom will not return.

It is truly a very great honor to be permitted to express the gratitude of the state to those who sacrificed themselves for all.

We have been authorized to expend whatever funds will be necessary. It is obviously up to us now to endeavor, as we have never before, in order that we may honor the occasion as we indeed have been honored by it.[16]

The state's offer to meet *Maccabaeus* expenses marked the first time the Society received public funds, and the only occasion up to the present time that such funds have been sufficient to meet all the usual expenses of a performance. Most significantly, the state's action was a welcome recognition, on an important state occasion, of the Society's role as a nondenominational organization representing the wide spectrum of Salt Lake interests and beliefs.

Enthusiastic chorus rehearsals resumed during September, and soon thereafter the selection of soloists was announced. Marjorie Warner was given the soprano role and a fellow Chicagoan, Edward Atchison, was engaged as tenor on Mrs. Warner's recommendation. Will Magginetti, a talented member of the Society chorus, sang the bass part. In announcing Magginetti's selection the *Tribune* noted that the Society had departed from its "custom heretofore employed of engaging talent entirely outside of the organization for the solos."[17]

In the absence of its conductor and not a few of its musicians, the Salt Lake Philharmonic Orchestra was quiescent during the war and most of 1919, so that the *Maccabaeus* orchestra of thirty-one pieces had to be drawn directly from the city's various theater orchestras, though with the faithful Arthur Freber in his usual role as concertmaster. Tabernacle organist J. J. McClellan was at the console for his first Society appearance, one he repeated for *Messiah* in 1920 and 1921 and for *The Creation* in 1925.

Maccabaeus constituted only the latter part of the evening's ceremony. The program was called to order by C. Clarence Neslen, chairman of the executive committee organizing the program. He was a member of the Society Board and in later years would serve as both Salt Lake City mayor and Oratorio Society president. The audience, estimated in the press at nine thousand persons, consisted mostly of servicemen and their families. B. Cecil Gates directed and Evelyn Buehler, a Society chorus member, lead the huge crowd in singing "America." President Heber J. Grant of the LDS Church offered an invocation, and Governor Simon Bamberger made a brief introductory address. Sergeant Axel Madsen and Chaplain B. H. Roberts addressed the assembly. Army and Navy service flags, made by the War Mothers of Utah, were presented to the members of a delegation that included representatives of every Utah county that had lost a son in the war.

It was a long program. By the time all speeches and awards were given, colors presented, hymns and anthems sung, and "taps" played, well over an hour had elapsed before the Society's performance began. Nonetheless, the majority of those attending seem to have remained throughout, and the *News* reported that this "first rendition in Salt Lake of Handel's noted work" was followed with "keen appreciation," adding that "nothing more fitting as an expression of victorious triumph after the war and as a future memorial to those who fell could have been chosen. Many a silent tear fell and many handkerchiefs were seen in that portion of the house reserved for the relatives of the boys who will not come back from 'over there.'"[18]

In the opinion of the *Tribune*, "the soloists were in superb voice, and the conclusion of every recitative or air brought a storm of applause." Mrs. Warner, it felt, had "seldom, if ever...sung with such entrancing purity of tone and fidelity of expression," while Atchison "grew in favor with the audience as the succeeding numbers for tenor were given." Even Magginetti, the Society chorus member turned soloist, "measured up well with the professional soloists who had made a long journey to participate. His base," the *Tribune* found, was "pronounced, flexible and highly pleasing," and he sang "with both spirit and understanding."[19]

The *News* found one of the finest features of the performance to be the training shown by the chorus of 215 voices, which led it to doubt that even "the great singing organizations in the big cities could have done any better." It was, the paper concluded, a performance marked with "vigor and life, as well as artistic effort."[20]

But as great as was the success of *Judas Maccabaeus*, and of other recent Society renditions, the years since 1913 had been arduous and in may ways disappointing years for Professor Coop. Now, in late 1919, he was a man well into middle age. The hours he had devoted to the Oratorio Society numbered in the thousands and though he had no doubt accomplished a great deal, much of his dream remained unfulfilled and he could scarcely be faulted if indeed he was discouraged. It must have seemed to the Professor that the Society's preeminence in the oratorio field was under deliberate attack from the Tabernacle Choir. And despite some slight if encouraging financial assistance from private donors and, most recently, for *Maccabaeus*, the Society was still almost entirely dependent on the donated work of himself, the Board, the chorus, and proceeds from ticket sales, so that of the six renditions the Society had given, only two met the professor's ideal of oratorio free to the public.

That he was already giving serious consideration to leaving the Society is not certain, but that he was unhappy with the current situation he made abundantly clear to a representative of the *News* who, at about the time the Society would normally have begun *Messiah* rehearsals, reported that Professor Coop, "when asked whether the Oratorio Society would undertake another work in the near future..., replied that he was seriously considering retiring from the field of musical endeavor unless some arrangements can be brought about whereby the proposition of giving these works to the public can be adequately financed and made remunerative to those who devote their time to the work of preparing and presenting them."[21]

Perhaps the statement most telling of the Professor's tempestuous feelings is one that came somewhat later, in the form of a letter to the *Tribune*. By rendering the impossibility of the situation in which he and many Utah musicians found themselves, his letter seems to mirror the kind of wrestling with conscience and love of place that must have caused him some little torment during these and coming months. "Salt Lake City has a musical reputation," he wrote.

> It was established by the Mormon Tabernacle Choir and extended by the tabernacle organ recitals. There is something significant in these facts.
>
> When one hears Salt Lake City spoken of in a musical way by outsiders, the large number of local toilers in the musical vineyard of these mountain slopes is not thought of.
>
> That array of gifted and giving personalities which has contributed not a little to the musical life and welfare of the community passes unobserved. One who has lived here and witnessed the endeavors of this...company...could not deny, if he would that certain men and women have given musical service that is comparable to nothing less than pure devotion, equal in self-sacrifice and perhaps equal in value to the service of those few upon whom fortune has hung a mantle of fame.
>
> Their names are unsung. Some have departed like the troubadours in Tannhäuser, their harps hanging at their sides. The contest held but one prize, anyway; there was only one Elizabeth. Others remain to pass in a similar way.

Following this allusion to Wagner's opera, which in view of the circumstances surrounding his University of Utah dismissal is so evocative, the direction of his remarks abruptly changed. "The point I intend to call attention to," he wrote, "is that a place or community rides to victory in the chariot of institution. Individuals come and go, but institutions may live forever," and "those who render inconspicuous service may be neglected....[but] this does not matter so much after all if they have kept the fires burning."

In conclusion he wrote that "one distant day Salt Lake City might attract the world to hear the great masterpieces of choral music...or, if this is too bold a dream, at least let us not wake up to the realization that we have neglected the opportunity to add to the splendid beginning."[22]

To whatever degree he felt personally the rebuke of Venus to Tannhäuser when she tells him the world will never forgive him, it is clear that the Professor could not abandon the Society, the love child of his mind, without providing for its continued existence—and by early November 1919 the *News* announced that *Messiah* preparations were again underway.[23]

Two innovations were tried for the January 1, 1920, rendition. First, the performance was held at 11:00 A.M., whereas it had never started earlier than mid afternoon. This was done because of the difficulty of finding sufficient instrumental musicians at the later hour, when all the theaters were open; but a disappointing turnout was blamed on this experiment, and it was not repeated. The second innovation met with more general approval. For the first time the organ, with McClellan at the console, accompanied choruses throughout the performance, making what the *News* called "a rare addition to the instrumentation."

With the participation of volunteers from other organizations the chorus was restored to three hundred voices, and the *News* in its review complimented it for being "remarkably well balanced, in sympathetic unison, finely voiced, accurate in attack, well trained in phrasing, simply great in its crescendos, fairly overpowering in the double fortes; while in the 'Hallelujah' chorus it was a thrilling inspiration."[24]

Out-of-town soloists were soprano Marie Partridge Price of San Francisco and bass-baritone Albert Borroff of Chicago, both experienced oratorio soloists of considerable reputation. Contralto Evelyn Buehler, the Society chorus member who had been lead singer for hymns and anthems during the memorial service preceding *Judas Maccabaeus*, sang the alto role; and Dr. William R. Worley, the popular Salt Lake tenor, made his second Society appearance.

It was less than five weeks later, with the death of Alfred Peabody on January 30, 1920, that the Society lost one of its most important founding members. He was also one of Salt Lake City's best loved musicians and the irony of his death is that he had passed through the most lethal period of the influenza epidemic in 1918 and 1919 with scarcely a cough. While others were bedridden, many dying, he remained at his post as secretary of three large Utah mining companies, leader of the Orpheus Club male chorus, organist of St. Mark's Cathedral, member of the board of directors of the Philharmonic Orchestra, and assistant director of the Oratorio Society—only to fall victim to the disease just as the danger seemed finally to have passed. He became ill on Tuesday and on Friday morning, at the age of fifty-four years, his life ended.

He was born in Capetown, South Africa, where his father was the American consul, and came to Salt Lake City in 1889. In a resolution of condolence to his family the Board of Directors wrote of their "belief that one so happily endowed with all the lovable and attractive qualities which so endeared Alfred H. Peabody to us is still one with us unseen."[25]

The Utah State Historical Society

The Utah State Historical Society

Above: The fact that the Salt Lake Tabernacle has benches rather than seats makes it very difficult to accurately estimate the size of any audience. A few thousand can appear to have filled it, while thousands more can be added by more tightly packing the benches.

Left: Edward P. Kimball was at the console of the Tabernacle organ the first time it was used to accompany an Oratorio Society *Messiah*.

CHAPTER ELEVEN

Wandering Minstrel

During the years immediately following its 1920 *Messiah*, the rendition with which Professor Coop had at first expressed reluctance to participate, the Society's fortunes improved steadily. The first important development concerned the Tabernacle Choir. After its poorly attended and lightly regarded *St. Paul*, it temporarily withdrew from the field of spring and summer oratorio. The Society, understandably encouraged, immediately reentered it with plans for the first of what eventually totaled six renditions of *The Creation* and one program dominated by *Creation* selections, all of which were given on the University of Utah campus.

The first of these productions was doubly important because, excepting the special case of *Judas Maccabaeus*, it was also the first for which the Society received either public funding or substantial financial assistance from the business community. Contributions from the city, the University of Utah, and from the Exchange Club totaled $1,450, and similar contributions in succeeding years enabled the Society to give all its university programs without charging admission.

The inaugural *Creation* of this series, like its University Musical Society counterpart of 1913, coincided with the school's hosting of another National Education Association (N.E.A.) convention. It was given at the "sunset hour," July 9, 1920, on the steps of the John R.

Park Administration Building, the entrance to which, with its white columns, portico, and wide stairway, provided an inviting setting for Haydn's masterpiece. Before it the expanse of walks and lawn accommodated many thousands, while below in the valley lay the city, and beyond that the immense lake reflecting the desert sky.

The audience, including conventioneers, was estimated at fifteen thousand persons. Herbert Gould, a noted Chicago bass, was engaged for the part of Raphael and Marjorie Dodge Warner returned to sing the part of Gabriel. Gould, in particular, would prove very popular with Salt Lake audiences, and during coming years would appear with the Society eight times more, a record no bass has yet exceeded. In fact, with the return from European war duty of John W. Summerhays for the part of Uriel, three of the most popular soloists in Society history were gathered for one rendition. Over the years, between them, they would account for forty-one solo appearances.

The chorus of three hundred was acclaimed one of the best ever; the orchestra, according to *The Salt Lake Tribune*, was "effective throughout, in genuine sympathy with the director and responsive to every demand of the moment." As a work of artistic merit, the *Tribune* felt, it "far surpassed any previous effort of the Salt Lake Oratorio Society." Even the perfections of nature, the *Tribune* found, contrived to add to the majesty of the performance. "Castles of clouds in the west were transformed by the setting sun to realms of roseate, golden glory, while far in the east, above the lofty peaks of the Wasatch, myriad of evanescent shades and colors shifted, and through the patches of clear sky looked down the changeless stars." At the conclusion of the performance hundreds from the audience surged forward to congratulate Professor Coop; and Fred M. Hunter, president of the N.E.A., declared that "this is the most wonderful and artistic work of music I have ever heard."[1]

Half a year later, for the 1921 *Messiah*, Summerhays was joined by Florence Jepperson, the contralto who had made such a favorable impression in 1917 and 1918. New soloists were soprano Christine Laugenhan of New York City and Frank M. Dunford, a Salt Lake-born bass who was at that time pursuing his career in Chicago. Especially well known in the Middle West for his concert, recital, and church solo work, he arrived in Salt Lake directly from a December 28 *Messiah* appearance with the Milwaukee Oratorio Society.

Never before, the *Tribune* reported in its lavish review, has the chorus "been so well balanced, so efficiently drilled; never before have the four soloists...measured up so well in artistry and comprehension of their roles; never before has the orchestra been so large and so generally satisfactory, and, of equal significance in making a general analysis, never before has an audience taxing the capacity of the Tabernacle listened with such close attention and shown such impressive evidence of community appreciation."[2]

Not withstanding these successive triumphs, however, Professor Coop almost immediately announced his decision to leave the Society. Early in January 1921 the *Tribune* quoted him as saying, "I am ready to stand aside. My personal interests demand that I devote myself to remunerative employment here or elsewhere."[3]

At first the import of this announcement seems not to have been fully appreciated by many among his admirers and supporters, and their initial reaction would have been more appropriately aimed at placating a man whose genius was perhaps overbalanced by temperament, than to accepting the word of one who truly spoke his mind. And to the outside observer, at least one with a Salt Lake perspective, there could have seemed little in his life to displease him. He was still the conductor of the prestigious Salt Lake Theater Orchestra, he had only recently succeeded to the directorship of the Orpheus Club, he had his students as an added source of income, and his Oratorio Society at last seemed thriving, so that there must have been many, far from perceiving the difficulties he confronted, who envied him.

The *Tribune*, more than ever his champion, editorialized on his behalf in the same article in which it announced his intention to leave the Society. Reviewing the Society's already impressive contribution to community music, and the financial difficulties that had often plagued it, the paper concluded that it was "a subject that challenges deep and sober thought—this record of the Salt Lake Oratorio Society." It reminded readers that deficits had frequently been met out of Professor Coop's pocket. It reminded them, also, that it was he, in addition to carrying a disproportionate responsibility for managing the Society, who had the full responsibility of training the chorus and rehearsing the orchestra:

> The big task preliminary to the rendition of an oratorio is getting the chorus into shape. The choral numbers are not only the most important parts of any great oratorio, but, of necessity, they must be sung by non-professional singers, men and women from many walks of life, who, with loyal devotion, worship at immortal music's shrine, finding reward only in the consolation and uplift that comes from breadth of view and communion with pure spirit speech.

For the director such training spells great sacrifice of both time and energy—the sopranos one time, altos another, then the tenors, then the bassos and finally the ensemble. Three weeks or a month are not sufficient. It requires three months at least to get the untrained members of the chorus into anything like satisfactory condition; even then they are largely sustained by the veterans who have assisted in the production year after year.

Then there is the orchestra to be considered. When one remembers that in Salt Lake the great majority of orchestra men must perforce spend the greater part of their time playing the light and transient music of the theater and motion picture house, the excellence of their work in handling the harmonies of Handel, Haydn and Beethoven is a matter for both congratulation and wonder....Those who enjoyed the artistic and satisfying New Year's day performance of Handel's masterpiece doubtless looked over the audience and thought: "With this crowd the society must make some money," yet such was not the case. The expenses of soloists, orchestra, advertising, printing, stamps, telegrams, and a few minor, yet essential, incidentals, virtually ate up the receipts. Had the price of admission been made commensurate with the worth of the performance, as is done in many cities smaller than Salt Lake, the same sized audience would have brought the society a few hundred dollars for contingent fund.

It chanced that climatic conditions were favorable. Had a storm broken at noon and continued throughout the day the musical director would have faced a mass of unpaid bills. There was no individual or organization to stand behind him. Mr. Coop handled none of the money, but had it not been forthcoming from the receipts the bills would have been his.

Drawing on the example set by public and business financing of the previous summer's *Creation*, the paper warned that if the city was to have *Messiah* year after year it must continue to do more to support the Society. Hasn't the time come, it asked, "that the municipality, as a corporation, or the Commercial Club, as the representative of the city's best interests, or a group of public spirited citizens of means and influence, awoke to the value of oratorio as a community uplift and furnished substantial and permanent support?"[4] And a week later the same paper took the city to task for failing to adequately support any of its musical organizations, warning that "without encouragement and support individual work cannot be indefinitely extended."[5]

At about this same time Professor Coop was chosen to be guest of honor at the annual Author's Club banquet. Of special satisfaction to him must have been the attendance there, among other dignitaries, of Dr. Joseph T. Kingsbury and W. W. Riter, two of the men who had, as university president and chairman of the board of regents respectively, participated in the decision to terminate the professor's career at the University of Utah. Toastmistress Margaret S. Roberts described Professor Coop as a leader "who handled minds and souls as his instruments, in the interpretation of the master spiritual music of the ages," adding that his *Messiah* was "the mightiest of sermons on the life of Christ and the greatest service to the city, state and to religion itself."[6]

With this outpouring of sympathetic understanding, the success of his current work, and in the absence of any further public announcements of his pending departure, especially, it must have seemed to many that the professor had been won back to the city and the Society. One circumstance, however, and one not widely comprehended at the time, indicates that his mind was made up and that his search for a way of implementing his departure, if not already complete, continued unabated.

This circumstance had to do with Marjorie Dodge Warner, the Chicago soprano and frequent Society soloist. During the years of Mrs. Warner's association with the Society she and Professor Coop had come not only to admire one another as musicians and artists, but to feel toward each other a personal regard and an abiding friendship. Finally, with Mrs. Warner's marriage coming to an end, this friendship was quite naturally developing in the direction of a committed and close relationship. Professor Coop, however, had already felt the bite of provincial disapproval when, his own first marriage ending, he had soon after been publicly humiliated and deprived of his teaching position with the insinuation in the press, at least, that the circumstances of his divorce had contributed to his dismissal. Remembering this unfortunate experience, and not wanting to experience it again or to subject Marjorie to anything resembling it, it seems unlikely that he could ever have seriously reconsidered his decision to leave Salt Lake.

In the meantime, with continued financial assistance from the city, civic organizations, and the university, another *Creation* was given on June 16, 1921, before what the *Tribune* described as "the largest assemblage of citizens ever drawn to one place in Salt Lake with a single motive." Estimates of the attendance ranged from twenty to as high as thirty thousand, "a seething sea of humanity," the *Tribune* said, "that became stilled as by magic when Mr. Coop lifted his baton and the first notes of the overture were heard." Both Gould and Summerhays returned for this performance, and they were joined by Chicago soprano Margery Maxwell. The performance was, the *Tribune* declared, "without disparagement to any of the others, the best, most artistic and thoroughly satisfactory of all," and as it drew to a close "nature, beneficent and loving, invested the scene with a glory and grandeur that was sublime, the sun had long since sunk to rest, but the glow of an ideal summer twilight still lingered in the western skies, while far above, from the east and south, kindly breezes swept from the moon her mantle of cloud, revealing the queen of night, attended by brilliant stars. The multitude stood hushed and reverent—to the auditors it did not seem fitting to go away and it was only after a stanza of 'America' and a verse of 'Just a Song at Twilight' that the exodus toward the city began."[7]

Throughout this period attempts were made to obtain for *Messiah* the kind of funding the two recent *Creations* had enjoyed, but the general feeling among those who might have provided it seems to have been that Tabernacle ticket sales were both appropriate and sufficient. In fact, since the first Tabernacle *Messiah* in 1917, revenues had almost always been adequate to meet expenses and even provide small amounts toward the Society's other activities, though this was to change radically over the next few years.

In 1922, particularly, the feared performance-day storm, which had been anticipated in the *Tribune* editorial quoted above, actually occurred. Snow fell steadily throughout the day, greatly reducing attendance and with it, revenues. Another factor which may have contributed to reduced attendance was the scheduling of *Messiah* for January 2, a Monday, rather than New Year's Day. This was necessary because, for the first time since the Society had begun using the Tabernacle, New Year's Day fell on the Sabbath, when LDS Church rules forbade use of the building for paid performances.

In all other respects the Society carried on with the same enthusiasm and efficiency that had marked most of its efforts since the end of World War I. The chorus at 350 voices and the orchestra of fifty pieces were both the largest yet presented for *Messiah*. Herbert Gould, after two *Creations*, made his first *Messiah* appearance. He was joined by Chicago soprano Florence Lang and by two Salt Lake singers, contralto Eunice Edwards Anderson and tenor Howard Frazee.

Every aspect of the performance was reviewed positively. The orchestra, made up mostly of Philharmonic members, was especially praised. After a fitful start in 1920 and a year's hiatus in 1921, the Philharmonic was once again holding regular rehearsals and the effect of these was striking. Tracy Y. Cannon, who would also appear in the 1923 and 1924 renditions, made his Society debut at the organ.

Shortly after *Messiah*, C. Clarence Neslen succeeded George D. Pyper as Society president. The crush of Pyper's duties as manager of the Salt Lake Theater, secretary of the Utah State Fair Association, and manager of the Salt Lake Musical Arts Society, as well as in several important leadership roles with the LDS Church, made it impossible for him to continue carrying the load of Society president, though he remained an important member of the Board of Directors until 1938. Neslen, since joining the Board in 1919, had also served as a Salt Lake City commissioner and more recently as mayor, in which capacity he had been instrumental in arranging city funding for the Society's *Creation* productions.

During preparations for the following summer's *Creation*, Professor Coop at last let it be known officially that he had accepted an appointment to the music faculty of the University of California at Los Angeles, and that he would be leaving Salt Lake City permanently at the beginning of the coming fall term. It must have been an especially gratifying appointment, freeing him of any suspicion of incompetence or unfitness of whatever kind that might have lingered as a result of his dismissal from the University of Utah. In addition, it finally brought to a resolution the conflicting feelings and ambitions with which he had been tormented since the disruptions of the war, and it relieved him of the anxiety he would have felt about having to make a life for himself and his bride-to-be in a community that still held a narrow view of propriety. For the little world of Salt Lake City music, however, especially for the Society, it was a time of great loss. Another of the city's most talented and prominent musicians, as had many before him, concluded that the future, if a future in music there was, lay elsewhere.

On the evening of June 20, as the 1922 *Creation* was about to begin, there was a wash of clouds and haze across the western horizon that gave the sunset a darkened, brooding aspect. "The whole rendition showed a tenseness of emotion creating an atmosphere that indubitably made itself felt on performers and audience alike," wrote the anonymous *Salt Lake Tribune* reviewer. "Never before did the chorus sing with such an accuracy of attack, such clear attention to phrasing and such brilliant and impressive interpretation, for it got deeper into the heart and soul of the mighty work than it has ever done in previous years."[8]

Marjorie Dodge, her name now shortened by divorce, was joined by Gould and Summerhays in the three solo roles, and though each of them would appear with the Society several times more, it was the last time together for this popular trio. The performance was once again supported by grants from the city, the Commercial Club, and the university; but, and this was taken as a very hopeful sign for the future, with a number of contributions from individuals and small businesses. At the very moment of his departure Professor Coop had brought the Society to the greatest heights of strength and prestige it had yet achieved.

Those who were to remain in Salt Lake, however, were faced with the task of finding some way to replace the devotion, skill, and vision he had lavished on the Society. It was a task that must have seemed, and perhaps was, impossible. Early in July the *Deseret News* observed that "no successor has been named in [Professor Coop's] place as director of the Salt Lake Oratorio Society, it being a matter as to whether another musician will care to devote the time and energy to the musical organization which Mr. Coop has made a matter of personal interest. It is hoped, however, by local citizens, that the society will not be allowed to perish but will rather be developed to even greater attainments in the future than have been accomplished in the past." A tentative agreement was extracted from Professor Coop, in fact, to the effect that if it were possible for him to do so, he would return to conduct the coming winter's *Messiah.*

Meanwhile, the *News* reported, the professor was widely entertained by his fellow musicians, friends, and admirers, among whom were some of the Utah's most prominent citizens. "Wednesday he was guest of honor at a luncheon at the Hotel Utah, given by a group of local musicians, Arthur Freber, Charles Shepherd, Bert Shepherd, Sterling Fogelberg and L. P. Christensen. Monday Ogden friends gave a sort of 'old home' supper at the Hermitage in Ogden canyon." The Reverend Mr. Carver "was toastmaster and speeches were made by Major Francis, [future LDS Church President] D. O. McKay and others. There were some 150 guests present. Miss Marjorie Dodge gave musical numbers during the evening. The Salt Lake theatre orchestra is also planning an affair in honor of Mr. Coop, for nine years director of the orchestra."[9]

With the professor's impending departure it was thought wise to reincorporate the Society. The structure of the organization remained essentially the same, with fifteen directors, but with only two vice-presidents rather than the three called for in 1915. The most telling aspect of this exercise was a statement by Professor Coop, in the form of an addendum to the new articles, consenting to the Society's use of the name "Salt Lake Oratorio Society," thus relinquishing any proprietary rights to the name he may have enjoyed while at the same time emphasizing the degree to which his own identity and that of the Society had been associated during the preceding years.

Finally, on August 21, Marjorie Dodge and Professor Squire Coop were married at the Hermitage by Society President C. Clarence Neslen, whose authority for performing the ceremony derived from his being both Salt Lake City mayor and an LDS bishop.

During the following autumn the Society seems to have made no attempt to replace Professor Coop. Instead, armed with the professor's promise to conduct the January 1, 1923, *Messiah* if it proved possible for him to leave his duties in California, the Society appealed directly to Dr. Ernest C. Moore, who was head of the UCLA campus. In a telegram[10] sent on December 1, 1922, Dr. Moore was informed that the

> DIRECTORS OF SALT LAKE ORATORIO SOCIETY ARE DESIROUS OF HAVING PROFESSOR SQUIRE COOP RETURN TO US DURING CHRISTMAS HOLIDAYS TO CONDUCT TENTH ANNUAL PRESENTATION OF THE MESSIAH. PROFESSOR COOP WAS ORGANIZER OF SOCIETY AND ALL MEMBERS AND PUBLIC GENERALLY ANXIOUS TO HAVE HIM RETURN FOR THIS SPECIAL OCCASION. WOULD APPRECIATE ANY ASSISTANCE YOU COULD GIVE US.

Dr. Moore replied by return telegram that he would "do what I can to assist you in arranging for Squire Coop's return."[11] Both Dr. Moore and Professor Coop were true to their word, and by mid December the Professor was conducting rehearsals in Salt Lake City.

The chorus, meanwhile, in anticipation of the Professor's arrival, was trained by J. Spencer Cornwall, who was a former student of Professor Coop's, a Society chorus member, and a future director of both the Society and the Salt Lake Tabernacle Choir.

Marjorie accompanied the Professor on his trip home in order to sing the soprano role. She was joined by two veterans, Provo contralto Florence Jepperson (Madsen) in her fourth Society appearance, and Summerhays in his sixth. The bass, a newcomer to the Society, was Gustave Holmquist of Chicago. A veteran of more than twenty years as a professional singer, he had most recently been the chief bass soloist for the Swedish Choral Society of Chicago and was said to have performed *Messiah* more than one hundred times. In the present season alone, this was his fifth *Messiah* .

In an era when every Society rendition was favorably reviewed, this performance was no exception. From the chorus of three hundred voices to the organist, the *Tribune* found scarcely a fault. The orchestra of forty pieces, it was agreed, showed marked improvement over earlier performances, a fact attributed "to the skill and musical intuition of Arthur Freber, concertmaster." And in addition to Freber's influence, the regular training the Philharmonic was receiving under the baton of Charles Shepherd was a contributing factor of no little importance.

A highlight of the afternoon was Holmquist's rendering of "The trumpet shall sound" which, accompanied by John Visser's trumpet obbligato, was considered remarkable for its brilliance, while the final "Amen" brought to a close what the *Tribune* described as a "distinct and unquestioned triumph."[12]

CHAPTER TWELVE

Home-Talent Conductors

During the eleven years beginning with the 1924 *Messiah* and concluding with its New Year's Day 1935 rendition, the Oratorio Society called on the services of five prominent young Salt Lake music directors. The first of these was Charles Shepherd, who had taken the baton of the Salt Lake Philharmonic Orchestra following Freber's resignation in 1917.

In late 1923, as Shepherd began preparing the Oratorio Society chorus for its New Year's Day performance, the principal problem faced by the Society was the Tabernacle Choir's decision to reenter the oratorio field with another rendition of *Elijah*. Though a date was never set, early statements indicated that it would come at a time clearly conflicting with Society plans. Negotiations were held and briefly it seemed the Society might be forced to abandon its annual rendition. In the end, however, an understanding was reached by which *Elijah* was postponed until the following spring.

Shepherd's *Messiah* featured the return of Gould and Summerhays. They were joined by Detroit soprano Lois Johnston and by contralto Doris Buriff of Salt Lake, who was head of the music department at Westminster College. The rendition was a noteworthy success, even by comparison with the recent splendid performances for which Professor Coop had been responsible. The chorus, maintained at three hundred voices, was commended for its "accuracy in attack, an ability in phrasing and a concept of correct volume," while the orchestra, comprising virtually the entire Salt Lake Symphony Orchestra (as the renamed Salt Lake Philharmonic was now known), was superb.[1]

The following summer Shepherd directed a program dominated by *Creation* selections, but including a chorus from *Judas Maccabaeus*, the "Jewel Song" aria from *Faust*, and two orchestral pieces. The only vocal soloist was Margaret Tout Browning of Ogden. Since singing with Professor Coop's University Musical Society in 1912 and 1913, she had become associated with the New York Metropolitan Opera, where she sang under the professional name of Margaret Romaine. She had also appeared widely in New York musicals and European opera, and she and her talented and successful sister Nannie were considered by some to rival even Emma Lucy Gates among Utahns important in national and even international music circles.

The mixed program, so unusual for the Society, may have reflected Shepherd's own taste, particularly his interest in orchestral music. But though records on this point are not numerous, it is certain that there were other considerations. Inclusion of the performance in National Music Week observances (which featured several days of concerts by various groups throughout the city), and as a special event on the concluding day of a national convention of Disabled American Veterans, had at least some influence. It is known, for instance, that the *Maccabaeus* chorus, "See the conquering hero comes," was for the benefit of the veterans. And among Society members themselves there had always been a faction that favored a more varied repertoire. The Society's original charter, after all, had defined it as an organization for the purpose of presenting "oratorios, operas, concerts, recitals, and the like."

The Salt Lake Tribune, in its initial response, represented itself as favorably disposed to virtually every aspect of the program. But a week later the same paper observed that "Haydn's *The Creation*...is a concept, an 'Idea,' in one sense an 'ideal,' devoted primarily to praise of Nature and Nature's God—a composition welding words long held as inspired to music scarcely less inspirational. It holds so much of entity and unity, of cogency and interrelated significance" the paper felt, "that to single out two solos and three choruses seems inevitably to destroy its worth." In the *Tribune*'s opinion, "classic orchestra selections, operatic solos and totally unrelated choral numbers" could in no way "conduce to the development of a psychic atmosphere that aids in appreciation of *The Creation*," not even under "the ideal physical and climatic conditions that have usually attended the rendition of the Haydn masterpiece by the Salt Lake Society."

In the same article, in a startling revision of its initial assessment of the chorus, the paper also first revealed what was to be a recurring problem for the Society for more than three decades to come. "Among many of the ablest and most experienced members of the chorus," it reported, "the impression prevailed that the work of the ensemble did not reach the standard attained in several previous years." The reason for this, it revealed, was that "the chorus, in anything like its entirety, was not present" and, evidently, many of those who were present were ill prepared for the work at hand.[2]

In the transition from Professor Coop to Charles Shepherd, chorus discipline had been lost. The charismatic leadership and singleness of vision Professor Coop had supplied had not been reestablished, and in the short term, at least, there seemed only one way in which it could be restored. Professor Coop, accompanied by Marjorie, returned to conduct the New Year's Day 1925 *Messiah*.

Since leaving Salt Lake, Professor Coop had been appointed chairman of the UCLA music department and Marjorie had also met with great success in California. Her July 1923 appearance in the Hollywood Bowl as soloist with the Los Angeles Symphony Orchestra scored a considerable success, which she at least matched by a return appearance during August 1924. In addition, she had spent several months in recital and concert appearances in Chicago and New York.

J. Spencer Cornwall, having proven himself as choral director in 1923, was appointed assistant conductor and undertook rehearsals until Professor Coop's arrival in mid December. Albert J. Southwick, like Cornwall a future Society conductor, made his debut as bass soloist. Completing the roster of soloists, besides Marjorie, were Florence Jepperson (Madsen) in her fifth Society appearance and Summerhays, who by now was a perennial favorite with Salt Lake audiences in both oratorio and opera. Frank W. Asper made his Society debut at the organ, which he would also play for *Messiah* every year through 1928, then in December of 1929 and 1933, and for both 1935 renditions.

Though the audience was considered to be on the small side, the performance was well received by reviewers. Southwick, especially, was found to be a promising talent with a voice of good range and excellent musicianship, and following the performance many in the audience pressed forward to congratulate the soloists and, particularly, Professor Coop.

The summer of 1925 found Professor Thomas E. Giles, Professor Coop's successor as head of the University of Utah Music Department, wielding the baton over a strictly conventional Society *Creation.* Professor Giles was a grandson of Thomas Davis Giles, a blind harpist who walked to Utah in 1856, and the son of Henry E. Giles, organist of the Provo Tabernacle Choir and founder of the music department at Brigham Young Academy (forerunner of Brigham Young University).

The chorus for Professor Giles' *Creation,* at 450 voices, was the largest yet presented by the Society. A month earlier many members of the Society chorus had sung with the Ogden Tabernacle Choir in its rendition of *The Creation,* and the Ogden singers' reciprocal participation accounts for the greatly expanded numbers presented at the June 30 Park Building performance. Combined with an orchestra of fifty-five pieces, it was one of the great spectacles ever witnessed on the University of Utah campus.

Soloists, besides the virtually obligatory Summerhays, were soprano Jane Burns Albert of Portland, Oregon, and bass John Claire Montieth of New York City. An innovation for this rendition was the inclusion of a two-pedal organ with Tabernacle organist McClellan at the keyboard. Another very special feature was a rendition, as a finale to the program, of the "Hallelujah" chorus from *Messiah.* George Careless, who was now eighty-five years old, was called from the audience to conduct it in commemoration of the Handel and Haydn Society *Messiah* at the Salt Lake Theater fifty years before. According to *The Salt Lake Tribune,* a storm had been threatening throughout the performance and as Professor Careless took up the baton, it finally began in earnest. "With the lightning flashes coming more frequently to punctuate the music and while the rain pattered more quickly about his bent shoulders, Mr. Careless swept orchestra and chorus into the glorious hymn with a fervor of passion and devotion that swayed the audience to complete forgetfulness of the warring elements."[3]

The following winter saw Professor Coop returning to conduct *Messiah*, but the highlight of the January 1, 1926, performance was the first of three Society appearances by Emma Lucy Gates (Bowen). It is not possible to overstate her importance to Utah music. From the time that she won the piano competition in the Great National Eisteddfod of 1895 in the Salt Lake Tabernacle until her death in 1951, she was one of its dominating forces. A granddaughter of Brigham Young, she was born in St. George in southwestern Utah, and following the musical promise exhibited by her prize-winning Eisteddfod performance, she was taken to Germany to study at the Berlin Royal Conservatory of Music. It was at the Royal Conservatory that her voice, theretofore considered unremarkable, was "discovered," and soon after she left the conservatory to study singing with Madame Corelli. On February 2, 1902, while still hardly more than a girl, she made her debut at Carnegie Hall. Later she sang at the Royal Opera House in Berlin, then regularly at His Majesty's Royal Opera House in Kassel and elsewhere, until the advent of World War I forced her return to the United States.

In Salt Lake she had given frequent Tabernacle concerts, had appeared with the Salt Lake Opera Company, and had been a featured soloist with both Arthur Shepherd's Salt Lake Symphony Orchestra and the later Salt Lake Symphony under Charles Shepherd. Probably her most noteworthy contribution to Salt Lake Music was the creation, with the assistance of her brother, B. Cecil Gates, of the Lucy Gates Grand Opera Company, which gave performances from 1918 through most of the 1920s.

Other soloists for 1926 were Summerhays, Gould, and Nan Butterfield, a well known Salt Lake church and concert artist said to know the contralto role so well, from appearing with so many other organizations, that she could sing it without reference to the score.

As a special feature requested by Professor Coop, Evan Stephens was invited to conduct the "Hallelujah" chorus. It will be recalled that once before, during the Society's Tabernacle debut in 1917, he had been called from the audience to take the baton for this most popular of all Handelian choruses, but this time it was Professor Coop's intention that the honor should be formalized by being announced in advance.

At this time, also, an amusing controversy arose over the question of applause. If newspaper accounts are to be believed, early Salt Lake audiences must have been as demonstrative, some might say as boisterous as any in America. They made their pleasure known with instantaneous, vigorous, and prolonged applause, and—most annoying of all to the devout—they seem to have considered it their privilege to interrupt *Messiah*, indefinitely if necessary, until the beleaguered artists consented to repeat a favored number. It was an acceptable practice for a band concert or a circus, some felt, and it had long annoyed Professor Coop. Able to stand it no longer, he directed that the 1926 program notes ask the audience to refrain from applause, a request that he repeated from the podium before the Overture was begun.

The *Tribune*'s reaction to this request offers ample evidence that it was a step not only necessary, but one the taking of which required some daring. "Many who were in the big audience Friday," the *Tribune* reported, "expressed opposition to the ban placed upon applause, feeling that it is the privilege of the silent participants to make known their approval of both the work and its interpreters. The request that the oratorio be received in silence was made because of the religious character of the composition, and in one sense this seems appropriate, but it is a deep-seated characteristic of any American audience to express in some manner approval of great music, regardless of its type."[4]

Whatever their feeling about the new restriction, the *Tribune* reported that the audience sat in compliant silence until the "Hallelujah" chorus. But when their old friend Professor Stephens took up the baton the strain was too great, and they erupted into rebellious applause.[5]

In the autumn of 1926, when it became evident that Professor Coop would not be available that year, J. Spencer Cornwall was appointed music director for the coming New Year's *Messiah*. In addition to having been choral director and assistant conductor for the Society, he was at that time director of the Mendelssohn Male Chorus and supervisor of music for the Granite School District. In his youth he had studied with J. J. McClellan, Hugh Dougall, and with Professor Coop; and in 1935, following the death of Anthony C. Lund, he would become Mormon Tabernacle Choir director.

The New Year's Day 1927 *Messiah* also saw the debut of another important Society figure. He was Harold H. Bennett, the new bass soloist, who would make a total of nine appearances with the Society, the last coming in 1950—following which he would spend several years on the Society's Board of Directors. He had been a student of W. W. Clive, a member of the Latter-day Saints University Orchestra, and at the time of this first Society appearance, which was his first major appearance as a vocal soloist in Salt Lake, he had only recently returned from a period of study in the East. In later years he would appear widely in Salt Lake musical events, particularly with the Tabernacle Choir and the Zion's Cooperative Mercantile Institution (ZCMI) Chorus. Other soloists, besides Summerhays, were Marjorie Coop and Mrs. Raymond Havens, a Kansas City contralto.

The performance, a marked financial disappointment, was noted for a chorus pronounced the best the Society had yet produced. The "Hallelujah," especially, had been inspiring to an audience which was, if nothing else, a practiced judge of "Hallelujahs," and the *Tribune* critic, waxing eloquent, wrote that "there are probably thousands who have noted in the 'Hallelujah' chorus an effect as though great golden bells were beating out a transcendental symphony. This effect," he said, "is attained occasionally" and it was "attained perfectly Saturday by the oratorio society singers. Resonantly, unmistakably, the sound of mighty chimes pealed from the choir seats, mingling in a gigantic harmony of unearthly beauty and power."[6]

Late in 1927 the Society was confronted with a serious new challenge from the Tabernacle Choir. On November 5 the *Deseret News*, under a headline reading "Oratorio *Elijah* To Be Presented By Choir in Dramatized Form," told readers that the Choir's coming "religious spectacle" would "mark a new epoch in Tabernacle Choir renditions," and that the "promoters of the project believe this presentation will be one of the outstanding big musical programs to be given in Salt Lake this winter."[7] The article went on to explain that the chorus would number three hundred voices, that a full symphony orchestra of more than fifty pieces would be used, and that much detailed attention was being given to the staging and costuming.

A week later the headlines reaffirmed that the Choir was "To Present *Elijah* on [a] Pretentious Scale."[8] The accompanying story outlined chorus revisions being made, announced that special lighting was being installed in the Tabernacle, and otherwise emphasized the elaborate nature of the planned rendition.

The Oratorio Society was understandably dismayed. Given the disturbing trend of recent years toward slighter attendance and greater expense, the Choir's ambitious plans seemed certain to diminish the audience it needed to meet costs, and to deny it access to the many singers it shared with the Choir and upon which it depended for the quality of its performances. Initially, the Choir showed no willingness to modify its plans and the Society Board of Directors, finding themselves powerless to dissuade the Choir, voted to abandon *Messiah* for at least the present year.

Within the music community, however, reaction was swift and forceful. Tabernacle organist Frank W. Asper, speaking as director of the Orpheus Club, said he and his singers considered the decision to suspend *Messiah* a calamity. Organist Edward P. Kimball (who also directed the Swanee Singers) and 1927 Civic Opera Director C. W. Reed both urged the Society to reverse itself. Under the pressure of these sentiments Professor Lund finally offered to postpone the Choir's *Elijah* if the Society would reconsider, and Professor Coop offered to return to Salt Lake at his own expense to both rehearse the chorus and direct the performance.

In the end the Society responded to this encouraging display of support, and rehearsals were resumed in early December. Three veteran soloists, Summerhays, Bennett, and Marjorie Coop, were joined by newcomer Georgia Standing, a Salt Lake contralto who was meeting with considerable success in New York City, where she currently made her home.

Pending Professor Coop's arrival, B. Cecil Gates took charge of training the chorus. By this time, in addition to conducting the Emma Lucy Gates Grand Opera Company, he was an assistant director of the Salt Lake Tabernacle Choir and head of the music department at the Utah State Agricultural College in Logan (now Utah State University).

Artistically the rendition proved a success fully equal to the Society's high standards. The audience, however, was no larger than it had been the year before, and the fact that there was no deficit was due not to increased revenues, but to the services of the director, the choral assistant, and the soloists, all of whom worked for either no fee or one that had been significantly reduced.

Following the 1928 *Messiah*, Gates was appointed music director and conductor for the coming year and in the spring preparations were begun for the first *Creation* since 1925. Emma Lucy joined her brother for this performance, given on July 17, in what was reported to have been her first *Creation* appearance anywhere—and the addition of Summerhays and Bennett made it an all Salt Lake cast of principals.

Another important personality made her *Creation* as well as her Society debut in 1928. Becky Almond, who appeared for the first time as pianist for this performance, would continue with the Society as a regular rehearsal accompanist, performance pianist for the 1947 *Messiah*, and ultimately as a board member until her death in 1984. Other highlights of her music career included an appearance as solo pianist with the Salt Lake Philharmonic Orchestra in 1917 and an assignment as accompanist for the Salt Lake Tabernacle Choir during its California-Pacific International Exposition appearance in 1935.

The preceding October the University of Utah stadium (since renamed Rice Stadium) had been completed and it was decided to give *The Creation* in this new structure. It was the first experiment ever made by any organization with using the stadium for a musical event, and though in future years it would become a popular location for summer musical entertainments, the Society found it far from satisfactory. In what one critic referred to as the vastness of the stadium, the sense of intimacy so important to the Society's sensitive interpretations was lost. But that, as the *Tribune* observed, was not all. "Soloists, orchestra and chorus alike worked under the...handicap...of having no background or sounding board to project the sounds, and prevent their dissipation and thinning" and "a large part of the inspirational effect...was lost."[9]

The *Tribune* noted other problems, as well. "All chance of soloists or chorus building up atmosphere was dispelled by the conduct of the crowd." Finding itself in a football stadium the audience acted as though it were at a football game. There were arrivals and departures throughout the performance, the *Tribune* reported, and a great deal of seat changing and talking. Finally, when the program was not more than two-thirds complete, an exodus to the parking lot began which, for the serious music lover, was the crowning annoyance to an evening that had been a long succession of distracting annoyances.[10]

Professor Gates also conducted the January 1, 1929, *Messiah*, for which Society veteran soloists Summerhays and Gould were joined by Kansas soprano Alice Gentle and Salt Lake contralto Jessie Evans (later the wife of LDS Church president Joseph Fielding Smith). The following summer, however, and not improbably due to the debilitating illness that but a few weeks later would force his resignation from the Agricultural College and ultimately take his life, he was unable to direct a second *Creation.* Substituting for him, Professor Thomas Giles returned to direct what has proved the last of the Society's University of Utah appearances. It was also the first rendition ever given two performances and the first to travel outside Salt Lake City.

Plans called for the initial performance to be given at the Park Building on July 16, 1929, and a day later on the shores of Salem lake in Utah County, but stormy weather forced postponement of the Park Building performance until the eighteenth.

Veteran soloists Summerhays and Bennett were joined by Utah lyric soprano Jessie Perry. Though this was Perry's first *Creation,* she had appeared with the Lucy Gates Grand Opera Company as Santuzza in *Cavalleria Rusticana,* also in the title role of *Aida,* and most recently she had sung the role of Natoma in a University of Utah production of Victor Herbert's opera of the same name.

On the afternoon of July 17 the chorus, soloists, and instrumentalists (well over three hundred in all) boarded a special Orem train on the old Salt Lake and Utah line for the trip south. Unlike the previous evening, there was no rain and the *Evening Herald* of Provo reported that "The natural amphitheater at the head of the charming little lake provided a perfect setting for a production of this kind, and expressions of delight were heard from audience and participants alike."[11] The next evening, though the weather was unsettled, the Park Building rendition was given in full, thus ringing down the final curtain on these University of Utah performances.

The following winter's *Messiah,* on December 29, 1929, was the first performed on a Sunday (though *Creation* had twice been given on that day), the first performed in December rather than on New Year's or the day after, and the first given absolutely free to the public; and surprisingly, all these innovations had to do with the Society's growing financial difficulties.

During recent years, with costs rapidly increasing, attendance at best holding even and sometimes declining, and with continued public resistance to higher ticket prices, one thing had become abundantly clear: *Messiah* could no longer be made to pay for itself on the basis of ticket sales alone. The solution adopted—perhaps the most radical imaginable, but the one most consistent with the Society's founding ideals—was to abolish the sale of tickets altogether, with it the illusion that *Messiah* was a profitable enterprise, and to appeal directly to Salt Lake businesses, clubs, churches, civic groups, government entities, and individuals for the necessary support. Had the Society more clearly perceived the severity of the coming world-wide economic disaster it might have been less anxious to follow this course; but in the closing weeks of 1929, even though the stock market crash was already underway, public and private assistance proved more than adequate.

The Society's confidence in staking its continued existence on the generosity of Salt Lake government and business entities was due largely to the efforts of one man, W. Jack Thomas, who almost singlehandedly laid the foundations of the Society's present-day base of financial support. He was a former student of Professor Coop and had been a member of the chorus since the first *Messiah* in 1915. He was also a member of the Tabernacle Choir, for which he would later become tour manager.

His talents for soliciting contributions first became evident to his Society colleagues in 1928, when he assisted F. W. Reynolds in what was the Society's most vigorous fund-raising effort to that time—and one that resulted in its first acknowledgment, in a program note, that "material assistance has been rendered, both financially and otherwise, by business firms and by public-spirited individuals of this city."[12] The next year, with Thomas taking full charge of solicitations, the Society was able at last to fulfill Professor Coop's dream of a *Messiah* free to all who would partake of it.

An added advantage of the new funding arrangement was that the Society was now able to schedule Sunday performances without violating the LDS Church prohibition against charging admission to the Tabernacle on the Sabbath. As Sunday seemed the day most appropriate for religious oratorio, and as it was also the day when the greatest number of people were free to attend, *Messiah* was thereafter given on that day, with the sole exceptions coming in 1933 and 1935 when, in the depths of the Great Depression, it twice became necessary to charge for some of the choicest downstairs seats.

As no permanent conductor had yet been found to replace Gates for this first Sunday rendition, Professor Coop once again came from Los Angeles. Pending his arrival, Ferenz Steiner, a recent resident of

Salt Lake City and a graduate of the Royal Conservatory at Budapest, was given charge of training the chorus. He was the organizer of the Chamber Music Society of Salt Lake City, with which he was cellist, and he had recently succeeded Asper as director of the Orpheus Club. Soloists, besides Summerhays, were Mary Early Sloman, a Salt Lake contralto; and two Los Angeles singers, soprano Melba French Barr and bass Tudor Williams.

The audience that crowded into the Tabernacle was estimated by the press to have been in excess of eight thousand, which if accurate would have made it the largest *Messiah* audience yet assembled, and one very nearly rivaling the nine thousand said to have attended the War Memorial *Judas Maccabaeus*. The performance ended with a second rendition of the "Hallelujah," with Professor Evan Stephens once again brought from the audience to conduct it.

The next year Albert J. Southwick became the fifth Salt Lake musician besides Professor Coop to lead the Society in public performance, and that he was one of the most successful is all the more impressive because of the many difficulties he confronted. He directed Society renditions, all of *Messiah*, on December 28, 1930; December 27, 1931; January 2 and December 31, 1933, and January 1, 1935.

At the time he accepted the Society baton he was the newly appointed music director of KSL, Salt Lake City's pioneer radio station. He was, in addition, a veteran bass with the Lucy Gates Grand Opera Company and with the University of Utah Opera, and he had recently succeeded Steiner as director of the Orpheus Club. In Logan, where he lived prior to coming to Salt Lake, he was conductor of the local Tabernacle Choir and head of the music department at Brigham Young College. At about the time he became Society music director, he was also appointed assistant Tabernacle Choir director under Anthony C. Lund, a position he held until Lund's death in 1935, and after which he served briefly as acting Choir director.

For several years following the panic of 1929, money available for all purposes in Salt lake City was sharply limited, and music necessarily stood far down the list of community priorities. *Creation* performances were beyond the Society's means, and even the *Messiah* budget, now totally dependent on contributions at a time when there was little to give, reached levels that were less than half those of recent years. In 1933 Southwick explained to the *Deseret News* that prior to the Great Depression some seven hundred dollars were spent on the orchestra alone. This figure, he said, was within three hundred dollars of the total thousand-dollar budget he had available for everything that was to be included in the 1933 production, whereas earlier budgets had reached levels of two thousand dollars and more. "Sometimes, he said, "it has floored me to tackle this great oratorio with but a part of the woodwind section," for instance, "which is scored for two clarinets, two flutes, two oboes, and two bassoons. Without all of the woodwind parts, the orchestra seemed as unbalanced as a choir singing without any tenor or alto sections."[13]

The first two Southwick renditions were given without the public becoming much aware of the Society's increasingly desperate straits. By the autumn of 1932, however, reserves exhausted and prospects for additional funding at best bleak, the directors announced that there would be no Christmas season *Messiah*—and had it not been for the action of the chorus members themselves, who assumed full financial responsibility and undertook even the organizational details for a January 2, 1933 rendition, the history of the Society might well have ended at that time.

Another destructive and intractable problem faced by the Society was the general decline of instrumental music. The period from the founding of Arthur Shepherd's Salt Lake Symphony in 1902 though early 1925, when Charles Shepherd's Orchestra gave its last concert, might well be considered a golden age of instrumental music. It was made possible by the proliferation, first of the vaudeville orchestra, then of the orchestras of silent movie theaters, and it ended when "talking" movies doomed those orchestras to obsolescence. Deprived of regular employment, competent musicians became a rarity, with most forced to move elsewhere for work or to pursue new careers.

Several amateur and student orchestras continued through the late 1920s and the 1930s, among them the McCune School of Music and Art Orchestra, Salt Lake Civic Orchestra, and the University of Utah Orchestra, but it is evident from the diminishing size of picked orchestras for the more important musical events, and from the tone of newspaper critiques of them, that the competency of the available material was well below that of only a few years before. In such short supply were musicians, in fact, that it was sometimes necessary to bring them from Ogden, Logan, and Provo to fill out a relatively small orchestra of forty pieces. By 1935 the instrumental situation had deteriorated to the point that not even the coaching and leadership wizardry of Arthur Freber, the Society's talented and steadfast concertmaster, could conceal it from the public, prompting the *Deseret News* to report of that year's rendition that the orchestra was so inadequate that it "at times hampered the production."[14]

Despite the many difficulties of this period, however, it included some of the Society's most exciting accomplishments. Foremost among these, certainly, were its *Messiah* broadcasts over KSL and the National Broadcasting Company network in 1930 and 1931. The first of these is also said to have been the first nationwide *Messiah* broadcast by any organization, and estimates were that the network's forty-six affiliated stations carried it to as many as twenty million listeners.[15] And another exciting occurrence of this period was the inclusion of parts of the 1930 rendition in a Paramount Studios sound news film.

The Society's radio career actually began under Professor Coop's baton with a local KSL broadcast of the December 1929 *Messiah*. In his history of the Tabernacle Choir, J. Spencer Cornwall includes a description of how contemporaneous Choir broadcasts were made, and the first Society broadcasts must have been similar. There was, Cornwall informs us, only one microphone used, which was placed at such a height before the Choir that the commentator had to make his announcements from the top of a stepladder. Heavy drapes were hung to prevent the sound dissipating into the greater portion of the building (where the audience would normally have been) and the choir seats were all covered with thick carpeting.[16]

In those early days of radio, before the availability of adequate recording devices, all transmissions were of "live" events. Since the Society's broadcast, unlike that of the Chorus, was of the actual public performance, a technique such as hanging drapes was out of the question. In general, in fact, the Society's technical problems would have been more formidable, but this humble 1929 experiment must have been successful or it would not have been repeated nationwide the following year.

To accommodate its eastern audiences NBC required that the 1930 rendition be given at 10 A.M., and in an abbreviated one hour version. These restrictions necessitated omission of the Overture and

Pastoral Symphony, as well as several numbers traditionally given by the Society; and, because the unusually early hour could not help but conflict with many church services throughout the city, a diminished audience was assured.

Herbert Gould, who was now generally agreed to be one of the country's foremost bassos, joined three singers with Salt Lake connections. The most significant of these would eventually prove to have been tenor Richard P. Condie and the young contralto, Annette Richardson Dinwoodey. Condie, who would become the eleventh Salt Lake Tabernacle Choir conductor in 1957, had sung for two years in European opera and as a soloist with the Boston Symphony. Dinwoodey's Society association, though not continuous, has lasted until the time of this writing, when she presently serves on the Board of Directors as vice-president for productions. In 1930 she was already the veteran of two years as a KSL Radio staff artist, appearing regularly on such programs as "Slumber" and "Midnight Hours." The soprano, Irene Kelly Williams, had been one of J. J. McClellan's promising piano students and was currently a vocalist with the Philadelphia Civic Opera. Another important artist made his first Society appearance in 1930. This was Alexander Schreiner, who was destined to become one of the most highly regarded of all Utah musicians.

The popular success of this broadcast warranted its being repeated the following year, with Summerhays and Bennett in the tenor and bass roles, Dinwoodey returning as contralto, and Margaret Anderson Bowen, another Salt Lake Singer, as the soprano.

The difficulties attendant on NBC's early hour and limited time were avoided in 1931 by giving two programs. The first, exclusively for broadcast, was sung at 7:30 A.M. on Sunday, December 20 (9:30 eastern standard time), in the required one-hour format. A week later it was repeated in expanded form, including both the "Overture" and "Pastoral Symphony," before an audience estimated by the papers (which by now seem always to have been exceedingly generous in this regard) to have been in excess of nine thousand and in which was seated ninety-two-year-old Professor Careless, the venerable grandfather of Utah oratorio.

Letters from throughout the country, both in 1930 and 1931, testify to the enthusiastic response enjoyed by the two broadcasts.

"You must have been inspired," wrote one Indiana listener to Dinwoodey, "when you sang 'He shall feed His flock like a shepherd,' the expression and feeling you put in the number was marvelous."[17]

Following the Society's near collapse in the autumn of 1932 its financial position, again due to Jack Thomas's almost herculean fund-raising efforts, began a slow improvement. In 1935 he was elected to the Board of Directors and his role as business manager made official, and though there have since been frequent periods of tight money, there have been none since 1932 so dire that frugal policies and occasionally the deep pockets of the Society's most devoted board members have been unable to insure at least an annual *Messiah.*

Repeat soloists for Southwick's three final Society renditions were Summerhays in January and December 1933; Bennett and Jepperson (Madsen), both in January 1933; Dinwoodey in December 1933; and Irene Williams in January 1935. They were joined by six new singers, who included Salt Lake sopranos Cora Thorne Bird in January and Jessie Arlene Williams in December 1933. Bird, a native of Springville, Utah, had been active in Salt Lake music circles since winning a Charles Shepherd-sponsored singing contest in 1914, while Jessie Williams had sung one of the leading roles in the Tabernacle Choir's 1928 *Elijah.* Los Angeles baritone Alexander Kisselburgh, who sang *Messiah* in December 1933, had at one time maintained a studio in Salt Lake, where he had been a popular church soloist. Among his credits were a recent appearance at Carnegie Hall.

The remaining soloists were contralto Frances Warren Haynes and tenor Thomas McGranahan, both of Los Angeles, and Arizona bass Rollin Pease, all of whom sang in the January 1935 rendition.

The five years Southwick spent as music director were probably as difficult as any the Society ever faced, and the *Deseret News*' assessment of his New Year's Eve 1933, rendition seems particularly apt as a tribute to his work on the Society's behalf. "Great credit belongs to Mr. Southwick," the paper felt, "for his dignified and compelling direction, the fine contrasts achieved, and the vigor and fire imparted by him to the interpretation of these superb choral numbers."[18]

Right: Professor Coop and Marjorie at their home in Southern California—not long after their marriage at the Hermitage in Ogden Canyon.

Courtesy of Elinor Coop Frost

Courtesy of Charles R. Neslen

Left: Salt Lake City Mayor C. Clarence Neslen succeeded George D. Pyper as Oratorio Society president in 1922. He served until 1936 and thereafter remained on the Board of Directors until 1938. From 1945 until 1966 he was an honorary director.

University of Utah Library Special Collections

Above: This 1920 rendition of Haydn's *Creation* was one of seven the Oratorio Society gave on the University of Utah campus from 1920 through 1929. Soloists in 1920 were Marjorie Dodge Warner, John W. Summerhays, and Herbert Gould. The conductor was Professor Coop. With the exception of the 1928 rendition (and excluding one performance of the 1929 rendition which was given at Salem Lake in Utah County) all were sung on the steps of the Administration Building (now Park Building) at the "sunset hour." Audiences were sometimes put at fifteen thousand and more.

University of Utah Library Special Collections

Facing Page, Bottom: Arthur Freber conducted the Salt Lake Philharmonic Orchestra from its second concert on December 14, 1913, until the final performance of the 1917 season. He was also concert master for every Oratorio Society rendition except one until his death in early 1951.

Right: Charles Shepherd conducted the Oratorio Society *Messiah* on January 1, 1924, and *Creation* the following summer. He was also conductor of the Salt Lake Philharmonic from Arthur Freber's resignation in 1917 until the orchestra's final concert on April 21, 1925.

University of Utah Library Special Collections

University of Utah Library Special Collections

University of Utah Library Special Collections

Utah State Historical Society

LDS Historical Department

Following Charles Shepherd, four more home-talent conductors took up the Society baton. These were Albert J. Southwick (**top left**), who conducted five *Messiahs*; Thomas Giles (**top right**), two *Creations*; B. Cecil Gates (**above left**), one each of *Creation* and *Messiah*; and J. Spencer Cornwall (**above right**), a single rendition of *Messiah*.

CHAPTER THIRTEEN

The Minstrel Comes Home

Within the Oratorio Society Professor Coop had at least three ardent supporters who had recently risen to positions of prominence on the Board of Directors. Besides Jack Thomas, who has already been discussed as the Society's chief fund-raiser, these were David E. Smith and Howard T. Anderson, both of whom were prominent Salt Lake physicians. All three had been students of the professor before the founding of the Society. All had participated in early Coop-directed oratorios, operettas, or both, and they had all sung in every chorus since the Society's founding.

In the autumn of 1935, combining forces with others among the directors who were either favorably disposed to him or becoming disenchanted with Southwick, these three prevailed upon the Board to invite Professor Coop home for an appearance as guest conductor. Southwick, agreeing to step aside for a year, remained with the Society and undertook early training of the chorus.

Professor Coop's homecoming *Messiah*, given December 29, 1935, was in some ways the Society's most enthusiastically received to that time, and the audience that flocked to the Tabernacle was probably the largest yet to attend *Messiah*. Press estimates ranged as high as ten thousand, though if anything approaching that number actually crowded into the building, they must have been piled onto one another's laps. The soloists, all proven Salt Lake favorites, were Emma Lucy Gates (Bowen), Annette Dinwoodey, John Summerhays, and Herbert Gould.

Especially popular with the large audience was the professor's request that it join in singing the "Hallelujah" chorus; and even the orchestra enjoyed an almost total respite from the criticism to which, increasingly, it was being subjected—though this came at the expense of being scarcely mentioned at all.

The Salt Lake Tribune called it a "sympathetic and competent rendition"[1] and Gail Martin, writing for the *Deseret News*, considered that the chorus had "attained effects of rare delicacy and ever-changing color." Behind the scenes, however, it seems there were now serious chorus difficulties. "If attacks at times were not as certain as they might have been," Martin revealed in his *News* review, "it was no fault of Mr. Coop. Handicapped by irregular attendance at rehearsals and the appearance at the final rehearsal of many whom he had not seen before...only his dominant personality and absolute mastery of the music saved the performance from disaster."[2]

Judging by press comment, the Southwick years, though they were otherwise troubled times, were years when the Society enjoyed a stable chorus of consistent quality; and it was only following Southwick's final rendition in January 1935 that the chorus was implicated in some mild and well-meaning criticism directed primarily at Southwick's directing. The *Deseret News* felt that "tempos too fast and lacking in repose robbed the choral numbers of their true dignity and beauty,"[3] and privately there may have been remarks from other quarters. Dr. Anderson, who had previously served several years as chorus president, took this criticism to heart and it was largely through his efforts that active recruiting of new and younger singers was begun in the autumn of 1935, as preparations were under way for Professor Coop's return—and ironically it was the chorus augmented by these singers that first betrayed what would prove to be deep-seated and intractable problems.

The next year Dr. Anderson succeeded Mayor Neslen as Society president and for the *Messiah* presented on December 27, 1936, he undertook much more aggressive reforms, including the request that large numbers of singers resign and apply for readmission on the basis of auditions. This somewhat heavy-handed tactic engendered such resentment that before long there was an outright revolt, and by the closing years of the 1930s and the early 1940s the Society was left with virtually no chorus organization of its own, so that only the participation of large numbers of Ogden, Logan, and Salt Lake Tabernacle singers allowed it to function in 1940 and 1941. In fact it was only the United States involvement in World War II, the accompanying three-year closing of the Tabernacle (1942-44), and the consequent hiatus in its own activities, that saved the Society from another serious threat of dissolution.

Meanwhile, when he stepped aside in 1935, Southwick anticipated resuming his place on the podium in 1936. This can be inferred from the dispute that arose among members of the Board of Directors. Finally, the matter of who was to conduct in 1936 had to be settled by secret ballot, which Professor Coop won by an undisclosed margin.[4]

This was the last time there would be a serious challenge to Professor Coop's role as the Society's conductor. In 1940, as perhaps his health should have become a consideration, the Society took the step of formally designating him "permanent conductor" and even in 1941, when he literally had to leave his sick bed, the Society was unwilling to appoint a substitute.

Southwick, even after it had become clear that his demotion from conductor to choral director was permanent, agreed to train the chorus for another year. Following this, in 1937, he was succeeded by Wade N. Stephens, an assistant Salt Lake Tabernacle organist and *Deseret News* music critic, who trained the chorus for the December 26, 1937, and January 1 and December 31, 1939, renditions. Stephens was also organist for all Society renditions from 1936 through the onset of World War II. In 1940 and 1941 Lisle Bradford, a charter member of the Society and by this time a well respected musical educator at East High School, assumed the choral directing responsibilities.

Sixteen soloists appeared in *Messiah* from 1936 through 1940. These included Society contralto veterans Georgia Standing in 1936 and Annette Richardson Dinwoodey in December 1939 and in 1940; tenor John Summerhays in 1937; bass-baritone Harold H. Bennett in 1936; and baritone Alexander Kisselburgh in 1937. Of the newcomers, contralto Elizabeth Brown in January 1939 and soprano Virginia Freeze Barker in 1940 were both Salt Lake singers. Brown, a 1932 graduate of Salt Lake's East High School, had been living in Chicago for several years where she was associated with that city's Civic Opera, while Barker had recently sung *Messiah* in Logan as well as three leading roles with the Civic Opera in Salt Lake. The only new contralto from outside Utah was Rosalie Barker Frye of Los Angeles in 1937.

New non-Utah sopranos, both from Los Angeles, were Blythe Taylor Burns in 1936 and January 1939; and Sylvia Margolin in 1937 and December 1939. Burns was a frequent soloist at the Hollywood Bowl where she was a favorite with one of Professor Coop's California colleagues, Los Angeles Philharmonic conductor Otto Klemperer; but it is Sylvia Margolin who is of greatest interest. A native of New York City, she had grown up in California and it was there, as a student at UCLA, that she first met Professor Coop. Following college she experienced considerable success as a concert soloist, both in California and on the East Coast. In the meantime the Professor's marriage to Marjorie Dodge, after a separation of several years, had ended in divorce, and in 1940 Sylvia and the professor were married—and in 1941 their only child, Sheila, was born.

Four tenors, all from outside Utah, made their Society debuts. They were Los Angeles singers Russell Horton in 1936 and Allan R. Lindquest in December 1939; Cleveland's Harold Haugh in January 1939; and Joseph Victor Laderoute of Canada in 1940.

New basses were Mark Love of Chicago in both January and December 1939, and Los Angeles-based Sten Englund in 1940. Englund, a native of Sweden, had at one time been a Salt Lake resident. Recently he had sung *Messiah* with the Pasadena Oratorio Society and the Los Angeles Philharmonic Orchestra.

Several times since 1929, when the Society gave its last pre-depression *Creation* at Salem Lake and the University of Utah, there had been discussions of resuming summer performances; but finances in the tight money climate of that era had invariably proven an insurmountable problem. So in 1937, When it was invited to give *Creation* at the expense of the Covered Wagon Days Celebration, an annual event commemorating the arrival of the Mormon pioneers in 1847, the Society enthusiastically accepted.

The first of what proved to be three successive Capitol Building *Creations* was given on July 21, 1937. The weather was as nearly perfect as could be hoped for with clear, warm skies and scarcely any breeze to scatter the music. Because of Dr. Anderson's reforms, the chorus was much smaller than in recent years; but it was still of sufficient quality to make a very favorable impression on both the audience and critics.

The difficulties that had so marred the first Capitol Building *Creation* in 1917, when a south wind combined with the building's inherent acoustical vagaries to carry the music away unheard, were insured against by reversing the relative position of audience and performers. This time the audience was seated on the steps that rise to the building's south entrance while chorus, soloists, and orchestra were placed on a platform below. With the addition of microphones, amplifiers, and speakers, this trapped a sufficient volume of sound to make the performance audible to all who attended.

It was for this first Covered Wagon Days *Creation* in 1937 that Sylvia Margolin, the future Mrs. Coop, made her Society debut. She was joined by a second Los Angeles singer, baritone Emery Darcy, who had come highly recommended to the Professor by Otto Klemperer, and the solo trio was completed by John Summerhays in his twenty-first Society appearance.

During this period the Society's use of non-Utah talent first became a matter of serious controversy. From the Society point of view, outside talent filled at least three functions. Foremost, it insured that the quality of soloists would be maintained at levels commensurate with those of the nation's principal music centers; and second, by continually presenting fresh talent, it maintained the public's interest. The third consideration had been discussed by Southwick in a 1933 interview with Gail Martin of the *Deseret News*:

"It has been," said Mr. Southwick yesterday, "the desire of a large part of the board that in choosing soloists non-Mormon members of the community be given equal representation with those professing the Mormon faith.

"To that end we have conscientiously bent our efforts, but as one checks over the field, one finds a preponderant number of Mormon singers. For example, in checking over the tenors capable of doing the part, one finds there are about two—[John] Summerhays and Richard Condie. Both are members of the Church.

"This does not mean to say that Mr. Summerhays and Mr. Condie are the only tenors in the field. There are other fine tenor voices, but either they are not prepared to sing the difficult tenor role, or if prepared, at this time they do not feel their voices to be in shape for this exacting service.

"Just the other day, we held a tryout for soprano soloists. Four were heard. Of this number, three were Mormons. So that even though we have tried to carry out the desire of the board in this particular as well as meet our own wish to make this a genuinely community project, we do not seem to have succeeded very well. However, if we employ an outside bass, this will bring down the average more nearly to the desired balance.[5]

This policy of balancing outside and non-Mormon singers against resident Mormon artists, though it was only a fractional consideration in selecting talent, seems to have been perceived by at least some Society critics as an intolerable bias against members of the LDS Church; and in time such pressure was brought to bear that the Society began to feel it was in danger of losing its funding. Few documents shed light on this situation, but Professor Coop's letter to the Board of Directors, while clearly stating his own position, gives a sense of the difficult atmosphere in which he wrote it:

I trust the following will be regarded as the expression of an honest desire to contribute a proper and a practical comment upon the situation in which the Salt Lake Oratorio Society finds itself.

If I am correctly informed, complaints have been made against the engagement of non-resident talent for the solo and directorial items of the public performances of the Society—and restrictions have been imposed on its current undertaking—the *Creation* performance in connection with the Covered Wagon Days Celebration.

As I regard this, the Society is confronted with a question foreign to its aims and purposes, to its ideals and to its history.

The Society was formed and has been fostered these twenty-seven years purely as a music-religious enterprise. Religion and music as put forth in its now classic tradition—the annual rendition of Handel's *The Messiah* and Haydn's *The Creation*—serve the universal appeal of love and beauty, ONLY THESE. This tradition has as its sole, beautiful objective the fostering of the brotherhood of man through singing Handel's *Messiah* and exulting in the praise of God in nature, by singing Haydn's *Creation*—again and again.

I respectfully submit that other considerations might taint this ideal. What have these spiritual and artistic intentions to do with restriction of persons and residence, or what have restrictions of place and persons to do with these ideals of universal good will and love of beauty.

It is my view that in true music and in pure religion, feeling and the soul of things divinely blest remove mental and physical boundaries, and these are replaced by something impersonal—nameless—placeless—boundless—as the true spirit of God itself.

However we may philosophize as to the ordination, divinity of Jesus Christ, or place him in the Humanist's conception, we all know that it was political or social or sectional hands that struck him down. He did not belong to their company, and I imagine that He is crucified again and again whenever man marks man with something less than fellowship.

The message of the Messiah is "Love ye one another"—Handel's music glorifies and promotes this sentiment—Jesus Christ was a Palestinian—Handel was a German.

The message in the *Creation* is "The marvelous world behold amazed, and to the ethereal vaults resound the praise of God." Moses, who is credited with the religious part of the text, was probably an Egyptian—Milton, with the lyrics, was an Englishman. Haydn, the composer of the music, an Austrian.

We do not discriminate against these revelators; should we do so against certain disciples in the re-creation of their art? Utah does not do this. Its friendly mutual relations with the outside world is too essential and close to its heart. Notable Utah men and women have been welcomed with open arms and given honors by the outside world. Utah is not less gracious and hospitable. The earnest of this attitude is illustrated in its importation of numerous concert artists presented in the auditoriums of the city and state and the respect shown for outside eminent men and women who are welcomed here to lecture, paint, sculpture, and build—brothers all in a world for all.

However, it should be noted that the Salt Lake Oratorio Society has not neglected its own resident or native artists when composing its roster of soloists and directors for its performances. It has always been the policy of the Society to present INSIDE and OUTSIDE soloists in equal ratio.

Before concluding his letter, Professor Coop made several additional points. The Society, he felt, was not a training school for apprentice soloists, and to use ill-prepared singers, subjecting them to harsh criticism, was more likely to do them harm than to further their fledgling careers. He added that the Salt Lake public had become sophisticated enough that it demanded both accomplished singers and the frequent novelty of new voices. But most of all, he felt, "the great oratorios are works of art" and "they should never suffer the restrictions of provincial, political or personal policies; but should have all the beauty and perfection possible from whomsoever to whomsoever."[6]

For the July 20, 1938, rendition, a year before Professor Coop wrote his letter, the selection of *Creation* soloists was consistent with previous Society policy. Blythe Taylor Burns returned from

Los Angeles to sing with two newcomers, baritone John H. Patrick of New York City and tenor James E. Haslam, who was business coordinator for Salt Lake City schools and a future Society board member. By the time of the July 19, 1939, rendition, however, and despite his letter to the Board of Directors, only Professor Coop himself, with his Los Angeles address, could be considered an outsider. The soloists, all Salt Lakers, were soprano Elizabeth Hayes Simpson of the Westminster College music department, tenor Haslam in a second Society appearance, and Albert J. Southwick, the former Society conductor and music director, in his final Society appearance.

As a group the soloists could have occasioned no complaint from the advocates of local talent. However, a further point of conflict arose in 1939 when festival officials accused the Society of overspending its budget (the Society felt the festival was disallowing legitimate expenses), and despite hopeful discussions in the spring of 1940, the Society and the committee found it impossible to reach agreement for a fourth rendition.

Meanwhile, on the recommendation of Jack Thomas, Dr. Adam S. Bennion was voted onto the Society's Board of Directors in 1936. He was at that time an assistant to the president of Utah Power and Light Company and a member of the Deseret Sunday School Union general board, and in 1953 he would be named an apostle of the LDS Church. Earlier in life he had pursued an education career in Salt Lake area high schools, then at the University of Utah.

Professor Coop, in particular, seems to have been pleased by Dr. Bennion's inclusion on the Board. In a letter the professor wrote to him shortly thereafter, he suggested that they were two men "spiritually off the same stick," and as though he anticipated the important role Dr. Bennion would play in Society affairs, he told him that "when I heard that you had accepted to be on the Board of Directors, I felt that the ideal person had been added" because, as he explained, until now there "has been no one strong, compelling person—a leader, powerful enough to harmonized the discordant items of personal feeling"—feelings, in fact, that were at that time leading to serious animosities among the directors.[7]

Approximately three years later, with the chorus reeling from one crisis to another, the Utah-versus-outside-talent controversy threatening the Society's funding, and internal dissension increasingly hindering the Board's ability to function, Dr. Anderson stepped aside as president. For several months Vice-president Alex E. Eberhardt, a native Kansan who first joined the Board in 1933, served as acting president and late in 1939 Dr. Bennion was elected the Society's fourth chief executive.

Soon after, Dr. Bennion demonstrated his grasp of his colleagues' strengths and talents by appointing Dr. Anderson to the post of production manager. In this capacity Dr. Anderson's extensive musical education and experience and his artistic sensibilities, instead of being lost to the Society because of a less than happy experience as president, were put to their most advantageous use, especially in the postwar era when he was almost solely responsible for relations with conductors and with the Society's increasingly important soloists.

During the final two years preceding World War II the Society was hindered, in addition to the difficulties already mentioned, by Professor Coop's rapidly deteriorating health. For the December 29, 1940, Messiah he was scheduled to take over rehearsals from Lisle Bradford on December first, but illness forced him to delay his arrival for more than a week and thereafter significantly curtailed his activities. For the first time in memory he was gently chastised, by Lesley Goates in his *Deseret News* review, for "having set all his tempos a little faster than usual," which was thought possibly to "account for the fact that the soloists and conductor were not always together;"[8] and not improbably such imperfections in his performance were attributable to his illness.

Chorus problems were masked somewhat by the participation of Ogden singers and of seventy-five voices from a short-lived organization known as the Salt Lake Junior Oratorio Society. This group was established with Dr. Lorin F. Wheelwright and Lisle Bradford as joint directors for the purpose of recruiting and training high school students, a task at which it seems to have been modestly successful. Following the performance Professor Coop commented that, "Our young members will work in well. They made a few mistakes today but they were mistakes of the mind and of the voice and not of the heart."[9]

One particularly promising aspect of the 1940 performance was its orchestra. Late in 1935, as part of President Franklin Delano Roosevelt's program to combat the effects of the Great Depression, the State Music Project for Utah was established under the Works Project Administration (W.P.A.). Reginald Beales, formerly a London and New York orchestra leader who was then a McCune School of Music and Art violin instructor, was appointed supervisor of the project and director of its new instrumental ensemble. This fledgling W.P.A. Orchestra (also known as the Utah State Sinfonietta) was organized in early 1936 and by mid March of that year had expanded from only four members to twenty. It's first public concert was given in Assembly Hall on May 11 of that year and by 1938 the orchestra had grown to more than forty members.

Early in 1940 the Utah State Symphony Orchestra was formed, giving its first concert in Kingsbury Hall on the University of Utah campus on May 8. The result of all this activity, which included more than one thousand performances given statewide between 1936 and 1940, was that large numbers of Salt Lake musicians were once again performing regularly and receiving compensation for doing so—with effects that were noted with satisfaction by Salt Lake music lovers.

Offsetting this good news, however, was Professor Coop's poor health and the accompanying decline of his spirits. In October of 1941 he phoned Dr. Bennion and asked to be excused from conducting the coming *Messiah*. Thereafter he sent a telegram, and a short while later the following letter:

> I want you to know—assuredly know—that my attitude has a basis of long thinking; that while at the present moment I am *hors de combat* from a very sorry sick spell which weakens my will, my desire for a leave of absence this year is more than a year old—perhaps two.
>
> You know, as I do, that the chorus problem has grown steadily worse and worse. I have had to hazard a performance with nondescript talent, untrained, and uncertain as to numbers—only the assistance of the Ogden singers saved our face, four times, in fact.
>
> This disgrace I felt, **do feel**, I cannot ever face again. Besides, to do so would risk a flop performance which would render 29 years of love's labor lost, or badly hurt.
>
> I think it is reasonable to expect that after all these years there would have developed a desire on the part of enough Salt Lake singers to stand side by side—Mormon, Gentile, who-so-ever, to sing Handel's glorious *Messiah* beautifully—increasingly so. In justice to the social minded there, I think we should admit that lack of competent organization is in part responsible for this, and unfriendly individuals and detracting efforts of other singing groups have certainly contributed to our difficulties. There may be some other causes.

It is this that has convinced me that it might be politic for me to step aside—once at least—and thus bring the situation into the open. Some provincial standards obtain in Salt Lake and as you have observed, we may, should, acknowledge this with intellectual candor. I do.

I am a little ashamed of my weakened spirit and the desertion from the side of you there who have so payless and praiseless held up my hands. Be assured my thought is more strategic than disloyal.

Excuse this penciled scribble. I am in bed. And am I tired of it? I am.[10]

Other documents indicate that Professor Coop hoped the Society would engage Lester Hinchcliff, the Ogden Tabernacle Choir leader who, with his chorus, had so frequently come to the Society's aid. The Society, however, was determined that Professor Coop would be on the podium, and redoubled efforts were made to improve the chorus and to otherwise address the difficulties to which the professor alluded in his letter.

Over the professor's health, however, the Society had no control. He continued to weaken and though he reluctantly agreed to conduct the performance, he was able to attend none of its rehearsals. As a consequence, Lisle Bradford was appointed associate conductor, and it was she, in addition to training the chorus, who lead it in performance, leaving Professor Coop the task of directing only soloists and orchestra.

One of the featured attractions of this last Coop *Messiah* was the inclusion of Metropolitan Opera star Richard Bonelli. He was a personal friend of then Salt Lake Mayor Ab Jenkins and it was largely through the efforts of Mayor Jenkins, who was also a member of the Society Board, that Bonelli appeared with the Society. Other soloists were contralto Ione Duncan, a Salt Lake Tabernacle Choir soloist, and Harold Haugh, the Cleveland tenor who was making his second Society appearance. The soprano was Sylvia Margolin, now Mrs. Coop, who was, with her husband, performing for the last time with the Salt Lake Oratorio Society.

The performance, the Society's twenty-ninth *Messiah* (including the private rendition in 1919), was given on December 28, 1941, three weeks to the day after the Japanese attack on Pearl Harbor. According to the newspapers more than ten thousand persons crowded into the historic building and overflowed into the adjacent Assembly Hall, where for the first time in Society history the music was carried on a public address system. Whatever the actual number, it was a larger audience than the huge turnout for Professor Coop's return in

1935. One last time they had come to the Tabernacle to hear the professor conduct the message of the Prince of Peace before that message was silenced in a world of guns, bombs, and death.

In 1942, because of the war, the Tabernacle was closed to the public. For awhile it was hoped that a performance might be given anyway, but early in December Dr. Bennion wrote to Professor Coop, telling him that "I have just released to the papers the accompanying notice [that Messiah would not be done]. The *Deseret News* for tonight has carried it in full and a similar notice no doubt will appear in tomorrow morning's *Tribune.* We had hoped (Jack [Thomas] and I), until day before yesterday," he told the professor, "that the Tabernacle might be opened especially for this performance which was to be dedicated to the soldiers who now crowd our city. After due consideration, however, the Presidency [of the LDS Church] decided that it is wiser not to use this edifice for public gatherings at the present time. We hate to break a tradition of thirty years, but we are all agreed that it would be a mistake to try to do it in one of the smaller halls, the largest of which will accommodate only about two thousand people."[11]

Recent *Messiah* renditions had been recorded by the Society as aids to improving future performances and these now provided the material for a series of three broadcasts that kept the Oratorio Society tradition alive throughout the dark days of the war. Presented by KSL on December 27, 1942; December 26, 1943; and December 31, 1944, they were the first Society broadcasts not originating live from the Tabernacle.

The 1942 version included, in addition to chorus numbers, solos by Mrs. Coop (Sylvia), by Salt Lake contralto Annette Richardson Dinwoodey, Ohio tenor Harold Haugh, and by Chicago and New York bassos Mark Love and Richard Bonelli. Wade Stephens was the featured organist and Joseph Kirkham the trumpeter. Dr. Bennion, who introduced the program, explained that had it not been for the war, the annual *Messiah* would be given that evening before "eight thousand lovers of music in the Salt Lake Tabernacle," and he concluded his remarks by suggesting

> that during the next hour you imagine yourself one of that great Tabernacle throng, Christian beyond all creed, listening to a chorus made up of singers of all faiths, under the inspired leadership of that great conductor, Squire Coop, as he builds chorus, orchestra, organ, soloists, into one great triumphal expression of musical eloquence.

And may we suggest that out beyond this experience you let your mind explore far horizons. Out where the men of Hitler, Hirohito, and Mussolini would trample human rights and subjugate men under a rule of hate and tyranny and terror. Against such forces, let us follow our own boys in their fight for freedom. To the sublime strains to which you are to listen, may we couple a prayer that the King of Kings may come to their aid and make possible a new day when we can sing again:

Glory to God in the highest,
And on earth—Peace,
Good will toward men.[12]

In subsequent broadcasts tenor John Summerhays and sopranos Elizabeth Hayes Simpson and Virginia Freeze Barker, all Salt Lake soloists, were added to the list of featured artists.

Late in 1942, before it had become certain that no Tabernacle *Messiah* could be given that year, Professor Coop wrote to Dr. Bennion explaining that "Since my last partial effort with the performance, and before—since September a year ago—I have not been well. I fear the strain [of conducting] again might retard further complete recovery."[13] Of course there was no *Messiah* that year and fate was such that he was never again called upon. Through the remaining years of the war his health showed no permanent improvement and late in August 1945, as the war was entering its final hours, the professor's condition worsened. For the last time he was admitted to Good Samaritan hospital in Los Angeles and two weeks later, at 3 A.M. on September 10, 1945, his life ended.

With the death of Professor Coop an epic in the history of the Salt Lake Oratorio Society was closed. He had taken the lead of such musical pioneers as George Careless and Evan Stephens. Following their example of cutting across all cultural and religious barriers, he created the Oratorio Society and shepherded it through its formative decades. In 1915 *Messiah* drew a few hundred to the Empress Theater. By the late 1930s and early 1940s it was able to attract to the Tabernacle audiences estimated by an enthusiastic press at eight, nine, even ten thousand persons. By doing so it gave eloquent testimony that the intervening years had been devoted not only to the building of the Society, but by season after season of patient teaching and example, to building an audience as well.

Oratorio Society of Utah Archives

University of Utah Library Special Collections

Top Left: Howard T. Anderson, M.D., assumed the presidency of the Oratorio Society in 1936. He was a lifelong Society member who had sung in the first *Messiah* and his was an important influence in the move to bring back Professor Coop as music director.

Top Right: In the pre-World War II days Professor Coop frequently flew between Salt Lake City and Los Angeles, a trip, in those pioneer days of commercial aviation, that was fraught with a far greater chance of adventure than that risked by today's travelers.

Courtesy of Richard Bennion

Above: Adam S. Bennion, the Society's fourth president, served in that position from 1939 until his death in 1958. His influence as an important business executive and member of the LDS Church hierarchy proved invaluable to the Society.

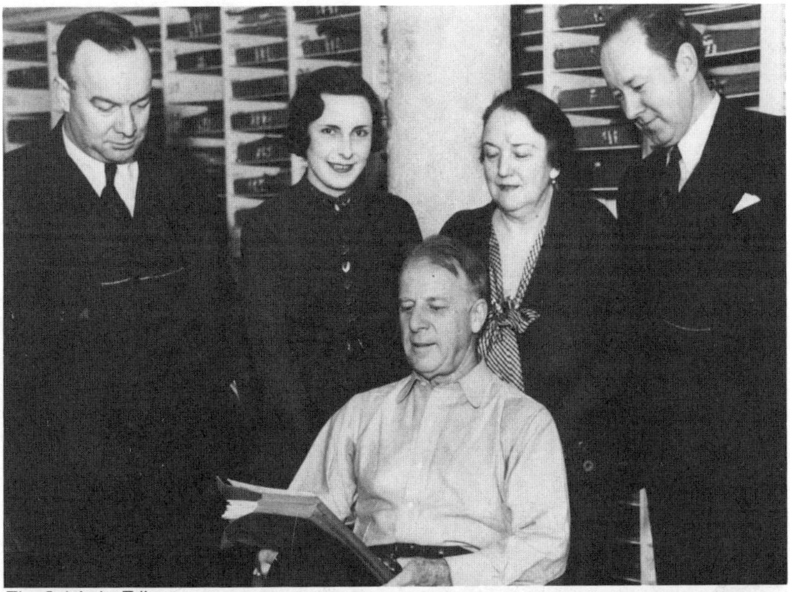

The Salt Lake Tribune

University of Utah Library Special Collections/ *The Salt Lake Tribune*

Top: (L-R) Tenor John W. Summerhays, contralto Annette Richardson Dinwoodey, soprano Emma Lucy Gates (Bowen), and bass Herbert Gould join Professor Coop (center) in preparing for the December 29, 1935 *Messiah*.

Bottom: Professor Coop rehearses the *Messiah* orchestra.

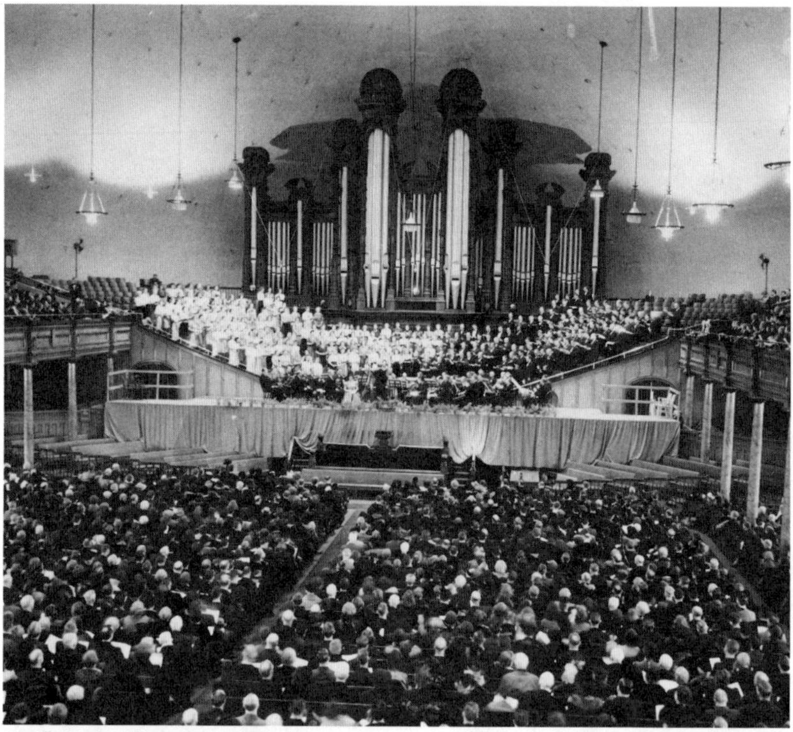

The Salt Lake Tribune

Above: This December 31, 1939, *Messiah* was the last for which Professor Coop's health allowed his full participation as both conductor and choral director. Singing the soprano part was Sylvia Margolin, who shortly after became the Professor's wife and eventually the mother of his only child. Other December 1939 soloists were Annette Richardson Dinwoodey in the alto part; Allan R. Lindquest, tenor; and Mark Love, bass.

Facing Page, Top: For this 1939 *Creation* the audience was seated on the south steps of the Capitol Building and the orchestra, chorus, and soloists on a platform below. It was a marked improvement over 1917, when the audience was placed below, musicians on the steps, and the music was carried away unheard by a stiff south breeze.

Facing Page, Bottom: This Barratt Hall rehearsal is typical of most held in the pre-World War II era, though other early sites included the Hotel Utah and the Odeon (a theater and dancehall at 25 E. North Temple).

University of Utah Library Special Collections/*The Salt Lake Tribune*

University of Utah Library Special Collections

PART THREE

The Oratorio Society of Utah

CHAPTER FOURTEEN

The Postwar Messiah

So long as Professor Coop lived, his ideas and wishes were decisive in shaping Society policy. Even during the Southwick years, when he took no active role in its activities, his influence was there, conscience-like, so that an independent leadership never fully matured. Following his death, however, the very men who until then had deferred to his judgment in almost every matter of importance found that now they must form a new center of gravity. If the Society was to survive, they would have to be the ones whose vision and energy would carry it into a new era.

Dr. Bennion, Alex Eberhardt, Jack Thomas, and Dr. Anderson rose to the challenge of this new situation with a degree of enthusiasm and dedication that not even Professor Coop himself could have found wanting. Respectively they were Society president; vice-president; business manager and director of finance; and production manager. Nominally, of course, their responsibilities and duties were much as they had been before the war, but now they were undertaken with a new sense of self-certain authority.

Their first task, in the closing months of 1945, was the difficult one of choosing a new conductor. Well versed in Society matters as they were, and in the social, cultural, and artistic intricacies of Salt Lake life, they were fully aware that the power naturally accruing to a permanent conductor could eventually prove a separate and potentially disruptive center of influence. They also knew that there was a very real danger, if the wrong man were chosen, of the Society's stagnating into mediocrity.

In the end these potential hazards were avoided by adopting a policy of inviting the most distinguished guest conductor for each rendition that the Society's means would allow. It was a policy, however, that displeased many Salt Lake musicians, including not a few who were otherwise well-disposed toward the Society. J. Spencer Cornwall, who by that time was in the midst of an illustrious career as Mormon Tabernacle Choir conductor, expressed his feelings in a letter he addressed to Dr. Bennion in early 1947.

Bringing in outside conductors, he argued, was in effect to break faith with local musicians who, as a consequence, would never have the opportunity of learning *Messiah*. His own experience was illustrative, he felt. Had not Professor Coop, Mayor Neslen, and other members of the Society had sufficient faith in his ability to allow him to conduct the 1927 rendition, he in all likelihood would not have been considered experienced enough to take on his present job with the Tabernacle Choir. He named several Salt Lake musicians he felt were qualified, adding that they would undertake *Messiah* with a prayer, not a cigarette, on their lips.[1]

Even discounting Cornwall's understandably pro-Mormon bias, it must be conceded that he made a valid point. As Professor Coop himself had demonstrated a quarter-century before, if talented Utah musicians could find neither employment nor honor at home, they would seek it elsewhere. But Salt Lake City was changing rapidly. Musically, at least, it stood at the threshold of a burst of activity and sophistication such as could scarcely have been dreamed possible. During the summer of 1945 the new Symphony Orchestra joined forces with the Tabernacle Choir for a rendition of *The Creation* in the University of Utah football stadium (at that time called Stadium Bowl), thus signalling an era of renewed competition in the oratorio field and serving notice to the Society that if it was to continue drawing crowds to the Tabernacle, it must take steps to assure its own excellence and the public's continued interest.

This Symphony and Tabernacle Choir *Creation* was only the first in a succession of important choral works that would greatly enhance the musical acumen of the Salt Lake choral enthusiast. During the decade beginning in late 1948, the orchestra and the combined choruses of the University of Utah presented Beethoven's

Missa Solemnis, Verdi's Requiem, Bach's *St. Matthew* Passion, Honegger's *King David* and *Joan of Arc at the Stake*, Handel's *Judas Maccabaeus* and *Israel in Egypt*, Robertson's Oratorio *From The Book of Mormon*, and a second rendition of *Creation*. Because of these, and other influences, the demands for excellence were to be keenly felt during the years ahead, and the competition for audiences often fierce.

It was the Symphony Orchestra, in fact, that set the example of importing conductors. Beginning in 1940, when Reginald Beales was succeeded as Utah State Symphony conductor by Chicagoan Hans Heniot, the orchestra had been conducted by non-Utahns. During the war years, especially, while its regular conductor was serving as an army band leader at nearby Camp Kearns, the baton was taken by a succession of guests, including Sir Thomas Beecham, Jose Echaniz, Albert Coates, and Christos Vrionides. Dr. Bennion, the Society's president, served on the Symphony board during this period and it seems not improbable, impressed as he must have been by the orchestra's success, that he was one of the leading advocates for adoption of a similar Oratorio Society policy.

Another weighty factor in the Society's decision to import conductors was the availability of one of the world's foremost orchestra leaders. During the mid 1920s Professor Coop had organized the Philharmonic Chorus to participate in Los Angeles Philharmonic Orchestra choral renditions. So successful was this enterprise that by some it was credited with having influenced William Andrews Clark, Jr., one of the orchestra's principal benefactors, to make a sizeable bequest to UCLA, the professor's employer. Professor Coop's association with the orchestra lasted many years and it was there that he came into frequent contact with Otto Klemperer, the eminent German conductor Clark had secured for the Los Angeles orchestra. On several occasions during the 1930s Klemperer was able to suggest the names of promising young vocalists who ultimately served the Society, and it was in part at least this interest in the Society, born of a friendship for Professor Coop, that led to the famous conductor's willingness to appear in the first postwar *Messiah* on December 30, 1945.

A native of Breslau (now Wroclaw, Poland), Klemperer was conductor of the German National Theater in Prague from 1907 until 1910, following which he had successive conducting appointments with opera houses in Hamburg, Strasbourg, Cologne, and Wiesbaden.

He was also first conductor of the Berlin State Opera and Philharmonic Choir from 1927 until 1933 when, because he was a Jew, his contract was cancelled by the Nazis. Leaving Germany then, he conducted the Los Angeles Philharmonic Orchestra from 1933 through 1939, and again during the 1941–42 season. He was also associated with the Pittsburgh Symphony and following the war he conducted the Budapest Opera, appeared as guest conductor throughout Europe and in Israel, conducted the Montreal Symphony, and finally the London Philharmonic, of which he became principal conductor for life in 1964.

The decision to forgo a regular conductor greatly enhanced the importance of the production manager. Dr. Anderson took upon himself the important tasks of arranging for soloists, deciding which numbers should be included, of what composition the orchestra was to be, coordinating details with the conductor, communicating the conductor's preferences to the choral director, and then assisting in their communication to the chorus. He was well suited to the task, both by temperament and by his considerable musical training. Early in life he studied both violin and voice, was a member of Romania Hyde's First Methodist Church Quartet, and a soloist in several early opera and operetta productions. His personal correspondence abounds with discussions of the minutiae of oratorio production and not a few of these letters from guest conductors and soloists, alluding to his musical expertise, indicate the high esteem in which he was held by the musicians with whom he became associated.

Lisle Bradford, who trained the chorus for the last two prewar renditions, continued in that capacity in 1945 with the title of associate music director.

Once the question of a conductor was resolved, two pressing problems remained. The first of these was to revive the business community's interest in supporting the Society financially. The second was gathering together a sufficiently large chorus to assure that the first postwar *Messiah* would be the kind of success that would launch the Society into a new era of excellence.

A happy resolution to neither of these problems seemed assured. In the case of finances, there had been a three-year lapse during which Salt Lake businesses had been spared Thomas's relentless solicitations, and in the interim, also, the new Utah State Symphony Orchestra had become a formidable competitor for available dollars. So the fact that the necessary funds were almost effortlessly raised was not only a tribute to Thomas's skill, but to the power of *Messiah* itself. Few events in the months following the war's end could have been looked forward to more enthusiastically, and the audience that ultimately attended the performance was reported by the newspapers to have been the largest ever to witness a Salt Lake *Messiah*. It filled every seat and crowded the aisles, Assembly Hall was filled to overflowing, crowds lingered on the grounds where the music was carried by a public address system, and hundreds, perhaps thousands more returned to their homes where the performance could be heard in a live KSL broadcast that was carried throughout most of the West.

The abysmal chorus problems of the prewar years were overcome with equally impressive results. By late October two hundred singers were in rehearsal. Subsequent invitations to Ogden and Provo singers added many more, and an appeal to the Tabernacle Choir swelled the final chorus to four hundred voices, a number that took second place only to the 1925 *Creation* chorus of 450 voices. Cornwall's cooperation in enlisting as many as possible of his Tabernacle Choir singers, in particular, was helpful and generous. He supplied a list of singers he thought would be interested and later made an announcement before the entire Tabernacle Choir in which he made clear that all members should feel free to participate with the Oratorio Society.

The performance was dedicated to the memory of Professor Coop and attended by his widow and their young daughter, Sheila. A letter from Mrs. Coop to Dr. Bennion, written while *Messiah* preparations were still underway, states as movingly as possible the sense of both loss and hope felt that autumn by the Society and its friends. "You have my sincere, heartfelt wishes," she wrote, "for an outstanding performance. It shall be. Yet, somehow, it will not be the same. The vital personality—the soul that was the Oratorio Society is gone from our sight. Surely, somewhere—somehow—he will be with you and the Society December 30, inspiring you to heights undreamed."[2]

Soloists in 1945, with one exception, were Society veterans. Annette Richardson Dinwoodey, one of the most popular home talents ever to have sung the alto part, had appeared with the Society six times from 1930 through 1940. Cleveland tenor Harold Haugh sang *Messiah* in 1939 and 1941, and Tudor Williams, a Los Angeles opera and oratorio bass, first appeared with the Society in 1929. Soprano Sara Carter, making her only Society appearance, was also from Los Angeles.

Haugh, especially, was to prove popular with Salt Lake audiences.

He held a Master of Sacred Music degree from the Union Theological Seminary in New York City and was widely considered one of the best American oratorio tenors of his time. In all, he made thirteen *Messiah* appearances with the Society, the last coming in 1955.

Two other important Society veterans returned to the Society in 1945. The first of these was the venerable concertmaster, Arthur Freber. With the exception of the December 1935 *Messiah*, when he was substituted for by West High School orchestra and band leader Kenneth C. Roylance, he trained every Society orchestra from the first in 1915 until his death in 1951. The other returning veteran was Tabernacle organist Alexander Schreiner, who made the first of his thirty-seven postwar Society appearances in 1945. One of America's foremost organists, he first appeared with the Society in its pioneering 1930 NBC broadcast, and again in 1933.

Messiah, when at last it came, was as well received by the critics as by the public. "Never before has the Salt Lake Oratorio Society welcomed such an audience, and never has its audience heard such a spirited and thrilling performance," wrote Conrad B. Harrison in the *Deseret News*. Judging by the thirty-four numbers included, it was a very long rendition by Society standards; but Klemperer kept the tempos rapid, even with the large chorus, and Harrison noted that the "most striking result of the Klemperer influence was the unity and balance of the entire company," which "performed with unquestionable authority." Maestro Klemperer's "moving and exhilarating tempi were stimulating and highly interesting to performers and listeners alike" and the "choral work was particularly thrilling" with attacks and releases so precise that they were "the envy of conductors who have long been striving for such unity."

The soloists were all praised, though Williams perhaps least of all, while Dinwoodey was cited for her intense interpretation of "He was despised" and the thrillingly clear resonance and pure quality of her voice in "He shall feed his flock."

One very gratifying aspect of this and other postwar renditions was the steadily improving orchestra. In Harrison's opinion, Concertmaster Freber "headed a group of outstanding musicians who performed with perfect precision and understanding," and of the chorus he added that Lisle Bradford had so well drilled the "music into the singers before Dr. Klemperer's arrival" that it freed the conductor to concentrate his attention on installing "expression and spirit into the ensemble."[3]

On the negative side was a problem that had surfaced once or twice before and that would plague the Society for some years to come. Since the beginning of free *Messiah* renditions in 1929, tickets had been distributed through downtown businesses. The purpose of this was twofold. Being the distributor of tickets was perceived to have advertizing and public relations value in exchange for which the participating businesses were willing to make generous contributions. Of equal importance, requiring tickets, even though they were free tickets, was used by the Society as an aid in controlling the size of the crowd that would have to be handled on performance day, especially in so far as it limited the number of people who might have to be turned away at the door.

In practice, however, this sometimes worked so poorly as to seem to work not at all. The problem was that in no case could every holder of a free ticket be counted upon to attend the performance. Consequently, there were always more tickets distributed than there were seats available in the Tabernacle. The more anxious the Society was for a large turnout or, conversely, the more it feared a light one, the more apt it was to distribute tickets far in excess of the available seating, as it did with unfortunate consequences in 1945.

One would-be member of the audience complained in a letter to Dr. Bennion that she and her family had been but few among thousands of ticket holders who were turned away from both the Tabernacle and Assembly Hall. In 1941, she wrote, her family had been refused admittance because it lacked tickets, and in 1945 despite having them. The solution she and many others suggested was that the Society sell its tickets. But this was a remedy that for both practical and sentimental reasons lay some years in the future, though in the immediately succeeding years the problem was somewhat alleviated by opening the final rehearsal.

On December 29, 1946, Dr. Klemperer conducted another Tabernacle *Messiah*, and the enthusiasm of the preceding year was undiminished. A second successive record breaking chorus was amassed—this time of 450 voices. For sheer size it was a *Messiah* chorus not yet surpassed by the Society and equalled only twice since, in 1955 and 1961. The audience, even with the Saturday night dress rehearsal opened to the public, was only slightly smaller than that of the preceding year. The program was again carried by KSL radio, as it has been most years since, and the public address system carried the music to Assembly Hall and throughout the grounds.

Harold Haugh returned in the tenor role. He was joined by Los

Angeles soprano Blythe Taylor Burns and Salt Lake bass Harold Bennett, both well known Society veterans. The only new voice was that of New York-based contralto Marie Powers, who had sung *Messiah* at Carnegie Hall and with the San Francisco Symphony Orchestra.

For its December 28, 1947, *Messiah* and again for its January 2, 1949, rendition, the Society called on the services of Alfred Greenfield, permanent conductor of the New York Oratorio Society. Organist, composer, and educator, as well as conductor, Greenfield was a prominent authority on *Messiah* and on oratorio interpretation and conducting generally. On December 20, little more than hours before his arrival in Salt Lake, Greenfield conducted the New York Oratorio Society in a Carnegie Hall world premier rendition of the newly completed J. M. Coopersmith version that is said to have been the first complete *Messiah* rendition ever given in the United States. It lasted three and one-half hours and required two intermissions.

It was Greenfield, with his progressive approach, who gave Utah its first real introduction to what had long been the twentieth century's changing concept of *Messiah*. Though shortened to a more manageable two hours, his Salt Lake renditions were strongly influenced by Coopersmith, the intent of which was to provide the basis for a performance more nearly approximating those of Handel himself. Horns and trombones were excluded from the orchestra while strings, oboes, bassoons, and organ were given greater emphasis than in Society renditions of past years. Another innovation was the inclusion of a piano modified to produce a sound similar to that of the harpsichord. For the 1947 rendition it was played by Becky Almond and in 1949 by Helen Taylor Johannesen; and it is noteworthy that in recent years the harpsichord itself, usually with Ricklen Nobis at the keyboard, has become a regular part of every performance.

Lowell Durham, music critic for *The Salt Lake Tribune*, wrote of the 1947 version that Greenfield had "directed a rendition which will not soon be forgotten. He introduced several innovations never heard in a previous local performance of this oratorio," including considerable added "ornamentation and a short vocal cadenza in two of the vocal arias." Durham found the most striking changes in the instrumentation. "A much more delicate orchestral coloring," he felt, "was the result....At times the instrumental accompaniment consisted only of [modified] piano, one stand of celli and one contrabass—needless to say the contrast proved most effective."[4]

Haugh sang the tenor solos for both Greenfield renditions and Barbara Stevenson, a leading soprano with the Philadelphia Opera Company, was also scheduled for both. In 1947, however, she was stricken with a debilitating throat ailment the day before the performance and Blythe Taylor Burns was flown from Los Angeles as a substitute. The bass part in 1947 was sung by Kansan Orcenith S. Smith, a promising student at Juilliard and the Union Theological Seminary. Welsh contralto Margaret Tan Williams, a specialist in religious music who had been one of the soloists in Greenfield's uncut *Messiah*, sang the alto role. A year later these parts were taken by two Utah singers, Society veteran Dinwoodey and an Ogden bass, C. Austin Seager, who had sung *Messiah* several times with Lester Hinchcliff and the Ogden Tabernacle Choir.

Of all the soloists in Greenfield's second Salt Lake *Messiah*, by far the greatest interest centered on Mrs. Dinwoodey. During Greenfield's 1947 Salt Lake visit the Society had arranged for him to hear her, and so impressed was he with her voice that he in turn asked her to audition with the New York Oratorio Society. The result was such that when Mrs. Dinwoodey appeared with the Salt Lake Society in its January 2, 1949, Messiah, she was fresh from having sung the alto solos in Greenfield's second uncut Carnegie Hall rendition.

An important feature of Greenfield's second rendition was the first inclusion since 1941 of "The trumpet shall sound," with the obbligato played by Keith Lowell Smith (who was also heard in both 1950 renditions and in 1951). Greenfield, a stickler for authentic detail, supplied a D trumpet and it may have marked the first time that such an instrument had been heard in a local *Messiah*. In past renditions, so far as is known, the cornet had always been substituted. The result of once having heard the proper instrument was a deep dissatisfaction, thereafter, with anything less. Consequently, the need for a D trumpet became a common carping point for newspaper music critics and a source of embarrassment for the Society, which in 1952 went so far as to include the aria accompanied by neither trumpet nor cornet.

That, it seems, was more than at least some *Messiah* enthusiasts were able to bear. In late 1953, in time for Utah Symphony trumpeter William Sullivan to play the part in the January 3, 1954, rendition, the Daynes family, proprietors of Daynes Music Company, presented the Society with a D trumpet bearing the inscription:

Presented to the
Salt Lake Oratorio Society
In Memorial
Royal W. Daynes

Royal Daynes, the reader will recall, was a founding director and early secretary of the Oratorio Society, as well as proprietor of Consolidated Music Company and the associated Consolidated Music Hall, scene of much early concertizing and other important musical activity. His membership on the Society Board of Directors lasted through 1938 and his active support of the Society continued until his death on December 5, 1950.

Sullivan proved so popular as trumpeter that he appeared in every Society *Messiah* through 1979. Edmund Cord played the obbligato in 1980, and thereafter the Society's present trumpeter, Edward Gornik, has rendered this service. Prewar trumpeters, or more accurately, cornetists, were L. P. Christentsen (1915); John Visser (1920, 1923); Clyde White (1924); John J. Fiala (1926, 1927, January and December 1929, 1930); Staff Sergeant William Bunburry (December 1933); Earl J. Bleak (January 1935); Seare Morrison (1937); and Joseph Kirkham (1941).

Though reviews of both Greenfield renditions were laudatory, not a few Salt Lake music lovers seem to have disapproved. The musically sophisticated might find innovation interesting, even exciting, but for those who felt about *Messiah* much as they felt about scripture, change bordered on heresy, and in this regard *Messiah* enthusiasts who objected to Greenfield found their voice almost a year after his final Salt Lake appearance. In an article headlined "Dr. Greenfield Snaps a Finger at Handel *Messiah* Tradition," the *Ogden Standard Examiner* noted that

> now is the time for all good friends of Handel's Oratorio, *The Messiah* to come to the aid of tradition. There is dirty work being done at the crossroads.
>
> Albert Greenfield, in conducting the New York Oratorio Society's 126th performance of the famous work, had the tenor soloist sing "Rejoice Greatly" instead of the soprano. He took away "He Was Despised" from the contralto and gave it to the soprano.
>
> New Yorkers were further startled when Greenfield had the basso instead of the soprano sing "Thou Art Gone Up on High" and the contralto rather than the soprano sing "How Beautiful Are the Feet."

Dr. Greenfield's variance from tradition shouldn't be much of a surprise to Utah Handel fans who heard his Utah *Messiah* performances. He thrust a piano into his orchestra. While the many expressed no objection to the piano's percussive utterance marring the rich flow of accompaniment from the bowed instruments a few protested. It made them mad, and we're wondering how New Yorkers like Dr. Greenfield's significant departures from ancient tradition.[5]

Unbeknownst to the Salt Lake public, Greenfield had written a letter to the Society in the autumn of 1948 that suggested making many of these same changes. But being more attuned to the conservative nature of Salt Lake audiences than Greenfield could have been expected to be, the Society respectfully declined.

Following Greenfield, the Society's next conductor was Dr. Thompson Stone, permanent music director of the Boston Handel and Haydn Society and another of the country's most distinguished conductors of oratorio. Dr. Stone's three renditions were given on January 1 and December 31, 1950, and January 2, 1955.

Soloists appearing with Dr. Stone, with three exceptions, were all Society veterans. January 1950 saw the return of Marie Powers in the alto part, Haugh as tenor, and Bennett as bass, while the single new voice was that of New York-based soprano Ruth Diehl, who had recently sung Handel's *Israel In Egypt* at Carnegie Hall. The following December Haugh and Blythe Taylor Burns were joined by two newcomers, Chicago contralto Lillian Chookasian and Iowa baritone Andrew White, both of whom proved Society favorites. Chookasian had recently sung *Messiah* at Carnegie Hall with Greenfield and White was a vocalist with the Fred Waring Orchestra. In January 1955 Chookasian, Haugh, and White were joined by soprano Barbara Stevenson, making an all-repeat quartet of soloists for that year's rendition.

Dr. Stone was personally no more averse to experimentation and innovation than was Dr. Greenfield. His own experience, however, had shown him that even Boston audiences were little more prepared to have their *Messiah* tinkered with than were those of Salt Lake. In a letter to the Society he explained that in England he had learned a great deal from studying an early *Messiah* score. But when he twice thereafter conducted it in Boston with the "original" instrumentation, it met with limited public favor and he had since reverted to the more familiar treatment. There was, however, one important change he did make in the program. "Would it be possible," he wrote to the Society in the fall of 1949, "to omit the alto aria, 'O though that tellest good tidings?'" He explained that in his opinion there were few contraltos who could sing it in a pleasing manner and that moreover, it was followed by a chorus that sang the same melody harmonized in a way that he found much more interesting.[6]

The chorus Stone referred to, in fact, had never been included by the Society until it was done by Dr. Klemperer in 1945, whereas the aria had been omitted only for the radically shortened 1930 NBC broadcast rendition. Now, at Dr. Stone's suggestion, the aria was dropped and the chorus retained with such pleasing results that, with occasional variations, it has been done this way in most renditions since.

There were other minor changes, but nothing in Stone's first rendition that seems to have shocked the "traditionalists" so much as had Greenfield's piano, and the *Deseret News* noted that "so excellent was the performance and so complete the balance on this New Year's Day that the individual more than ever was lost in significance of music and text."[7]

The *Tribune*'s Lowell Durham, commenting on the second Stone rendition, observed that Dr. Klemperer had been essentially an orchestral conductor, Greenfield a choral conductor "whose specialization left considerable to be desired." Disregarding whether or not this was a fair assessment of the two musicians, Durham found in Dr. Stone a conductor able "to strike a pleasing medium. His experience and knowledge of the score," wrote Durham, "combine to make him one of the outstanding baton-wielders to appear in our city."[8]

By 1955, however, when he made his final Society appearance, even Stone had become too radical for some Salt Lakers. Harrison, in the *News*, regretted cuts in "The trumpet shall sound," as well as unusual tempos and dynamics in "For unto us a child is born," and in the concluding "Amen."[9] Durham, who had studied with Stone, felt constrained to observe that "like guest conductors of previous seasons, he had his own particular bag of interpretative tricks....This always makes for interest on the part of the experienced listener. At the same time it keeps the performers on their toes. I, for one," he added, "don't go along with the purists who claim exclusive knowledge to 'THE' correct interpretation of any particular composer or work"—and the result of such minor tempests, of course, was not to diminish interest in *Messiah*, but to enhance it.[10]

CHAPTER FIFTEEN

The Thor Johnson Era

The 1950s and 1960s continued to be a period of growth and change for the Oratorio Society. There were conflicts with the proliferating new musical organizations, all of which were struggling to establish themselves, and there were painful compromises the Society would be forced to make. Inevitably the years would continue to take a toll of its oldest members and longest associations, one by one severing the living links with the earliest years of its history.

There would continue to be changing *Messiah* fashions, too, and conductors whose ideas would be even more radical than those of Greenfield and his "percussive" piano. In fact Dr. Thor Johnson, the conductor who immediately succeeded Greenfield and Stone for the December 30, 1951, rendition would eventually prove one of the Society's most radical—and this despite the fact that in his first rendition he was one of its most traditional. His eight *Messiahs* are the most given by any of the Society's guest conductors and second only to Professor Coop's nineteen renditions—and from his first to his last in 1973, the Johnson *Messiahs* span almost a quarter of a century.

Dr. Johnson's father was a Moravian minister, his mother a pianist and music teacher. The result was a musician impressive not only for his fine conducting, but for the sense of reverent mission he brought to his work. Of his Tabernacle appearances he said "there is something—some undescribable quality—which makes a non-Utahn feel very honored when he receives an invitation to take part in the musical life of this community. I am certain," he explained, "that it is closely identified with the privilege of performing sacred music in a sacred place. This sensation is inescapable."[1]

Another important personality made his first Society appearance in 1951. This was the great Chinese bass, Yi Kwei Sze, who is thought by many to be the finest bass ever to have sung with the Society. Born in Shanghai, he escaped from the Japanese during World War II and came to the United States in 1947. In 1949 and 1950 he sang *Messiah* at Carnegie Hall and by 1950 had become associated with the San Francisco Opera.

The only Society veteran among the 1951 soloists was Lillian Chookasian, whose deeply colored contralto voice and spiritual delivery were fast making her a favorite with Salt Lake audiences. Of the other soloists, Chicago soprano Maude Nosler had been a soloist with the Bach Choir of St. Louis and the St. Louis Symphony Orchestra; and the tenor, Alexander Haggar of Detroit, had at one time been a student at the University of Utah.

Dr. Johnson proved an immediate success with Salt Lake critics. Durham lavished him with enthusiastic comments in his *Tribune* review and Conrad Harrison did likewise in the *Deseret News*. "The inspiring message of *The Messiah* lifted the hearts of many thousands of listeners Sunday in a traditional Yuletide production," Harrison wrote of the performance, which he characterized as "direct and traditional in almost every regard"—an observation, in those days, that was tantamount to saying that the rendition was "properly" done.[2]

Regrettably, one change was forced on the Society that year. The death of Concertmaster Arthur Freber, on March 22, 1951, closed one of the Society's longest associations. His contribution to the Society, the city, and to the musical profession, could hardly be over estimated, and his loss was keenly felt. In his absence the Society turned to Reginald Beales, founding conductor of the Utah State Sinfonietta and the Utah W.P.A. Symphony Orchestra, who had served the Society as associate concertmaster in the late 1930s. Beales continued as concertmaster through 1955, when he was succeeded by Dr. David A. Shand, a Utah Symphony assistant conductor, University of Utah choral director, and, for several years, choral director of the Oratorio Society. Dr. Shand, in turn, was succeeded in 1961 by Kenneth Kuchler, assistant concertmaster of the Utah Symphony and music director and conductor of the Westminster Community Orchestra. Kuchler has ever since retained the position, with the single exception of the 1981 Messiah when he was substituted for by William Preucil.

Seven years elapsed between Dr. Johnson's first and second Society appearances, during which time two new guest conductors were introduced. The first of these was Sir Ernest MacMillan, who conducted on December 28, 1952, January 3, 1954, and December 18, 1955. Canada's most distinguished musical son, MacMillan was conductor of the Toronto Symphony Orchestra and director of the Mendelssohn Choir of Toronto. He was also the first Canadian elected a Fellow of the Royal College of Music of England.

Under MacMillan's baton the only new voice added to the Society's list of guest soloists was that of Los Angeles soprano Jean Fenn, who was a frequent soloist with the San Francisco Opera Company. A favorite with MacMillan, she sang in all three of his Society renditions, as did Lillian Chookasian and Harold Haugh. Yi Kwei Sze sang the bass part in 1952 while Andrew White returned in 1954 and 1955.

MacMillan was a serious student of Handel, especially of *Messiah*, which he conducted annually for a national Canadian broadcast, and he gave Salt Lakers a valuable insight into his attitude toward the work in a short article published in the *Tribune*. He pointed out that *Messiah* had in the past been a much misunderstood work around which traditions of all kinds clustered "like barnacles." He conceded that the Crystal Palace Handel festivals, with their thousands of singers and instrumentalists, must have created inspiring effects, but in his opinion such effects were "unsuited...to the pellucid delicacy of the lighter numbers and [tended] to necessitate too pedestrian a tempo." He pointed out that such choruses as "For unto us a child is born" and "His yoke is easy" are "largely adaptations from a book of duets set to Italian words about nothing in particular, and that they therefore call for a comparatively light bel canto style." By comparison, he said, the "great climaxes like those associated with the words 'Wonderful Counselor, Mighty God' (which do not appear in the duets and which belong rather to the English side of Handel) are thrown into high relief." He concluded by pointing out that Handel "had a rare feeling for the human voice.

Seldom does he write a passage ungrateful to a singer and his skill in laying out choral passages with a view alike to expression, balance and color can be compared only with the feeling of a Tschaikowsky for the orchestra."[3]

Thus warned, *Messiah* enthusiasts were treated to a series of uniquely MacMillanesque performances, with spirited tempos, sharp contrasts, and rapid transitions from number to number. In addition, MacMillan's affinity for the organ led him to make greater use of it than had been done in prior years, particularly in accompaniment for soloists.

It was between MacMillan's first and second appearances that the Society lost its popular choral director, Lisle Bradford. Her death in 1953 left the Society temporarily without a designated choral director and for the January 1954 rendition her assistants, Dr. David E. Smith, Albert Eccles, and Dr. David A. Shand, undertook the job jointly—and with creditable results. Later in 1955 Dr. Shand was named permanent choral director and given complete charge of the chorus, a position he held until his resignation in 1961.

By the time of MacMillan's final Salt Lake rendition the solo quartet consisting of Fenn, Chookasian, Haugh, and White had become so popular with Salt Lake audiences that it was referred to as "The Dream Quartet." Fittingly, it was this foursome that joined the Society chorus for its first postwar network broadcast on December 18, 1955. The program was part of a series of annual CBS *Messiah* renditions that had included performances by the Reorganized Church of Jesus Christ of Latter Day Saints from Independence, Missouri, and most recently the Worcester (Massachusetts) Choral Society and Symphony Orchestra. Unlike the first two Society network broadcasts—which went live to their radio audiences—this performance was to be recorded, then edited from two hours to a length of ninety minutes, before being released later the same day.

With MacMillan on the podium the Society gave a *Messiah* that was in every respect worthy of a CBS broadcast. In the *News* Harrison wrote that MacMillan's "conception of the *Messiah* remains one of sincerity and understanding" putting "dynamics to effective use,"[4] and Durham, in his *Tribune* review, added that "there were refinements of style new to the annual undertaking, such as were heard during the 16th-note runs in 'For unto us A child is born' and 'His yoke is easy.' They came off with clarity and definition and...in keeping with the spirit of the text."[5]

Letters from listeners across the nation echoed this enthusiasm. "I wish to tell you how clearly and lovely the *Messiah* came in at Houston," wrote one listener. "All day Monday 'The King of Kings and Lord of Lords' thrilled me and moved me to tears at the reality of it all,"[6] and a Harrisburg, Pennsylvania listener wrote that she wanted "to thank you for the great pleasure and inspiration you have given me in broadcasting the *Messiah* last evening."[7]

While still enjoying the recognition that had come with the CBS performance, the Society was invited to present the "Hallelujah" chorus for NBC Television's *Wide Wide World* program. On New Year's Day 1956 the chorus, 400 voices strong, assembled in the foothills overlooking Salt Lake City, the winter-locked ramparts of the Wasatch Mountains rising behind them. Dr. Shand conducted and Alexander Schreiner accompanied as the Society was telecast live from coast-to-coast in the closing segment of a ninety minute telecast that had included scenes from important Washington, D. C., locations and other sites across the nation.

The very early performance date that had been chosen for MacMillan's final *Messiah* in December 1955 was unprecedented at that time. It was dictated, in part, by a CBS requirement calling for a pre-Christmas day rendition; but there were other and less congenial reasons that should be noted. In 1949, 1950, and 1951 the Utah Symphony, which had been giving its concerts in the Tabernacle since the beginning of the 1947–8 season, scheduled Christmas week concerts the Society felt interfered intolerably with its schedule of final rehearsals. Following the January 1, 1950, *Messiah*, the Board of Directors addressed a letter to Bishop Isaacson of the Presiding Bishopric of the LDS Church explaining that

> through thirty-four annual renditions the Salt Lake Oratorio Society's *Messiah* has become a tradition in this community as the spiritual climax to each year's holiday week.
>
> This outstanding rendition by a nonsectarian chorus of 400 voices is offered free to the music lovers of our state. Each year we add a substantial number of new singers to the group, who have to become acquainted with the conductor—a leader of national repute—who comes in for the last week of rehearsals. When he arrives, many experienced singers come in, too, for this final week, who must become familiar with his direction.
>
> I am sure I do not need to stress with you that to perfect the performance of this mixed voluntary group, to have them synchronize with the orchestra and with the work of the soloists...requires the work of a full week. In the final stages of rehearsal to move this great chorus to other

buildings with different seating arrangements, threatens the quality of the finished performance dreadfully. Through your courtesy, prior to last year, we have heretofore regularly had the benefit of the use of the Tabernacle.

Remembering the difficulties of last year, we are fearful that the schedule already set up for this year is going to make it particularly hazardous to carry out our plans. In the week in question, Monday night is Christmas; Wednesday night the Utah Symphony performance is scheduled, to which many of our singers subscribe; Thursday night is regular [Tabernacle] Choir practice, with which we do not want to interfere; Saturday night will be celebrated as New Year's Eve; and our performance is the following day.

Under these circumstances we appeal to you in an effort to have the Symphony Concert held at some time other than this Christmas week. You may be sure we shall appreciate whatever consideration you give this request.[8]

Failing to receive satisfaction in 1950, the Society found itself in the position of having to make the same plea in the spring of 1951, to which Bishop Isaacson responded in a letter addressed to both Jack Thomas of the Society and David Romney, manager of the Utah Symphony. "Now, Brother Thomas and Brother Romney," the bishop wrote, "may I suggest you two brethren get together and talk this out, and then after you have discussed this in detail, will you come to my office together so that we can get these dates properly scheduled and approved by the committee."[9] As a result of this letter an agreement was reached whereby the Symphony would complete its scheduled December 26 concert, but in future years would refrain from scheduling Christmas-week concerts.

This respite from the pressure of increasingly numerous holiday season entertainments was only temporary, however. In 1955, the same year as the MacMillan CBS broadcast, the Utah Symphony combined with the University of Utah's new ballet (later known as Ballet West) to present the first annual rendition of Tchaikovsky's *Nutcracker* in Kingsbury Hall on December 27, 28, 29, 30, and 31. This program, incorporating the complete Utah Symphony Orchestra, has been repeated every year since with an increasingly ambitious schedule of performances. In 1955 only the unusually early *Messiah* date prevented *Nutcracker* from conflicting with the Society's plans, but the Society recognized the threat it posed for the future: musicians could hardly be expected to attend the Society's important evening rehearsals while simultaneously playing in *Nutcracker*.

Friction with the Symphony and the Ballet was averted for

several years more by the Society's decision to continue with pre-Christmas renditions, which it did through 1959; but attendance levels for this period were disappointing and, suspecting that audiences had found it difficult to adjust to the earlier *Messiah* dates, the Society scheduled its next rendition for January 1, 1961. By reluctant accommodation on all sides, a schedule was arranged which allowed the Society sufficient access to musicians for rehearsals and performance, without the musicians having to rush too hectically from *Nutcracker* to *Messiah* and back again. Symphony Manager Herold Gregory did raise the Society's collective blood pressure, however, by suggesting that for the Society the Brigham Young University Orchestra would be good enough.[10]

For a total of five years, through December 27, 1964, the Society clung to its post-Christmas dates before finally bowing to the inevitable consequences of ever increasing musical activity. Thereafter, from December 19, 1965, through December 17, 1972, it gave its performance on the Sunday preceding Christmas. Two exceptions came in year's when Christmas Eve and Sunday coincided, at which times *Messiah* was given on the second Sunday before Christmas. Beginning with the first double *Messiah* rendition in 1973, and again bowing to the unpleasant reality of being unable to compete for musicians, the Society was forced to set its performance dates back another week. Thereafter all performances have fallen on the second Saturday and Sunday before Christmas, with exceptions occurring in 1976 and 1977, when Christmas fell on the weekend and *Messiah* was given during the weekend immediately preceding.

Meanwhile, for the December 23, 1956, and December 22, 1957 *Messiah* renditions, the last before the return of Dr. Johnson, the Society's guest conductor was Karl Kritz, associate conductor of the Pittsburgh Symphony Orchestra and musical director of the Pittsburgh Civic Light Opera Association.

In 1956 the only veteran soloist was bass Andrew White. He was joined by soprano Carole Larsen, a native Salt Laker then living in Los Angeles; by Chicago contralto Ruth Slater, who was especially noted for her Bach and Handel interpretations; and by Raymond Manton of San Francisco, who had charmed Salt Lake music lovers with his interpretation of the tenor role in a recent Utah Symphony rendition of Mahler's *The Song of the Earth*.

In 1957 the solo quartet included both White and Chookasian, who were joined by a pair of newcomers. These were coloratura-soprano Sylvia Stahlman of New York City, who had sung with the San Francisco and Chicago Lyric Operas; and Leslie Chabay, a Hungarian tenor who had appeared with both the San Francisco and the New York Metropolitan Operas.

After the excitement generated by MacMillan's lively renditions, the verdict on Kritz was friendly, but not enthusiastic. He was credited with being a workmanlike conductor whose control of the orchestra was superb, but whose handling of the chorus lacked inspiration and force. "Routinely good" and "almost mechanical at points," is how Harrison described him in 1957. A lack of thrilling climaxes and choral contrast were most regretted.[11]

In 1958, on the other hand, the return of Dr. Johnson presented Salt Lakers with one of the few conductors who could make them forget their infatuation with MacMillan. For the next six years Dr. Johnson's personality and musicianship dominated *Messiah* with performances on December 21, 1958; December 20, 1959; January 1 and December 31, 1961; December 30, 1962; and December 29, 1963; after which ten years would pass before he returned for his final *Messiah*, and the Society's first double rendition, on December 15 and 16, 1973.

A total of twenty-one soloists sang with Dr. Johnson between 1958 and 1973. Of them, only four had appeared with the Society prior to 1958. These were basses Yi Kwei Sze, who sang in Johnson's 1959 and 1962 renditions, and Andrew White, who made the last of his eight Society appearances in 1958 and in December 1961; contralto Annette Richardson Dinwoodey, who made her ninth and final appearance in 1959; and tenor Harold Haugh who completed his Society career with an eleventh performance in 1958.

Four of the newcomers were Utah singers. These were tenor Glade Peterson, who sang in 1959; sopranos JoAnn Ottley, who made her Society debut with Dr. Johnson in 1973, and Lucretia Ferre, whose single Society appearance came in 1962; and bass Robert Peterson, whose 1973 performance with Johnson was but one of six Society appearances he made between 1968 and 1983. At the time of his first Society appearance Glade Peterson was leading tenor with the Zurich Opera in Switzerland. Mrs. Ottley was a soloist with the Tabernacle Choir. Ferre was living and working in New York where she had recently sung *Messiah* at Town Hall, and Robert Peterson, though an Omaha native, had grown up in Salt Lake City where he attended the University of Utah until winning a scholarship to the Juilliard School.

The other new sopranos were Toronto singers Ilona Kombrink in 1958, 1959, and 1963, and Lois Marshall in 1963; and Frances McCann of Los Angeles in January 1961. Kombrink had sung with Dr. Johnson at Wisconsin's Peninsula Music Festival and Marshall, whose voice had been pronounced "phenomenally perfect" during a recent concert tour of Australia, had also toured widely in Europe. McCann, an instant favorite with Salt Lakers, was a leading soprano with the San Francisco Opera.

The five singers who made their Society debuts in the alto part were contraltos Jean Handzlik in December 1961 and Margery Mackay in 1963, both of Los Angeles; San Diego contraltos Mary MacKenzie in 1961 and 1962, and Christina Krooskos in 1973; and San Francisco mezzo-soprano Margot Helmuth Blum in 1958. Handzlik had toured as featured soloist with the Roger Wagner Chorale; MacKay was a soloist with the New York City Opera; MacKenzie was with the Metropolitan Opera; Krooskos, a frequent soloist at the Hollywood Bowl and with the San Francisco Opera, had recently sung Verdi's *Requiem* with the Utah Symphony; and Blum, another San Francisco Opera soloist, was scheduled to tour nationally with the San Francisco Opera Quartet.

Besides Glade Peterson, Dr. Johnson's new tenors were New Yorkers David Lloyd in January and December 1961 and James Wainner in 1963 and 1973; and John McCollum of Ann Arbor, Michigan, in 1962. Lloyd was associated with the New York City Opera; Wainner had sung the American premier of Stravinsky's *Threni*; and McCollum had sung *Messiah* at Carnegie Hall.

The two non-Utah bass soloists were Los Angelean Robert Oliver in January 1961; and Kenneth Smith of Stamford, Connecticut, in 1963. Oliver had so impressed Stravinsky that he wrote a part especially for him in *Threni* that ranged from middle B-flat to low E-flat and for which Oliver received enthusiastic praise in the Venice International Music Festival premier of that work. Smith, a bass-baritone, had been associated with the Chicago Lyric and New York City Operas, and in 1962 sang the role of Brigham Young in an NBC telecast of Leonard Castle's opera, *Deseret*.

One of the exciting events during Dr. Johnson's tenure with the Society was the full two-hour CBS radio network broadcast of the

1959 rendition. Replacing, as it did, the regular weekly broadcast of the New York Philharmonic Orchestra, it was an important tribute to the Society's growing prominence. It was recorded in live performance on the afternoon of December 20 and released nationwide the following Saturday at 8:30 P.M. (eastern standard time).

Harold Lundstrom, the new *Deseret News* music critic, wrote of it that "Thor Johnson directed a performance of Handel's *The Messiah* with such loving care and dedication Sunday afternoon that it not only officially ushered in Christmas week perfectly, but also transformed the great oratorio into a highly spiritual experience." The effect, he said, of "a quartet of excellent soloists, an orchestra of 55 players and Alexander Schreiner, organist, and William Sullivan, trumpeter, was almost overwhelming." Johnson's conducting, he continued, was "energetic, to the point, and with a sweep that evoked from the singers and the musicians the big curve, the splendid stride, of Handel's magnificent stately phrases."[12]

Other broadcasting milestones were passed while the Society was under Dr. Johnson's baton. The December 31, 1961, rendition was recorded and one year later, on Christmas Day, broadcast by New York shortwave station WRUL to Europe, Africa, South America, Mexico, and parts of Asia. Similar international broadcasts were made for several years thereafter, either by WRUL or by another New York station, WNYW. In 1962 KSL first broadcast the Society *Messiah* in FM stereo, a service it has repeated most years since, and for several years FM broadcasts were followed by a taped rebroadcast on KSL-AM.

Unfortunately, taped broadcasts of all kinds came to an end following the 1966 performance. This was the result of a musicians' union order prohibiting the recording of any performance or rehearsal in which its members participated, unless the Society was willing to forgo an annual subsidy for musicians' salaries it received from the Music Performance Trust Funds of the Phonograph Industries. So strict was the union's stance that the Society was no longer allowed to make recordings even for its own use, which in past years had provided it with an important tool for criticizing and improving each year's performance—and which had, of course, provided material for the wartime *Messiah* broadcasts.[13]

During most years Dr. Johnson's renditions differed little in content from those of other Society conductors. In both 1961 renditions and in 1962 he did include "And with his stripes," a chorus the

Society had previously sung only three times; and in December 1961 and in 1962 he omitted the chorus "All we like sheep," which had been included every year since 1936. In 1959 and January 1961 he also omitted the recitative "He that dwelleth" and the aria "Thou shalt break them." It was not until his final rendition in 1973, however, that he departed radically from the usual Society selection, performing several numbers included in the Prout edition but never before sung by the Society, and dropping others that had been sung every year since the Society's first.

During the ten years that passed between his seventh *Messiah* and his Society finale in 1973, Dr. Johnson's conception of *Messiah* underwent considerable change. Where he previously leaned toward romantic interpretation with its large choruses and massed instrumentalists, he came to more and more appreciate the baroque. He was particularly influenced by a new edition of the work published in 1965 by the English musicologist and educator, Watkins Shaw, and when approached by the Society during the spring of 1973 he agreed to conduct only if the Society, in turn, would agree to a performance differing sharply from those of prior years.

The chorus was pared to 240 voices, the smallest for *Messiah* since the troubled days preceding World War II; and only two orchestras, those for the 1920 and 1941 renditions, are known to have been smaller than the 37 pieces used in 1973. Deleted numbers were the choruses "His yoke is easy" (which had been given every year since 1936), "Behold the Lamb" (every year since 1939), "Surely He hath born our grief" (omitted only once before), and "With His stripes" (given only irregularly); and the arias "Come unto Him" (omitted neither before nor since) and "He was despised" (sung in all but two previous renditions).

Some of these numbers were not easily relinquished by the Society. "I hope you will not think me presumptuous in sending you this revised outline of our program," Dr. Anderson wrote in an early August letter. "As you can see I have added...TWO NUMBERS that the S.L.O. Society's Board Members said must be in the program as they have been traditional: 'Come unto him' & 'He was despised.'"[14] Dr. Anderson went on at length as to the attachment Salt Lakers had for these numbers and of the unpleasant consequences certain to follow their omission. But thinking Dr. Anderson presumptuous or not, as the case may have been, Dr. Johnson was adamant: the rendition would be as he wanted it, or he would not conduct it.[15]

Eight numbers from the Prout edition were included that had never been sung by the Society, seven of which have not since been done. These were the choruses "The Lord gave the word," "Their sound is gone out into all lands" (done by Johnson as a tenor aria), "Let us break their bonds asunder" (as aria and chorus), and "But thanks to God who giveth us the victory;" the arias "Thou art gone up on high" and "If God be for us, who can be against us;" the duet "O death, where is thy sting;" and the recitative "Then shall be brought to pass."

Two choruses that had been only infrequently sung were also included. These were "All we like sheep" and "Lift up your heads, O ye gates." In addition, Dr. Johnson added a solo quartet, "Break forth into joy, glad tidings!" that does not occur in the Prout edition. Another innovation was the singing of a variant form of "O thou that tellest good tidings to Zion" by the contralto alone, rather than as the chorus or the combined aria and chorus usually presented by the Society.

Largely as a result of Johnson's final *Messiah*, there are only two numbers included in the Prout edition that have not yet been used by the Society in one form or another. These are the recitative "Unto which of the angels" and the chorus "Let all the angels of God worship Him." It is interesting to note that in 1973 these were originally among the numbers to be included, but probably because of urgent complaints that recent performances had run longer than Salt Lake audiences could endure, they were dropped in the only compromise to which Dr. Johnson is known to have consented that year—and due to their relative obscurity, they may not be heard in Salt Lake for many years to come.

Interestingly, there were no lamentations for sorely missed numbers in 1973. No shocked outcries condemned the smaller orchestra, the prominent use of the harpsichord, the unfamiliar ornamentation brought to many of the solos, or the inclusion of obscure numbers. In large part this was due to the work of the whole succession of Society conductors, each of whom had insisted on departures from Salt Lake tradition that would mark the rendition his own. Taking full advantage of this wider tolerance that he and his colleagues had forged, Dr. Johnson turned his final Salt Lake *Messiah* into what Lundstrom called "a gold mine, filled, for sure, with many nuggets of musical excellence in both the new as well as the traditional elements."[16]

Meanwhile, as Dr. Johnson was leading the Society to ever greater heights, other important changes were taking place. Early in

1958 death took Dr. Bennion, the Society's fourth president. He was succeeded by Henry D. Moyle who was, like Dr. Bennion, an apostle of the LDS Church. Not himself noted as a musician, his interest in the Society seems to have sprung mainly from a love of the scriptures and the great spiritual strength and beauty he found embodied in Handel's music. He was a native of Salt Lake City and had served for many years as a member of the University of Utah Law School faculty.

In June 1959, only a few months after accepting the Society presidency, Apostle Moyle was set apart as Second Counselor to LDS Church President David O. McKay. This important new post in the Church hierarchy greatly increased the demands on his time and when, little more than a year later, he was elevated to the post of first counselor to succeed the late J. Reuben Clark, Jr., it became difficult for him to continue with the Society.

For this reason Apostle Moyle was succeeded, during December 1960, by Harold B. Lee, who was another member of the Council of the Twelve and a future president of the LDS Church. Unfortunately, Apostle Lee had scarcely begun his association with the Society when he became embroiled in a dispute the Society was having with Dr. Shand, the Society's choral director and concertmaster.

Dr. Shand, it seems, had assumed that his work with the chorus would lead to his eventually conducting *Messiah*. His qualifications were probably not less than those of men conducting important renditions elsewhere in the country, and as choral director he had gained the respect of the Society, the critics, and of musicians throughout the local community. The Board of Directors, however, considered that its policy of engaging important outside conductors was essential to the continued success of the Society; and since they felt certain no promise had been made to Dr. Shand, his desire to conduct was frustrated.

In the ensuing controversy, President Lee felt that his name and Church position were used unfairly in denying Dr. Shand, as well as in the Society's subsequent request that Dr. Shand resign as choral director. As a result, Apostle Lee's resignation followed closely upon that of Dr. Shand and thereafter the Board turned to its own membership for a new president.

In early October 1961 Nicholas G. Morgan, Sr., was elected. A Salt Lake native, he had been a director since 1958. He was also a trustee of the Utah State Historical Society and had at one time been president of the National Society of the Sons of the Utah Pioneers.

Reprintd with permission of the*Deseret News* /University of Utah Library Special Collections

Above: Otto Klemperer (lower left), the world famous German conductor who directed the Society *Messiah* in its first two postwar renditions, gathers at the piano with Professor Coop's widow and daughter (Sylvia and Sheila) and 1945 *Messiah* soloists Tudor Williams (L) and Harold Haugh.

Facing Page, Top: Alfred Greenfield (third from left), conductor of the New York Oratorio Society, directed the Salt Lake Society's 1947 and 1949 *Messiahs*. With him are 1947 soloists (L-R) Orcenith Smith, bass; Margaret Tan Williams, contralto; and Harold Haugh, tenor.

University of Utah Library Special Collections/*The Salt Lake Tribune*

University of Utah Library Special Collections

Above: Dr. Thompson Stone (holding score), the Society's third postwar conductor, was permanent music director of the Boston Handel and Haydn Society. He conducted the December and January 1950 and the Janurary 1955 *Messiahs*. With him are December 1950 soloists (L-R) bass Andrew White, tenor Harold Haugh, soprano Blythe Taylor Burns, and contralto Lillian Chookasian.

University of Utah Library Special Collections

University of Utah Library Special Collections

Above Left: Dr. Thor Johnson is joined in the Salt Lake Tabernacle by Alexander Schreiner, the renowned Tabernacle Choir organist who played for every postwar Society *Messiah* but one through the 1977 rendition. Johnson, who was perhaps the best-loved of the Society's postwar conductors, presided over eight *Messiah*s between 1951 and 1973.

Above Right: (L-R) Production Manager Howard T. Anderson, Business Manager and Finance Director W. Jack Thomas, and President Adam S. Bennion brought the Oratorio Society through the difficult years of transition following Professor Coop's death.

Facing Page, Top: Sir Ernest MacMillan (bottom center), the Society's fifth postwar conductor, was the first Canadian elected a Fellow of the Royal College of Music of England. He was conductor of the Toronto Symphony Orchestra and director of the Mendelssohn Choir of Toronto. With him (L-R) are bass Andrew White, Salt Lake trumpeter William Sullivan, tenor Harold Haugh, and soprano Jean Fenn, all of whom appeared with MacMillan in 1954 and December 1955.

Facing Page, Bottom: (L-R) Tenor Alexander Haggar, contralto Lillian Chookasian, soprano Maude Nosler, and bass Yi Kwei Sze sang in the first Thor Johnson *Messiah* in 1951.

University of Utah Library Special Collections/*The Salt Lake Tribune*

University of Utah Library Special Collections/*The Salt Lake Tribune*

Courtesy of Ann Bennet Lowden

Courtesy of Mrs. Dinwoodey

University of Utah Library Special Collections

Utah State Historical Society/*The Salt Lake Tribune*

Above: Alexander Schreiner and Oratorio Society Secretary Emma Thomas at the Tabernacle organ with (L-R) Dr. David Shand, Dr. Howard T. Anderson, and W. Jack Thomas behind them.

Facing Page, Top: These 1946 *Messiah* soloists are (L-R) tenor Harold Haugh, contralto Marie Powers, soprano Blythe Taylor Burns, and Salt Lake bass Harold H. Bennett.

Facing Page, Bottom Left: Salt Lake contralto Annette Richardson Dinwoodey shortly after her appearance with Alfred Greenfield and the New York Oratorio Society in that organization's second full-length *Messiah* rendition—which was only the second U. S. rendition to utilize Handel's full score.

Facing Page, Bottom Right: Lisle Bradford, a charter member of the Society who had sung in every *Messiah* since the Society's first, was one of its most devoted members. She served at various times as a chorus officer, section director, choral director, assistant conductor, and associate music director, and her death in 1953 was deeply felt by the Society.

University of Utah Library Special Collections

Left: Following Dr. Adam S. Bennion, two more apostles of the LDS Church served as president of the Oratorio Society. The first of these was Henry D. Moyle from 1958 through 1960.

Right: The third apostle of the LDS Church to serve as president of the Oratorio Society was Harold B. Lee in 1960 and 1961.

LDS Historical Department

CHAPTER SIXTEEN

The Nielson Chorus

By the time of Dr. Shand's resignation as choral director early in 1961, the Oratorio Society was once again the victim of vexing chorus problems. Even its own singers were lax in their rehearsal attendance, but more troublesome yet was the continued dependence on large numbers of outside singers who had no particular allegiance to the Society. These, on the assumption that they already knew *Messiah*, assumed also that they need attend only a final rehearsal or two.

For obvious reasons this made even slight changes in *Messiah* interpretation difficult to achieve. Prior to World War II, when Salt Lake's musical experience was limited and all performances were either conducted by Professor Coop or by a handful of other Salt Lake musicians, innovation was not an important concern. Following the war, however, the inflexibility of the chorus tended to negate much of the value that even the more insular and tradition bound of Salt Lake music lovers were coming to recognize as inherent in the Society's use of heralded guest conductors.

In hopes of correcting these difficulties, the Society turned to Dr. Jay E. Welch as its new choral director. He was an assistant professor of music at the University of Utah and an assistant to Tabernacle Choir Conductor Richard P. Condie, whom he would eventually succeed in that post. The course of events was such, however, that

Dr. Welch resigned as choral director after a single season and it fell to his successor, John Marlowe Nielson, to build the chorus into the truly fine organization it subsequently became.

At the time he joined the Society in 1962 Nielson was an instructor in the music department at the University of Utah. He had founded the University Chorale in 1952 and he was also director of the University's Men's Chorus. In addition, he was director of the Orpheus Club, which had previously been headed by both Professor Coop and Alfred H. Peabody, the latter being the Society's earliest treasurer and choral assistant.

Nielson was first approached by the Society at the time of Dr. Shand's resignation in 1961, but Dr. Welch, the musician with the more extensive background, was chosen over him. A year later, following Welch's resignation, he was again contacted and the directorship definitely offered. As Nielson relates it, he had combined his Orpheus Club and University Male Chorus singers for a concert in Assembly Hall. Dr. Anderson attended, and after the concert, Nielson recalls, "he sought me out, hurriedly made a few congratulatory remarks and then said, 'You are our man, I'll talk to you later.' He seemed to take for granted that I would accept; and, of course, he was right."

The Society could hardly have been more fortunate in its choice of a new choral director, nor could the new director have taken over at a more difficult time. Nielson recalls that the first rehearsal was held with dishearteningly few singers. "We persevered until two or three weeks before *Messiah*," he says, "and still the chorus was not more than two hundred or so.

"I was told not to worry, folks from the Tabernacle Choir would come in and others that 'knew' *Messiah*. Well, many did come in, but I was appalled by the result. I thought it was a sloppy attempt. Dr. Thor Johnson, the guest director, was unhappy, the critics were unhappy, I was unhappy. Only Dr. Anderson was optimistic and thought we did the best we could under the circumstances. His enthusiasm and faith never waned."[1]

A small furor was aroused within the Society by Harold Lundstrom's *Deseret News* comments about that first Nielson-trained chorus. Echoing criticisms from some of the darker prewar days, he wrote that "the chorus members know that Dr. Johnson was disappointed because he was not getting through to them with his suggestions at the rehearsals, and he returned to Northwestern University

Sunday evening still extremely disappointed. And with reason." In Lundstrom's opinion it was "a chorus that, somehow, failed to blend, indicating that the various sections were not listening for or to each other; frequently they sang more as a lay congregation rather than as a chorus of trained singers."[2]

Whether this was true or not (and there were certainly legitimate questions raised as to the degree of its truth), there can be little doubt that 1962 marked the nadir of the Society's postwar choral efforts. *The Salt Lake Tribune*, in fact, did not deign to give the performance a by-lined review.

Thereafter, Nielson moved quickly to establish his chorus as a cohesive, disciplined body with a stable membership and a high degree of confidence in its own ability. Reforms were instituted, including auditions and a strict policy on attendance; recruitment and training of new singers was begun; and advanced training for veteran members provided. Many of these changes had been tried in the past—but with less than happy results. This time, however, no doubt due to the diligence and understanding Nielson brought to his task and the unqualified backing he received from Jack Thomas, Dr. Anderson, and the other members of the Board, chorus members responded with enthusiasm.

In 1965 the chorus spirit and its sense of unified purpose were so far improved that the members voted a five-dollar annual membership fee to help the Society meet the cost of its productions. Since then this fee has been increased twice: first to seven and one-half dollars and recently to ten. Similar assessments had been set forth in the Society's bylaws in 1915, but the Board, perhaps candidly facing its dependence on outside singers who would balk at paying fees, had immediately voted to suspend them, and there is no record of their having been assessed at any time during the intervening years.

By 1969 the Nielson chorus was so well established that the Society was able to do something it had accomplished only twice before in its history—something that required its knowing who its chorus members would be well in advance of the performance. For the first time since 1927 and 1929 the entire chorus personnel was listed in the program notes, as it has been every year since.

Enthusiastic chorus members frequently refer to the privilege of working with a director of Nielson's ability and training, and for many it is this feeling of friendship, loyalty, and gratitude toward him that explains their continued chorus membership. No doubt expressing the sentiments of many, Janet Young Hammond, a twenty-plus-year veteran of the chorus, exclaims that "it is a treat to be trained by such directors as John Marlowe Nielson and to be exposed to the great guest directors that we've had." Valena M. Berntson, herself the veteran of fifteen years, adds that "he creates an atmosphere which makes you want to give your all and perfect the talent you have."[3]

In 1964, at a time when Nielson was already making rapid progress with the chorus, the Society engaged Walter Susskind, one of its best-loved guest conductors. A native of Prague, he enjoyed not only an international reputation as a fine conductor, but was also a noted concert pianist and a composer of widely recognized merit. When Czechoslovakia was occupied by the Nazis at the onset of World War II he adopted England as his new home, eventually becoming principal conductor of the Scottish National Orchestra. Following the war he spent several years in Australia, then followed Sir Ernest MacMillan as conductor of the Toronto Symphony Orchestra and director of Toronto's Mendelssohn Choir. For the Society he conducted *Messiah* seven times, with performances on December 27, 1964; December 19, 1965; December 17, 1967; December 22, 1968; December 21, 1969; December 20, 1970; and December 19, 1971.

Though Susskind was an appreciative student of early Handel scores, he pointed out to the *Tribune*'s Michael Fox that Handel's own renditions were given for small audiences in small halls for which chorus and orchestra of limited size were adequate. With *Messiah* we, on the other hand, make a compromise, he told Fox, when we adapt the work to our larger halls and audiences, and this sense of compromise perhaps best characterizes the Susskind approach.[4]

Of the sixteen soloists who sang *Messiah* with Susskind, six have already been mentioned in connection with the Johnson renditions. These were contraltos Mary MacKenzie, who sang with Susskind in 1964, and Christina Krooskos in 1969 and 1970; tenors John McCollum in 1964 and 1967, and James Wainner in 1968, 1970, and 1971; and bass-baritones Kenneth Smith in 1964 and Robert Peterson in 1968 and 1970.

Three sopranos made their *Messiah* debuts with Susskind. The first of these was Leona Gordon of the San Francisco Opera who sang in the 1964, 1965, and 1970 renditions. She was also scheduled in 1968, but a serious bout with influenza forced the last minute substitution of Los Angelean Nancy Bramlage, whose performance merited a return engagement the following year. In 1967 and 1971 the soprano was Nöel Rogers of Ann Arbor, Michigan, who was a frequent vocalist with the Aspen Summer Music Festival in Colorado.

New contraltos were Peggy Coburn in 1965 and 1968, Donna Peterson in 1967, and Louise Parker in 1971. Coburn, who made her home in Los Angeles, had sung at Carnegie Hall and the Hollywood Bowl; Peterson was in her eighth season with the San Francisco Opera; and Philadelphian Louise Parker, one of America's promising young vocalists, had sung a Carnegie Hall rendition of Bach's *St. Matthew* Passion with Stokowski.

Two new tenors sang with Susskind. These were Chicagoan Walter Carringer in 1965 and Paul Mayo of Los Angeles, who substituted for an ailing James Wainner, in 1969. Carringer was a soloist with the Robert Shaw Chorale while Mayo's oratorio experience included roles in *Messiah, Israel in Egypt,* and *Judas Maccabaeus.*

New bassos were Raymond Michalski of New Jersey, who appeared in 1965, 1967, and 1969; and Philip Booth of Washington, D. C., in 1971. Michalski was a member of the Lincoln Center Young Artists Group and later joined the Metropolitan Opera. Booth, a soloist with the Western Opera Theater, had recently sung *L'Enfance du Christ* with the Choral Society of Washington, D.C.

Susskind's Salt Lake debut in 1964 drew the first overflow audience in several years and Lundstrom, in his *News* review, related that at "about two minutes to 2 P.M. Sunday afternoon, Dr. Howard T. Anderson announced to all those persons standing in the Tabernacle that if they wanted to find seats, there were some available in nearby Assembly Hall....How many took advantage of the invitation, I do not know. But," Lundstrom wrote, "if several hundred or thousand other music patrons not present had known what kind of a performance Walter Susskind was going to lead...the Assembly Hall would also have been filled to overflowing." Lundstrom found "the sweep and control of Mr. Susskind's conducting...moving and convincing" and "his range of dynamics...hair-raising...and the final climax...shattering in its overwhelming impact."

His assessment of the chorus must have been especially gratifying, both to the Society and to Nielson, who had worked untiringly to reform it. "For many weeks," Lundstrom wrote, "the 400 singers had been carefully prepared by John Marlowe Nielson [and his assistants], Kenly Whitelock and Wesley Mason, and they were more equal to the task than they have been in several years."[5]

It is impossible at this remove to point to one Susskind rendition as having been best. Certainly that of 1965, celebrating the Society's fiftieth birthday, was one of the most impressive. In addition, the performance was not only broadcast to the large KSL audience and to the far-flung audience of WRUL Short Wave, it was also videotaped by KSL-TV for release one week later, on December 26. The chorus, improving noticeably each year, was lauded by Jim Fitzpatrick of the *Tribune* as being "the main reason for the brilliance of the performance." He noted that "the perfect precision and the clear enunciation were remarkable and the vitality and zest of the singers' efforts were infectious."[6]

For Lundstrom it was "Susskind's profound musicality, his refusal to take the lowliest 16-note for granted, an avoidance of both exaggeration and routine," that resulted in "as exciting a performance as the most avid Handel buff could want."[7]

During his years with the Society Susskind was responsible for the inclusion of three numbers that had not been previously sung. For the anniversary rendition he added the recitative "All they that see Him laugh Him to scorn," and the chorus "He trusted in God that He would deliver him;" and in 1970 he added an abbreviated version of "Since by man came death," a chorus that has been included every year since.

His farewell performance with the Society in 1971 was probably the most difficult and courageous ever given in a Tabernacle *Messiah.* Certainly not since 1941, when Professor Coop was called from his sickbed to lead the last prewar rendition, had a conductor overcome such physical suffering. Unknown to Society Vice-president Michael Megeath, who made the customary introductory remarks prior to the performance, Susskind had been taken suddenly ill, and following his introduction failed to take the podium. After an awkward moment of waiting, punctuated by a nervous cough or two and the rustling of programs from the huge audience, Dr. Maurice Taylor, the assistant production manager, went back stage to find out what the trouble was.

"I'm just too sick to go on," Susskind told him.

The only alternative would have been for Nielson to conduct the performance, which he could no doubt have done. But it was Susskind, not Nielson, that the thousands who packed the Tabernacle and overflowed into the Assembly Hall had come to see and hear. Not knowing what else to do, Dr. Taylor said, "You have to go on. You've been announced."

Confronted with the seemingly inexorable logic of this assertion, Susskind pulled himself together, made his way to the podium, and proceeded to give what many felt to be the most inspiring performance of the seven he conducted in the great hall.

The rendition was also his most nearly romantic, "perhaps...a bit too romantic a reading for strict Handelians," Lundstrom wrote in the *News*, "but if you like the way Klemperer conducts Mozart as though it were Beethoven and if your favorite Jewish composer is Mendelssohn rather than Mahler, then you would have enjoyed the lushness of Sunday's performance." In addition to every other aspect, the chorus was roundly praised. In 1970 Lundstrom called it the best Society chorus he had yet heard; by 1971 his enthusiasm was even greater. He was especially impressed with its extraordinary intensity and accuracy.[8]

The continuity of the Susskind years was interrupted only once. Following his 1965 *Messiah* he tentatively agreed to return to Salt Lake in 1966, but his fulfilling this engagement, it was understood by all parties, might be prevented by a European tour that was then being arranged for him and for which not all dates had yet been made final. As it turned out, a concert in Antwerp on December 18 made it impossible for him to conduct *Messiah*, which was scheduled for the Tabernacle on that same day. At Susskind's suggestion the conductor of the Indianapolis Symphony Orchestra, Izler Solomon, was engaged in his place.

A native of St. Paul, Minnesota, Solomon was one of the most highly regarded American-born conductors of his generation. He had been associated with the Lansing (Michigan) and Illinois Symphonies, Chicago Women's Symphony, the Columbus Philharmonic, and the New Orleans Summer Symphony, and he was director of the Aspen Festival orchestra in Colorado.

The Solomon rendition, which included Society veteran soloists Leona Gordon, Peggy Coburn, James Wainner, and Raymond

Michalski, represented perhaps a more technical treatment than those of recent conductors. "An interesting musical composition rather than a state occasion or a necessary time to meditate," is how one critic characterized it.[9] For the first time in four years, and only the seventh since 1915, it included the chorus "And with his stripes we are healed." Omitted for the first time since 1936 was the popular chorus "All we like sheep have gone astray"—and though it was missed by many, it was not reinstated until the final Johnson rendition in 1973. Since then, however, it has been included most years.

Following Solomon, Susskind returned for five more renditions. Thereafter, he was also scheduled to conduct the December 17, 1972, rendition, an appearance that had already been announced by the Society when he suffered a serious hand injury that necessitated rescheduling of all his concert dates and cancellation of the Salt Lake engagement.

In Susskind's place the Society turned to Dr. Crawford Gates, a musician who was especially dear to Salt Lake audiences. Though not actually a native of Utah—he was born in San Francisco—Dr. Gates had strong ties with the Mormon heartland. His name alone, by recalling Emma Lucy and B. Cecil Gates, linked him with the earliest of Utah pioneers and the most exalted of early Utah musical traditions. From 1950 through 1966 he was a member of the Brigham Young University music faculty, heading the department from 1960 until he left in 1966 to accept the position of artist in residence at Beloit College in Wisconsin. Since 1966 he had also been music director and conductor of the Beloit Symphony Orchestra and his guest conducting included repeated appearances with the Utah Symphony. He was best known to Salt Lakers, however, as composer of the musical play *Promised Valley*, which was presented every summer by the LDS Church.

Soloists for Gates 1972 *Messiah* were soprano Nancy Bramlage, contralto Marvellee Cariaga, Utah tenor Glade Peterson, and bass Philip Booth. Of these, only Cariaga had not previously sung *Messiah* with the Society. A resident of Corona del Mar, California, she was a frequent vocalist with the Monday Evening Concerts in Los Angeles and had sung three successive Christmas *Messiah*s with the Pasadena Symphony Orchestra.

Dr. Gates disappointed none among those of his admirers lucky enough to hear him. The newspapers reported that both the Tabernacle and Assembly Hall were filled at least thirty minutes before the program was scheduled to begin, and that hundreds of ticket holders waited at the doors in hopes room would be found for them.

It was the first time in many years that the Society had suffered the embarrassment of turning away ticket holders in such numbers. Subsequently, it received a flood of letters critical of its method of handling attendance, some of them renewing the suggestion first made in 1945 that the Society resort to the methods of supply and demand capitalism by charging a small admission.

At that time, however, the solution the Society felt itself compelled to adopt was that of presenting double performances, the first of which was the Dr. Johnson finale in 1973. At first, from the perspective of the public, these amounted to little more than issuing tickets for the Saturday night dress rehearsal, which had been periodically opened to the public since the late 1940s. Nonetheless, the mere formality of calling a rehearsal a performance greatly increased the fees and salaries that had to be paid soloists and musicians, and it was not long before the Saturday performances were treated as seriously by both the Society and the public as were those on Sunday.

Following the double Johnson rendition in 1973, the Society's next guest conductor was Dr. Louis Lane, who conducted *Messiah* on December 14–15, 1974, December 13–14, 1975, and December 17–18, 1977. He was currently the resident associate conductor, under Lorin Maazel, of the Cleveland Orchestra, co-director of the Cleveland Orchestra's Blossom Festival School, director of the Akron Symphony Orchestra, and principal guest conductor of the Dallas Symphony.

Veteran Society soloists who sang with Dr. Lane were contralto Louise Parker, bass Philip Booth, and soprano JoAnn Ottley, all in 1974; contralto Christina Krooskos in 1975; tenor James Wainner in both 1974 and 1975; and bass Gary Kendall (whose 1976 Society debut is noted in Chapter Seventeen) in 1977.

Those making their Society debuts were soprano Ariel Bybee and baritone Gene M. Larson in 1975; and soprano Sung Sook Lee, mezzo-soprano Carole Walters, and tenor Dan Marek, all in 1977. Among these newcomers were two with Utah connections. Bybee, who was a member of the San Francisco Opera and the Western Opera Theater, was a graduate of Brigham Young University; and Larson, a Provo native and the music director and conductor of the Alhambra Playhouse in Pleasant Grove, Utah, had sung roles in two joint Ballet West and Utah Symphony productions of Orff's *Carmina Burana* and in a 1974 Brigham Young University rendition of Mussorgsky's *Boris Godunov.*

Lee, the 1977 soprano, was an eleventh hour substitute for Shigemi Matsumoto, who was prevented from singing by the sudden death of her father. Born in Korea, Lee was noted for her work in opera and oratorio, and she was scheduled to sing an upcoming *Messiah* with the Seattle Symphony. Walters, who grew up in South Dakota and Canada, was the leading mezzo-soprano of the Aachen State Theater in Germany and Marek, originally from Oklahoma, was associated with the Metropolitan and New York City Operas.

Dr. Lane's first rendition, in 1974, dropped ten of the numbers Dr. Johnson had added the year before and restored six of those Johnson had cut. He also made two additional changes which bore no evident relation to what Johnson had done. Beginning in 1974, for the first time since the Society's founding, the chorus "And He shall purify the sons of Levi" was included; and in another first, beginning in 1975, "But who may abide the day of His coming" was sung as an alto rather than as a bass aria.

His interpretation was more in keeping with the modern ideas than with the romantic, and Lundstrom described it as having "a spacious airy acoustic that combined with an outstanding quality of performance;" and a chorus, he wrote, "large as it was," that "was sparkling clear and, indeed, almost made the whole show," which was "full of extraordinary intensity, vigor, and enthusiasm."[10]

It was for Dr. Lane's 1977 rendition that Alexander Schreiner made the last of his thirty-nine Society appearances at the great organ. Since the war he had missed only the 1967 *Messiah*, when Dr. Robert Cundick (who was also the 1978 and 1979 organist) substituted. Other postwar organists have been John Longhurst in 1980; Parley L. Belnap from 1981 through 1983; James Drake from 1984 through 1986; and Linda Margetts in 1987.

An important Society milestone was passed in the mid 1970s when the Society adopted its new name, the **Oratorio Society of Utah.** The reason for such a startling change after so many eventful years seems to have had more to do with state bureaucracy and the upcoming United States Bicentennial Celebration, than with any inner processes of the Society. The nationwide observances were to include the participation of many regional performing arts groups, for which considerable amounts of money had been made available by Washington and by the various states—including Utah. Of course the Oratorio Society, as Utah's oldest continuously active independent musical organization, was hopeful of participating. A number of possible oratorio performances were discussed by the Board of Directors and suggested to the Utah Bicentennial Commission, including both Tabernacle renditions and renditions elsewhere in the state. Understandably, competition for the available funds was keen and the principal objection to the Society's application was that as an organization it was not sufficiently representative of the state as a whole.

Both the Bicentennial Commission and the Utah Institute of Fine Arts suggested the Society should alter its name to include the word Utah, and in August 1975, after more than fifty years as the Salt Lake Oratorio Society, the new name was adopted. Unfortunately, the Society received none of the hoped-for funding, and its contribution to the celebration, a Tabernacle rendition of Mendelssohn's *Elijah* (see Chapter Eighteen) given free to the public during June, 1976, was paid for from its own funds.

There were other important Society changes in the late 1960s and early 1970s, especially in the membership of the Board of Directors. Deaths and retirements resulted in new presidents, a new business manager, new secretary, and several new directors. The first to leave the Society was Emma Thomas, who retired in 1969 as secretary for both the Board of Directors and the chorus. The former post she had held since 1964, the latter since 1929. As chorus secretary she was succeeded by Helen Wilcox who remained in that post until the spring of 1987, when she was succeeded by Merle Lowe. The new secretary of the Board was Harvey S. Ross, the Society's current vice-president for chorus relations. Not long after Emma's retirement, Richard G. Horak took over her husband Jack's fund raising activities under the office of vice-president for finance—though Jack Thomas remained an influential member of the Board until his death on August 29, 1973. Soon thereafter the death of Dr. Anderson, on July 18, 1974, severed the final living link between the Society and its earliest origins.

The tribute paid Dr. Anderson by Harold Lundstrom in his

Deseret News column could with little modification be applied to the Thomases and to the many others who devoted their time and love to the Society:

If there was a deficit he, with a few other devoted friends, made up the deficit from their own purses.

He traveled from coast to coast frequently, listening to and hunting for the high quality of soloist talent that has helped the Oratorio Society's productions attain national recognition.

Through his long service Dr. Anderson also had the exciting experience, as well as the good fortune, to be associated with many distinguished choirmasters, conductors, and other competent musicians.

That association and training extended for more than half a century, and I doubt that any lay singer and practicing physician ever knew the musical challenges of Handel's *Messiah* better than he. He had a hundred and one perceptive observations about virtually every chorus and aria anyone wanted to discuss with him....

It is difficult to think of sitting in the Tabernacle this Saturday and Sunday and not seeing white-haired Dr. Anderson on the stand. But his influence will be felt—as well as missed.

Over and over again, Dr. Anderson demonstrated his worth to the Oratorio Society which he fostered with every ounce of devotion.[11]

At the time of Dr. Anderson's death the Society had already lost its seventh president, Nicholas G. Morgan, Sr. He died on November 17, 1971, and during the remainder of his term was substituted for by Vice-president Michael Megeath. The following winter, when the Board held its elections, Megeath was chosen to succeed Morgan. He was a native of Wyoming who had joined the Society Board in 1969, soon after coming to Salt Lake as assistant public relations director for Mountain Fuel Supply Company. Unfortunately, Megeath's tenure as Society president was the shortest of any who have yet held that position. On April 16, 1972, he died suddenly at home of a heart ailment.

The Society's next president was Jack Everett Holmstrom. A native of Sweden, he came to the United States with his parents in 1917 and retired as a vice-president of First Security Bank of Utah in 1971. He served the Society as president through 1982, when he was succeeded by the current president, Richard G. Horak. A native of Omaha and budget director for Mountain Fuel Supply, Horak became a Salt Lake resident in 1946. He is a graduate of the University of Utah and a lieutenant colonel in the Air Force Reserve.

CHPTER SEVENTEEN

Contemporary Messiah

It was in 1973, as the Society was preparing for its first double Messiah, that the idea of charging admission became a serious topic of discussion. Inflation was beginning to push costs rapidly upward, and the double performances represented another sharp increase in outlays, so not surprisingly several directors (perhaps even a majority) favored selling tickets. The main obstacle to doing so, however, was Dr. Anderson. Having presided as chorus president at the time of the first free *Messiah* in 1929, he was strongly opposed—and even at this late date his influence on the Board was sufficient to veto any such proposal.

For this reason the idea languished until after the Doctor's death, by which time the combination of recession and even more alarming increases in the rate of inflation had become a serious threat. In 1975 the Society faced *Messiah* expenses of nearly fifteen thousand dollars and finally, with the support of the Board of Directors, then Vice-president Horak addressed a letter to LDS Church authorities explaining the Society's difficulty and requesting permission to charge for both the Saturday and Sunday performances of the coming rendition. Disappointingly for the Society, permission was refused, though it was gladly extended for any day but Sunday.

The following year, however, a letter written by Annette Richardson Dinwoodey, who joined the Board in 1972, resulted in a more favorable response. On condition that some accommodation be made for those unable to pay, permission was granted in a letter of July 30, 1976, over the signature of F. Michael Watson, assistant secretary to the First Presidency of the LDS Church. Soon after, on December 18–19, 1976, a forty-five-year tradition of free *Messiahs* came to an end.[1] Prices ranged from $2.00 through $6.50 for the best seats, and by the 1987 rendition had increased to a range of from $6.00 to $12.00.

The conductor for this first paid rendition, whose single Society appearance fell between the second and third Louis Lane renditions, was Dr. Mischa Semanitzky. He was assistant conductor of the Pittsburgh Symphony Orchestra and musical director and conductor of both the Pittsburgh Youth Symphony and the Pittsburgh Ballet Theater.

Soloists were JoAnn Ottley, Christina Krooskos, Henry Price, and Gary Kendall, of whom only the Texas tenor, Price, has not been previously mentioned. He had recently appeared on a nationally televised "Live From the Met" rendition of *The Barber of Seville* with Beverly Sills and with a televised "In Performance at Wolf Trap" rendition of *La Traviata.*

Semanitzky's performance was well received and the audience, despite having to pay for tickets, was not much smaller than those of recent years. In content the program differed somewhat from the preceding Lane renditions. The chorus "His yoke is easy" and the aria "He was despised" were dropped and "How beautiful are the feet" was first sung as a soprano aria, then repeated as a duet for soprano and alto.

The orchestra of forty pieces was small by comparison to Society orchestras of the 1950s and 1960s, when nearly sixty instruments were not unusual. Its reduced size, which had begun with Dr. Johnson's 1973 rendition, reflected the widespread trend toward smaller ensembles, though in part it was also the result of the Society's pinched budget during this period of tight money and inflation. But even with so few players, Semanitzky managed a lushness of sound that prompted the *Deseret News* critic to pronounce him "consistent in persuading the orchestra to approach its score in the romantic vein," though others professed to be most impressed by his baroque touches.[2]

Following Semanitzky, and then Lane's final *Messiah*, the decade of the 1970s was completed by guest conductors Walter Hendl, who appeared with the Society on December 16–17, 1978; and Sandor Salgo on December 15–16, 1979, and December 13–14, 1980. Hendl, a native of New Jersey, may be remembered by Salt Lakers as having been one of the musicians seriously considered as a possible conductor and music director for the Utah Symphony at the time Maurice Abravanel was chosen for that position. He had been an instructor of conducting at the Juilliard School, director of the Eastman School of Music, music director and conductor of the Dallas Symphony and the Chautauqua Orchestra in New York State, and by the time of his Society engagement in 1978 was orchestral director of the Erie Philharmonic in Pennsylvania.

Hendl's selection by the Society was the result of an impression he made on Grant Johannesen, Utah's internationally renowned pianist. Johannesen, who later joined the Society Board of Directors and who remains a Society consultant as of this writing, "discovered" Hendl in Pennsylvania. As Hendl related it to William S. Goodfellow, *Deseret News* music critic, "Johannesen came to Erie to solo in the *Emperor* Concerto last year. I'd done *Messiahs* for the last two years straight there, and he was impressed enough with my work to put me in touch with the Oratorio Society here."[3]

The only veteran soloist in the Hendl rendition was Dan Marek. The others were San Francisco Opera soprano Shigemi Matsumoto, who had been forced to forgo singing in the 1977 *Messiah* because of her father's death; contralto Victoria Grof of the New York City Opera; and bass-baritone Edward Pierson, another New York City Opera singer, who had captivated Salt Lake audiences with his starring role in a 1976 Pioneer Memorial Theater rendition of *Show Boat.*

Hendl's interpretation was less self-consciously energetic than many of recent years, his tempos slower, both vocal and orchestral tones clearly articulated, which allowed the music, as Wetzel described it in the *Tribune*, "to unfold and develop naturally, without haste."[4] These fine effects were purchased at a price, however—at least from the standpoint of many a listener. Where orchestra and soloists benefited, the fire and drama of swelling choruses, for instance, was diminished.

Sandor Salgo, the 1979 and 1980 conductor, began his musical career in his native Hungary. In 1939 he emigrated to the United States and at the time of his Society appearances he was music director of the Marin (County, California) Symphony and director of the Carmel Bach Festival and the Music at the Vineyards series at Saratoga, California.

Three Society veterans sang solo parts with Salgo. These were James Wainner, who made the last of his twelve Society appearances in 1979; JoAnn Ottley in 1980; and Edward Pierson in both 1979 and 1980. Newcomers were soprano Ronit Kalisky in 1979; mezzo-soprano Jane Bunnell in 1979; and mezzo-soprano Linn Maxwell and tenor Dana Talley in 1980.

Kalisky, who was born in Israel, had appeared with both the New York Lyric and the Philadelphia Opera Companies; Bunnell had sung *Israel in Egypt* at the Washington Cathedral and *Messiah* with the Richmond Symphony; Maxwell's recent engagements included *Elijah* with the Chicago Symphony and the *St. Matthew Passion* at Lincoln Center with Musica Sacra; and Talley had recently sung *Judas Maccabaeus* at Carnegie Hall. Interestingly, Tally was first trained as a baritone at the Juilliard School. In 1977, however, he entered the Busseto International Competition in Italy where he won the special prize for Verdi tenor voices, and a tenor he had since remained.

In content the Salgo rendition differed from those of immediately preceding years principally in the omission of the solo quartet, "Break forth into joy, glad tidings," that had been included for the first time by Dr. Johnson in 1973 and, in abbreviated form, repeated most years since. Musically, the performance approached the leisurely pace that had characterized Hendl's *Messiah*, though with a more effective use of choral climaxes.

Salgo's 1980 rendition was more conservative, even, than that of the preceding year, and partly, at least, this was due to its being telecast nationally as a Public Broadcasting Service Christmas special. It was by all measure the most seen and heard Society *Messiah*, and it was the most difficult project the Society had yet undertaken. Artistically, and in quality of sound and image reproduction, it far surpassed the effort of 1965, when KSL had taped the Society *Messiah* for local telecast. The cost alone, which ran in the neighborhood of sixty thousand dollars, presented an all but insurmountable obstacle. It was nearly three times the largest amount previously raised by the Society for a single rendition, and until the LDS Church generously offered to meet the greater share of it, the Society's ability to undertake such a project remained in doubt.

Preliminary discussions with officials of the University of Utah's Public Broadcasting Service (PBS) affiliate, KUED-TV, began as early as 1975, and continued periodically through 1978 and early 1979, when the first serious efforts were made to locate a sponsor and to work through the many other difficulties such a program entailed. By early 1980 the LDS Church, through the agency of its Deseret Management Corporation, had stepped forward as the principal sponsor and negotiations were begun with instrumental musicians, whose union rules strictly governed their participation in recorded and televised productions.

Not since 1977, when a program of vigorous re-auditioning had been used to restrict the chorus to its finest voices, had the Society presented a chorus of more than three hundred. These relatively small ensembles were appropriate to the trend of presenting Handel with generally reduced forces, and in 1979 *Messiah* was done with only 269 voices, the fewest since the difficult days of 1941. For the televised rendition, however, it was felt that visual considerations, if not those of the music, called for a full Tabernacle choir loft, so that recruitment of additional singers was begun during the summer and autumn. As a result, a chorus of 341 voices was used with such pleasing results that it was kept at about that level for three years thereafter, before the trend towards smaller numbers resumed.

Principal technical personnel for the PBS telecast were John Hesse and Allyson Beecher, respectively KUED-TV producer and executive producer, and Kirk Browning, the director.

Highly regarded for his work with musical productions, Browning's directorial career began with NBC in 1949, where he worked on the NBC Opera, Bell Telephone Hour, Producer's Showcase, and the Toscanini NBC Orchestra. Since the early 1960s he had been a free lance director, and his PBS credits included several "Live From Lincoln Center" performances, a Heifetz special, and others. In his professional capacity he had visited Salt Lake once before, to direct a television special of the Ballet West and Utah Symphony *Nutcracker* that was aired by PBS in 1975.

The difficulty of televising any live performance from the Tabernacle will be immediately evident to anyone who has been inside the building. There are no backstage or other areas in which cameras and related paraphernalia can be suitably hidden, nor are there the high balconies immediately overlooking a stage that are frequently found in other concert halls. Except for a relatively narrow gallery that runs around the sides and one end of the oval building, spaces are completely open and the orchestra and choir loft backed by the enormous organ with its thousands of pipes. Wherever cameras might be located, they would be in full view and hampered by a seriously limited range of mobility.

Nonetheless, in an interview with the *Tribune*'s Paul Wetzel, Browning explained that "one of the disciplines we have is that we do it under performance conditions." He told Wetzel that "if you brought a *Messiah* into a studio, you could arrange it somewhat to suit the cameras a little bit more." But, he said, when you do it in a performance situation, you're pretty much disseminating the program, rather than interpreting it for camera."

One technique that was used by Browning was the inclusion of a painting and etchings by the nineteenth century French painter and graphic artist, Paul Gustave Doré. He explained that he had "found a painting called 'The Triumph of Christianity over Paganism,' the top half of which is a perfectly marvelous kind of sunburst of Christian symbols with the Messiah and the Cross." To Browning it seemed ideal for what he called a "signature picture" for *Messiah*. Then, he said, he heard that Doré had also illustrated the Bible and found that those illustrations would be perfect for cutaway scenes and as introductions to the various numbers, giving the television viewer the kind of supplementary material that is usually provided the concert goer by the printed program.[5]

It was the Sunday performance of the Society's 1980 rendition that was taped live—a performance, notwithstanding the conservative pace, that was generally acclaimed to have been one of the Society's finest. In addition, it was for Salgo a personal triumph similar to that which Walter Susskind had in 1971—when Susskind pulled himself back from the brink of physical collapse to conduct what many considered the finest of his Society renditions.

Salgo's difficulty was the result of an unusual reaction to antibiotics he suffered during the week preceding the performance. It seriously limited his participation in rehearsals and raised doubts about his ability to conduct. He rebounded at the last moment, however, for what Dorothy Stowe in the *Deseret News* called "a highlight of his career" at the head of a musical organization that was "at a peak of choral excellence."

She called it a "mighty musical edifice to the mission of the Saviour" that culminated in the "final brilliant apotheosis of the resurrection." The chorus was "balanced..., with rolling bass and a soprano tone stiletto clear yet pear-shaped in resonance." The "florid passages," she found, were "clearly articulated, pianissimos communicative, fortissimos galvanic in effect."[6]

Soloists and orchestra were also praised. JoAnn Ottley was credited with intelligent and beautifully controlled interpretations; Maxwell with an appropriately dark voice and fine diction. Talley was noted for his control and Pierson was said to have "practically spit nails in 'Why do the nations so furiously rage.'"[7]

Messiah was first viewed over PBS on Christmas Eve and the home audience in Salt Lake had the added pleasure of an FM simulcast with the sound coming over the University of Utah's public radio station, KUER-FM. It was telecast again on Christmas Day, 1980, and subsequently re-released on December 20 and 25 of both 1981 and 1982, and for a final viewing on December 17, 1983.

After Salgo's last Society appearance, five new guest conductors presented the seven remaining Tabernacle *Messiahs* that have been completed through the time of this writing. Varujan Kojian conducted the December 12–13, 1981 rendition; Sir Charles Groves that of December 11–12, 1982; Ling Tung conducted on December 10–11, 1983; Uri Mayer took the baton on December 15–16, 1984, and December 12–13, 1987; and William Noll appeared on December 14–15, 1985, and December 13–14, 1986.

At the time of his Society appearance in 1981 Kojian was in his second season as conductor and music director of the Utah Symphony. A Beirut, Lebanon, native of Armenian extraction, he became assistant concertmaster with the Los Angeles Philharmonic and later rose to the position of assistant conductor. At the urging of Zubin Mehta, conductor of the Los Angeles orchestra, he studied conducting at the Vienna State Music Academy, after which he accepted the post of associate conductor of the Seattle Symphony. In 1973 he became principal guest conductor of Stokholm's Swedish Royal Opera, where he remained until joining the Utah Symphony in 1980. His *Messiah* marked only the third time that the conductor of a Salt Lake City symphony orchestra had accepted an invitation to wield the Society baton—the first two occasions being when Charles Shepherd, conductor of the Salt Lake Philharmonic, took the podium for both *Messiah* and *The Creation* in 1924.

Sir Charles Groves, the Society's 1982 conductor, was one of the English-speaking world's most distinguished musicians. Born in

London, he began his musical career as a choir boy at St. Paul's Cathedral Choir School. From 1963 through 1977 he was conductor of the Royal Liverpool Philharmonic Orchestra and of the English National Opera in 1978 and 1979. He was, in addition, credited with having conducted virtually every major orchestra and most of the important festivals in England and Europe.

Ling Tung, the 1983 guest conductor, was music director of the Grand Teton Music Festival. To Salt Lakers he was well known for having twice conducted the Mormon Tabernacle Choir in Teton Festival renditions of the Brahms and Verdi Requiems. He was also the second important Shanghai-born musician to appear with the Society, the first having been Yi Kwei Sze.

Uri Mayer, who conducted in 1984 and 1987, was a native of Transylvania in Romania. In New York he attended the Juilliard School, in 1970 became assistant conductor of the American Symphony Orchestra at Carnegie Hall, and at the time of his Society *Messiah* was in his third year as music director and chief conductor of the Edmonton Symphony Orchestra in Alberta, Canada.

William Noll, the 1985 and 1986 conductor, was director of the Providence Opera Theater in Rhode Island, conductor and music director of The Choral Guild of Atlanta, The Opera Orchestra of Atlanta (of which he was founder), and co-artistic director and principal conductor of the Atlanta Civic Opera Association.

Twenty-four soloists participated in the final seven *Messiah* renditions covered here. Society veterans among them were Linn Maxwell in 1981 and 1982, JoAnn Ottley in 1981 and 1984, Dana Talley and Gary Kendall in 1982, Robert Peterson in 1983, Philip Booth in 1984, and Dan Marek in both 1983 and 1984.

Of those making their *Messiah* debuts, only mezzo-sopranos Carla Cook in 1983 and Lani Poulson in 1984, and contralto Doris Madsen Brunatti in 1987 were Utah singers. Cook, a graduate of the University of Utah and formerly a member of the music faculty of Utah State University, was associated with the San Francisco Opera Company. Poulson, a Utah winner of the Metropolitan Opera Auditions, had recently pursued her career in the Netherlands where she was scheduled to record Mahler's *Kindertotenlieder* with the TROS Radio Orchestra in Hilversum. Brunatti had appeared with the Utah Opera, Pro Musica, and the Edmonton (Alberta, Canada) Symphony Orchestra in Beethoven's Ninth Symphony.

New sopranos for this period were Susan Belling, 1982; Linda Cusanelli, 1983; Mary Rawcliffe, 1985; Mary Burgess, 1986; and Lorna Haywood, 1987. Belling had sung *Messiah* with the Ann Arbor Festival and with the National Symphony at Kennedy Center; Cusanelli was associated with the Seattle Opera; Rawcliffe had recently sung *Messiah* in the Hollywood Bowl and a series of concerts with the Los Angeles Philharmonic; Burgess had distinguished herself with Carnegie Hall renditions of *Elijah*, Haydn's *St. Cecilia* Mass, and Mozart's Mass in C Minor; and Haywood had recently sung Britten's *War* Requiem, Beethoven's Ninth Symphony, Mozart's *Don Giovanni*, and Ravel's *Shéhérazade*.

Besides the three Utah singers, new soloists in the alto role were mezzo-soprano Karen Brunssen in 1985 and contralto Judith Farris in 1986. Brunssen had recently sung roles in Haydn's Mass *In Time of War*, Schubert's Mass in E Flat, and Beethoven's *Missa Solemnis*; and Farris, besides numerous operatic roles, had portrayed Nettie in a Kennedy Center production of *Carousel*.

New tenors were Frank Little in 1981, Curtis Rayam in 1985, and Rodney Nolan in 1986 and 1987. Little was a frequent soloist with such opera companies as the Metropolitan, Chicago Lyric, and the Philadelphia, and at the time of his Society appearance had recently sung Mozart's Requiem Mass with the Utah Symphony; Rayam's international reputation was enhanced by his 1984 performance of the title role in a Salzburg Festival rendition of Mozart's *Idomeneo*, in which he alternated with the renowned Metropolitan Opera tenor Luciano Pavarotti; and Nolan had recently made his European debut in Berio's *La Vera Storia* at the Florence May Festival.

The new bass-role soloists were Jon Enloe in 1981, Michael Burt in 1985, David Power in 1986, and Mark Pedrotti in 1987. Enloe had sung roles in 35 operas and in a total of 175 performances with the Houston Grand Opera Association; Burt, an Englishman, was a regular soloist with the Masterwork Society at Avery Fisher and Carnegie Halls; and Pedrotti, a New Zealander and a graduate of the University of Toronto Opera department, had appeared at Carnegie Hall and extensively in Europe. Power, a Salt Lake singer discussed below, was added when illness disabled the scheduled baritone.

From 1981 through 1987 there was no Dr. Johnson to champion the inclusion of seldom-heard numbers and the *Messiah* of these years is not exceptional for its changes in content. Both Kojian and Mayer conducted essentially the same numbers as their predecessors, though Mayer did add the aria "O thou that tellest good tidings" in 1987, a number that had not been included since the early postwar years. Noll's renditions differed primarily in that he restored numbers dropped by either Groves or Tung. Groves' 1982 changes included the aria "But who may abide," which most years since 1915 had been sung by the bass but which Lane, Semanitzky, and Hendl presented as an alto aria. Groves, in the first time this innovation had been tried by the Society, presented it as an aria for both alto and bass. He also dropped the chorus "And with His stripes" and included the abbreviated form of Dr. Johnson's solo quartet, "Break forth into joy, glad tidings"—the only time since 1978 that this non-Prout number has been included. In 1983 Tung dropped the chorus "And He shall purify," added "He trusted in God" and the recitative "All they that see Him," and these three changes have since remained in effect. He also abbreviated the aria "He was despised" and dropped the aria "Why do the nations so furiously rage," the latter of which was restored by Noll in 1985. And also in 1985, Noll presented the chorus "His Yoke is easy" as a concertino choir, the bass recitative "Thus saith the Lord" by both alto and bass, and in 1986 restored "And with His stripes" to the program.

In other ways too, of course, each conductor put his own distinctive mark on the work. Kojian's striving for subtlety and contrast, Groves' combination of the Watkins Shaw score and the baroque orchestra with a straightforward English choral interpretation, Tung's subtle handling of the orchestra, Mayer's comfortable tempos and dramatic nuance, the intensity and lyric sweetness of Noll. Each year *Messiah* presented a new experience for the Salt Lake devotee of this most famous of oratorios. Picking the best or the most interesting would be an impossible task. Innovation one listener considers unfortunate, another finds inspired; none can agree on tempo. One of the most unusual renditions, and the one which best illustrates the remarkable adaptability of *Messiah*, was the first performance of the 1986 rendition.

It is the only Society *Messiah* that has ever been sung without a full complement of soloists. In other years there had been close calls when illness or personal tragedy necessitated last minute substitutions, but only in 1986 did the difficulty strike so suddenly and so late as to make substitution impossible. Kevin McMillan, a Canadian baritone who had been engaged to sing the bass role, greatly impressed Society members during rehearsals and there was every reason to believe his would rank among the fine voices ever to have sung that part in Salt Lake City. His credentials included appearances with Musica Sacra, the Boston Handel and Haydn Society, and the New England Bach Festival Chorus, and he was a winner of the voice competition of the New York Oratorio Society, with which he had sung at Carnegie Hall.

Late in the afternoon of the first evening's performance McMillan was stricken with a throat infection that precluded his participation. Every effort was made that could be made on such short notice to find another singer both willing and able to take the part that night, but none was available. Rodney Nolan, the tenor, saved the performance from ruin by singing several of the important bass numbers, including "Thus saith the Lord of Hosts," "But who may abide," "Behold, I tell you a mystery," and "The trumpet shall sound." Scheduled numbers that had to be omitted were "For behold, darkness shall cover the earth," "The people that walked in darkness," and "Why do the nations so furiously rage."

Nolan's performance was little short of a triumph. So charmed were some among the audience, in fact, that they wondered if the tenor voice were not the more appropriate for those numbers—and of course Handel himself was not averse to arranging the score to fit a favored artist, or one who happened to be the only one available.

For the Sunday night performance the Salt Lake baritone, David Power, was found and the program restored to the proportions originally intended by the Society and its guest conductor.

This last-minute difficulty was the kind of brush with artistic disaster that keeps every performing arts organization humbly beholden to the fates and the muses. Even after seventy-two years of presenting annual performances the Society had not become immune to the vagaries that plague and occasionally ruin such endeavors.

University of Utah Library Special Collections/*The Salt Lake Tribune*

Budd L.. Bingham

Above: This view from the Choir loft shows the enormous audience gathered for Walter Susskind's first Salt Lake *Messiah* in 1964. One of the largest crowds to attend *Messiah* in the postwar era, it was put by some writers at as many as ten thousand persons.

Facing Page, Top: Walter Susskind puts a *Messiah* orchestra through final rehearsals. With Thor Johnson and Professor Coop himself, he was one of the Oratorio Society's all-time favorite conductors and from 1964 through 1971 conducted seven *Messiah*s and both the Society's Aspen, Colorado, *Christ on the Mount of Olives* and *Elijah.*

Above: John Marlowe Nielson trained the Oratorio Society Chorus from 1962 until his retirement in early 1987, in the process transforming it into the independent organization the Society now enjoys.

University of Utah Library Special Collections

Courtesy of Marjorie Morgan

Courtesy of John Megeath

Above: Nicholas G. Morgan, Sr., (L) succeeded Harold B. Lee as Society president in 1961. He served in that position until his death in 1971, when he was succeeded by Michael Megeath (R), whose own term was cut short by his sudden death in 1972.

University of Utah Library Special Collections/*The Salt Lake Tribune*

Utah State Historical Society

Above: Izler Solomon, one of the most highly regarded American-born conductors of his generation, conducted *Messiah* in 1966. Soloists were (L-R) bass Raymond Michalski (standing); and contralto Peggy Coburn, soprano Leona Gordon, and tenor James Wainner (all seated).

Facing Page, Top: This 1980 *Messiah*, one of two conducted by Sandor Salgo, was telecast nationwide by University of Utah television station KUER and the PBS Network for four consecutive years—the last telecast coming in 1983.

Above: Crawford Gates, though a San Francisco native, had strong family, musical, and religious ties to Utah and his Tabernacle *Messiah*, conducted for the Society in 1972, was one of the exciting events in recent Society history.

KUED

Busath Photography

Courtesy of Ling Tung

Above Left: Carla Cook, a Salt Lake City mezzo-soprano who had recently made her Carnegie Hall debut with the National Orchestra, sang the *Messiah* alto role in 1983.

Above Right: The 1983 *Messiah* conductor was Ling Tung, the Grand Teton Music Fesitval's Shanghai-born music director. He was also founder of the Philharmonic Orchestra of Philadelphia.

Richard Schramm

Lawrence Cooper

Wallace Ackerman

William Smith

Top Left: Lani Poulson, a Salt Lake mezzo-soprano with an impressive European as well as American reputation, sang the *Messiah* alto role in 1984.

Top Right: Mary Burgess, the 1986 *Messiah* soprano, had recently sung *Elijah*, Haydn's *St. Cecilia* Mass, and Mozart's Mass in C Minor at Carnegie Hall.

Above Left: Dana Talley, who sang the tenor role in both the 1980 and 1982 *Messiahs*, was a regular soloist with the New York Metropolitan Opera.

Above Right: Judith Farris, the 1986 contralto, was noted for her ability in opera, recital, oratorio, and even broadway musicals.

CHAPTER EIGHTEEN

Expanding Horizions

During the post-World War II era, besides its annual *Messiah*, the Society presented four other large choral works in a total of fourteen renditions. These were Beethoven's *Christ on the Mount of Olives*, Bach's *St. Mark* Passion, Mendelssohn's *Elijah*, and a final rendition of the Society's prewar summer standard, *The Creation*. Besides the Tabernacle, renditions were given at the Aspen Summer Music Festival, in the LDS Church's Temple View Theater, on the Brigham Young University campus in Provo, in Salt Lake's new Symphony Hall, at Edmonton in the Canadian provence of Alberta, and in the Holy Land.

The Society was slow to undertake these exciting new projects, however, and a quarter of a century passed between its last prewar *Creation* and its first rendition of *Mount of Olives* on April 16, 1965. Throughout this time there were periodic discussions of reviving summer renditions, but financial considerations, competition from other programs, and difficulties with the pre-Nielson chorus prevented this talk's leading to an actual performance.

In the end, it was the occasion of the Society's fiftieth birthday celebration, combined with the splendid progress John Marlowe Nielson was making with the chorus organization, that emboldened the Society to undertake its first non-*Messiah* oratorio of the postwar era—the aforementioned *Mount of Olives*. The choice of this oratorio, from a Society point-of-view, was especially appropriate. It had been the first oratorio presented by Professor Coop and the University of Utah Musical Society on April 21, 1911, and because of the close association between the Musical Society of Professor Coop's time and the origins of the Oratorio Society, the Coop *Olives* had in the past frequently been claimed as a Society rendition.

On the other hand there are reasons why the Society had gone so many decades without being seriously tempted to undertake this work and why it has seldom been performed in Salt Lake City by other organizations. Simply put, it had never managed to become very popular with Salt Lake audiences, particularly by comparison to such favorites as *Messiah*, *Elijah*, and *The Creation*—and probably as a result of this, the Society's 1965 rendition enjoyed a somewhat less than enthusiastic reception.

Jim Fitzpatrick, writing in the *Tribune*, called it "a strange work, struggling between the Italian opera and the fulsome German romanticism to which Beethoven is the key," and added that "the performance in the Salt Lake Tabernacle was marked for its earnestness, its unquestioned sincerity and the sense that the performers were as uncertain as the composer when it came down to what it means."[1]

The composition of *Olives* came at the end of Beethoven's first period, before his genius had fully matured, it is said, and it is frequently faulted for a lack of appropriate reverence and a heavy reliance on operatic technique. In *The Oxford History of Music*, for instance, W. H. Hadow writes of it that though it is commonly called an oratorio, "it more nearly resembles a musical passion play, if we could imagine one written by an un-Christian hand. The figure of our Lord is treated without reticence or restraint, the style is 'not only secular but in certain places actually sparkling': the great 'Alleluia' at the close is purely pantheist, as different from Handel's as Goethe is from Milton." Despite this, however, Hadow concedes that "if we are indifferent to the title and unmoved by the impropriety of treatment, we must acknowledge that the music is of high interest and value."[2]

The brevity of *Olives*, which allows it to be performed in about one hour, encourages its being sung in combination with other works. Thus the 1965 Society rendition, given in the Tabernacle on Good Friday, was followed by the closing number from part one of *The Creation*, which includes the chorus "The heavens are telling the Glory of God" alternating with the solo trios "The day that is coming" and "In all the lands resounds the word." This, in turn, was followed by the final chorus of Part Two, "Achieved is the glorious work."

Guest conductor for the first Society *Olives* was Dr. Hans Lampl, Vienna-born conductor of the Compton Symphony Orchestra and chorus master for the Laguna Beach Opera Festival, both of which are located in Southern California. Of the soloists only Leona Gordon had previously appeared with the Society. The others were tenor Ronald Christensen, who was director of the Ogden Symphonic Choir, and bass Alan Ord, a vocal student at Brigham Young University.

Press criticism was uniformly negative. In the *Deseret News* Keith Burris, virtually echoing Fitzpatrick's *Tribune* comments, suggested that "because *Mount of Olives* so closely parallels operatic structure, it is difficult not to dramatize superficially,"[3] and this was a trap into which Burris thought Ord, in particular, had sometimes fallen.

Nonetheless, this performance, which was so little appreciated at home, ultimately led to the Society's first invitation to sing at an important music festival outside Utah. In 1965 the Society was still recording all its performances for purposes of critical evaluation, and the following winter, when Walter Susskind was in Salt Lake to conduct his second *Messiah*, he was so impressed with the *Olives* recording that he wondered if the Society might not be interested in performing the same work with the Aspen Music Festival in Colorado, where Susskind was permanent music director. At his urging, Dr. Anderson was put in touch with James N. Cain, Aspen Festival executive director, whose enthusiasm turned out to be the equal of Susskind's own.

It was a particularly difficult problem transporting the chorus to Colorado, housing and feeding it there, plus the myriad other organizational problems attendant on any Society production. But largely as a result of Dr. Anderson's efforts, the difficulties were overcome and the Society sang *Mount of Olives* with the Aspen Festival Orchestra and soloists on July 23, 1967. Two Bach compositions were also included on the program. These were "Choral Fantasia" from Cantata No. 79, "God the Lord is Sun and Shield;" and Cantata No. 131, "Out of the Darkness, Call I Lord to Thee."

Olives was conducted by Susskind, of course, and the three soloists, all of whom had previously sung with the Society, were

Nöel Rogers, John McCollum, and Yi Kwei Sze. Because of the small festival stage, a chorus of only 150 singers could be accommodated, but this seems to have in no way diminished the quality of the performance. In a special article for the *Deseret News* Lenore Sagon wrote that it "never disclosed that it was doctors, lawyers, teachers, housewives, and secretaries who were singing. All of them sounded as if singing were their vocation."[4] The finest tribute, however, came in a letter from James Cain to Dr. Anderson, in which he wrote that "never have we experienced a chorus that has been so beautifully trained as yours."[5]

Since Aspen the Society has given *Mount of Olives* twice more—in the Tabernacle on March 18, 1973, and in a double rendition that opened in the Tabernacle on May 8, 1981, and was repeated the next day on the Brigham Young University Campus in Provo.

The 1973 program included another Bach composition, the little known *St. Mark* Passion. Unlike that composer's familiar *St. John* and *St. Matthew* Passions, neither the original nor any copy of the original score of *St. Mark* has survived, and as a consequence the work went for two hundred years without being heard—until the world premier of a reconstructed version was given in Stuttgart, Germany, in 1964.

The existence of this new version, though far from representing the complete Passion, was due to the research of Dr. D. Hellmann of Mainz, Germany, who, with assistance from the Bach Institute in Göttingen and the help of several musicologists from Gutenberg University, compiled it from a surviving draft of the libretto and several fragments of the music.

Guest conductor for both the Passion and *Mount of Olives* was Dr. Lara Hoggard, who was holder of the William Rand Kenan Chair in the music department of the University of North Carolina and director of choral activities for the Festival of Three Cities in Vienna, Austria. Through his scholarly interest in the works of Bach he had become acquainted with Dr. Hellmann, and it was Dr. Hoggard who brought the *St. Mark* Passion to the United States for its Western Hemisphere debut with the Midland-Odessa (Texas) Symphony and Chorale in 1967. The Society rendition was sung in German, though the program notes were supplied with an English translation prepared by Dr. Hoggard and Hugo Lentze of Münster, Germany.

Veteran Society soloists were James Wainner and JoAnn Ottley. They were joined by contralto Jean Ann Wolbert, who was affiliated with the Fred Waring Singers, and Utah baritone Gene Larson, who had sung the role of Jed in recent productions of *Promised Valley.*

The 1981 *Mount of Olives* was part of a program billed as the "All Beethoven Concert." Featured, in addition to *Olives*, were the seldom heard Beethoven composition for piano, chorus, and orchestra, *Choral Fantasia*; and one of the few nonchoral pieces ever presented by the Society, Beethoven's Sonata in E Flat Major Opus No. 31. At the keyboard for both pieces was Utah's renowned concert pianist, Grant Johannesen.

The guest conductor was Dr. Ralph G. Laycock, professor of music and director of the Philharmonic Orchestra at Brigham Young University, and conductor of the Utah Valley Symphony Orchestra. The soloists, all with Utah connections, were soprano Donna Dalton, contraltos Rose Cook and Cathryne Ball, tenors Roger Summerhays and Verdi White, Jr., and bass Rick Picket. Dalton had sung with the Utah Symphony; Cook was a soloist with the Mormon Tabernacle Choir; Ball, Summerhays, and White were members of the John Marlowe Nielson founded Pro Musica, a choral ensemble specializing in baroque and other less frequently performed compositions; and Picket had recently sung a solo part in a Pro Musica rendition of Berlioz's *The Childhood of Christ.*

In no case has the Society received the acclaim for one of its Salt Lake *Olives* renditions that it received for its Aspen performance, but the reaction of the *Tribune*'s Paul Wetzel to this final Society effort in 1981 must be counted as the most negative to which it has ever been subjected—for any oratorio at any time. The thrust of his attitude was made clear in his opening remarks. "The man of the hour," he wrote, "was Grant Johannesen, who single-handedly rescued the concert presented by the Oratorio Society of Utah Friday night from musical disaster." Of *Mount of Olives* itself he wrote, "I would like nothing better than to be tactful in my comments about the oratorio, but to be perfectly frank, I've tried in vain to find something positive to say about the performance. So I'll apologize in advance to those who will be hurt by what they are about to read." He faulted the performance for lacking interpretive statement, for technical problems, a ragged, muddy chorus that was devoid of transparency, multiple orchestral problems, and soloists who "did well to hold themselves together and plow forward in the face of accompaniment which was more a hindrance than support." He even objected to the "insipid English version of the original German," which happened to be the same Prout edition of the text that had always been used for Society renditions, including the acclaimed Aspen rendition. Of *Fantasia*, he averred that "Johannesen presented a studied and powerful statement of the piano part. As for the rest, it went better than the oratorio but suffered many of the same flaws."[6]

About one thing he was certainly correct, the Society, including both its directors and its chorus members, were hurt by what they read in his column, and not a little mystified. At least two letters published in the *Tribune*'s "Public Forum" column took him to task, and the *Deseret News* critic, Dorothy Stowe, though less than totally enthusiastic about the performance, found much that was positive, including her observation that *Olives* "is crowned by a towering 'Hallelujah' which found the large chorus at a pitch of power and glory." She also wrote that the soloists had given generally praiseworthy performances without any suggestion that they had in the process been forced to overcome orchestral obstacles.[7] But whatever the basis of Wetzel's negative review, it is obvious that *Mount of Olives* is not an oratorio that finds a large, or a critically enthusiastic following in Salt Lake City, and this seems particularly true when it is rendered by the Oratorio Society of Utah.

By way of contrast to its Salt Lake reception, the Aspen Festival *Olives* was such a marked success that the Society was invited to return to Aspen in 1968 to participate in a rendition of *Elijah*.

This perennially popular oratorio was given its first Salt Lake City production at the Tabernacle by J. J. McClellan and his Salt Lake Choral Society on January 27, 1909. It had since been rendered many times by the Tabernacle Choir and more recently by the Utah Symphony with the combined choruses of the University of Utah.

The conductor for the Society's Aspen rendition on July 21 was once again Walter Susskind; and the three soloists who had sung *Mount of Olives* with the Society the year before were joined by mezzo-soprano Claudine Carlson, who was an assisting artist in residence with the Festival program.

As final Aspen preparations were being made, arrangements were also being concluded for a special one hour version to be given in the LDS Church's Temple View Theater. This program was presented on July 28, just one week after the Aspen performance, and it was the inaugural oratorio for the twenty-five-hundred-seat outdoor theater which once faced the historic Mormon temple from a site now occupied by the new LDS Church office building.

The conductor was the Society's own John Marlowe Nielson. Under his direction were a thirty-piece orchestra and the personnel of the Society's Aspen chorus. Soloists were soprano Lila J. Stuart, tenors Val J. Stuart and Kenly W. Whitelock, and bass-baritone Robert Peterson, all singers with Utah ties. Peterson, already mentioned in connection with *Messiah*, was making the first of his six Society appearances; Val Stuart and Whitelock had both sung roles in a recent Utah Symphony rendition of Honegger's *Judith*, and Lila Stuart was on the faculty of the University of Indiana opera workshop.

Both the Aspen and the Temple View renditions were marked successes. In Salt Lake *Elijah* drew an audience that filled all standing room as well as those strategic locations outside the theater from which the performance could be heard. Harold Lundstrom, in his *Deseret News* review, called it a command performance for those Salt Lakers not fortunate enough to have been present at the acclaimed Aspen performance. In order to affect the radical cuts demanded by the one-hour format, while at the same time retaining the dramatic continuity inherent in *Elijah*, large portions of the performance were narrated by Gordon Owen, a prominent Salt Lake media executive and a member of the Society Board. These numbers included the alto solos as well as all or parts of various others.

A year later, on July 13, 1969, the Temple View Theater was the scene of a second abbreviated *Elijah* with Nielson once again conducting and Gordon Owen narrating. Soloists, all Salt Lake singers, were soprano Cohleen Bischoff, tenor Glade Peterson, and bass Don Watts. Both Bischoff and Watts had sung Handel's *Israel in Egypt* with the Utah Symphony and Glade Peterson, mentioned above in connection with his 1959 and 1972 *Messiah* appearances, was still widely engaged in European opera.

Subsequent Society *Elijah* productions were given in the Salt Lake Tabernacle on June 27, 1976; June 5, 1977; April 23, 1978; in Salt Lake's new Symphony Hall on June 6, 1985; in Edmonton, Canada, on September 13 and 14, 1985; and in Israel on June 29 and 30, 1987.

Guest conductor for the 1976 and 1978 renditions was Dr. Daniel L. Martino, who was director of Fine Arts at Weber State College in Ogden and chairman of the Utah State Institute of Fine Arts. Glade Peterson returned to the Society for the 1976 *Elijah*. He was joined by Donna Dalton, who also sang in the 1981 *Mount of*

Olives, and by contralto Alyce Rogers and bass-baritone Harold Enns. Rogers had sung frequently with the Portland and Vancouver Opera Companies and Enns was associated with the San Francisco Opera.

For Martino's 1978 rendition the soloists were Ronit Kalisky, Victoria Grof, James Wainner, and Edward Pierson, all of whom have already been mentioned in connection with their *Messiah* appearances. A novelty of this performance was the addition of a boy soprano, Ricky Tanner, to sing the part of the youth in Number 19, which begins with Obadiah singing "O man of God, help thy people," after which Elijah sends the youth to watch for the cloud that rises from the waters "like a man's hand" to end the draught that has afflicted Israel. The only Utah soloist in the 1978 rendition, Ricky lived in Ogden with his parents, Mr. and Mrs. Gary Tanner. He had previously sung with Eugene Ormandy and the Philadelphia Orchestra, with the Utah Symphony, and on tour with the Mormon Tabernacle Choir.

Both Martino renditions were generally well received. A performance reaching heights "of exciting and enchanting choral beauty,"[8] Lundstrom wrote of the 1976 rendition, and Stowe called the 1978 version "an *Elijah* with the burnished sonority of an old violin."[9] Only the *Tribune* faulted Martino, for what it seemed to consider a lack of choral precision,[10] but judging by the enthusiastic ovations the *Tribune*'s was an opinion not shared by the audience.

The 1977 *Elijah* was conducted by Dr. Jay E. Welch, the Society's former choral director. Besides Henry Price and Edward Pierson (both mentioned above for their *Messiah* performances), the soloists were New York-based soprano Elaine Bunse and Salt Lake contralto Darleen Merrihew. Bunse had sung frequent oratorio roles on the East Coast and Merrihew was a soloist with the Tabernacle Choir. Criticism of the performance was uniformly positive, with the only serious complaint reserved for an unseasonably warm evening in which the audience suffered as "Elijah suffered in the wilderness."[11]

The conductor for both 1985 *Elijah* renditions was Uri Mayer, music director and principal conductor of the Edmonton Symphony Orchestra, who also conducted the Society's 1984 and 1987 *Messiahs*. Among soloists for the Symphony Hall rendition was Rodney Nolan, the tenor whose last minute heroics later saved the 1986 *Messiah*. He was joined at Symphony Hall by sopranos Nancy Fox-Hoover and

Pamela Dale Watkins; contralto Wendy White; and baritone James Dietsch. Fox-Hoover had sung *Elijah* with the Detroit Symphony; Watkins, the only Salt Lake singer, was a musical assistant aiding Nielson in training the Society chorus and a frequent soloist with Nielson's Pro Musica; White, a winner of the National Metropolitan Opera Auditions, had sung with the Lyric Opera of Chicago; and Dietsch had appeared at Town Hall and with the New York City Opera.

The only Symphony Hall soloist to travel north with the Society was Miss Watkins. She was joined by Salt Lake soprano JoAnn Ottley, who was making her eighth Society appearance. The three Canadian soloists were mezzo-soprano Jennifer Jestley, tenor Glyn Evans, and bass Don Garrard. Jestley had most recently sung Egk's *La Tentation de Saint Antoine* with the Manitoba Chamber Orchestra; Evans had appeared several times with the Toronto Mendelssohn Choir; and Garrard, a recipient of The Queen's Jubilee Medal for Outstanding Artistic Achievement, had made operatic and concert appearances throughout Europe and the Americas.

Critically, the Symphony Hall *Elijah* was one of the Society's best received efforts. "A choral triumph,"[12] the *Tribune* writer called it, and the *News* was equally enthusiastic. Three months later, in Canada, the Society fared perhaps less well. One writer described the choral sound as "a bit muffled,"[13] for instance, but it is not unlikely that this can be attributed to the Jubilee Auditorium, in which *Elijah* was performed. Though in size it is approximately equal to Salt Lake's Symphony Hall, it is a multi-purpose building and compares favorably with neither Symphony Hall nor the Tabernacle. Inherent acoustical properties dictated the seating of both chorus and Edmonton Symphony Orchestra far back on the stage, where neither could be heard to best advantage.

The Symphony Hall chorus numbered two hundred voices and one hundred thirty-five singers traveled north in September, accompanied by a large contingent of Society officers, choral assistants, friends, and relatives. Most traveled by plane, though a considerable number made the more than twenty-two-hundred-mile round trip by automobile. One group of eleven, who traveled north in a rented van, startled customs officials at the Canadian border crossing by suddenly breaking into that nation's national anthem, "Oh Canada." Following the final *Elijah* performance the Society's Canadian sojourn concluded with a trip on chartered buses through the spectacular

Canadian Rockies in the vicinity of Banff, Lake Louise, Athabasca Glacier, and, finally, to Calgary.

The Society's only post-World War II rendition of Haydn's *Creation* was given on June 11, 1972. The guest conductor was Dr. Hans Lampl, who had first appeared with the Society as conductor of the 1965 *Mount of Olives*. Soloists, all Society veterans, were Nancy Bramlage, James Wainner, and Robert Peterson. The cost of production was born by the chorus, which provided funds from its recently instituted annual membership fees, and the program was given free to the public in the Salt Lake Tabernacle.

In contrast to Dr. Lampl's first Society effort, the coolly regarded *Olives*, *Creation* was very well received. In the *Deseret News* Lundstrom called the rendition "an endless succession of delights," adding that "the guest conductor...knows that *The Creation* abounds in colorful instrumentation and in harmonies and modulations that were startling for their time and still seem pretty startling in their contexts today."[14] In virtually every respect, from chorus to orchestra, soloists to conductor, the success of the performance was unqualified, and at its conclusion the audience showed its appreciation with a prolonged standing ovation.

Without question the most thrilling events in the postwar period, for those fortunate enough to participate, were the Society's trips to the Holy Land for *Messiah* performances on June 8 and 9, 1983; and again in 1987 for performances of *Elijah* on June 29 and 30. Such an excursion as these had long been a cherished dream and as early as 1973 tentative plans were made by at least some Society singers to participate with Dr. Crawford Gates in Jerusalem and Tel-Aviv *Messiah* renditions that were to have been given under the auspices of the (U.S.) National Federation of Music Clubs. Unfortunately, the outbreak of war between Israel and her neighboring states in October of that year forced cancellation of Dr. Gates' project. Later, the Society began preparations for a 1975 tour that was to have included Jerusalem performances of *Mount of Olives* and *Messiah* during Easter Week; but this plan also had to be abandoned when it proved impossible for a sufficient number of chorus members to participate.

Finally, in late 1982, the Society was invited to tour the Holy Land by Benjamin Navon, Israeli consul general in Los Angeles, and by Shmuel Zurel, consul for Israeli Tourism Affairs. The entire trip, *Messiah* particularly, was made an official part of the thirty-fifth anniversary celebration of the 1948 founding of the Jewish state. It was, additionally, put under the patronage of Samuel W. Lewis, United States Ambassador to Israel, and Abraham Sharir, Israeli cabinet minister for tourism. By proclamation of Utah Governor Scott M. Matheson it was made an official cultural exchange between the state of Israel and the state of Utah; and in a separate resolution the Forty-fifth Legislature of the State of Utah extended official "recognition and gratitude for the outstanding contribution made to the state, by the Oratorio Society of Utah."

Travel and lodging costs were largely absorbed by individual chorus members, with only limited assistance from Society funds and from a number of contributions made to the Society specifically for this project. The party enplaned from Salt lake City on June 4 and after a seven-hour delay In New York that was occasioned by the Jewish Sabbath, they boarded an El Al 747 for the flight to Ben Gurion Airport in Tel-Aviv, where they arrived on June 5.

On Monday, June 6, while sightseeing, the chorus gave an impromptu concert in the ancient amphitheater at Caesarea, approximately thirty miles from Tel-Aviv. This structure, built by King Herod and surrounded by the ruins of a more recent crusader fortress, is located only a few hundred feet from the Mediterranean Sea, and the chorus, singing Israeli folk songs it had prepared before leaving Salt Lake, attracted a crowd of several hundred persons. Then from the nearby sea an Israeli war plane flew close by, its thundering engines a reminder of the still festering hostilities that lingered in the wake of the previous year's invasion of Lebanon.

Other informal concerts were given atop Masada, where early in the Christian era Jewish warriors killed themselves rather than accept defeat and enslavement at the hands of the Romans; on the Mount of Beatitudes where Christ spoke the Sermon on the Mount; and on a tour boat drifting on the Sea of Galilee.

On the evening of June 7 the Society was officially welcomed by the Israeli government at a cocktail party and reception hosted by the municipality of Tel-Aviv, and the next day it gave its first *Messiah.* One hundred forty-five members of the Society chorus joined the Kibbutz Chamber Orchestra, conductor Amos Meller, and four Israeli soloists at the Fredric R. Mann Auditorium. Meller was music advisor and conductor of the Ramat-Gan Chamber Orchestra, the oldest chamber ensemble in Israel. A native-born Israeli, he had studied at Juilliard and the Manhattan School of Music. The soloists, all of whom sang regularly with the principal Israeli ensembles, were soprano Hadassa Ben-Haim, contralto Hanna Zur, tenor Victor Schwartz, and bass Mordechai Shvurun.

Included in the audience of three thousand was Mrs. Sally Lewis. She was substituting for her husband, Ambassador Lewis, who had been called home to Washington. Others were Arthur Berger and Robert Peterson, respectively charge d'affaires and cultural attache of the United States Embassy; the United States Embassy press attache; some thirty-five embassy employees; and several important Israeli dignitaries.

In a manner reminiscent of early Salt lake renditions, the performance was frequently interrupted by applause from the very enthusiastic audience, and at the program's conclusion there was a prolonged standing ovation while special bouquets were given to the conductor and soloists, to Society music director John Marlowe Nielson, and to tour organizer Karen Winder who, with then Society Vice-president Richard G. Horak, had handled the myriad travel, lodging, and other details for the ten-day tour.

The next day in Jerusalem the Society's reception was of an entirely different sort. Outside Binyaney Ha'uma, the auditorium in which the Society was to perform, some two hundred pickets protested use of the Jewish Agency owned hall for performance of what they considered an anti-Jewish oratorio. Their placards carried such messages as SHAME TO THE POISON OF CHRISTIANITY and THIS IS NOT THE MESSIAH WE ARE WAITING FOR.[15] They also chanted, sang songs, and shouted "The lord of Israel is alive! The people of Israel are alive!"[16]

The demonstrators, yeshiva students (roughly the Jewish equivalent of Christian Bible students) evidently acting with the encouragement of their rabbi—who had told them they could not remain silent—objected to the inclusion of parts of the *Messiah* libretto in program notes, which they considered tantamount to distributing Christian propaganda. They also demanded that the concert be relocated to Abu Ghosh "where," *The Jerusalem Post* reported in an evident reference to some other Utah group, "the Mormon singers have previously performed."[17]

The demonstration was by no means confined to the outside of Binyaney Ha'uma. Soon after the concert began hecklers shouted slogans from positions scattered throughout the audience and during the alto solo, "O thou that tellest good tidings to Zion," the stage was invaded by protestors and the program interrupted for several minutes while police were called in to eject the troublemakers.

Thereafter only a few shouting incidents marred the performance until after a brief intermission, when what was potentially the most dangerous incident of all occurred during the chorus, "Lift up your heads." Lee Case, a chorus member who was accompanied to Israel by his wife, recalls those moments in vivid terms. "I remember," he says, "seeing a young man on my left in the audience get up and run to the stage at which time he grabbed the Israeli flag and attempted to hurl it into the audience. It fell well in front of the first row," Case recalls, but "he picked it up again and hurled it javelin style, with sharp pointed end, at the audience for a second time. To my horror the flag, shaft, point and all, were headed straight for my sweetheart's chest. At the very last moment possible the woman next to her grabbed it Wonder Woman style and arrested the forward travel of the deadly shaft."[18]

Ronald L. Jones, another chorus member, remembers that one of the protestors called out from the balcony that it was not the Society to which they objected. Rather, their anger was really directed toward their own government, as Jones recalls the protestor's words, "for letting us sing about Christ in a public building." Dorothy Stowe, who accompanied the Society for the *Deseret News*, wrote that "'Why do the nations so furiously rage together' took on added significance for Jew and Gentile alike, when punctuated by violence and dissent. The 'Hallelujah' chorus brought forth a storm of rhythmic clapping, compelling a repeat."[19]

Once the last zealot had been expelled, in fact, the performance became one of the most intensely felt the Society had ever given. Even Case, despite the danger it had posed to his wife, remembers the Jerusalem *Messiah* as a positive experience. "The concert moved forward despite the attempts to stop it," he recalls, "with a mutual interaction of the audience with the performers. At the conclusion we all sang, as one, the Israeli national anthem, then adjourned. This will always be a major highlight in my musical experience."

Most members of the audience were deeply embarrassed by the evening's disruptions, of course, and both during intermission and after the performance, which ended with a standing ovation, there were many Israelis who made a point of offering their heartfelt apologies. To each Society member the minister of tourism, Abraham Sharir, sent a rose and letter expressing his special thanks. An invitation was also extended to sing at the home of Israeli President Chaim Herzog on the following Sunday.

In *The Jerusalem Post* Sharir was reported as having condemned the disruption as a "shameful act by a small number of extremists," adding that "we have taken steps to limit the bad impression, but the damage has been caused."[20] In the *Deseret News* Stowe reported Sharir as having said that *Messiah* is not a religious work,[21] which must have come as something of a revelation to many in the Society, but by which he no doubt meant that it was not a work intended to win converts or to offend non-Christians. It was Stowe, also, who expressed as well as possible the feelings of most Society members and of many Israelis when she wrote that "Just as a broken bone sometimes knits stronger than before, the disruptions of Thursday's *Messiah* has led to an outpouring here of warmth and regard for the visiting Utah Oratorio Society, forging deeper bonds of friendship."[22]

The most compelling proof of Stowe's optimistic assessment lies in the fact of the Society's return trip to Israel in 1987, when it joined the Jerusalem Symphony for *Elijah* performances on June 29 at Kibbutz Ein Hashofet (eighty miles northwest of Jerusalem) and a day later in Jerusalem itself. For this 1987 trip, Jewish sensitivities were at least partly assuaged by all members of the Oratorio Society party having accepted the Society's pledge to engage in no activity that could be interpreted as proselytizing for Christ.

Conductor for these performances was Uri Mayer, who also conducted the Society's 1984 and 1987 *Messiah*s and its two 1985 renditions of *Elijah*. Soloists included three Salt Lake singers. These were Karen Anderson, soprano; David Arnold, tenor; and the Society's 1987 *Messiah* contralto soloist, Doris Madsen Brunatti. The part of Elijah was sung by bass-baritone Andrew Wentzell of New York.

From Israel the Society traveled to Cairo, Egypt, where concerts of American show tunes, opera choruses, Egyptian folk songs, and patriotic American pieces were given at the Marriott Hotel on July 2, at American University on July 3, and at both the Cairo American College and the United States ambassador's private residence on July 4.

CHAPTER NINETEEN

The Heart of the Society

People are the heart of any choral organization. In their multitude they have played such a prominent role in the Oratorio Society of Utah that in places its history reads a little like the telephone book or the census. But though some hundreds have been named, and most of those identified by profession, affiliation, or musical contribution, they represent only a small portion of the thousands who have involved themselves in the more than seventy-two years of the Society's history. In the appendix that follows this chapter, more than six thousand Oratorio Society chorus members are identified. They include in excess of two thousand each of sopranos and altos, nearly a thousand tenors, and almost fourteen hundred basses. Yet even these are only a part of those who have sung with the Society.

For most years prior to the 1950s few chorus lists survive. Only for the period from 1927 through 1934 have systematic role books come down to us, and chorus lists were printed in the newspapers for only the 1916 and 1917 *Messiah*s and the 1917 and 1929 *Creation*s, which leaves almost a quarter of the Society's history for which virtually no names are available.

Besides chorus members, one hundred twenty-six persons have been on the Board of Directors. Eighty more can be identified as having served the chorus organization as assistants, accompanists, choral directors, or chorus officers. Add to these even a thousand unknown chorus members and the Oratorio Society of Utah numbers a small army marching in the service of sacred oratorio and in that of one of Salt Lake City's oldest and proudest musical traditions.

During the winter and spring of 1985 and 1986, chorus members were asked to fill out a questionnaire, on which much of the following information is based. At that time the chorus had a membership of 300, and of these 174 members responded—representing some fifty-eight percent of the total. Their answers show the chorus to consist of an intensely musical group of people who are otherwise very diverse in their interests, professions or trades, backgrounds, and places of origin. Among them are four with Bachelor of Arts degrees in music, four more with music minors, and two Master of Arts degrees in music or music education. One hundred thirty-five more have had formal training in voice, instrumental music, or both—some of them many years of institutional and private instruction. Sixty-seven members play an instrument. Another sixty-three play at least two, and many play four, five, and even more.

One hundred eighteen chorus members reported that they participated with musical organizations other than the Oratorio Society. By far the most frequently mentioned of these was singing with a church or LDS ward or stake choir, in which ninety members participated. Other frequently mentioned organizations were the Murray Symphony Chorale, Pro Musica, the Utah Symphony Chorus, West Valley Chorale, Utah Opera, and the Mormon Tabernacle Choir.

The majority, some one hundred, were Utah natives, while the remainder hailed from twenty-three states and eight foreign countries. Not all members currently live in the immediate Salt Lake City area and several commute significant distances in order to attend rehearsals and performances. Laurie Williams Sowby, who drives the eighty-mile round trip from her home in American Fork, calculates that in her fourteen years of membership she has logged nearly thirteen thousand miles. "I'm always glad I came," she says. "In the concerts there are always some absolutely thrilling moments. Then I know it's all worth it."[1] Glen R. Schmidt makes the approximately one-hundred-sixty-mile round trip from Logan while Doris and Darla Lynne Alsop and Sidney R. Atkin all travel some seventy miles from Tooele and back. Others drive from Orem in the south and Farmington, Layton, Clearfield, and Ogden in the north.

Responding singers, in their commercial lives, fit into some seventy job classifications. Not surprisingly, in a part of the country where family life is highly regarded, homemaker topped the list as the most frequently mentioned principal occupation with twenty-seven respondents. Other popular occupations were public school teaching, secretary, accounting, and nursing. There were also doctors, lawyers, a policeman, professors, and many more.

During an era when the would-be chorus member has a wide variety of important organizations from which to choose, the nonsectarian aspect of the Society is less important than it was in earlier years. So not surprisingly, the chorus reflects the population at large by being predominantly LDS, but Protestants, Catholics, various evangelicals, as well as persons who profess no religious preference at all, are well represented, as they have regularly been on the Board of Directors.

One of the most noteworthy characteristics of chorus members is loyalty, especially as it is extended over a period of many years. One member, Helen Wilcox (who until recently was chorus secretary), began singing with the Society more than forty-seven years ago. Rene Urry Price has sung with the Society for forty-three years. Others who had sung more than forty years, as of the 1987 *Messiah*, were Jeanne Wignall Ames, Joyce Orlob Evans, Mildred V. Thelin, Barbara J. Alvey, and the Society's only blind chorus member, A. Ray Trimble.

Of the questionnaire respondents, twenty-one had been chorus members from thirty to thirty-nine years, fifty-nine from twenty to twenty-nine years. In all, seventy-six had sung with the Society for more than ten years; and for all respondents, the average length of time in the chorus was more than ten and one-half years. Sometimes, of course, membership was interrupted. Myrna Griggs, for instance, sang with the Society for three years in the late 1950s, following which she left Utah; and some twenty-five years later, upon her return, she rejoined the chorus and is now in her sixth year of membership. Elaine McDonald sang *Messiah* every year from 1950 through 1956, quit to raise her boys, then rejoined in 1975.

In addition to the remarkable longevity of many memberships, belonging to the chorus is often a family tradition. Thirty-nine respondents report having relatives currently in the chorus and forty-one are related to past members. Barbara J. Alvey says that it was because of her grandfather, Frederick C. Fuller, that as a child she attended her first *Messiah*. "I was so thrilled," she says, "that I hoped someday to belong to this group." She reports that her grandfather "was born in 1867 and was the forerunner in our family to begin a love affair with music. He was among the first to sing with Squire Coop and the Oratorio Society. He sang with the Oratorio and the Tabernacle Choir for forty years." Her invitation to join the chorus came from another Society old-timer. As an East High School student she was a member of the girls' chorus and the a cappella choir. Impressed with her ability, the high school chorus leader, who was the Society's own Lisle Bradford, invited her to join the *Messiah* chorus and, as she says, she has been "a loving and loyal member ever since—never missing a performance." One of her most cherished possessions, she adds, is her grandfather's *Messiah* score "which he used from the time he started until he retired due to illness in his late seventies."[2]

Another familial relationship is represented by Albert J. Southwick, Jr., who is himself a veteran of more than twenty-five years. The reader will recall that his father, in addition to being music director and Messiah conductor from 1930 through 1935, was twice a Society soloist and also choral director for the December 1935 and the 1936 *Messiah*s.

Nothing, in fact, more completely reveals the spirit of the chorus than do the words of its members themselves. Faye S. Patrick remembers that when she was thirteen years old she "went to my first *Messiah* performance and loved it. I sat there and said 'some day I'm going to sing in that.' I remember Harold H. Bennett as the bass soloist." In 1967, after two years of voice lessons, she says, "I got the courage to audition and I was so thrilled that I made it. Dr. Anderson auditioned me," she says, adding that "being able to sing *Messiah* each year and having the association of friends I've made has meant a great deal to my life. The trip to Israel was a highlight of my life which I will never forget. I moved into a smaller apartment to cut down on my expenses in order to pay the loan I got to make that trip." She says she feels "the Oratorio Society has become better with Marlowe Nielson as our director and I love him for all he has taught me. I only wish," she adds in a sentiment shared by many, that "we could still perform the *Messiah* without charge as we used to do. It was more special as a gift for Christmas to the public."[3]

Loretta Henderson, reminiscing about joining the chorus, says "I remember the day as if it were yesterday. Dr. Anderson was the person who auditioned me." The accompanist, she says, "didn't think that I had the ability to sing the music. Dr. Anderson," however, told her "to report for rehearsal." She says, "I have been a member since that time and have only missed one performance of *Messiah* because I was in California during the holidays, but even then I attended all the rehearsals I could." She adds that she doesn't know whether she loves *Elijah* or *Messiah* the most. "All I know," she confides, "is when I sing those two oratorios I feel as though my voice is not mine. Something happens to me spiritually when I come to practice and during performances that raises my voice and capabilities to their highest levels. I feel as though God has a hand in pulling out the best of my special gift from him—my voice."[4]

Kent Barry has a very special reason for valuing his Society membership. Though Louis Lane in 1975 and William Noll in 1985 and 1986 were his favorite conductors, he says, "nonetheless, the highlight for me was the 1980 performances which were conducted by Sandor Salgo." He was so moved by the "feeling of love and well being" with which the music had filled him that he proposed to his girlfriend while they were still on the Temple grounds. He says "I could contain my feelings no longer, and genuinely felt confident about the timing." They married, he adds, on the following February twenty-eighth.[5]

Joyce Orlob Evans says that "music is for me the closest thing to heaven. There is so much more music in me than my limited vocal ability can express that it is frustrating. The Oratorio Society has given me such wonderful opportunities to express what I can. The training from John Marlowe has been invaluable, as have the associations with choice people. I feel heaven blessed to have sung my way through life. Hopefully, there will be a place for me in the heavenly choirs;"[6] and Jane P. Brown adds that "some of the most worshipful experiences I've had have been in performances with the Society."[7]

"It's relaxing, it's uplifting, it's fun meeting good friends," says A. Ray Trimble, the Society's blind singer. "It gives me a chance to learn and a chance to grow. I enjoy the music, even though I can't see the conductor, and the people in the Society are super fine. I'd rather sing than eat."[8]

Elrena Nielsen says that she especially loved the Aspen trip. "It was raining with thunder and lightning before we sang, she remembers, "but it stopped while we sang and started after. The Lord," she says, "was with us."[9] And Jayna Friberg, remembering a more recent Society trip, says that "Besides the concert in Jerusalem, I will always hold dear the singing of the 'Hallelujah' chorus while crossing the Sea of Galilee and singing 'God Of Our Father' on the Mount of Beatitudes."[10] Julie L. Williams remembers the Holy Land trip also, especially the eventful Jerusalem performance. She says "The first time we performed the *Messiah* back home after that experience, especially "O Thou that tellest good tidings to Zion," and got all the way through without interruption, I can say that I truly experienced the gratitude that I should always feel when I think 'I live in America' and of what being an American really means. It is a lesson I will never forget."[11]

Vying with the chorus for the honor of being the center of Society activity and the principal source of its energy, is the Board of Directors. Over the decades this group of dedicated Society members—many of whom, like Dr. Anderson, the Thomases, Dr. Smith and others, were also chorus members—has taken on the year-round drudgery of organizing and staging *Messiah* and the other oratorios which the Society has from time to time had the means of producing. It has faced the perpetual problem of raising money, keeping audiences interested, finding exciting new soloists and conductors, protecting Society turf from competing organizations, and coping with the various press, musical, social, and governmental establishments.

The present Board of Directors (following the 1987 *Messiah*) is comprised of thirteen members. Of these, former President Jack Everett Holmstrom, President Richard G. Horak, and Vice-president for Productions Annette Richardson Dinwoodey have already been discussed. Of the remaining members, the one with the most years service is Vice-chairman Maurice J. Taylor, a prominent Salt Lake physician who joined the Board at the invitation of Dr. Anderson in 1969.

Edith S. Anderson, the present chairman, is the widow of Dr. Anderson. Since the early 1960s she has taken an active role in Society matters and before assuming her present post she served as assistant production manager.

Treasurer John D. Banchero joined the Board in 1977; and

Advertising Vice-president Eleanor Muth, a general merchandise manager for the J. C. Penney Company, joined in 1979. In 1984 the Society's present vice-president for chorus matters, Gerald B. Trapp, joined the Board. He is vice-president and general manager of the Intermountain Network, which is affiliated with radio stations throughout the Mountain West. Also joining the Board in 1984 was Dr. Rodney H. Brady, who in commercial life is president and chief executive officer of Bonneville International Corporation, the parent company of KSL radio. He is also the former president of Weber State College in Ogden, Utah.

In 1987 the names of three new directors were announced. These were Bill Peters, Elizabeth Evans, and Jayna Friberg. Evans is the Board's present secretary while Friberg, a seven-year veteran of the Society chorus and a sales service manager for Salt Lake's KTVX Television, is vice-president for administration.

The Board also includes three emeritus members. These are Harvey S. Ross, a board member since 1969; former Utah State Supreme Court Chief Justice J. Allan Crockett, who joined the Board in 1968 and who also sang with the chorus for many years beginning in 1928; and the Society's recently retired music director of twenty-five years, John Marlowe Nielson.

A number of other directors from the past, in addition to those discussed in the preceding chapters, warrant mentioning. In all, eight Salt Lake City mayors have been associated with the Oratorio Society Board. The first of these, of course, was C. Clarence Neslen (1920–28), who joined the Board in 1919 and served as the Society's second president from 1922 through 1936. After stepping down as president he continued as a director until 1938 and as an honorary director until 1966. The next mayor to serve was Louis Marcus (1932–1936), who was a director in 1934 and 1935. Another was Mayor John Wallace, who also served on the board of the old Salt Lake Philharmonic Orchestra. He first joined the Society Board in 1931 and was appointed mayor in 1938 to complete the unexpired term of Mayor E. B. Erwin.

A 1934 reincorporation of the Society altered the articles of incorporation to automatically extend ex-officio membership to all serving Salt Lake City mayors—a provision that stayed in effect until the early 1980s when it was superceded by yet another revision of the articles. Those who accepted ex-officio membership were

Mayor Erwin (1936–38), Ab Jenkins (1940–44), Earl J. Glade (1944–56), Adel F. Stewart (1956–1960), J. Bracken Lee (1960–1972), and E. J. Garn (1972–1974).

Besides such prominent LDS leaders as Dr. Adam S. Bennion, Henry D. Moyle, Harold B. Lee, and George D. Pyper, the Board has included a number of important non-LDS ecclesiastics. The Catholic community was represented by the Rt. Rev. Msgr. Patrick F. Kennedy, rector of the Cathedral of the Madeleine, from 1945 through 1960. He was followed, in 1961 through 1970, by the Rt. Rev. Msgr. Patrick Maguire, pastor of Our Lady of Lourdes Church. The Rev. Ward W. Reese, rector of St. Paul's Episcopal Church, was one of the early directors of the Society, serving in 1915 and 1916. Rev. Stanley A. Curtis, pastor of the First Methodist Episcopal Church (now part of the United Methodist Church), was a director during the 1920s; Rev. Robert D. Steele, president of Westminster College, was a director from 1945 through 1951; and the Rev. Earl L. Riley, pastor of the First Baptist Church, served on the Board from 1965 through 1970. The Jewish community has been represented, besides Mayor Marcus, by Mrs. Ernest Bamberger, who served as vice-president from 1923 through 1925.

Several persons prominent in the administration of public education have served the Society. In addition to Dr. Bennion, whose teaching and school administration career is mentioned above, the Board of Directors has benefitted from the participation of Dr. E. G. Gowans, state superintendent of public instruction, who was vice-president in 1915 and 1916; George N. Child, superintendent of schools for the Salt Lake Board of Education, who was vice-president from 1923 through 1931; and Ernest Hanson, assistant superintendent of schools for Salt Lake, who served as a director from 1939 through 1947.

It is clear from the record that at times the Board as a whole has been the guiding force of the Society, equally clear that at other times it has been little more than window dressing while a small clique of its members made the important decisions and carried forward most of the day to day organizational and promotional tasks. From the Society's founding in 1914–15, for instance, until his departure in 1922, the preponderance of power lay in the hands of Professor Coop. At the same time, however, the actual running of the Society—because of the professor's absorption with the chorus—was left to individual directors and to committees, and minutes of this period indicate that virtually everyone on the Board was delegated some part in the Society's day to day activities. From 1922 through the onset of World War II the Board as a whole continued to take an active role—though not always with unanimity. Deprived of Professor Coop's vision, rival factions sometimes disputed the purpose and spirit of the organization. On one occasion the Board became so demoralized that only the energetic intervention of the chorus saved the Society from dissolution.

Following World War II control of the Society was concentrated in the hands of Dr. Bennion, Dr. Anderson, Jack Thomas, and Alex Eberhardt, and only as they were one by one recalled by death did the Board resume the sharing out of its functions. In recent years, by way of contrast, the Board has met monthly throughout the year and every member has had assigned duties, insuring full and active participation by all. The result of this has been to develop a specialist for every aspect of Society operations, from administration through fund raising, public relations, productions, and chorus relations. In effect, the Society now operates much as does any modern organization, public or private—from a well-defined hierarchical structure.

If people form the heart of the Oratorio Society, the unfortunate corollary is that money is its life's blood. Without it, no matter how willing and talented its members, little can be done; and in its long history the results of financial anemia have been all too obvious and frequent. Opportunities, especially in the early years, were lost, renditions were given without adequate forces—sometimes skimping on the orchestra, sometimes on the quality of soloists; unfortunately, at times, on both.

Since World War II no financial crises have occurred of such magnitude as to threaten the existence of the Society, though on a number of occasions Dr. Anderson, the Thomases, and others were forced to assume responsibility for sizeable deficits. Beginning in the early 1970s steps were taken to establish a permanent fund, the income from which would supplement other revenues and, most importantly, help insulate the Society from the unavoidable year to year variations in the level of contributions and, later, ticket sales.

Unfortunately, at the very time this fund was being established the inflationary environment of the 1970s and early 1980s was pushing the cost of oratorio production to heights undreamed of only a few years earlier. The 1974 *Messiah* cost something in excess of nine thousand dollars.[12] By 1985, even though the size of the orchestra had been reduced by about thirty percent and other economies implemented, the cost had risen to more than thirty-four thousand dollars—an amount two thousand dollars in excess of income.[13]

But even at these relatively astronomical levels, the Society's financial requirements are modest by comparison to some of Salt Lake City's other performing arts organizations; and this may prove the Society's greatest strength in the years ahead, which seem to be emerging as a lean time for any arts organizations dependent upon grants, contributions, or ticket sales to sustain themselves. A recent *Tribune* article noted that the Utah Symphony, with a budget of a little more than five million dollars for the fiscal year ending August 31, 1987, faced a deficit of a half-million dollars. Ballet West, Salt Lake's nationally acclaimed professional dance company, also faces grave difficulties, as do several other organizations.[14]

While preparations were beginning for the Society's 1987 *Messiah* on December 12–13, Professor John Marlowe Nielson stepped aside as choral director in favor of his assistant, Dr. Morris F. Lee. The historical record reveals that this marked a traditionally dangerous time for the Society. Singers form allegiances, they become used to doing things in certain ways, and for many of them it is difficult to change their loyalty from one leader to another. Compared to some of the abrupt and not altogether amiable changes of past years, however, the transfer from Professor Nielson to Dr. Lee must be seen as one of the Society's most orderly and carefully considered. Dr. Lee has been associated with the Society as Professor Nielson's assistant since 1984 and Professor Nielson, since retiring, has continued as director emeritus—thus ensuring a sense of continuity and stability for the chorus organization.

Dr. Lee is a graduate of the University of Utah, where he also received his Ph.D. He studied piano with Oscar Wagner at Juilliard, composition with Utah composer Leroy Robertson—whose *Book of Mormon Oratorio* is a favorite with Salt Lakers—and he is currently director of music programs at Cottonwood High School.

As we have seen, the origins of the Oratorio Society of Utah lie deep in the musical traditions of the pioneers, Mormon and non-Mormon alike. Historically and spiritually the Society has become the keeper of a nonsectarian choral tradition that was begun in the

1870s under the baton of George Careless. During the 1880s and 1890s this tradition was nurtured by Thomas Radcliffe and Evan Stephens, then by the Spring Music Festivals of the present century's first decade. From there it passed to Professor Coop's University of Utah Musical Society and, following the difficulties of 1913, went with the professor to his new Salt Lake Oratorio Society.

Along with its predecessor organizations, the Society served as one of the healing forces that helped Salt Lake overcome the mistrust and misunderstanding that set Mormon and non-Mormon communities against each other during the late 1800s and the early years of the present century. For those who know and understand this history, the Society cannot help but be an important symbol of the struggle for understanding that finally triumphed in the cordial relations now prevailing.

In the process of achieving this goal the Society has established a Christmas season *Messiah* tradition that is as much a part of the fabric of Salt Lake cultural life as it would be possible for any musical event to become. Originally the special dream of one man, Professor Squire Coop, the work of the Society has become a monument to the many thousands who have lent it their voices and their own dreams. As Professor Coop said of it many years ago, when it was still very much a Cinderella organization, its acceptance and survival yet in doubt, "It is an orphan, a love-child, bestowed in love and love bestowing. May it not falter as the years go by."[15]

Reprinted with permission of the *Deseret News*

Oratorio Society of Utah Archives

Above: (L-R) Oratorio Society President Jack Everett Holmstrom, Vice-president for Administration Edith S. Anderson, Karen Winder of AAA World Wide Travel, and Music Director John Marlowe Nielson go over plans for the Society's 1983 tour of the Holy Land.

Left: Salt Lake tenor Glade Peterson, in addition to his *Messiah* roles in 1959 and 1972, sang the part of Obediah in the Society's 1969 Temple View and 1976 Tabernacle *Elijahs*.

Busath Photography

Robert Clayton

Lisa Kohler

James R. Kriegsmann

Top: (L-R) Salt Lake soprano JoAnn Ottley, in addition to six *Messiahs*, sang in the 1973 *Mount of Olives* and the Edmonton, Canada, *Elijah*. Robert Peterson, an Oklahoma native who studied at, and later jointed the faculty of, the University of Utah, appeared in the 1968 Temple View *Elijah*, 1972 *Creation*, and in four *Messiah* renditions.

Above: (L-R) Tenor Rodney Nolan and baritone James Dietsch both sang in the 1985 Symphony Hall *Elijah*.

Courtesy of Mr. Horak

Harold Ecker Photography

Courtesy of Pat Lees

Above Left: Richard G. Horak joined the Board of Directors in 1972 as Vice-president for Finance and in 1983 was elected president.

Above Right: Dr. Morris F. Lee was appointed choral director in 1987.

Left: Becky Almond, a graduate of the Utah Conservatory of Music and a teacher at the McCune School of Music, began her Oratorio Society association with a 1928 appearance as *Creation* pianist. She served as rehearsal accompanist fom 1933 through 1961 and as a member of the Board of Directors from 1972 until her death in 1984.

Courtesy of Helen Wilcox

Courtesy of Merle Lowe

Courtesy of the Oratorio Society of Utah

Top: Helen Wilcox (L) joined the chorus in 1934 and served as chorus secretary from 1969 until 1987. She was succeeded in this important post by Merle Lowe (R), who first sang with the chorus in 1950.

Above: In this 1985 photograph Society Board members are (L–R) Jerry Trapp, now vice-president for chorus matters; Vice-president for Productions Annette Richardson Dinwoodey; Vice-president for Advertising Eli Muth; Marcia Price, secretary; President Richard G. Horak; the Board's present chairman, Edith S. Anderson; and Treasurer Richard D. Banchero.

APPENDIX A

Chronology of Performances

Native, resident, formerly resident, and subsequently resident conductors and soloists are marked with an asterisk.

1915 Jan 1 *Fri* **MESSIAH**
Empress Theater
Cond & Mus dir: *Squire Coop
Sop: *Della Daynes Hills
Alto: *Edna Cohn
Tenor: *Coyle Crosby Tullar
Bass: *Willard Andelin
Concert M: Arthur Freber
Trumpeter: L.P. Christensen
Chorus: 140

1916 Jan 1 *Sat* **MESSIAH**
Salt Lake Theater
Cond & Mus dir: *Squire Coop
Sop: *Fay Loose Stiehl
Alto: *Edna Lamb Williams
Tenor: Farquhar Murray
Bass: *Willard Andelin
Concert M: Arthur Freber
Chorus: 172

1917 Jan 1 *Mon* **MESSIAH**
Salt Lake Tabernacle
Cond & Mus Dir: *Squire Coop
Sop: Marjorie Dodge Warner
Alto: *Florence Jepperson
Tenor: *Dr. William R. Worley
Bass: *Ray M. Russell
Concert M: Arthur Freber
Chorus: 214
NOTE: Professor Evan Stephens conducted the "Hallelujah" chorus.

1917 May 13 *Sun* **CREATION**
State Capitol Bldg—south steps
Cond & Mus Dir: *Squire Coop
Gabriel: Marjorie Dodge Warner
Uriel: *John W. Summerhays
Raphael: *Fred E. Smith
Concert M: Arthur Freber
Chorus: 350

1918 Jan 1 *Tue* **MESSIAH**
Salt Lake Tabernacle
Cond & Mus Dir: *Squire Coop
Sop: Marjorie Dodge Warner
Alto: *Florence Jepperson
Tenor: *Fred C. Graham
Bass: Harold Dale Sauerer
Concert M: Arthur Freber
Organist: Edward P. Kimball
Chorus: 300

1919 Jan 1 *Wed* **MESSIAH**
Odeon Theater
Cond: *Alfred H. Peabody
NOTE: This was a private performance necessitated by the 1919 influenza epidemic. Margaret Summerhays and Walter Wallace sang solo parts and Squire Coop, arriving unexpectedly from New York, joined in as a member of the chorus.

1919 Oct 8 *Wed* **MACCABAEUS**
Salt Lake Tabernacle
Cond & Mus Dir: *Squire Coop

Sop: Marjorie Dodge Warner
Tenor: Edward Atchison
Bass: *Will Magginetti
Concert M: Arthur Freber
Organist: J.J. McClellan
Chorus: 215

1920 Jan 1 *Thur* **MESSIAH**
Salt Lake Tabernacle
Cond & Mus Dir: *Squire Coop
Sop: Marie Partridge Price
Alto: *Evelyn Buehler
Tenor: *William R. Worley
Bass: Albert Borroff
Concert M: Arthur Freber
Organist: J.J. McClellan
Trumpeter: John Visser
Chorus: 300

1920 July 9 *Fri* **CREATION**
University of Utah Park Bldg.
Cond & Mus Dir: *Squire Coop
Gabriel: Marjorie Dodge Warner
Uriel: *John W. Summerhays
Raphael: Herbert Gould
Concert M: Arthur Freber
Chorus: 300

1921 Jan 1 *Sat* **MESSIAH**
Salt Lake Tabernacle
Cond & Mus Dir: *Squire Coop
Sop: Christine Laugenhan
Alto: *Florence Jepperson
Tenor: *John W. Summerhays
Bass: *Frank M. Dunford
Concert M: Arthur Freber
Organist: J.J. McClellan
Chorus: 300

1921 June 16 *Thur* **CREATION**
University of Utah Park Bldg.
Cond & Mus Dir: *Squire Coop
Gabriel: Margery Maxwell
Uriel: *John W. Summerhays
Raphael: Herbert Gould
Concert M: Arthur Freber
Chorus: 300

1922 Jan 2 *Mon* **MESSIAH**
Salt lake Tabernacle
Cond & Mus Dir: *Squire Coop
Sop: Florence Lang
Alto: *Eunice Edwards Anderson
Tenor: *Howard Frazee
Bass: Herbert Gould
Concert M: Arthur Freber
Organist: Tracy Y. Cannon
Chorus: 350

1922 June 20 *Tue* **CREATION**
University of Utah Park Bldg.
Cond & Mus Dir: *Squire Coop
Gabriel: Marjorie Dodge
Uriel: *John W. Summerhays
Raphael: Herbert Gould
Concert M: Arthur Freber
Chorus: 300

1923 Jan 1 *Mon* **MESSIAH**
Salt Lake Tabernacle
Cond: *Squire Coop
Sop: Marjorie Dodge
Alto: *Florence Jepperson (Madsen)
Tenor: *John W. Summerhays
Bass: Gustave Holmquist
Concert M: Arthur Freber
Organist: Tracy Y. Cannon
Trumpeter: John Visser
Chor Dir: J. Spencer Cornwall
Chorus: 300

1924 Jan 1 *Tue* **MESSIAH**
Salt Lake Tabernacle
Cond & Mus Dir: *Charles Shepherd
Sop: Lois Johnston
Alto: *Doris Buriff
Tenor: *John W. Summerhays
Bass: Herbert Gould
Concert M: Arthur Freber
Organist: Tracy Y. Cannon
Trumpeter: Clyde White
Chorus: 300

1924 June 29 *Sun* **CREATION**
University of Utah Park Bldg.
Cond & Mus Dir: *Charles Shepherd
Sop: *Margaret (Tout Browning) Romaine
Concert M: Arthur Freber
Chorus: size unknown
This was a mixed program consisting of the following:
"Hallelujah" (*Messiah*) chorus
"March Slave" (Tschaikowsky) orchestra
"Jewel Song" (Gounod's *Faust*) sop
"Conquering hero" (*Maccabeus*) chorus
Prelude, 3rd act, *Loengrin* orchestra
"Marvelous work" (*Creation*) sop & chorus
"Awake the harp" (*Creation*) chorus
"With verdure clad" (*Creation*) sop
"Heavens are telling" (*Creation*) chorus

1925 Jan 1 *Thur* **MESSIAH**
Salt Lake Tabernacle
Cond: *Squire Coop
Sop: Marjorie Dodge
Alto: *Florence Jepperson (Madsen)
Tenor: *John W. Summerhays
Bass: *Albert J. Southwick
Concert M: Arthur Freber
Organist: Frank W. Asper
Chor Dir: J. Spencer Cornwall
Chorus: size unknown

1925 June 30 *Tue* **CREATION**
University of Utah Park Bldg.
Cond & Mus Dir: *Thomas Giles
Gabriel: Jane Burns Albert
Uriel: *John W. Summerhays
Raphael: John Claire Monteith
Concert M: Arthur Freber
Organist: J. J. McClellan
Chorus: 450
NOTE: A rendition of Handel's "Hallelujah

Chorus", directed by George Careless, was an added feature of the evening's program.

1926 Jan 1 *Fri* **MESSIAH**
Salt Lake Tabernacle
Cond: *Squire Coop
Sop: *Emma Lucy Gates
Alto: *Nan Butterfield
Tenor: *John W. Summerhays
Bass: Herbert Gould
Concert M: Arthur Freber
Organist: Frank W. Asper
Trumpeter: John J. Fiala
Chor Dir: J. Spencer Cornwall
Chorus: size unknown
NOTE: Evan Stephens conducted the "Hallelujah" chorus.

1927 Jan 1 *Sat* **MESSIAH**
Salt Lake Tabernacle
Cond & Mus Dir: *J. Spencer Cornwall
Sop: Marjorie Dodge
Alto: Mrs. Raymond Havens
Tenor: *John W. Summerhays
Bass: *Harold H. Bennett
Concert M: Arthur Freber
Organist: Frank W. Asper
Trumpeter: John J. Fiala
Chorus: 300

1928 Jan 2 *Mon* **MESSIAH**
Salt Lake Tabernacle
Cond: *Squire Coop
Sop: Marjorie Dodge
Alto: *Georgia Standing
Tenor: *John W. Summerhays
Bass: *Harold H. Bennett
Concert M: Arthur Freber
Organist: Frank W. Asper
Chor Dir: B. Cecil Gates
Chorus: 300

1928 July 17 *Tue* **CREATION**
University of Utah stadium
Cond & Mus Dir: *B. Cecil Gates
Gabriel: *Emma Lucy Gates (Bowen)
Uriel: *John W. Summerhays
Raphael: *Harold H. Bennett
Concert M: Arthur Freber
Chorus: 250

1929 Jan 1 *Tue* **MESSIAH**
Salt Lake Tabernacle
Cond & Mus Dir: *B. Cecil Gates
Sop: Alice Gentle
Alto: *Jessie Evans
Tenor: *John W. Summerhays
Bass: Herbert Gould
Concert M: Arthur Freber
Organist: Edward P. Kimball
Trumpeter: John J. Fiala
Chorus: 300

1929 July 17 *Wed* **CREATION**
Salem Lake, Utah County
Cond & Mus Dir: *Thomas Giles
Gabriel: *Jessie Perry
Uriel: *John W. Summerhays
Raphael: *Harold H. Bennett
Concert M: Arthur Freber
Chorus: 258

1929 July 18 *Thur* **CREATION**
University of Utah Park Bldg.
NOTE: This was a repeat of the previous evenings program with the same personnel.

1929 Dec 29 *Sun* **MESSIAH**
Salt Lake Tabernacle
Cond: *Squire Coop
Sop: Melba French Barr
Alto: Mary Early Sloman
Tenor: *John W. Summerhays
Bass: Tudor Williams
Concert M: Arthur Freber
Organist: Frank W. Asper
Trumpeter: John J. Fiala
Chor Dir: Ferenz Steiner
Chorus: 275
Broadcast: The first broadcast of a Society Messiah was presented live by Salt Lake station KSL-AM on this date and most performances since have been carried locally by Salt Lake City radio stations.

1930 Dec 28 *Sun* **MESSIAH**
Salt Lake Tabernacle
Cond & Mus Dir: *Albert J. Southwick
Sop: *Irene Kelly Williams
Alto: *Annette Richardson Dinwoodey
Tenor: *Richard P. Condie
Bass: Herbert Gould
Concert M: Arthur Freber
Organist: Dr. Alexander Schreiner
Trumpeter: John J. Fiala
Chorus: 300
Broadcast: Live nationwide via KSL and the NBC in a specially shortened one hour version.

1931 Dec 20 *Sun* **MESSIAH**
Salt Lake Tabernacle
NOTE: This was a special one hour version of the program presented one week later, and was done especially for live nationwide broadcast over the National Broadcasting Company network. The public was not in attendance.

1931 Dec 27 *Sun* **MESSIAH**
Salt Lake Tabernacle
Cond & Mus Dir: *Albert J. Southwick
Sop: *Margaret Anderson Bowen
Alto: *Annette Richardson Dinwoodey
Tenor: *John W. Summerhays
Bass: *Harold H. Bennett
Concert M: Arthur Freber
Organist: Edward P. Kimball
Chorus: 300

1933 Jan 2 *Mon* **MESSIAH**
Salt Lake Tabernacle
Cond & Mus Dir: *Albert J. Southwick
Sop: *Cora Thorne Bird
Alto: *Florence Jepperson (Madsen)
Tenor: *John W. Summerhays
Bass: *Harold H. Bennett
Concert M: Arthur Freber
Organist: Alexander Schreiner
Chorus: 250

1933 Dec 31 *Sun* **MESSIAH**
Salt Lake Tabernacle
Cond & Mus Dir: *Albert J. Southwick
Sop: *Jessie Arlene Williams
Alto: *Annette Richardson Dinwoodey
Tenor: *John W. Summerhays
Bass: Alexander Kisselburgh
Concert M: Arthur Freber
Organist: Frank W. Asper
Trumpeter: Staff Sgt. William Bunburry
Chorus: 250

1935 Jan 1 *Tue* **MESSIAH**
Salt Lake Tabernacle
Cond & Mus Dir: *Albert J. Southwick
Sop: *Irene Kelly Williams
Alto: Frances Warren Haynes
Tenor: Thomas McGranahan
Bass: Rollin Pease
Concert M: Arthur Freber
Organist: Frank W. Asper
Trumpeter: Earl J. Bleak
Chorus: 300

1935 Dec 29 *Sun* **MESSIAH**
Salt Lake Tabernacle
Cond: *Squire Coop
Sop: *Emma Lucy Gates (Bowen)
Alto: *Annette Richardson Dinwoodey
Tenor: *John W. Summerhays
Bass: Herbert Gould
Concert M: Kenneth C. Roylance
Organist: Frank W. Asper
Chor Dir: Albert J. Southwick
Chorus: size unknown

1936 Dec 27 *Sun* **MESSIAH**
Salt Lake Tabernacle
Cond: *Squire Coop
Sop: Blythe Taylor Burns
Alto: *Georgia Standing
Tenor: Russell Horton
Bass: *Harold H. Bennett
Concert M: Arthur Freber
Organist: Wade N. Stephens
Chor Dir: Albert J. Southwick
Chorus: 150

1937 July 21 *Wed* **CREATION**
State Capitol Bldg—south steps
Cond: *Squire Coop
Gabriel: Sylvia Margolin
Uriel: *John W. Summerhays
Raphael: Emery Darcy
Concert M & asst cond: Arthur Freber
Chorus: 150

1937 Dec 26 *Sun* **MESSIAH**
Salt Lake Tabernacle
Cond: *Squire Coop
Sop: Sylvia Margolin
Alto: Rosalie Barker Frye
Tenor: *John W. Summerhays
Baritone: Alexander Kisselburgh
Concert M: Arthur Freber
Assoc Concert M: Reginald Beales
Organist & Chor Dir: Wade N. Stephens
Trumpeter: Seare Morrison
Chorus: 200

1938 July 20 *Wed* **CREATION**
State Capitol Bldg—south steps
Cond: *Squire Coop
Gabriel: Blythe Taylor Burns
Uriel: *James E. Haslam
Raphael: John H. Patrick
Concert M: Arthur Freber
Asst Cond: Wade N. Stephens
Chor Dir: Lisle Bradford
Melvin Peterson
Lydia White Boothby
Chorus: 200

1939 Jan 1 *Sun* **MESSIAH**
Salt Lake Tabernacle
Cond: *Squire Coop
Sop: Blythe Taylor Burns
Alto: *Elizabeth Brown
Tenor: Harold Haugh
Bass: Mark Love
Concert M: Arthur Freber
Asst Concert M: Reginald Beales
George Groneman
Organist & Chor Dir: Wade N. Stephens
Chorus: 250

1939 July 19 *Wed* **CREATION**
State Capitol Bldg—south steps
Cond: *Squire Coop
Gabriel: *Elizabeth Hayes Simpson
Uriel: *James E. Haslam
Raphael: *Albert J. Southwick
Concert M: Arthur Freber
Chorus: 250

1939 Dec 31 *Sun* **MESSIAH**
Salt Lake Tabernacle
Cond: *Squire Coop
Sop: Sylvia Margolin
Alto: *Annette Richardson Dinwoodey
Tenor: Allan R. Lindquest
Bass: Mark Love
Concert M: Arthur Freber
Organist & Chor Dir: Wade N. Stephens
Chorus: 300

1940 Dec 29 *Sun* **MESSIAH**
Salt Lake Tabernacle
Cond: *Squire Coop
Sop: *Virginia Freeze Barker
Alto: *Annette Richardson Dinwoodey
Tenor: Joseph Victor Laderoute
Bass: Sten Englund
Concert M: Arthur Freber

Organist: Wade N. Stephens
Chor Dir: Lisle Bradford
Chorus: 200

1941 Dec 28 *Sun* **MESSIAH**
Salt Lake Tabernacle
Cond: *Squire Coop
Assoc Cond & Chor Dir: *Lisle Bradford
Sop: Sylvia Margolin
Alto: *Ione Duncan
Tenor: Harold Haugh
Bass: Richard Bonelli
Concert M: Arthur Freber
Organist: Wade N. Stephens
Trumpeter: Joseph Kirkham
Chorus: 235

1945 Dec 30 *Sun* **MESSIAH**
Salt Lake Tabernacle
Cond: Dr. Otto Klemperer
Sop: Sara Carter
Alto: *Annette Richardson Dinwoodey
Tenor: Harold Haugh
Bass: Tudor Williams
Concert M: Arthur Freber
Organist: Dr. Alexander Schreiner
Assoc Mus Dir: Lisle Bradford
Chorus: 400

1946 Dec 29 *Sun* **MESSIAH**
Salt Lake Tabernacle
Cond: Dr. Otto Klemperer
Sop: Blythe Taylor Burns
Alto: Marie Powers
Tenor: Harold Haugh
Bass: *Harold H. Bennett
Concert M: Arthur Freber
Organist: Dr. Alexander Schreiner
Assoc Mus Dir: Lisle Bradford
Chorus: 450

1947 Dec 28 *Sun* **MESSIAH**
Salt Lake Tabernacle
Cond: Alfred Greenfield
Sop: Blythe Taylor Burns
Alto: Margaret Tann Williams
Tenor: Harold Haugh
Bass: Orcenith S. Smith
Concert M: Arthur Freber
Organist: Dr. Alexander Schreiner
Assoc Mus Dir: Lisle Bradford
Chorus: 350

1949 Jan 2 *Sun* **MESSIAH**
Salt Lake Tabernacle
Cond: Alfred Greenfield
Sop: Barbara Stevenson
Alto: *Annette Richardson Dinwoodey
Tenor: Harold Haugh
Bass: *C. Austin Seager
Concert M: Arthur Freber
Organist: Dr. Alexander Schreiner
Trumpeter: Keith Lowel Smith
Assoc Mus Dir: Lisle Bradford
Chorus: 400

1950 Jan 1 *Sun* **MESSIAH**
Salt Lake Tabernacle
Cond: Dr. Thompson Stone
Sop: Ruth Diehl
Alto: Marie Powers
Tenor: Harold Haugh
Bass: *Harold H. Bennett
Concert M: Arthur Freber
Organist: Dr. Alexander Schreiner
Trumpeter: Keith Lowel Smith
Assoc Mus Dir: Lisle Bradford
Chorus: 350

1950 Dec 31 *Sun* **MESSIAH**
Salt Lake Tabernacle
Cond: Dr. Thompson Stone
Sop: Blythe Taylor Burns
Alto: Lillian Chookasian
Tenor: Harold Haugh
Bass: Andrew White
Concert M: Arthur Freber
Organist: Dr. Alexander Schreiner
Trumpeter: Keith Lowel Smith
Assoc Mus Dir: Lisle Bradford
Chorus: 350

1951 Dec 30 *Sun* **MESSIAH**
Salt Lake Tabernacle
Cond: Dr. Thor Johnson
Sop: Maude Nosler
Alto: Lillian Chookasian
Tenor: Dr. Alexander Haggar
Bass: Yi Kwei Sze
Concert M: Reginald Beales
Organist: Dr. Alexander Schreiner
Trumpeter: Keith Lowel Smith
Assoc Mus Dir: Lisle Bradford
Chorus: 400

1952 Dec 28 *Sun* **MESSIAH**
Salt Lake Tabernacle
Cond: Sir Ernest MacMillan
Sop: Jean Fenn
Alto: Lillian Chookasian
Tenor: Harold Haugh
Bass: Yi Kwei Sze
Concert M: Reginald Beales
Organist: Dr. Alexander Schreiner
Assoc Mus Dir: Lisle Bradford
Chorus: 400

1954 Jan 3 *Sun* **MESSIAH**
Salt Lake Tabernacle
Cond: Sir Ernest MacMillan
Sop: Jean Fenn
Alto: Lillian Chookasian
Tenor: Harold Haugh
Bass: Andrew White
Concert M: Reginald Beales
Organist: Dr. Alexander Schreiner
Trumpeter: William Sullivan
Assoc Mus Dirs: Dr. David E. Smith
Albert Eccles
Dr. David Shand
Chorus: 380

1955 Jan 2 *Sun* **MESSIAH**
Salt Lake Tabernacle
Cond: Dr. Thompson Stone
Sop: Barbara Stevenson
Alto: Lillian Chookasian
Tenor: Harold Haugh
Bass: Andrew White
Concert M: Reginald Beales
Organist: Dr. Alexander Schreiner
Trumpeter: William Sullivan
Chor Dir: Dr. David A. Shand
Chorus: 450

1955 Dec 18 *Sun* **MESSIAH**
Salt Lake Tabernacle
Cond: Sir Ernest MacMillan
Sop: Jean Fenn
Alto: Lillian Chookasian
Tenor: Harold Haugh
Bass: Andrew White
Concert M: Reginald Beales
Organist: Dr. Alexander Schreiner
Trumpeter: William Sullivan
Chor Dir: Dr. David A. Shand
Chorus: 400
Broadcast: Recorded by CBS for nationwide release at 9 p.m. the same day.

1956 Jan 1 *Sun* **HALLELUJAH**
The Society chorus, directed by Dr. David A. Shand, appeared on the NBC-TV program WIDE WIDE WORLD singing the Hallelujah Chorus.

1956 Dec 23 *Sun* **MESSIAH**
Salt Lake Tabernacle
Cond: Karl Kritz
Sop: Carole Larsen
Alto: Ruth Slater
Tenor: Raymond Manton
Bass: Andrew White
Concert M & Chor Dir: Dr.David A. Shand
Organist: Dr. Alexander Schreiner
Trumpeter: William Sullivan
Chorus: 400

1957 Dec 22 *Sun* **MESSIAH**
Salt Lake Tabernacle
Cond: Karl Kritz
Sop: Sylvia Stahlman
Alto: Lillian Chookasian
Tenor: Leslie Chabay
Bass: Andrew White
Concert M & Chor Dir: Dr.David A. Shand
Organist: Dr. Alexander Schreiner
Trumpeter: William Sullivan
Chorus: 400

1958 Dec 21 *Sun* **MESSIAH**
Salt Lake Tabernacle
Cond: Dr. Thor Johnson
Sop: Ilona Kombrink
Alto: Margot Helmuth Blum
Tenor: Harold Haugh
Bass: Andrew White
Concert M & Chor Dir: Dr.David A. Shand
Organist: Dr. Alexander Schreiner
Trumpeter: William Sullivan
Chorus: 400

1959 Dec 20 *Sun* **MESSIAH**
Salt Lake Tabernacle
Cond: Dr. Thor Johnson
Sop: Ilona Kombrink
Alto: *Annette Richardson Dinwoodey
Tenor: *Glade Peterson
Bass: Yi Kwei Sze
Concert M & Chor Dir: Dr.David A. Shand
Organist: Dr. Alexander Schreiner
Trumpeter: William Sullivan
Chorus: 400
Broadcast: recorded by CBS for a two-hour release at 8:30 P.M. (EST) on Saturday, December 26, 1959, in place of the usual New York Philharmonic Symphony broadcast. In Salt Lake City it was heard on December 27 at noon and again at 10 P. M.

1961 Jan 1 *Sun* **MESSIAH**
Salt Lake Tabernacle
Cond: Dr. Thor Johnson
Sop: Frances McCann
Alto: Mary MacKenzie
Tenor: David Lloyd
Bass: Robert Oliver
Concert M & Chor Dir: Dr.David A. Shand
Organist: Dr. Alexander Schreiner
Trumpeter: William Sullivan
Chorus: 450

1961 Dec 31 *Sun* **MESSIAH**
Salt Lake Tabernacle
Cond: Dr. Thor Johnson
Sop: Ilona Kombrink
Alto: Jean Handzlik
Tenor: David Lloyd
Bass: Andrew White
Concert M: Kenneth Kuchler
Organist: Dr. Alexander Schreiner
Trumpeter: William Sullivan
Chor Dir: Dr. Jay E. Welch
Chorus: 375
Broadcast: Recorded and broadcast the following Christmas (1962) by WRUL of New York (short wave) to Europe, Africa, South America, Mexico, and parts of Asia.

1962 Dec 30 *Sun* **MESSIAH**
Salt Lake Tabernacle
Cond: Dr. Thor Johnson
Sop: *Lucretia Ferre
Alto: Mary MacKenzie
Tenor: John McCollum
Bass: Yi Kwei Sze
Concert M: Kenneth Kuchler
Organist: Dr. Alexander Schreiner
Trumpeter: William Sullivan
Chor Dir: John Marlowe Nielson
Chorus: 350
Broadcast: First FM broadcast, by KSL.

1963 Dec 29 ***Sun*** **MESSIAH**
Salt Lake Tabernacle
Cond: Dr. Thor Johnson
Sop: Lois Marshall
Alto: Margery Mackay
Tenor: James Wainner
Bass: Kenneth Smith
Concert M: Kenneth Kuchler
Organist: Dr. Alexander Schreiner
Trumpeter: William Sullivan
Chor Dir: John Marlowe Nielson
Chorus: 350
Broadcast: Recorded for release by WRUL New York (short wave) at 1:00 P.M. (EST) on January 1 to Europe, the British Isles, South Africa, Mexico, South America and Australia.

1964 Dec 27 ***Sun*** **MESSIAH**
Salt Lake Tabernacle
Cond: Walter Susskind
Sop: Leona Gordon
Alto: Mary MacKenzie
Tenor: John McCollum
Bass: Kenneth Smith
Concert M: Kenneth Kuchler
Organist: Dr. Alexander Schreiner
Trumpeter: William Sullivan
Chor Dir: John Marlowe Nielson
Chorus: 400
Broadcast: Recorded for release by WRUL New York (short wave) at 2:40 P.M. (EST) on January 1 to Europe, the British Isles, South Africa, Mexico, South America and Australia.

1965 Apr 16 ***Fri*** **MOUNT OF OLIVES**
Salt Lake Tabernacle
Cond: Dr. Hans Lampl
Seraph-Gabriel: Leona Gordon
Jesus-Uriel: *Ronald Christensen
Peter-Raphael: Alan J. Ord
Concert M: Kenneth Kuchler
Organist: Dr. Alexander Schreiner
Chor Dir: John Marlowe Nielson
Chorus: 225
The program also included two choruses from Creation: "The heavens are telling the wonder of His work" and "Achieved is the glorious work."

1965 Dec 19 ***Sun*** **MESSIAH**
Salt Lake Tabernacle
Cond: Walter Susskind
Sop: Leona Gordon
Alto: Peggy Coburn
Tenor: Walter Carringer
Bass: Raymond Michalski
Concert M: Kenneth Kuchler
Organist: Dr. Alexander Schreiner
Trumpeter: William Sullivan
Chor Dir: John Marlowe Nielson
Chorus: 400
Broadcast: Videotaped for release December 26 on KSL-TV, Channel 5, in Salt Lake City and retelecast on Christmas day, 1966. Taped for release by WRUL New York (short wave) at 2:40 P. M. (EST) on December 25 to Europe, the Bristish Isles, and South Africa; and on the following Sunday to Mexico, South America and Australia.

1966 Dec 18 ***Sun*** **MESSIAH**
Salt Lake Tabernacle
Cond: Izler Solomon
Sop: Leona Gordon
Alto: Peggy Coburn
Tenor: James Wainner
Bass: Raymond Michalski
Concert M: Kenneth Kuchler
Organist: Dr. Alexander Schreiner
Trumpeter: William Sullivan
Chor Dir: John Marlowe Nielson
Chorus: 350
Broadcast: Recorded for release by WNYW New York (short wave) at 1:30 P.M. (EST) on December 24 to Europe, the British Isles, South Africa, Latin America, and Australia; and to the New York City area on WRFM New York in stereo at the same time and date.

1967 July 23 ***Sun*** **MOUNT OF OLIVES**
Aspen, Colorado, Mus Festival
Cond: Walter Susskind
Seraph: Nöel Rogers
Jesus: John McCollum
Peter: Yi Kwe Sze
Chor Dir: John Marlowe Nielson
Chorus: 150
The program also included the following by Bach: 1."Choral Fantasia" from Cantata No. 79, "God the Lord is sun and shield"; and 2. Cantata No. 131, "Out of the darkness call I to Thee."

1967 Dec 17 ***Sun*** **MESSIAH**
Salt Lake Tabernacle
Cond: Walter Susskind
Sop: Nöel Rogers
Alto: Donna Peterson
Tenor: John McCollum
Bass: Raymond Michalski
Concert M: Kenneth Kuchler
Organist: Dr. Robert N. Cundick
Trumpeter: William Sullivan
Chor Dir: John Marlowe Nielson
Chorus: 350

1968 July 21 ***Sun*** **ELIJAH**
Aspen, Colorado, Mus Festival
Cond: Walter Susskind
Widow: Nöel Rogers
Angel: Claudine Carlson
Obediah: John McCollum
Elijah: Yi Kwei Sze
Chor Dir: John Marlowe Nielson
Chorus: 122

1968 July 28 *Sun*	**ELIJAH**
Temple View Outdoor Theater	
Cond & Chor Dir:	*John Marlowe Nielson
Widow:	*Lila J. Stuart
Obediah:	*Val J. Stuart
Elijah:	*Robert Peterson
A Voice:	*Kenly W. Whitelock
Narrator:	*Gordon Owen
Concert M:	Kenneth Kuchler
Chorus: 110	
1968 Dec 22 *Sun*	**MESSIAH**
Salt Lake Tabernacle	
Cond:	Walter Susskind
Sop:	Nancy Bramlage
Alto:	Peggy Coburn
Tenor:	James Wainner
Bass:	*Robert Peterson
Concert M:	Kenneth Kuchler
Organist:	Dr. Alexander Schreiner
Trumpeter:	William Sullivan
Chor Dir:	John Marlowe Nielson
Chorus: 350	
1969 July 13 *Sun*	**ELIJAH**
Temple View Outdoor Theater	
Cond & Chor Dir:	*John Marlowe Nielson
Widow:	*Cohleen Bischoff
Obediah:	*Glade Peterson
Elijah:	*Don Watts
Narrator:	*Gordon Owen
Concert M:	Kenneth Kuchler
Chorus: 130	
1969 Dec 21 *Sun*	**MESSIAH**
Salt Lake Tabernacle	
Cond:	Walter Susskind
Sop:	Nancy Bramlage
Alto:	Christina Krooskos
Tenor:	Paul Mayo
Bass:	Raymond Michalski
Concert M:	Kenneth Kuchler
Organist:	Dr. Alexander Schreiner
Trumpeter:	William Sullivan
Mus Dir:	John Marlowe Nielson
Chorus: 316	
1970 Dec 20 *Sun*	**MESSIAH**
Salt Lake Tabernacle	
Cond:	Walter Susskind
Sop:	Leona Gordon
Alto:	Christina Krooskos
Tenor:	James Wainner
Bass:	*Robert Peterson
Concert M:	Kenneth Kuchler
Organist:	Dr. Alexander Schreiner
Trumpeter:	William Sullivan
Mus Dir:	John Marlowe Nielson
Chorus: 363	
1971 Dec 19 *Sun*	**MESSIAH**
Salt Lake Tabernacle	
Cond:	Walter Susskind
Sop:	Nöel Rogers
Alto:	Louise Parker
Tenor:	James Wainner
Bass:	Philip Booth
Concert M:	Kenneth Kuchler
Organist:	Dr. Alexander Schreiner
Trumpeter:	William Sullivan
Mus Dir:	John Marlowe Nielson
Chorus: 395	
1972 June 11 *Sun*	**CREATION**
Salt Lake Tabernacle	
Cond:	Hans Lampl
Eve-Gabriel:	Nancy Bramlage
Uriel:	James Wainner
Adam-Raphael:	*Robert Peterson
Concert M:	Norma Lee Madsen
Organist:	Dr. Alexander Schreiner
Trumpeter:	William Sullivan
Mus Dir:	John Marlowe Nielson
Chorus: 187	
1972 Dec 17 *Sun*	**MESSIAH**
Salt Lake Tabernacle	
Cond:	*Dr. Crawford Gates
Sop:	Nancy Bramlage
Alto:	Marvellee Cariaga
Tenor:	*Glade Peterson
Bass:	Philip Booth
Concert M:	Kenneth Kuchler
Organist:	Dr. Alexander Schreiner
Trumpeter:	William Sullivan
Mus Dir:	John Marlowe Nielson
Chorus: 405	
1973 Mar 18 *Sun*	**OLIVES & ST. MARK PASSION**
Salt Lake Tabernacle	
Cond:	Dr. Lara Hoggard
Seraph:	*JoAnn Ottley
Jesus:	James Wainner
Peter:	*Gene M. Larson
Contralto (Passion):	Jean Ann Wolbert
Concert M:	Kenneth Kuchler
Organist:	Dr. Alexander Schreiner
Mus Dir:	John Marlowe Nielson
Chorus: 240	
1973 Dec 15-16 *Sat-Sun*	**MESSIAH**
Salt Lake Tabernacle	
Cond:	Dr. Thor Johnson
Sop:	*JoAnn Ottley
Alto:	Christina Krooskos
Tenor:	James Wainner
Bass:	*Robert Peterson
Concert M:	Kenneth Kuchler
Organist:	Dr. Alexander Schreiner
Trumpeter:	William Sullivan
Mus Dir:	John Marlowe Nielson
Chorus: 384	
1974 Dec 14-15 *Sat-Sun*	**MESSIAH**
Salt Lake Tabernacle	
Cond:	Dr. Louis Lane
Sop:	*JoAnn Ottley
Alto:	Louise Parker
Tenor:	James Wainner
Bass:	Philip Booth
Concert M:	Kenneth Kuchler
Organist:	Dr. Alexander Schreiner
Trumpeter:	William Sullivan
Mus Dir:	John Marlowe Nielson
Chorus: 414	

1975 Dec 13-14 *Sat-Sun* MESSIAH
Salt Lake Tabernacle
Cond: Dr. Louis Lane
Sop: *Ariel Bybee
Alto: Christina Krooskos
Tenor: James Wainner
Bass: *Gene M. Larson
Concert M: Kenneth Kuchler
Organist: Dr. Alexander Schreiner
Trumpeter: William Sullivan
Mus Dir: John Marlowe Nielson
Chorus: 421

1976 June 27 *Sun* ELIJAH
Salt Lake Tabernacle
Cond: *Dr. Daniel L. Martino
Widow: *Donna Dalton
Angel: Alyce Rogers
Obediah: *Glade Peterson
Elijah: Harold Enns
Concert M: Kenneth Kuchler
Organist: Dr. Alexander Schreiner
Mus Dir: John Marlowe Nielson
Chorus: 206

1976 Dec 18-19 *Sat-Sun* MESSIAH
Salt Lake Tabernacle
Cond: Dr. Mischa Semanitzky
Sop: *JoAnn Ottley
Alto: Christina Krooskos
Tenor: Henry Price
Bass: Gary Kendall
Concert M: Kenneth Kuchler
Organist: Dr. Alexander Schreiner
Trumpeter: William Sullivan
Mus Dir: John Marlowe Nielson
Chorus: 397

1977 June 5 *Sun* ELIJAH
Salt Lake Tabernacle
Cond: *Dr. Jay E. Welch
Widow: Elaine Bunse
Angel: *Darleen Merrihew
Obediah: Henry Price
Elijah: Edward Pierson
Concert M: Kenneth Kuchler
Organist: Dr. Alexander Schreiner
Mus Dir: John Marlowe Nielson
Chorus: 254

1977 Dec 17-18 *Sat-Sun* MESSIAH
Salt Lake Tabernacle
Cond: Dr. Louis Lane
Sop: Sung Sook Lee
Alto: Carole Walters
Tenor: Dan Marek
Bass: Gary Kendall
Concert M: Kenneth Kuchler
Organist: Dr. Alexander Schreiner
Trumpeter: William Sullivan
Mus Dir: John Marlowe Nielson
Chorus: 366

1978 Apr 23 *Sun* ELIJAH
Salt Lake Tabernacle
Cond: *Dr. Daniel L. Martino
Widow: Ronit Kalisky
Angel: Victoria Grof
Obediah: James Wainner
Elijah: Edward Pierson
The Youth: *Ricky Tanner
Concert M: Kenneth Kuchler
Organist: Dr. Robert N. Cundick
Mus Dir: John Marlowe Nielson
Chorus: 275

1978 Dec 16-17 *Sat-Sun* MESSIAH
Salt Lake Tabernacle
Cond: Walter Hendl
Sop: Shigemi Matsumoto
Alto: Victoria Grof
Tenor: Dan Marek
Bass: Edward Pierson
Concert M: Kenneth Kuchler
Organist: Dr. Robert N. Cundick
Trumpeter: William Sullivan
Mus Dir: John Marlowe Nielson
Chorus: 280

1979 Dec 15-16 *Sat-Sun* MESSIAH
Salt Lake Tabernacle
Cond: Sandor Salgo
Sop: Ronit Kalisky
Alto: Jane Bunnell
Tenor: James Wainner
Bass: Edward Pierson
Concert M: Kenneth Kuchler
Organist: Dr. Robert N. Cundick
Trumpeter: William Sullivan
Mus Dir: John Marlowe Nielson
Chorus: 269

1980 Dec 13-14 *Sat-Sun* MESSIAH
Salt Lake Tabernacle
Cond: Sandor Salgo
Sop: *JoAnn Ottley
Alto: Linn Maxwell
Tenor: Dana Talley
Bass: Edward Pierson
Concert M: Kenneth Kuchler
Organist: John Longhurst
Trumpeter: Edmund Cord
Mus Dir: John Marlowe Nielson
Chorus: 341
Broadcast: Videotaped by the Public Broadcasting Service for nationwide release Christmas Eve. In Salt Lake City the program was simulcast by KUER-FM. Retelecasts were made on April 18 and 19, and December 20 and 25, 1981; December 25, 1982; and on December 17, 1983.

1981 May 8 *Fri* **ALL BEETHOVEN**
Salt Lake Tabernacle
Cond: *Dr. Ralph G. Laycock
Seraph: *Donna Dalton
Jesus: *Roger Summerhays
Peter: *Rick Pickett
Alto: *Rose Cook
Contralto: *Cathryne Ball
Tenor: *Verdi White, Jr.
Guest Pianist: *Grant Johannesen
Concert M: Kenneth Kuchler
Organist: Dr. Parley L. Belnap
Mus Dir: John Marlowe Nielson
Chorus: 191
The program included 1. *Christ on the Mount of Olives*; 2. Sonata in E Flat Major Opus 31; and 3. *Choral Fantasia.*

1981 May 9 *Sat* **All BEETHOVEN**
Brigham Young University Harris Fine Arts Center with the same program and personnel as the preceding evening.

1981 Dec 12-13 *Sat-Sun* **MESSIAH**
Salt Lake Tabernacle
Cond: *Varujan Kojian
Sop: *JoAnn Ottley
Alto: Linn Maxwell
Tenor: Frank Little
Bass: Jon Enloe
Concert M: William Preucil
Organist: Dr. Parley L. Belnap
Trumpeter: Edward Gornik
Mus Dir: John Marlowe Nielson
Chorus: 300

1982 Dec 11-12 *Sat-Sun* **MESSIAH**
Salt Lake Tabernacle
Cond: Sir Charles Groves
Sop: Susan Belling
Alto: Linn Maxwell
Tenor: Dana Talley
Bass: Gary Kendall
Concert M: Kenneth Kuchler
Organist: Dr. Parley L. Belnap
Trumpeter: Edward Gornik
Mus Dir: John Marlowe Nielson
Chorus: 345

1983 June 8 *Wed* **MESSIAH**
Mann Auditorium (Tel Aviv)
Cond: Amos Meller
Sop: Hadassa Ben-Haim
Alto: Hanna Tzur
Tenor: Victor Schwartz
Bass: Mordechai Shvuron
Mus Dir: John Marlowe Nielson
Chorus: 145

1983 June 9 *Thur* **MESSIAH**
Binyaney Ha'uma (Jerusalem)
The same program and personnel as the preceding day.

1983 Dec 10-11 *Sat-Sun* **MESSIAH**
Salt Lake Tabernacle
Cond: Ling Tung
Sop: Linda Cusanelli
Alto: *Carla Cook
Tenor: Dan Marek
Bass: *Robert Peterson
Concert M: Kenneth Kuchler
Organist: Dr. Parley L. Belnap
Trumpeter: Edward Gornik
Mus Dir: John Marlowe Nielson
Chorus: 326

1984 Dec 15-16 *Sat-Sun* **MESSIAH**
Salt Lake Tabernacle
Cond: Uri Mayer
Sop: *JoAnn Ottley
Alto: *Lani Poulson
Tenor: Dan Marek
Bass: Philip Booth
Concert M: Kenneth Kuchler
Organist: James Drake
Trumpeter: Edward Gornik
Mus Dir: John Marlowe Nielson
Chorus: 284

1985 June 16 *Sun* **ELIJAH**
Symphony Hall (Salt Lake City)
Cond: Uri Mayer
Widow: Nancy Fox-Hoover
Angel: Wendy White
Obediah: Rodney Nolan
Elijah: James Dietsch
The Youth: *Pamela Dale Watkins
Concert M: Kenneth Kuchler
Mus Dir: John Marlowe Nielson
Chorus: 180

1985 Sept 13-14 *Fri-Sat* **ELIJAH**
Jubilee Auditorium (Edmonton, Alberta)
Cond: Uri Mayer
Widow: *JoAnn Ottley
Angel: Jennifer Jestley
Obediah: Glyn Evans
Elijah: Don Garrard
The Youth: *Pamela Dale Watkins
Concert M: James Keene
Asst Concert M: Broderyck Olson
Mus Dir: John Marlowe Nielson
Chorus: 133

1985 Dec 14-15 *Sat-Sun* **MESSIAH**
Salt Lake Tabernacle
Cond: William Noll
Sop: Mary Rawcliffe
Alto: Karen Brunssen
Tenor: Curtis Rayam
Bass: Michael Burt
Concert M: Kenneth Kuchler
Trumpeter: Edward Gornik
Organist: James Drake
Mus Dir: John Marlowe Nielson
Chorus: 269

1986 Dec 13-14 *Sat-Sun* MESSIAH
Salt Lake Tabernacle

Cond:	William Noll
Sop:	Mary Burgess
Alto:	Judith Farris
Tenor:	Rodney Nolan
Bass:	David Power
Concert M:	Kenneth Kuchler
Trumpeter:	Edward Gornik
Organist:	James Drake
Mus Dir:	John Marlowe Nielson

Chorus: 253

1987 June 29 Mon ELIJAH
Kibbutz Ein Hashofet, Israel

Cond:	Uri Mayer
Widow:	*Karen Anderson
Angel:	*Doris Madsen Brunatti
Obediah:	*David Arnold
Elijah:	Andrew Wentzell
Concert M:	Yigal Tuneh

1987 June 30 Tue ELIJAH
Henry Crown Hall, Jerusalem
The same program and personnel as the preceding evening at Kibbutz Ein Hashofet
Chorus (both nights): 85

1987 Dec 12-13 *Sat-Sun* MESSIAH
Salt Lake Tabernacle

Cond:	Uri Mayer
Sop:	Lorna Haywood
Alto:	*Doris Madsen Brunatti
Tenor:	Rodney Nolan
Bass:	Mark Pedrotti
Concert M:	Kenneth Kuchler
Trumpeter:	Edward Gornik
Organist:	Linda Margetts
Chor Dir:	Dr. Morris F. Lee
Asst Chor Dir:	Mark Pearce

Chorus: 214

APPENDIX B

Officers, Directors, and Chorus Officials

Presidents

George D. Pyper	1914-1921	Harold B. Lee	1960-1961
Mayor C. Clarence Neslen	1922-1936	Nicholas G. Morgan, Sr.	1961-1971
Dr. Howard T. Anderson	1936-1939	Michael Megeath	1972
Dr. Adam S. Bennion	1939-1958	Jack Everett Holmstrom	1972-1982
Henry D. Moyle	1958-1960	Richard G. Horak	1983-

Other Officers and Directors

Adkinson, H. M. *Dir.*	1919-1920	Beckstrand, Agnes Dalquist *Dir.*	1915-1921
Alder, Mae *Sec.*	1917	Bennett, Harold H. *Dir.*	1950-1975
Aldous, Heber K. *Dir.*	1936-1947	Bennion, Dr. Adam S. *Dir.*	1936
Alexander, Mrs. Danniel *Dir.*	1914-1916	Bennion, Mrs. Harden *Dir.*	1917-1918
Almond, Becky *Dir.*	1972-1984	Bird, M. A. (Denny) *V.P.*	1972
Alter, J. Cecil *Dir.*	1926-1928	*Asst. Production Mgr.*	1972-1973
Anderson, Edith S. *Dir.*	1972-1973	*Production Mgr.*	1974-1979
Asst. Production Mgr.	1974-1975	Boothby, Lydia White *Dir.*	1929-1931
V.P. for Administration	1976-1986	Bradford, Lisle *Dir.*	1933-1952
Chairman	1987-	Bradey, Dr. Rodney H. *Dir.*	1984-
Anderson, Ethel *Dir.*	1939	Bruneau, A. J. *Dir.*	1926-1928
Anderson, Dr. Howard T. *Dir.*	1926-1936	Burris, Rev. L. Gerald *Dir.*	1972-1974
Executive Sec.	1939-1940	Callister, Louis H. *Dir.*	1969-1971
Production Mgr.	1941-1972	Campbell, Robert S., Jr. *Dir.*	1979-1986
Asst Production Mgr.	1974	Cannon, George Nibley *Dir.*	1966-1970
Atchison, H. M. *Dir.*	1921	Chance, Ethel S. *Dir.*	1917-1918
Backman, Gus *Dir.*	1961-1970		1921
Bamberger, Mrs. Ernest *V.P.*	1923-1925	*Sec.*	1919-1920
Banchero, John D. *Treas.*	1977-	Child, George N. *V.P.*	1923-1931
Banker, Paul E. *Treas.*	1923	Christopulos, P. G. *Dir.*	1981
Bansbach, Phillip A. *Dir.*	1917-1918	Coop, Squire *Music Dir.*	1915-1922
Beason, Ross *Dir.*	1926-1928		1935-1945
		Honorary Dir.	1923-1934

Cornwall, J. Spencer	*Music Dir.*	1927
Crockett, Justice J. Allan	*Dir.*	1968-1984
	Emeritus Dir.	1985-
Curtis, Rev. Stanley	*Dir.*	1923-1925
Davis, May Belle T.	*V.P.*	1916
	Sec.	1917-1920
Daynes, Royal W.	*Dir.*	1915
		1924-1938
	Sec.	1916
Dinwoodey, Annette Richardson	*Dir.*	1972-1975
		1977-1979
	Asst. Production Mgr.	1976-1977
	Artistic Dir.	1983
	V.P. for Production	1984-
Druehl, Mrs. Hugo	*V.P.*	1914-1916
Eberhardt, Alex E.	*Dir.*	1933-1934
	Treas.	1935
	V.P.	1936-1962
Ensign, Horace	*Dir.*	1915
Erwin, Mayor E. B.	*Ex-officio Dir.*	1936-1937
Evans, Elizabeth	*Sec.*	1987-
Fitzpatrick, John	*Dir.*	1929-1933
Friberg, Jayna	*Dir.*	1987
	V.P. for Administration	*1987-*
Garn, Mayor E. J.	*Ex-officio Dir.*	1972-1974
Garrigues, Louise	*Dir.*	1986-1987
Gates, B. Cecil	*Music Dir.*	1928-1929
Giles, Thomas	*Music Dir.*	1925
		1929
Glade, Mayor Earl	*Ex-Officio Dir.*	1945-1955
Gorham, Mrs. A. J.	*V.P.*	1915-1916
Gowans, Dr. E. G.	*V.P.*	1915-1916
Gregerson, Mrs. Grant	*Dir.*	1940
Hanson, Ernest	*Dir.*	1939-1947
Haslam, James E.	*Dir.*	1940-1947
Hodgson, Mrs. W. S.	*Dir.*	1919-1921
Holmstrom, Jack Everett	*Dir.*	1971
	Dir	1987-
	Chairman	1983-1986
Horak, Richard G.	*V.P. for Finance*	1972-1982
Howard, John C.	*Dir.*	1923-1925
Jenkins, Mayor Ab	*Ex-Officio Dir.*	1940-1941
Johannesen, Grant	*Dir.*	1979-1981
Johnson, Edna Evans	*Dir.*	1933-1935
Kahn, Mrs. Jacob	*Dir.*	1926-1931
Kennedy, Patrick F.	*Dir.*	1945-1960
Kirkham, Oscar	*Dir.*	1914-1916
Lang, D. J.	*Dir.*	1914-1916
Lee, Mayor J. Bracken	*Ex-Officio Dir.*	1961-1971
McCowan, Joseph H.	*Dir.*	1939-1950
McMahon, Mrs. C. H.	*V.P.*	1916-1921
Maguire, Rt. Rev. Msgr. Patrick A.	*Dir.*	1961-1965
Marcus, Louis	*Dir.*	1934-1935
Martin, Gail	*Publicity Dir.*	1937-1938
Megeath, Michael	*Dir.*	1969-1971
	V.P.	1971
Miller, J. B.	*Dir.*	1923-1926
Morgan, Nicholas G., Sr.	*Dir.*	1958-1960
Morris, George Q.	*Dir.*	1915-1916
	V.P.	1917-1920
Mullins, T. J.	*Dir.*	1933-1936
Muth, Eleanor	*Dir.*	1979-1983
	V.P. for Advertising	1984-
Neslen, Mayor C. Carence	*Dir.*	1919-1922
		1937-1938
	Honorary Dir.	1945-1966
Nielson, John Marlowe	*Emeritus Dir.*	1987-
Owen, Gordon	*Dir.*	1965-1968
	V.P. for Promotion	1969-1970
Parry, Mrs. P. M.	*Dir.*	1924-1931
Peabody, A. H.	*Treas.*	1914-1921
Peters, Mrs. A. S.	*Dir.*	1917-1918
Peters, Bill	*Dir.*	1987
Peterson, William	*Dir.*	1945-1950
Plummer, Mrs. Charles G.	*Dir.*	1931-1947
Price, Marcia P.	*Dir.*	1984-
Pyper, Geroge D.	*Dir.*	1923-1934
	Honorary Dir.	1935-1938
Rampton, Anthony L.	*Dir.*	1978-1982
Reese, Rev. W. W.	*Dir.*	1915-1916
Reynolds, F. W.	*Dir.*	1917
		1926-1931
	Sec.	1923-1925
Rich, Maj. Gen. Maxwell E.	*Dir.*	1965-1970
Richards, Joseph	*Dir.*	1935
Riley, Rev. Earl L.	*Dir.*	1965-1970
Ross, Harvey S.	*Treas.*	1969-1972
	Sec.-treas.	1973-1977
	Sec.	1977-1979
	Chorus Coordinator	1980-1983
	V.P for the Chorus	1984-1986
	Emeritus Dir.	1987-
Salinger, Herbert	*Dir.*	1915-1916
Saville, Irene	*Sec.*	1935
Shelton, Sherry	*Dir.*	1979
Shepherd, Charles	*Music Dir.*	1924
Simmons, LeRoy D.	*Dir.*	1939-1945
		1966-1969
Simpkin, Mr.	*Dir.*	1917
Sitzer, Emily	*Dir.*	1916
Smith, Mrs. A. E.	*Dir.*	1919-1920
Smith, Dr. David E.	*Dir.*	1933-1935
	Sec.	1935-1939
Southwick, Albert J.	*Music Dir.*	1930-1935
Spencer, John D.	*Dir.*	1917-1919
Steele, Rev. Robert D.	*Dir.*	1945-1951
Stephens, Harold M.	*Dir.*	1923-1925
Stewart, Mayor Adiel F.	*Ex-Officio Dir.*	1956-1959
Stewart, Charlotte	*Dir.*	1921-1939
Stoven, Beverly	*Sec.*	1976
Taylor, Dr. Maurice J.	*Asst. Production Mgr.*	1969-1972
	Dir.	1972-1981
		1987-
	Executive V.P.	1982-1983
	Vice-chairman	1984-1986

Thomas,		
Emma Lindsay	*Asst. Sec.*	1937-1938
	Dir.	1939-1963
		1969
	Sec.	1964-1968
Thomas, Kate	*Sec.*	1915
	Dir.	1916-1939
Thomas, Mathonihah	*Dir.*	1915-1916
Thomas, W. Jack	*Dir.*	1933-1935
		1969-1973
	Treas.	1936
	Finance Chairman	1937-1938
	Business Mgr., Finance	1939-1968
Trapp, Gerald B.	*Dir.*	1984-1985
	Sec.	1986
	V.P for Chorus	1987-
Tyler, Mrs. Warwick A.	*Dir.*	1919-1920
		1923-1926
	Sec.	1921-1922
		1927-1930
Walker, Alex. H., Jr.	*Dir.*	1978-1979
	Sec.	1980-1984
Wallace, Mayor John M.	*Dir.*	1931-1938
		1970
Watkiss, Dorothy B.	*Dir.*	1978
Watson, Mrs. George H.	*Dir.*	1933-1937
Welch, Dr. Jay E.	*Dir.*	1962-1968

Chorus Officials

Alder, Mae	*Sec.*	1915-1917
Alexandria, Olga	*Sec.*	1940
	Asst. Sec.	1941
Alleman, Joan	*Monitor*	1985-
Almond, Becky	*Accompanist*	1933-1961
Anderson, Edith S.	*Asst. Secretary*	1968
Anderson, Dr. Howard T.	*Pres.*	1925-1933
Andrus, Jay O.	*Choral Asst.*	1967
Beattie, Ross		
	Asst. Arrangements sec.	1938
Bond, Richard G.	*Monitor*	1938-1939
Boothby, Lydia White		
	Junior Section Dir.	1938
Bowers, John D.	*Librarian*	1916
Bradford, Lisle	*Chorus Officer*	1929-1934
	Junior Section Dir.	1935-1941
	Choral Dir.	1940-1941
	Assoc. Music Dir.	1945-1953
	Asst. Conductor	1941
Bunting, Dorothy	*Monitor*	1965-
	Asst. Sec.	1983-
Butler, Velma	*Asst. Sec.*	1978-1979
Carrol, Mary	*Chorus Officer*	1939
	Soprano Section Dir.	1940-1941
Chance, Ethel	*V.P.*	1916
Christensen, Sue	*Accompanist*	1960
Cornwall, J. Spencer	*Choral Dir.*	1923
		1926
	Asst. Conductor	1925
Cunningham, Betty	*Monitor*	1985-1986
	Sec.	1987-
Day, Philip A. Jr.	*Asst. Music Dir.*	1980-1984
Eccles, Albert	*Asst. Music Dir.*	1951-1953
	Assoc. Music Dir.	1954-1961
	Asst. Choral Dir.	1961-1963
	Choral Coordinator	1964
Evans, Elizabeth P.	*Asst. Sec.*	1985-
Duncan, Leah	*Asst. Sec.*	1928-1929
Gates, B. Cecil	*Chorus Asst.*	1915
	Choral Dir.	1927
Gregerson, Mrs. Grant	*President*	1939-1940
Hahn, Naomi	*Asst. Sec.*	1968-1982
Hales, Dr. Bernell	*Chorus Asst.*	1967-1969
Hanson, Peggy W.	*Musical Asst.*	1984-
Hanson, Ernest M.	*Chairman*	1941
Haslam, James E.	*V.P.*	1939-1940
	V-Chairman	1941
Hays, Lucille Young	*Sec.*	1941
James, John	*Chorus Officer*	1929
Johannesen, Helen Taylor		
	Accompanist	1949
Johnson, Edna Evan		
	Chorus Officer	1929
Kirkham, El Moine	*Asst. Librarian*	1938-1939
Kirkpatrick, Ms G. D.		
	Asst. Superintendant	1939
	Alto Section Dir.	1941
	Asst. Choral Dir.	1945
Kurr, Dr. Doreen	*Asst. Music Dir.*	1973-1976
Lee, Dr. Morris F.	*Asst. Music Dir.*	1984-1986
	Music Dir.	1987-
Lowe, Myrle	*Asst. Sec.*	1980-1987
	Sec.	1987-
McConkie, James	*Librarian*	1938-1939
Mason, Wesley L.		
	Part Rehearsal Dir.	1964
Maxwell, Morris	*Arrangements Sec.*	1938
Mixter, C. T.	*Chairman*	1923
	General Sec.	1924-1938
Morris, Barbara	*Asst. Sec.*	1938-1939
Nielson, John Marlowe	*Choral Dir.*	1962-1969
	Music Dir.	1969-1987
Olsen, Chris	*Music Asst.*	1987-
Parks, Dorothy L.	*Monitor*	1985-
Peabody, Alfed H.	*Chorus Asst.*	1915-1921
	Acting Music Dir.	1919
Pearce, Kelly	*Part Rehearsal Dir.*	1964
Pearce, Mark	*Asst. Choral Dir.*	1987-
Peterson, Melvin	*Junior Section Dir.*	1938
Powell, Jerry	*Accompanist*	1961-1962
Powell, Mrs. Jerry	*Chorus Asst.*	1967
Rasmusson, C. V.	*President*	1916
Rowland, R. Stephen	*Chorus Asst.*	1967
Schreiner, William	*Superintendant*	1938-1939
Shand, Dr. David A.		
	Asst. Music Dir.	1951-1953
	Assoc. Dir.	1954
	Choral Dir.	1955-1957
	Music Dir.	1958-1961

Silviera, Norma	*Monitor*	1985-
Smith, Dr. David E.	*Chorus Officer*	1929-1932
	Tenor Section Dir.	1941
	Asst. Choral Dir.	1945-1950
	Asst. Music Dir.	1951-1953
	Assoc. Music Dir.	1954-1961
	Asst. Choral Dir.	1961-1963
Smith, Leona Stone	*Monitor*	1985-
Smith, Richard F.	*Musical Asst.*	1984-
Snow, Charlene Scowcroft		
	Accompanist	1967
	Musical Asst.	1977-
Southwick, Albert J.	*Choral Dir.*	1935-1936
Stark, Lorrie Lou	*Monitor*	1984-
	Asst. Sec.	1984-
Steiner, Ferenz	*Choral Dir.*	1929
Stephens, Wade N.	*Choral Dir.*	1937-1939
	Asst. Conductor	1938
	Accompanist	1938
	Asst. Choral Dir.	1950
Syphus, Myron	*Accompanist*	1964
Thomas, Ann Davies		
	Asst. Music Dir.	1952
Thomas, Emma Lindsay	*Sec.*	1929-1968
Thomas, W. Jack	*Sec-treas.*	1928-1929
	Business Mgr.	1929
Twitchell, Royce	*Accompanist*	1968-
	Musical Asst.	1970
Watkins, Pamela D.	*Musical Asst.*	1984-
Watts, Ardean	*Accompanist*	1963
Welch, Dr. Jay E.	*Choral Dir.*	1961
Wheelwright, Sterling		
	Asst. Choral Dir.	1935-1941
	Junior Section Dir.	1940-1941
Whitelock, Kenly W.		
	Part Rehearsals Dir.	1964-1966
	Musical Asst.	1967-1972
Whitelock, Susan	*Asst. Sec.*	1968
Whitney, R. Roene	*Monitor*	1985-
Wilcox, Helen	*Sec.*	1969-1987
	Chorus Consultant	1987-
Wood, Dorothy Marie	*Monitor*	1985-
Young, Wanda	*Monitor*	1938
	Asst. Sec.	1939
Zancanella, Patricia	*Monitor*	1985-

APPENDIX C

Charter Members and Members of the Chorus

Charter Members of The Salt Lake Oratorio Society

Alder, Mae C.	Ebaugh, W. C.	Miller, Minnie	Sutherland, Leona
Amott, Leona	Evans, Elva	Morton, William P.	Swensen, H. W.
Ashton, Donald	Glore, Cora	Nuttall, William T.	Thomas, Elthira
Berry, Josephine A.	Goff, Harold	Olson, Sam W.	Thomas, Ethel
Borden, Geraldine	Gorham, Mrs. A. J.	Peterson, Melvin	Thomas, Evangeline
Borden, Mrs. W. E.	Granque, J. G., Jr.	Rasmussen, C. V.	Thomas, Kate
Bowers, John D.	Guyon, Arua	Reese, Ward W.	Thomas, Lillian E.
Bradford, Lily Pye	Houtz, Evans B.	Rich, G. R.	Thomas, Mathonihah
Bradford, Lisle	Johnson, Elizabeth M.	Richards, Joseph E.	Thomas, R. Kendall
Browning, J. S.	Johnson, Mrs. Ida L.	Ross, Virginia D.	Tipton, Hattie
Chance, Ethel S.	Kesler, Violate	Russell, Ellen	Tuckett, Ethel
Cornwall, C. C.	Kesler, Vivian	Salinger, Herbert	Tyler, Mrs. Warwick A.
Crandall, Ivy Evans	King, Rose V.	Sandburg, H. C.	Walkingshaw, Jane
Davis, Emma	Kirkpatrick, Grace C.	Smith, D. E.	Watson, A. W.
Daynes, Royal W.	Lewis, Lucy	Smith, Winifred	Whiteley, Marjorie
Dean, Irene B.	Lindsay, Emma	Stephens, Mildred	Williams, R. C.
Dean, Jasper H.	Lindsay, O. S.	Summerhays, Florence	Williams, Sarah M.
Druehl, Mrs. Hugo W.	Madsen, Franklin	Summerhays, Lillian	Wise, George C.
Duvall, Ruth	Mattell, H. H.	Suthorland, J. R.	

The Chorus of the Oratorio Society of Utah

Sopranos

Abbott, Mrs. C. E.
Ackerlind, Cleo Despaine
Adams, Carolyn Truman
Adams, Ellen Jean
Adams, Joan
Adams, Joyce R.
Adams, Lucile
Adams, Nellie
Adams, Violet L.
Adamson, Lorna M.
Adamson, Myrtle
Adkin, Olive L.
Aft, Lorna
Aird, Eva
Alexandria, Olga
Alfreds, Joan
Allan, Juanita
Allart, Johanna
Alleman, Joan
Allen, Dorothy
Allen, Florence
Allen, Gwen
Allen, Joy
Allen, Linda
Allen, Mary E.
Allen, Mary Rose
Allen, Patricia
Allen, Ruby L.
Allen, Ruelen
Allen, Ruth M.
Allen, Zavenda
Alseen, Mrs. A.
Alsop, Darla L.
Alsop, Donna
Alsop, Doris
Alt, Ora Rew
Amann, Margie A.
Amott, Joan C.
Andersen, Lynda
Anderson, Andrea
Anderson, Annie M
Anderson, Barbara
Anderson, Billie L.
Anderson, Bonnie Rae
Anderson, Donna
Anderson, Elizabeth
Anderson, Elna Jean
Anderson, Gloria K.
Anderson, Hertha Bixley
Anderson, Judy K.
Anderson, LeArta L.
Anderson, Lou Ann J.
Anderson, Marjory
Anderson, Mary Jane
Anderson, Pearl
Anderson, Venita
Anderson, Verna
Anderton, Brenda H.
Anthony, Linda
Apostol, Bessie
Arbogast, Jacqueline
Armstrong, Cynthia
Armstrong, Linda
Arney, Harriet E.
Arstellar, Alys V.
Asay, Marilyn Loreen
Ashby, Nancy L.
Ashton, Alice
Athay, Shirley
Atkin, Ellen
Atkin, Gladys
Ault, Linda
Ayres, Edith
Baak, Olga
Backman, Edith
Bacon, Bonnie Jean
Baddley, Mary Lynn
Baggaley, Charlotte
Bagley, Fern J.
Bahl, Sylvia
Bailey, Jean
Bair, Laura
Baird, Trudy
Baird, Mrs. W. E.
Baker, Lola
Baker, Nancy
Ball, Shauna
Ballard, Edna
Ballard, Emma Jean
Ballard, LaRae
Ballard, Nellie H.
Bane, Margaret M.
Bangerter, Nola M.
Banwell, N. Kim
Barber, Betty
Bardwell, Ora
Barger, Ms.
Barker, Annette
Barker, Ilamae H.
Barlow, June
Barlow, Ray
Barlow, Virginia
Barnes, Jeanne
Barnett, Mary
Barr, Joan
Barrett, Gayle J.
Barron, Gladys
Barrus, Leola
Barrus, Noama
Barrus, Nora
Bartlett, Jane
Bartlett, Loretta
Barton, Annie
Barton, Doris
Barton, Joan Alfreds
Barton, Lenora
Barton, Marie
Barton, Marnee Rose
Basinger, Jean
Bastian, Marlene
Bates, Lavon
Bauer, Ora
Bauman, Gwen
Baxter, Annamae
Beal, Mrs. T. A.
Beam, Minnie
Bean, Annette S.
Bean, Carma Ann
Bean, Consuela
Bean, Dorothy
Bean, Minnie
Bear, Betty
Beard, Joan
Beatie, Sue
Beatty, Esther
Bebermeyer, Martha
Beckstead, Gundhild
Beckstead, Ruth
Beesley, Karine
Beesley, Sharol
Beesley, Sherry
Beins, Diane
Bell, Julia
Bell, Verla
Bellamy, Almina
Bellamy, Elizabeth
Belliston, Ara
Belnap, Mary Elen Bennett
Belnap, Maxine
Bennett, Barbara
Bennett, Elaine
Bennett, Francis
Bennett, Joan
Bennett, Marilyn
Bennett, Mary Elen
Bennett, Rose
Bennion, Becky L.
Bennion, Carolyn
Bennion, Florence
Bennion, Karla Pack
Bennion, Linda
Bennion, Lucile
Bennion, Mabel
Benson, Arvilla Clark
Benson, Beverly
Bently, Louise
Berg, Gertrude
Berg, Mae V.
Bergeson, Ethel
Berglund, Diane
Berndt, Grace E.
Berndt, Shirley
Berntsen, Valena
Berry, Josephine
Best, Carol D.
Best, Carrie D.
Bettes, Debbie
Bettess, Deborah
Betts, Leatha A.
Beyer, Julia
Biener, Ida
Bienert, Lilly
Billeter, Rose
Billings, Julia
Billings, Maxine
Bingham, Carolyn
Bircumshaw, Peggy
Bird, Alice B.
Bird, Alice R.
Bird, Barbara
Bird, Hazel S.
Bishop, Carolyn M.
Bishop, Dorothy
Bisnert, Lily G.
Bitner, Ella
Bixby, Hertha M.
Bixby, Leila
Bjorndal, Marilyn
Black, Cynthia L.
Black, Florence S.
Black, Joan
Black, Joanette Ferrell
Black, Louie H.
Blackhurst, Janet
Blain, Elizabeth N.
Blake, Lola
Blamires, Jeneil
Blatter, Lorene
Bleakley, Mrs. W. S. J.
Blindauer, Donna
Block, Henen Waite
Blomquist, Kathryn
Bogner, Suzanne
Bohle, Beorgia
Bohlin, Marjean
Bollinger, Rose
Bonner, May
Borden, Frances B.
Borden, Frances Canady

Borden, Mrs. W. E.
Borgquist, Lilian
Boulter, Charmaine M.
Bow, Dorothy Allen
Bowen, Agnes
Bowen, Barbara
Bowen, Emma
Bowen, Jeanne
Bowen, Lucile Ross
Boweres, Etta
Bowers, Carma D.
Bowers, Ruth
Bowman, EthelThomas
Bown, Mrs. John
Boyce, Karen
Bracken, Ida
Bradford, Kay
Bradford, Lily
Bradford, Lisle
Bradley, Fanny R.
Bramblett, Mary
Bremls, Christine L.
Brewer, JoAnn
Brewerton, Laurinda P.
Brewerton, Lucille
Briggs, Jane
Brigham, Janet
Bringhurst, Elizabeth
Brinton, Connie
Brinton, Leann
Bronson, Donna
Bronson, VaLois
Brough, Norena
Brower, Josephine
Brown, Cherry S.
Brown, Debra
Brown, Diane
Brown, Dorothy
Brown, Elaine
Brown, Elizabeth
Brown, Elsie
Brown, Esther Smith
Brown, Jane
Brown, LaPriel S.
Brown, Louise
Brown, Ora
Brown, Shirley Fay
Brown, Suzanne
Brown, Mrs. Tanner L.
Browning, Margaret Tout
Bruce, Bonnie
Bruno, Shirley
Brunson, Merrilee
Bryan, Rae
Buckley, Elizabeth
Buckley, Jeannine H.
Bult, Mary Louise
Bunn, Fanny Louise
Bunting, Dorothy
Burgener, Velda
Burgess, Kitty L.
Burkhardt, Ruth

Burnham, Barbara
Burns, Grace
Burris, Geneva
Burris, Jane
Burton, Annette
Burton, Annie
Burton, Connie M.
Burton, Dorothy
Burton, Edith
Burton, Ida
Burton, Valois Putnam
Butcher, Betty
Butcher, Vilate
Butler, Mary
Butler, Velina L.
Butler, Velma
Butts, Cherry
Buxton, Teresa Louise
Byer, Julia
Caffall, Annie D.
Cahoon, Matilda
Calkins, Vinnie
Call, Sandra M.
Callihan, Phyllis
Cameron, Ada M.
Cameron, Anita Z.
Campbell, Charlotte
Canada, Dorothy
Canady, Frances
Canatelli, Virginia
Cannon, Amelia T.
Cannon, Flora M.
Cannon, Ina Garff
Cannon, Marian
Cannon, Winifred S.
Capener, Ann
Cardall, Ann
Carey, Beatrice
Carland, Kathleen M.
Carlson, Jeneale
Carman, Virginia
Carr, Laura Annamae
Carr, Linda
Carr, Linda L.
Carratelli, Virginia A.
Carter, Blanche
Carter, Golda
Cassity, ValJeanne
Castane, Laura Carr
Castano, Laura
Cate, Chris M.
Cawley, Elaine
Cecala, Patricia
Chadwick, Barbara
Chadwick, Mrs. W. W.
Chamberlain, Merlyn
Chambers, Sylvia
Chance, Ethel
Chandler, Mrs. Jessie L.
Chapman, Donna
Chatwin, Vilate Butcher

Chipman,Nellie Adams
Chipman, Betty Jeanne
Chipman, Vichie
Christensen, Betty
Christensen, Bonnie Robinson
Christensen, Helen
Christensen,Kathryn A.
Christensen, Laraine J.
Christensen, Madelyn
Christensen, Marie D.
Christensen, Marlene Hewlett
Christensen, Mary Jo
Christensen, Pat
Christensen, Rhea Dean
Christensen, Sue
Christenson, Madelyn
Christenson, Sue
Christian, Bonnie
Christiansen, Bonnie
Christiansen, Shannan
Christie, Melba M.
Christopher, Della
Chytraus, Jeraldine
Cicerone, Violet
Circuit, Della C.
Clance, Ethel S.
Clapham, Barbara
Clapham, Elizabeth
Clapham, Gudrun
Clark, Arvilla
Clark, Delores
Clark, Ellamae
Clark, Frances
Clark, Jacquita
Clark, Merrilee Hillam
Clark, Mrs. Fred G.
Claus, Yvonne
Clawson, Pat
Clayton, Alberta
Clayton, Ethel
Clayton, Janell
Clayton, Vera
Clegg, Phyllis
Clemensen, Mrs. G. V.
Clinger, Susan
Clissold, Carrol
Clyde, Mary Ann
Coates, Connie
Coates, Connie Eastwood
Cole, Louise M
Colladay, Margaret
Collett, Kathleen
Colyar, Beth
Combs, Susan
Cone, Betty
Cone, Beverly
Cone, Catherine
Cook, Louise A.
Cook, May D.

Cook, Wilma
Coolbaugh, Carolyn H.
Cooley, Carolyn
Coomans, Nellie
Coombs, Marion
Coplin, Kris
Copling, Winefred
Coppock, Mrs. E. L.
Corak, Marlene
Corbett, Melba
Cordner, Marjean
Cornia, Merlynn
Cornwall, Mary
Cornwall, Mrs. Spencer
Cosby, Annita
Cosgrove, Nell
Couzens, Charlotte J.
Couzens, Jessie M.
Cowan, Ann M.
Cox, Ella E.
Cox, Mrs. W. M.
Cracroft, Terese Williams
Crandall, Ivy Evans
Crandall, Nancy
Crapo, Alice
Cricks, Willa Mae
Crocker, Shirleu
Crofts, Barbara
Croper, Vera
Crosby, Dorothy
Crosgrove, Nell
Crotch, Lilly N.
Crotch, Lily May
Crow, LaRena
Cufflin, Vinnie Calkins
Cull, Marion
Cummings, C. Jean
Cummings, Catherine
Cummings, Catherine J.
Cummings, Florence
Cummings, Irene S.
Cummings, Joanne
Curtis, Elda
Curtis, Leona
Cushing, Judy
Cushing, Lillie S.
Cutler, Geneve
Cutler, Joan
Cutler, Sue
Cutler, Sylvia J.
Dahl, Helga E.
Dahle, Myrtle
Dahnken, Eve
Dalley, Beverley H.
Dalton, Annie
Dalton, Kathie L.
Dame, Mary S.
Damon, Ethelynn
Darger, Ann
Darger, Frances

Darger, Peggy
Darling, Dorothy
Davenport, Ruth Ann
Davidson, Irene
Davies, Mrs. Busby
Davies, Darlene Katwych
Davies, Fay
Davila, Lola
Davis, Ann
Davis, Barbara
Davis, Beulah
Davis, Mrs. Busby
Davis, Cindy P.
Davis, Dora Dunyon
Davis, Eileen
Davis, Elthura Kimball
Davis, Emma
Davis, Esther
Davis, Hazel
Davis, Joanne S.
Davis, LaJon
Davis, Laura Jacobson
Davis, Ranae T.
Davis, Ruth
Dawson, Connie Gunderson
Dawson, Elizabeth
Dawson, Elsie
Day, Sandra
De Haas, Katherine
De Lange, Helen
Dean, Irma Browning
Dearing, Pat
Debendiner, Leonore E.
DeBruin, Anna
DeBruin, Martina
Decker, Dawna M.
Decker, Jo Ann
Decker, Louise L.
Decker, Mary
Decker, Mrs. L. C.
DeGroot, Elsa
DeHaan, Cheryl
Dehenham, Louise
DeHoop, Ann
Delin, Florence
Deloney, Wilma
Delson, Rene
Denkema, Ada
Denkers, Joyce A.
Denney, Minke
Denton, Beverly
Deppe, May
Derbidge, Dora
Derrickson, Frankie
DeSpain, Cleo
Despain, Evon
Devereaux, Frances
DeVine, Alice
Devitt, Agnes
Dickman, Diane
Dodderidge, Phyllis
Doelle, Myrtle
Donaldson, Edna
Donaldson, Isabell
Donaldson, Melba
Done, Elizabeth
Donnan, Lorrie
Donoviel, Vera
Doran, Jane
Dorins, Jacoba
Dorius, Luana Monson
Dorius, Nora
Dorsey, Beulah
Dotterer, Jane
Doubleday, Mrs. H
Douglas, Jestina
Draper, Frances R.
Driggs, Mrs. H. R.
Driggs, Jean
Druce, Joyce
Dubach, Marjorie
Dubois, Mari Ann
Dubois, Mariann S. O.
Duffin, Mirjam
Duncan, Aurora H.
Duncan, Hortense
Duncan, Kim
Dunford, Merlyn
Dunn, Elizabeth Anne
Dunyon, Dora
Duvall, Ruth
Dykman, Virginia
Dymock, Jeri
Eager, Ver Dawn
Earnshaw, Sarah Dee
Easter, Esther
Eastwood, Connie
Eaton, Mrs. George A.
Eccles, Barbara
Eccles, Caroline
Eccles, Carolyn
Eccles, Fay S.
Eccles, Mary Ethel
Eddington, Bonnie Rae
Edmonds, Diana
Edmunds, Mrs. J. W.
Edmunds, Victoria
Edwards, June A.
Edwards, Lori Jo
Edwards, Rachel W.
Egan, Mrs. A. T.
Ekstrom, Lorna M.
Elias, Dorothea
Eliason, Clara
Ellis, Kathryn
Elmer, Frances
Empey, Hilda Cox
Ence, Arlene
Engelhardt, Denise
Engelhardt, Ruth Helen
Engster, JoAnn
Engstrom, Rozella
Epperson, Loretta
Epperson, Virginia
Erickson, Mrs. A. G.
Erickson, Florence
Erickson, Yvonne
Ernshaw, Sara Dee
Eschler, Ruth
Esperson, Bonnie
Ethington, Lois L.
Ethington, Loretta
Eugster, JoAnn
Evans, Arda Lou
Evans, Bernice
Evans, Edna
Evans, Elizabeth
Evans, Georgia K.
Evans, Joyce
Evans, Virginia
Evertson, Ms.
Fackrell, Jan
Fairclough, Vivienne
Falsetti, Rose
Fariello, Laura M.
Farnsworth, Berneice
Farnsworth, Elaine
Farr, Alice Irene
Farr, Karma S.
Farr, Mayme
Farrell, Gladys
Farrell, Josephine B.
Faux, Annette
Fechser, Ida
Felicetti, Kathy A.
Fellows, Thelma
Felt, Jane
Fenton, Marybell
Fenton, Myrna
Fenwick, Jo
Feragen, Elaine
Ferguson, Ada L.
Ferguson, Jane
Ferguson, Sherri Stapley
Ferrell, Evelyn A.
Ferrell, Joanette
Ferrell, Josephine
Ferrell, Louise
Ferrell, Patricia
Ferrell, Tess
Feser, Bonnie Jean
Fetzer, Juana
Fiedel, Walli L.
Findley, Annette
Finlinson, Luella W.
Finnell, Christine
Firmage, Ruth
Fischer, Annemarie
Fitzen, Amy L.
Fleetwood, Lisa
Fleisch, Marian
Fleming, A. Modessa
Fletcher, Josephine B.
Fletcher, Marian
Flink, Elisabeth
Flores, Marnee
Floto, Alice T.
Floyd, Violet
Folks, Betty
Fonnesbeck, Luna
Forsgren, Louise
Forsherg, Edith
Forsyth, Emily E.
Fortie, Lorna
Fortie, Phyllis
Foulger, Etna H.
Fowler, Esther
Fox, Jeanne M.
Fox, Lucy G.
Francis, Connie
Francis, Gloria
Francis, Mrs. Jack
Frates, Mrs. Frank
Frazier, Ivy M.
Free, Florence
Freeman, Elaine
French, Gwen Standing
French, Jacqueline
Friberg, Jayna
Frink, Elaine F.
Frost, Cathi
Frost, Kathy
Frost, Mrs. R. P.
Fullmer, Valletta
Furner, Duffie
Gabbott, Kathryn
Gabinet, Sandra
Gaillac, Annette Louise
Galbraith, Lela P.
Galland, Chris M.
Gallegos, Renee
Gardner, Gladys
Gardner, Joyce
Gardner, Kathleen H.
Gardner, Kathy
Garff, Ina
Garff, Minnie
Garner, Ellen
Garner, Joyce Lurie
Garr, Alice Irene
Garrett, Delora G.
Garrison, Natalie Olsen
Garvin, Margaret
Garvin, Marguerite
Garvin, Minke
Garwin, Minke Denney
Gasser, Anna
Gedge, Margaret
Gee, Bernice
Gee, June
Geis, Idella
Geis, Tess
Geitheil, Frankie H.
Gerrard, Bertha
Gessel, Edna
Geving, Sandra
Gibb, Wanda
Gibbs, Rose
Gibson, Ann

Giers, Helen
Giers, Mrs. H. E.
Giles, Georgina
Giles, Sibyl
Giles, Vera
Gill, Pauline E.
Gillis, Anna
Gillmor, Florence
Glade, Barbara
Glasgow, Mary Ann
Glines, Shirley Brown
Glochner, Hilda
Goaslind, Rueleen W.
Goetmulder, Betty
Goff, Marion W.
Golding, Gladys
Goodro, Julie
Goodspeed, Muriel L.
Gorder, Joyce
Gordon, Brenda D.
Gordon, Jerry K.
Gordor, Joyce Ohlin
Gore, Cora
Goring, Helen
Gotepas, Lucy
Graff, Elizabeth H.
Graham, Eliza B.
Graham, Elizabeth B.
Grand-Pre, Jean L.
Grant, Grace
Grant, Joyce
Grassli, Michaelene
Grayson, Kathleen
Green, Atilla S.
Green, Mrs. F. W.
Green, Lucy
Green, Otilla
Green, Peggy
Green, Thelma G.
Green, Theola
Greenwood, Louise
Gregerson, Marie
Gregerson, Merle
Griffin, Jayne
Griffith, Marion C.
Groberg, Jean
Groesbeck, Linda
Grossen, Lucille Marie
Grove, Helen
Grover, Corinne
Grundig, Marie
Guerther, Evelyn
Guerther, Renate
Guertler, Christa
Gull, Lavern
Gull, Marion
Gundersen, Melani
Gunderson, Carrol
Gunn, Fanny Louise
Gunn, Nancy
Gunn, Vivian
Gunnerson, Connie
Gunnerson, Evelyn

Gustafson, Diane
Gustaveson, Jane
Gutheil, Frankie H.
Gwaltney, Lillian
Gygi, Ruth
Haberberg, Evelyn A.
Hackwell, Marie
Hadlock, Theresa
Hafen, Barbara
Hahn, Mary Jean
Hale, Rosalind
Hales, Susanna
Hall, Dora
Hall, Exie Webb
Hall, Florence M.
Hall, Gaylynne
Hall, Jean L.
Hall, Katherine
Hall, Valerie N.
Haltiner, Alma Ellis
Halvorsen, Margene
Hamblin, Emmy A.
Hamilton, Barbara
Hamilton, Connie Deane
Hampton, Ray M.
Hampton, Zora
Hancock, Janice
Hansen, Annette
Hansen, Deborah C.
Hansen, Eileen
Hansen, Florence
Hansen, Francille B.
Hansen, Lorraine
Hansen, Louise E.
Hansen, Martha
Hansen, Peggy
Hanson, Josephine
Hanson, Marie Barton
Hanson, Marlene
Harding, Evelyn
Harding, Renee
Hardman, Hazel
Hardy, Nellie Joy
Hardy, Renee
Hardy, Ruth B.
Hardy, Shirlene
Harkness, Elaine
Harline, Ida N.
Harman, Irene
Harmon, Bernice
Harmon, Mary Ann
Harper, Annie
Harper, Cathrine
Harris, Ann
Harris, Barbara
Harris, Elaine
Harris, Myrna Mae
Harris, Terry Ruth
Hartine, Olive
Hartman, Elvia
Harwood, Virginia
Hatch, Annette

Hatch, Karen B.
Hatch, Mary Ann
Hawker, Pam
Hawkins, Ina
Hayes, Beverly
Hayes, Marsha
Hazzard, Mrs. A. S.
Head, Ireta
Heagren, Rose
Heath, Beryl L.
Heath, Darlene
Heath, Terry
Hegessy, Mercedes
Hegewald, Ulrike
Heiman, Betty
Heimen, Phila
Heinhold, Carol Ann
Helgesen, Susan J.
Hellewell, Edith
Helpworth, Christine
Hemkas, Sylvia R.
Hence, Rachel Ann
Henderson, Betty
Henderson, Bonnie C.
Henderson, Irene
Henderson, Loretta
Henderson, RaNae
Hendricksen, Sylva R.
Hendrickson, Rose
Henerson, Eva May
Henrikson, Gretchen
Heppler, Eleanor
Heppley, Hulda
Hepworth, Christine
Herrin, Marion
Hess, Chloe
Hester, Irene
Heuish, Ann
Hewlett, Margaret
Hey, Miriam
Heyborne, Marjorie
Heyn, Renate
Hiatt, Aurora Duncan
Hickman, Olive
Hicks, Melva Jean
Hicks, Ray
Higginson, Nina
Higgs, Afton
Higgs, Lucile
Hildrith, Gailya
Hill, Derilys
Hill, Janice Ray
Hill, Joyce
Hill, Louise
Hills, Della Daynes
Hinckley, Beulah
Hinckley, Elizabeth Scofield
Hinkley, Hortense
Hinkley, Ila B.
Hinkley, Janice
Hinkley, Margaret
Hinkley, Peggy L.

Hinkson, Helen
Hintze, Jeannine L.
Hirth, Lois
Hisatake, Thelma M.
Hoel, Jennie
Hoffar, Mrs. William
Hogan, Betty Jean
Hogan, Patsy
Holdaway, Nellie B.
Holdaway, Ortell
Holfeld, Barbara
Hollings, Bessie
Hollingshead, Edna
Hollingshead, Lillace
Hollis, Mary
Hollstein, Lynne
Holmes, Viola R.
Holt, Hedwig
Holt, Janet D.
Holt, LueGene Tibbetts
Homer, Helen
Horman, Birdie
Horman, Carol L.
Horne, Virginia
Horsen, Helen
Horsley, Violet
Hosking, Annette
Howard, Beverly
Howard, Olivia
Howard, Orchid-Marie
Howard, Rose
Howe, Elaine
Howe, Marline
Howell, Candace Lea
Howell, Jean
Howell, Kathryn
Howell, Mary
Howell, Mary P.
Hubbard, Margaret
Hubbard, Sarah
Huch, Carol
Hughes, Gloria
Huish, Ann V.
Hull, Joyce
Hultman, Carol Jane
Hume, Bonnie
Humphreys, Helen
Hunt, Clarissa
Hunt, Mary
Hurd, M.
Hutchings, Carol
Hyde, Betty
Hyde, Marge
Hyer, Jeen
Ineichen, Nancy
Ingram, Noreen
Inman, Karen K.
Innes, Marilyn
Ipsen, Beatrice W.
Ipson, Lois
Ipson, Marilyn
Ipson, Virginia
Isaacson, Lollie

Isgreen, Louise
Ison, Angela
Iversen, Janet A.
Jackson, Carol
Jackson, Judith W.
Jackson, LaRue
Jackson, Merle
Jacob, Judi
Jacobs, Minnie
Jacobsen, Deanne
Jacobson, Laura
Jacobson, Mary Agnes
Jaqumer, Lois
Jellings, Linda
Jellings, Linda Sue
Jenkins, Elizabeth
Jenkins, Julia
Jenkins, Patricia V.
Jenks, Cathie
Jennings, Dorothy
Jensen, Blanche
Jensen, Hazel
Jensen, Helen Loye
Jensen, Margaret L.
Jensen, Marjorie R.
Jensen, Martha S.
Jensen, Mildred
Jensen, Mona
Jensen, Phyllis
Jensen, Venita
Jentzsch, Carol
Jeppson, Pat
Jeri, Dymock
Jerrell, Joyce
Jewett, Edith L.
Jewkes, Fredwyn
Johansen, Margaret
John, Betty C.
Johnson, Afton
Johnson, Ann Marie
Johnson, Beryl F.
Johnson, Charlotte
Johnson, Dolores
Johnson, Edna Evans
Johnson, Effie
Johnson, Elizabeth
Johnson, Elizabeth M.
Johnson, Ellen B
Johnson, Evelyn
Johnson, Frances
Johnson, Inga
Johnson, Janice
Johnson, Jewel
Johnson, Jill
Johnson, Jo Beth
Johnson, Judy L.
Johnson, Linette
Johnson, Lora
Johnson, LuRaine
Johnson, Mabel
Johnson, Mary L.
Johnson, Nancy Daniella
Johnson, Nancy Lee
Johnson, Nellie
Johnson, Norma
Johnson, Peggy
Johnson, Sharon
Johnson, Sheila Diane
Johnston, Isadora L.
Jonas, Dorothy
Jones, Betty M.
Jones, Eleanor
Jones, Helen B.
Jones, Mrs. J. Henry
Jones, Linda
Jones, Lorraine
Jones, Melba
Jones, Melba Read
Jones, Mildred
Jones, Orlene
Jones, Pat
Jones, Mrs. Ralph M.
Jones, Mrs. Vernon
Jongkles, Jeanette
Joplong, Ethel E.
Judd, Gwenyth
Judd, Jeanette
Judkins, Jill
Justisen, Camile
Kaege, Eugenie V.
Kari, Nakling
Karren, Edna
Katwyk, Darlene
Katz, Mary T.
Keil, Kunig
Keller, Helen
Keller, Katherine
Keller, Lucy
Kelm, Mrs. A. C.
Kendall, Ruth
Kenier, Maude
Kennard, Dorothy
Kennard, Rose
Kennard, Ruth
Kenner, Maude
Kercher, Germa M.
Kesler, Susannah E.
Keys, Sandra
Kienke, Kathryn Rae
Kilbourne, Shirlee
Kilbourne, Shirley
Kimball, Mrs. A. F.
Kimball, Mrs. A. L.
Kimball, Mrs. A. P.
Kimball, Carlin
Kimball, Dorothy
Kimball, Irene M.
King, Mona M.
King, Rose
Kingsbury, Mary
Kirk, LaVern
Kirk, Mabel
Kistner, Dixie
Kitley, Helen
Klein, Ruth
Knapp, Gladys
Knell, Mary L.
Knight, Delores
Knight, Mildred
Knudsen, Kay
Kobs, Barbara
Koch, Katarina
Koch, Mae Dorius
Koch, Zetha
Koch, Zether
Koop, Ramona
Kraft, Christine
Krantz, Jaydene P.
Krantz, Saundra
Krauser, Erna H.
Krogh, Pat
Kruse, Lillian Thorn
Kunz, Belva S.
Kunz, Claudette
Kunz, Virginia Pollard
Kuri, Doreen
Lacey, Barbara M.
Laker, Anna
Lakerveld, Shirley R.
Lamb, Jane
Lamb, Ruth W.
Lambert, Kathleen
Lamberty, Ruth H.
Lamborn, Grace
Lang, Ruth L.
Lange, Beverly M.
Langley, Linda
Langley, Linda L.
Langton, Bonnie
Lanners, Norita
Larsen, Elaine
Larsen, Ellen
Larsen, Katherine T.
Larsen, Mabel
Larsen, Ruth
Larson, Katherine
Larson, Marjory
Larson, Melba
Latimer, Anne G.
Latimer, Clara
Latimer, Emily G.
Latino, Josephine
Laughlin, Annette J.
Laughton, Annette
Laurence, Beth
Law, Ethel
Law, Pauline R.
Lawrence, Mrs. Gayle R.
Lawrence, Sherry
Lawson, Mrs. H. H.
Lawson, Thora
Layton, Shirley
Lazenby, Mildred
Leader, Maude
Leavitt, Merle
Lee, Alice
Lee, Linda
Lee, Marilyn
Lee, Vesta
LeeMaster, Helen P.
Leetham, Jeila
Lefler, L. Marilynn
Leigh, Yvonne
Leininger, Gretchen
Leishman, Marjorie
Lentz, Caroline A.
Lentz, Carolyn
Lewis, Anne Marie
Lewis, Gwen
Lewis, Janet S.
Lewis, Lucy
Lewis-Gibson,Jeanette
Lickey, Mary Brent
Lieber, Miriam
Liechty, Arlene M.
Lies, LaMarti
Lietjen, Ruby Brown
Limarz, Jeannette
Limberg, Mary Alice
Lindberg, Saga
Lindberg, Viola
Linde, Erna
Lindman, Diane
Lindman, Mary Louise
Lindorff, Jo Ann
Lindsay, Linda Lou
Lindsay, Mae
Lindsey, Viona R.
Linnarz, M. Jeannette
Linsey, Renate
Linton, Bernice
Linton, Jean
Linton, Mary
Lisdel, Jane
Little, Christine
Livingston, Louise
Lloyd, Olive
Lloyd, Rehon
Lohner, Margaret
Lollin, Linnie F.
Longe, Genevieve
Love, Clara
Lovendale, Connie O.
Low, Colleen
Lowden, Adrienne
Loy, Alma Lorene
Lozo, Vivian
Luckau, Ruth
Luckey, Frances
Luderer, Flora J.
Luderer, Wally
Lugo, Geraldine
Luke, Diane
Luke, Evelyn
Lukenbach, Mary E.
Lund, Lillian
Lund, Wildene
Lundberg, Merry Alice
Lundquist, Ruth
Lundskog, Margie

Lyman, Coral	Manns, DeAna	Minen, Connie B.	Nelson, Julie
Lyman, Isadora F.	Manookin, Dorothy	Mitchell, Beth C.	Nelson, Lou Etta
Lyman, Mrs. J. T.	Mantle, Ivi	Mitchell, Donna	Nelson, Marian S.
Lyman, Libbie	Manville, Lillian	Mitchell, Loretta	Nelson, Marie Rotzlor
Lyman, Trine A.	Manwaring, Pat	Moench, Melodie	Nelson, Mary
Lynch, Florence	Manwill, Linda	Moesching, Erva	Nelson, Mary Jane
Lyon, Alice	Mapes, Dorothy	Moffat, Patricia	Nelson, Melva
Lyon, Fern	Marin, Dorothy G.	Moise, Alice	Nelson, Pearl Straup
Lyon, Katherine	Marks, Mrs. G. E.	Monfrooy, Kathleen	Nelson, Rose
Lyon, Linda G.	Marks, Narita	Monson, Casse	Nelson, Teckia
Lyon, Margie	Marks, Urita	Monson, Inez	Nelson, Vanesa
Lyon, Norma Ray	Marley, Cora	Monson, Luana Jeanne	Nelson, Zora B.
Macadam, Joyce	Marshall, Dawn	Monson, Marian	Nemelka, Barbara
McAllister,	Marshall, Mrs. E. F.	Montgomery, Suzanne	Neumann, Elvira
Kathleen Collette	Marshall, Mrs. E. T.	Moody, Jane T.	Newell, Barbara
McCallister,	Marshall, Mary W.	Moore, Mrs. Henry I.	Newman, Elvira
Kathy Bloomquist	Marshall, Ruth	Moore, Joycelyn	Nicholes, Lois
McCausland, Helen	Marsteller, Alys	Moore, Mabel	Nicholes, Lois N.
McCleary, Casse M.	Marti, Dawna	Moore, Mavis	Nicholes, Jeanette H.
McClellan, Mary Jo	Martin, Dorothy	Morgan, Alta	Niederhauser, Ella
McCredy,Maria Barone	Martin, Marie	Morgan, Fanny	Nielsen, Afton
McDonald,Ada Russell	Martin, Walli	Morgan, Georgeva G.	Nielsen, D.G.
McDonald, Elaine	Martindale, Lila P.	Morgan, Jan	Nielsen, Mary Ann
McDonald, Lori	Martindale, Lilia	Morgan, Janice	Nielson, Dolores
McDougal,	Martineaux, Ann	Morgan, Sharon	Nielson, Jean
Elizabeth Moulton	Martinsen, Pearl	Morganis, Elsie	Nielson, Judith
McDougal, Evelyn	Marx, Loretta	Morr, Barbara L.	Nielson, Violet
McEntire, Carole	Marx, Marva	Morr, Miriam	Nielson, Virginia
McFarlane, Helen	Mash, Joan E.	Morrell, Lois	Nierderhand, Erica H.
McFarlane, Janice	Massion, Mrs. Lois	Morris, Evelyn	Noall, Lillian
McGavock, Jean	Mather, Jean	Morris, Ida	Nordberg, Elsie
McGreger, Phyllis H.	Mathews, Wanda B.	Morris, Joan	North, Alta
McIntyre, Jerilyn	Matson, Beverly	Morris, Myrthine	Nunley, Sandra T.
McIntyre, Nancy	Matson, Laurel Anne	Morris, Ruth M.	Nutter, Agnes
Mackay, Dixie	Maxfield, Pearl	Morris, Mrs. William	Nyberg, Jean B.
McKay, Dixie L.	May, Joye	Morse, Kay	O'Carrol, Mary
McKell, Jean	Mayo, Arvella	Mortensen, Lucy M.	O'Carrol, Mary H.
Mackie, Ann	Mehl, Mabel E.	Mortensen, Mary L.	O'Neil, Dorothy
McKinnon, Lillian	Mellus, Joyce	Mortenson, Linia	O'Neil, Dorothy E.
McMaster, Clara	Mendenhall, Jane	Moss, Marilyn	O'Neill, Mae
McMillan, Linda B.	Merril, Carol	Moulton, Donna	Obert, Susan
McMillin, Sherry	Merrill, Marge	Moulton, Evelyn	Obert, Susan C.
McMullin, DeNai	Merrill, Sandra	Mount, Barbara Anne	Oblad, Leone
McMullin, Sherry	Mertens, Shirley	Mount, Beryl M.	Ohlson, Barbara
McNamara, Elmeda	Mes, Minie	Moyer, Bernice	Oldham, Phyllis R.
Robinson	Metcalf, Gail Elaine	Mueller, Hannelore	Oleson, Mrs. G.
McPherson, LaPreal	Meyers, Janice	Mueller, Katherine	Oliver, Florence B.
McRae, Carol	Micklejohn, Mickie	Muggleston, Kathleen	Oliverson, Carol
McVey, Norma J.	Midgley, Lucile	Mugleston, Shirley K.	Ollsen, Lucile
Madsen, Alice	Midgley, Pat	Munoz, Myrtle Dahle	Olsen, Donnetta
Madsen, Lois Bullock	Miles, Eunice G.	Myers, Janice L.	Olsen, Gloria
Madsen, Marguerite	Miles, Rae	Myers, Mariana	Olsen, Loretta
Madsen, Marianne	Millard, Lorna	Naegle, Ruby	Olsen, Natalie
Madsen, Phillis	Miller, Anita	Nak, Delia	Olsen, Wanda S.
Malan, Kathleen	Miller, Dorothy	Nakling, Kari	Olsen, Wanda Young
Mallette, Nada	Miller, Elva	Nance, Sally	Olson, Alice Irene
Mallory, Sheila	Miller, Jay	Naukjoks, Edith	Olson, Doral Rae
Maniwell,	Miller, Martha	Naylor, Eleanor	Olson, Jean
Connie Brinton	Miller, Minerva G.	Neal, Edith	Olson, JoAnn
Mann, Lorinda L.	Miller, Patricia	Needham, Anna B.	Omer, Danielle
Mann, Nancy	Miller, Tressa L.	Neff, Helen L.	Orlob, Maurine
Manning, Ann	Milner, Annie W.	Nelson, Carol W.	Ormsby, Grace S.

Osborn, Mrs. C. M.	Peterson, Christa	Ray, Janice	Robinson, Mary A.
Osborn, Ella W.	Peterson, Janet	Ray, Mrs. Lucian	Robinson, Sadie
Osborn, Louise	Peterson, Melba	Ray, Margaret	Robison, Pearl
Osguthorpe, Allyce S.	Peterson, Nancy J.	Ray, Ruth Velene	Roden, Diane
Osguthorpe, Bernice	Peterson, Patsy	Ray, Virginia	Rodgers, Cora
Osness, Carol	Peterson, Peggy	Raymond, Carol	Rodgers, Jo Ann
Oss, Bonnie Jean	Peterson, Rilla W.	Read, Clytie	Rodgers, Sally
Ostermiller, Bernice	Pettigrew, Caroline	Read, Lucy R.	Rogers, Alrene B.
Ostertag, Marianne T.	Pettigrew, Edith Ann	Reber, Christine S.	Rogers, Mrs. Coran
Overly, Connie	Pettigrew, Mary Carol	Redford, Janice	Rogers, Janet
Owen, Ruby N.	Pettit, Patricia	Reed, Barbara	Rogers, Lillis J.
Pack, Karla Mae	Petty, De Lone	Reed, Jean	Rogers, Lucile
Pack, Mary Lou	Pfaff, Shauna Ball	Reed, Linda	Rogers, Patricia
Pack, Valaine	Pfeifer, June C.	Reed, Marian A.	Rollins, Joan
Paget, Cindy	Phillips,	Reed, Nyla	Rollins, Kerril Sue
Palfreyman, Helen	Pauline Thomas	Reed, Sarah K.	Romney, Emma Lou
Palmer, Beverly	Pierce, Louise	Rees, Marjorie	Rosen, Linda
Palmer, Faye	Pingree, Patricia	Rees, Phyllis C.	Rosenhan, Erma
Palmer, Sarah	Pixton, FayAnn	Reese, Mary M.	Rosenhan, Erusa
Palmer, Sue	Pixton, Natalie	Reese, Noralee	Ross, Lucile
Palmer, Susan Evelyn	Plaas, Kristina M.	Regnier, Annette F.	Rossiter, Betty
Paluso, Eva	Platt, Noel A.	Reid, Mrs. C. W.	Rossiter, Minnie
Papworth, Isabelle J.	Plescia, Rae	Reiley, Josephine	Rossiter, Venus R.
Park, Karla Mae	Poch, Ollie	Reiman, Jolene	Rotzler, Marie
Park, Martha Jo	Politovitz, Nona	Reynolds, Eleanore J.	Roubicek, Eva M.
Parker, Barbara Jean	Pollard, Ruby	Reynolds, Julie Anne	Rowland,Mrs.Lewis B.
Parker, Jackie O.	Pollard, Ruth	Rhees, Carol	Rowley, Aleene S.
Parkinson,	Pollard, Virginia	Rhoades, Diana	Rudy, Miriam
Mrs. Harold B.	Pond, Terry L.	Rhoades, Diane	Rupper, Virginia
Parkinson, Marilyn	Pope, Lucile	Ribner, Mrs. Rose	Rushforth, Kay
Parks, Dorothy	Porter, Beverly	Rice, Fuchia	Rushton, Nancy Jo
Parr, Joan	Porter, Sadie	Rice, Twila	Rushton, Virginia
Parry, Dorothy R.	Poulton, Annie	Rich, Mamie	Rusmussen, Ann
Parry, Linda May	Prance, Elizabeth Jean	Rich, Oive N.	Russell, Linda
Parsons, Shirley	Prance, Elizabeth R.	Rich, Mrs. William L.	Russell, Margaret J.
Patrick, Faye	Price, Avon A.	Richard,	Sackett, Charlotte O.
Patterson, Janice	Price, Mrs. Joseph P.	Mrs. H. Handrey	Safford, Jeanne
Patterson, Joyce	Pronty, Alvira	Richards, Alice	Sagebeil, Kercher
Paulsen, Bonnie	Pugmire, Laura	Richards, Mrs. H. V.	Salmon, Irene
Pearce, Agnes	Pugsley, Nellie	Richards, Marjorie	Sanborn, Susanne
Pearce, Mary Lynne	Pulley, Carol	Richards, Romay	Sandall, Leonora
Pearson, Evelyn	Pulver, LaVena	Richards, Mrs. T. C.	Sandberg, Norma
Pearson, Gussie	Purrington, Joy	Richards, Telle C.	Sanders, Georgia
Pearson, Mrs. John	Pursley, Tanya Kim	Richards, Wanda	Sandom, Vinnie H.
Pearson, Nancy Rae	Putman, Valois	Richardson, Nora P.	Sanone, Detta H.
Peck, Karla Mae	Putnam, Janice	Richardson, Sonia L.	Sansom, Vinnie H.
Peck, Marnelle	Pyper, Afton	Richardson, Virginia E.	Sargent, Alice
Peck, Marnie	Quigley, Nellie	Richman, Carole	Savage, Cherie
Peck, O. Shirley	Quistberg, Jeanine	Ricks, Jeanette	Saville, Adele
Peck, Shirlene	Quistberg, Judy	Rigley, Joanne	Saville, Betty Jean
Pederson, Arlene	Raad, Lucy R.	Ririe, Connie	Saville, Dora
Pederson, Jennie	Ralph, Frances	Ritchie, Vera	Saville, Ione
Peggs, Ireane D.	Ranch, Georgine	Ritley, Helen	Saville, Mrs. Leslie
Pence, Carlene	Randall, Beryl	Roberts, Glenda	Saville, Pat
Pendleton, Rulene	Randall, Karen	Roberts, Ilene	Schaerrer, Jane
Penrose, Marjory	Rankin, Ethel L.	Roberts, Kathleen	Schaferle, Mary Helen
Perkins, Billie J.	Rasmussen, Anne	Robertson, LaNore	Schauerhamer, Sue
Perkins, Donna	Rasmussen, Margaret	Robinson, Bonnie	Schaum, Hilda
Persons, Katherine B.	Rasmusson, Von	Robinson, Florence	Scheiner, Merle
Petersen, Karen	Ratz, Mary T.	Robinson, Jackie	Schick, Alice L.
Peterson, Adell	Rawlins, Carol	Robinson, Loretta	Schick, Alice Louise
Peterson, Ann	Rawson, Janet	Robinson, Lottie	Schmelter, Crista

Schmidt, Clara	Simpson, Mrs. Andrey	Soper, Lucille	Stoker, Karen
Schmidt, Evelyn	Simpson, Audrey	Sorensen, Irene	Stokes, Winnie
Schmidt, Gerda	Simpson, Elizabeth Hayes	Sorg, Kathleen A.	Stonoish, Florence E.
Schoenhals, Carol	Sinclair, Gladys	Sorg, Kathy	Stovall, Lucile
Schoepf, Marie	Sinefis, Amy	Spall, Florence	Strachan, Diane S.
Schreiner, Julianne	Sirrine, Marilyn Davis	Sparks, Janeen	Straup, Pearl
Schreiner, Merle A.	Sjostrom, Evalyn	Spencer, Emaline	Straup, Viola Holmes
Schumann, Allie	Sjostrom, Lillian N.	Spencer, Florence	Strecker, Wanda E.
Schumann, Alma	Skidmore, Helen	Spencer, Joan	Streeper, Mildred
Scopes, Mary Aye	Skinner, Joan W.	Spencer, Mary C. Pettigrew	Streeter, Mrs. Randolph
Scott, Judith	Slagowski, Betty	Spiker, Patricia	Strickley, Dora Jane
Scott, Mrs. Sara E.	Slagowski, Janette	Spilker, Christa	Strong, Joyce
Seal, Dolores	Slagowski, LaFaun	Spiller, Mrs. R.	Strong, LaPriel
Seaman, Edna	Slater, Marie A.	Spilsbury, Lezlee Ann	Stroud, Mary Ann
Seaman, Vicki Lee	Slight, Gayle	Spitko, Dolores	Stuman, Betty Ann
Seamons, Elvina H.	Sloan, Shauna W.	Springer, Janna	Sugden, Verda
Seamons, Julene H.	Smethurst, Joan	Squires, Victoria	Sullivan, Kathryn W.
Searing, Kathleen	Smiley, Sherril	Stack, Catherine E.	Summerhays, Alleyne
Searle, Nadine R.	Smith, Adelade	Stam, Emmy	Summerhays, Florence
Seely, Lucy B.	Smith, Anna	Stam, LaVern	Summerhays, Margaret
Self, Beatrice D.	Smith, Beverly	Standing, Gwen French	Summerson, Margaret
Self, Camilla	Smith, Mrs. D. E.	Stands, Ms.	Sundstrom, Elizabeth
Seltzer, Emily	Smith, Dianne	Stapley, Diane	Swallow, Cheryl
Sessions, Bertha	Smith, Dixie	Stapley, Sherrie	Swan, Helen J.
Sewalson, Mary Anne	Smith, Elaine	Stark, Lorrie Lou	Swan, Margaret
Shafer, Bonnie	Smith, Esther Julia	Stark, Mary Baker	Sweet, Martha Jane
Sharon, Frances	Smith, Florence S.	Stark, Nanna May	Swensen, Tracy Lee
Sharp, Chloe	Smith, Grace	Starks, Betty	Swenson, Doloris
Sharp, Luella F.	Smith, Jean Ann	Steadman, G. Valarie	Swenson, Geraldine
Sharp, Nearah	Smith, Kathryn Young	Steadman, Ruth	Swenson, Lynda
Sheets, Mrs. R.	Smith, Kelly	Steadman, Valarie G.	Swenson, Tracy
Sheffield, Charlotte	Smith, Leda	Steele, Erma E.	Syphus, Sharlene
Sheldon, Elizabeth C.	Smith, Leonora S.	Steinaker, LaMon	Taggart, Blanche
Shelledy, Dolores	Smith, Lovena	Steinmetz, Evelyn	Tanner, Gayle
Sheranian, Rose	Smith, Lydia H.	Stenoish, Florence	Tanner, Joan
Sherman, Rosa	Smith, Marjory Helen	Stephan, Olive	Tanner, Joyce
Sherwood, Mary	Smith, Mary Carol	Stephens, Esther Davis	Tarr, Alice Irene
Shewell, Kris E.	Smith, Mary S.	Stephens, Laura M.	Tarver, Ruth
Shewell, Victoria	Smith, Melba	Stephens, Marsha Gayle	Tate, Charlene
Shields, Helen	Smith, Minnie	Stephenson, Karalee G.	Tate, Joyce
Shimizu, Junko	Smith, Patricia	Stevens, Betty	Taylor, Anna
Shimmin, Jacquie	Smith, Rose	Stevens, Erma	Taylor, Edna
Shipp, Roberta	Smith, Rosemary	Stevens, Esther	Taylor, Esther
Shirts, Linda	Smith, Sylvia	Stevens, Jennie	Taylor, Jean
Shockley, Verna Lee	Smith, Wilma	Stevens, Ruth	Taylor, Joyce
Short, Irene	Smith, Winnifred	Stevens, Violet M.	Taylor, June Burns
Showalter, Ann	Smithen, Rose	Stevenson, Marilyn	Taylor, Lela
Shrader, Bonnie Lue	Smurthwait, Mary	Stewart, Ann Huish	Taylor, Lillian
Shuman, Della	Smurthwaite, Diane	Stewart, Diane	Taylor, Lola G.
Shurtliff, Carol Jean	Snell, Ivy B.	Stewart, Emma	Taylor, Marilyn
Shurtliff, Emily	Snethen, Marie C.	Stewart, Grace	Taylor, Mary Jean
Shurtliff, Lillian	Snow, Denice	Stewart, Jessie	Taylor, Sharon
Shutt, Doris	Snow, Patricia	Stewart, Mary	Tefteller, Anne T.
Shutt, Vera	Snow, Phyllis	Stewart, Myra	Tegge, Elvira H.
Siegmann, Ella	Snyder, Ruth Ann	Stewart, Valoise	Terry, Jennette
Sigley, Mary	Soderberg, Jean	Stewart, Vera	Terry, Virginia
Silveira, Norma Marie	Sohn, Hannah	Stocker, Wanda	Thalman, Joy M.
Simmons, Ruth	Sohn, Larina	Stockman, Mrs. D. D.	Thayn, Patricia E.
Simons, Barbara	Sondeno, Katherine Louise	Stockseth, Virginia Gunn	Thomas, Afton
Simons, Crista	Soopes, Mary		Thomas, Delight
Simper, Beatrice			Thomas, Ethel
Simper, LaRue			Thomas, Jean

Thomas, Jennie	Veasy, Hazel	Welling, Mrs. H. S.	Wilson, Barbara
Thomas, Mrs. Julian	Verde, Catherine	Welling, Leah	Wilson, Janice
Thomas, Lillian	Verniew, Lucill	Wells, Madelyn B.	Wilson, Marie
Thomas, Pauline	Vincent, Norita S.	Wells, Mary Garff	Winn, Cherry Ann
Thomas, Polly	Visser, Mirjam	Weseman, Elizabeth	Winn, Irma W.
Thome, Caroline Paul	Voegeler, Annie E.	Westmoreland, Melodee Ann	Winsor, Viola E.
Thompson, Anita	Voelker, Eleanore	Westwood, Rhea	Winter, Nancy
Thompson, Audrey	Voris, Evelyn	Wetzel, Alice	Wiscomb, Flora
Thompson, Diana	Voris, Peggy H.	Wetzel, Mrs. V.	Wiseman, Elizabeth
Thompson, Lissa K.	Vorkink, Connie	Wetzel, Virtue C.	Wiseman, Louise
Thompson, Violet	Voyles, Evelyn	Weyler, Evelyn	Wojtowicz, Nancy
Thompson, Willissa	Wach, Elizabeth O.	Wharton, Mary Ellen	Wood, Carol
Thomson, Audrey	Wadsworth, Reva	Wheeler, Alison	Wood, Dorothy
Thomson, Dixie	Wadsworth, Reva M.	Wheeler, Veneta	Wood, Geraldine Chytraus
Thorn, Jessie L.	Wahlen, Sherry L.	Whipple, Inez Lou	Wood, Karen
Thorn, Lillian	Waite, Helen E.	Whitaker, Maurine	Wood Kathleen
Thornell, Robyn Jean	Wakefield, Anne	Whitchurch, Mary J.	Wood, Mrs. Joseph
Thornley, Alice	Waldron, Enid W.	White, Barbara Eccles	Wood, Loretta S.
Thornton, Debbie	Walker, Ada	White, Dorothy J.	Wood, Picola
Thornton, Joan E.	Walker, Cherri Ann	White, Dorothy Jane	Wood, Sarah
Thornton, Lorraine	Walker, Marian	White, Geneva	Woodbury, Jilate
Thornton, Peggy Lee	Walker, Pearl E.	White, Viola	Woodhouse, Sandra
Thorpe, Annette C.	Walkingshaw, Pauline	Whitelock, Ingeborg	Woodland, Dianne
Thorpe, Shanna	Wall, Linda Lee	Whitman, Virginia	Woodruff, Shirley
Throckmorton, Elsie	Waller, Pauline	Whitney, Roene	Woods, Emily S.
Thurman, Ena	Walton, Jetta	Whittier, Mary	Wooley, Carol
Tibbitts, Joycelyn	Walton, Phyllis	Whitton, Eluned	Woolley, Marilyn
Tibbitts, Lue Gene	Ward, Winonia	Wignall, Jeanne	Woolley, Wendy K.
Tietjen, Ruby	Wards, Evelyn	Wilcox, Elen M.	Woolsey, Enid
Timothy, Agnes	Wark, Marilyn	Wilcox, Helen	Woolsey, Grace Welch
Tingey, Judy Kay	Warner, Mrs.	Wilcox, Louise	Worsley, Emma
Tipton, Hattie	Warner, Agnes B.	Wilcox, Marie	Worsley, Grace
Tischner, Fran	Warner, Darlene	Wilde, Dolores	Worth, Lily May
Tischner, Pat	Warner, Hester	Wilkin, Rose F.	Wren, Rylma
Tisdel, Jane	Wasden, Mamie L.	Wilkins, Rose	Wride, Prudence
Tobias, Virginia M.	Watkins, Lynn	Wilkinson, Suzanne	Wright, Genevieve
Tobiason, Virginia	Watkins, Pamela	Willard, Nancy	Wright, Jeralynn
Todd, Blanche	Watkins, Sidney A.	Willardsen, Dorothy Beck	Wright, Jerry
Todd, Eleanor	Watson, Elaine	Wille, Baerbel	Wright, Karen
Topping, Isabel	Watson, Kathryn	Wille, Klara	Wright, Lillian
Torres, Mary	Watson, Louise	Williams, Anna	Wright, Marci
Truman, Carolyn	Watson, Marilyn Jayne	Williams, Betty	Wright, Mitzi D.
Tuckett, Phyllis	Watts, Ruth	Williams, Charlie	Wright, Noreen Ingram
Tyler, Louanne	Watts, Ruth L.	Williams, Dianne	Wugh, Martha
Tyler, Mrs. W. A.	Wauschope, Donna	Williams, Dorothy	Wynn, Irma W.
Uhlenberg, Beverly	Weart, Hilda	Williams, Gayle	Yazdani, Carolyn
Valtri, Mrs. Ben	Weaver, Elizabeth	Williams, Holly	Young, Jeanet
Van Dam, Martha	Weaver, Sylvia	Williams, Janet H.	Young, Malta
Van Der Meyden, Bonnie	Webb, Janice	Williams, Julie	Young, Mary R.
Van Der Meyden, Connie	Weber, Gladys M	Williams, Katherine	Young, Renee
Van Der Weil, Ms.	Weber, Louise A.	Williams, Margaret	Young, Valeria B.
Van Gelderen, Sherrie	Weeks, Veronica	Williams, Marguerite	Young, Wanda S.
Van Horn, Nellie	Wegener, Anna M.	Williams, Marjorie	Young, Wilma
Van Lyes, Andrea	Wehili, Ursula	Williams, Marsha	Zachres, Janet
Van Noy, Coleen	Weiss, Gerri	Williams, Susan N.	Zancanella, Pat
Van Soters, Joan Parr	Wekson, Beatrice	Williams, Utahna	Zielke, Loria
Van Tielen, Hanna	Welch, Donna	Williamson, Mary	Zoetmulder, Betty
Van Tussenbrock, Kathy	Welch, Gertrude	Willis, Gayle	Zunbrun, Edna
Van Zelin, Willy	Welch, Grace	Willoughby, Ardis	
	Welch, Lonna	Wilson, Ann	
	Welch, Sereta		
	Weller, Miriam M.		

Altos

Aagard, Rita L.
Aamodt, Ruth
Abegg, Louise
Abrams, Veloy
Acheson, Lynnette
Adams, Ann
Adams, Dorothy
Adamson, Kathleen
Adamson, Nancy B.
Adamson, Sheri
Adler, Mae C.
Adolf, Arlis M.
Aird, Eva
Alder, Diane
Alder, Mae C.
Alder, Rita V.
Aldous, Elma Y.
Aldous, Millie
Aldous, Mrs. Ralph
Aldredge, Kathryn
Alfreds, Vera L.
Alleman, Alma F.
Allen, Florence
Allen, Mary E.
Allison, Doris
Allred, Bernice
Allred, Cheryl M.
Alston, Lillian
Alvey, Barbara
Ames, Jeanne
Ammott, Leone
Anderson, Annie
Anderson, Birdie
Anderson, Elizabeth G.
Anderson, Ellen
Anderson, Elsie
Anderson, Erika
Anderson, Ethel
Anderson, Eunice Edwards
Anderson, Ilene S.
Anderson, Jo Ann
Anderson, Joyce H.
Anderson, Julie C.
Anderson, Kathleen
Anderson, Leesa
Anderson, Lou Ann
Anderson, Mrs. Levar
Anderson, Shirley
Anderson, Suzanne
Anderson, Valane
Andrew, Winifred
Andrus, Dorothy
Andrus, Ruth C.
Angel, Mildred
Angell, Margie
Angelos, Caryl B.
Angerbauer, Betty
Anlersen, Elsie V.
Anton, Marie
Aragoni, Eugenia
Arbuckle, Cornelia
Archibald, Karen V.
Arnell, Bonnie Mae Peterson
Arnold, Elaine W.
Arnold, Margaret
Arntz, Janis M.
Arrington, Linda K.
Ashton, Janiel
Ashton, Leah
Ashton, Mary Ruth
Ashton, Pattie
Asper, Marguerite
Asplund, Mable
Assay, Marrilyn Loreen
Ayland, Florence
Azleth, Ann
Bacon, Bonnie Jean
Bacon, JoAnne
Badger, Doris M.
Baer, Mary Lynn
Baer, Rebecca Jane
Baer, Rienkje
Bagley, Elaine
Bagley, Marie
Bagley, Marta K.
Bahr, Sherrie E.
Bailey, Lucy G.
Bailey, Ruth J.
Bair, Janice
Baird, Madge
Baker, Moneta A.
Baker, Moneta S.
Baker, Ruth E.
Bakker, Audrey
Bakker, Verla B.
Ball, Cathryne B.
Ball, Cathryne S.
Ballard, Katheryn
Banks, Dale
Barber, Cora Rideout
Bard, Wilma
Barker, Geralda
Barker, Joanne
Barkley, Sarah E.
Barlow, Lois
Barlow, Patricia
Barlow, Patricia L.
Barnett, Marlene
Barnett, Mary
Barnett, Pat
Barnhart, Diane
Barns, Mary Alice
Barr, Alicia
Barr, Lois
Barrus, Norene
Barrus, Patt Lee
Bartko, Margot
Barton, Beth
Basinger, Jane
Basinger, Norma Jean
Bates, Beth
Bates, Margo
Batson, Marjorie Larson
Baumberger, Eloise
Baxter, Donna R.
Baxter, Susan
Beach, Lois
Beach, Mary
Beales, Jean Alaine
Bean, Helene
Bear, Helen
Beatty, Dorothy S.
Beazer, Christine
Beck, Dorothy Ence
Beck, V. Marie
Beeley, Joan B.
Beesinger, Lucille
Beesley, Evangeline
Beesley, Janice
Behunin, Joan
Beless, Edith
Bell, Bonnie
Bell, Faye B.
Bell, Mary
Bell, Melva J.
Bell, Pat Wakefield
Bell, Rose Marie
Bell, Sandra S.
Belliston, Donna
Belliston, Elizabeth Ann
Belliston, Iris
Belnap, Mary Elen
Belt, LuAnn
Belt, Nellie
Bement, Edna M.
Bench, Lanez
Beninberger, Eloise
Beninberger, Marjory
Benjamin, Gertrude E.
Benjamin, Mrs. Warren
Bennett, Ann
Bennett, Elaine
Bennett, Lily
Bennett, Mary Elen
Bennett, Shamra
Bennett, Susan
Bennion, Ann
Bennion, Bernice
Bennion, Carolyn
Bennion, Esther
Bennion, Florence
Bennion, Jean
Berger, Addie
Bergeson, Truda
Berndt, Kristie
Bernstein, Shalene W.
Bernstiel, Elke
Berrett, Eleanor
Berry, Mildred
Beuhler, Evelyn
Biesinger, Margaret
Billiston, Elizabeth
Bingham, Helen
Bintz, Dottie C.
Bird, Colleen M.
Bird, Ethel
Bishop, Brenda
Bishop, Mamie
Bitner, Helen
Bitner, Joan
Bitton, Betty
Black, Evelyn Peach
Black, Joan
Blackburn, Clyda
Blackemore, Erma
Blackhurst, Joan
Blake, Margeret R.
Blanchard, Gay N.
Blau, Henrietta
Bliss, Mrs. Walter
Blomquist, Dorothy
Bly, Joan A.
Boede, Irene
Boelter, Ethel
Boer, Rienkje
Boffinger, Ilene M.
Boggess, Marilyn
Bogh, Julia M.
Bollter, Ethel
Bolster, Carol E.
Bolto, Agnes
Booth, Betty
Booth, Elizabeth
Booth, Ida S.
Bott, Henrietta
Bowen, Betsy
Bowen, Elizabeth
Bowen, Saura J.
Bower, Winifred
Bowers, Jerry
Bowles, Allene
Bowman, Alice
Bowman, Nina N.
Boyd, Evelyn B.
Boyer, Donita
Boyer, Vivian D.
Bracken, Effie
Bradford, Gerri
Bradford, Afton
Bradford, Beth
Bradford, Lisle
Bradshaw, Josephine C.
Brady, Jean E.
Bratt, Barbara
Bresinger, Margaret

Brewer, Glennice C.	Butters, Sharolyn	Child, Alta	Cone, Catherine
Brewer, Judy L.	Bywater, Ila	Child, Carol C.	Conner, Rachel
Brienart, Ida E.	Cagle, Eila D.	Childs, Pauline O.	Conover, Ina
Brines, Myrtle	Cahoon, Mrs. L. B.	Christensen, Barbara Paul	Cook, Elsie
Brinton, Jane	Cahoon, Marion Jane	Christensen, Betty Jo	Cook, Idonna H.
Broadbent, June	Calderwood, Edna	Christensen, CloAnn Mason	Cook, Mabel
Brown, Ada	Calderwood, Mildred	Christensen, Joan	Cook, Myrtle
Brown, Bessie	Caldwell, Lois	Christensen, Marie D.	Cook, Susan
Brown, Beverly	Call, Ann	Christensen, Marie H.	Cook, Wilma
Brown, Delilah	Call, Carolyn	Christensen, Opal	Coombs, Mildred E.
Brown, Gayle	Call, Cathryn	Christensen, Pat	Coombs, Shirley
Brown, Irma	Callihan, Linda	Christensen, Verda	Coon, Mary
Brown, Jean	Calvert, Myrna Lee	Christenson, Barbara	Coon, Vickie Lee
Brown, LaRue	Cameron, Betty	Christian, Dorothy	Cooper, Darlynn
Brown, Margaret S.	Cameron, Grace	Christiansen, Irene	Cooper, Elaine
Brown, Maryetta	Campbell, Carolyn	Christiansen, Terie Jujean	Cordery, Eva Hook
Brown, Orpha S.	Campbell, Gayle B.	Christisonn, Barbara A.	Cordon, Carol
Brown, Sue J.	Campbell, Joanne	Christopher, Mrs. M. A.	Cornwall, Cleone
Brown, Thelma	Canady, Frances E.	Christopherson, Ann A.	Cornwall, Clo Donaldson
Browning, Etta	Cannon, Jean	Christopherson, Dagmar	Cornwall, Lottie
Bruce, Wanza	Cannon, Margaret S.	Christopherson, Effie	Cornwall, Millicent
Brumit, Helen	Capener, Ellen Edgington	Christopherson, Joan	Cornwall, Shirley W.
Brunatti, Doris M.	Caplain, Mrs. Ruth	Church, Annette B.	Corpron, Christine Vivian
Bruner, Susan L..	Captain, Mrs. Gus	Churchtown, Jane M.	Corry, Beth
Brunnt, Helen	Cardon, Carol	Churchtown, Kathleen A.	Cottrell, Joan H.
Brunson, Monti Rae	Carlisle, Mary H.	Clapin, La Vern	Covey, Marilyn
Brynola, Dorothy	Carlson, Erma Pendleton	Clapp, Martha	Cowan, Corene
Buehler, Miss	Carlson, Ingrid	Clark, Bettie Wiscomb	Cowley, LaVon C.
Buehler, Evelyn	Carlson, Jean	Clark, Carol Lauraine	Cox, Patricia R.
Buie, Connie C.	Carlson, Loraine	Clark, Estella	Craig, Louise
Bullen, Nancy	Carlston, Barbara Hull	Clark, Esther Marlene	Crandall, Alice
Burdette, Betty	Carlston, Janet	Clark, Helen E.	Crandall, Alice M. S.
Burdette, Beverly W.	Carman, Mary Jane G.	Clark, Karen R.	Craven, Joyce B.
Burgener, Patricia	Carmichael, Dorothy Ann	Clark, Marjorie	Craven, Yvonne
Burgess, Lurrene	Carpenter, Winifred	Clarke Jerrie	Crawford, Jane
Burgon, LaRee	Carr, Barbara	Clarke, Ruth	Crawford, Peggy
Burgoyne, Ann	Carr, Beverly F.	Claus, Rienkje	Creer, Jennie
Burgoyne, Julia B.	Carratelli, Virginia A.	Clausing, Brenda	Crisman, Connie Leonudakis
Burnett, Marge	Carrigan, Ann	Clawson, Barbara	Crofts, Marcia R.
Burnham, Suzanne	Carroll, Charleen	Clawson, Beth Bates	Cromar, Rozella
Burningham, Joan	Carver, Agnes	Clawson, Gertrude R.	Crosby, Marcia
Burns, Ariel	Carver, Julia	Clawson, Z. Claire	Cross, Ada
Burns, Grace	Cary, Barbara	Clayton, Patricia	Culley, Mrs. John
Burris, Arnel	Case, Delores	Clegg, Delma	Cullimore, Sandra V.
Burrows, Abbie	Casper, Diane	Cline, Jenalyn G.	Cullimore, Venice
Burrows, Amelia Church	Casper, Lu Dawn	Coffey, Sally K.	Cullingworth, Lillian B.
Burrows, Annette	Cazakas, Barbara	Cohn, Edna	Cundick, Adrienne
Burrows, Jesse K.	Cederstrom, Beth R.	Cole, Gay	Cunningham, Elizabeth N.
Burrows, Nancy A.	Chadwick, Barbara	Cole, Nell	Cunningham, Mrs. V. E.
Burrows, Naomi	Chamberlaine, Amelia	Collett, Roberta	Curtis, Alice
Burt, Shanna	Chamberlin, Lucy	Collier, Avis J.	Curtis, Bardella
Burton, Elaine	Chambers, Leone	Collier, Gladys E.	Curtis, Dorothy
Burton, Janice	Chapman, Theone B.	Collier, Virginia	Curtis, Elsie
Burton, Mary	Chappuis, Emily	Collingwood, Lucy	Curtis, Ilsa
Burton, Mildred	Charles, Norma J.	Collingwood, Ruth	Curtis, Sandra L.
Busath, Beth	Chatelain, Sharon	Colt, Virginia	Curtis, Shauna
Busath, Karen	Cheshire, Lydia M.	Colyar, Avis	Cushman, Emma
Bushnell, Shaun N.	Chesley, Gwen W.		
Butcherest, Alice	Chew, Dorothy		
Butler, Beth			
Butler, Margot			

Cutler, Durella	Dickerson,Mrs. Roy E.	Engar, Kristie B.	Field, Mrs. Logan
Cutler, Eunice	Dixon, Crissie P.	England, Charlotte	Fife, Joan
Cutler, Kate W.	Dixon, Deena R.	England, Lara	Fitt, Linda
Cutler, Sharlene	Domack, Sue	England, Rae Bryan	Flandro, Beverly
Dalby, Frances	Donavan, Sheri A.	English, Sherryl	Flanigan, Joy Carol
Dalebout, Diana	Done, Valerie	Ensign, Ivie	Flatley,
Dalrymple, Louise	Doran, Jane	Ensign, May Wood	Kathleen Nancy
Dalton, Kathie L.	Doras, Elke B.	Epperson, Mrs. L. T.	Fleming, Betty Lou
Dangerfield, Fay	Dowse, Julie	Epperson,	Flemming, Hazel
Daniels, Sarah	Doyle, Mary S.	Margaret Ann	Fletcher, Rosanne
Dansie, Dorothy	Dozie, Ardieva	Epperson, Ruby	Fletcher,
Dansie, Tasma	Draney, Lois	Erekson, Erica Ann	Sandra Louise
Davidson, Inge S.	Draper, Dorothy	Erickson, Gwendolyn	Flint, Alice H.
Davidson, Irene	Draper, LaMar	Erickson, Melba	Flora, Elmia
Davidson, Trude E.	Drummenhausen,	Erickson, Violet	Florence, Glade
Davie, Valerie	Esther	Ernshaw, Elva	Florence, Shirley
Davies, Dawna	Dumayne, Anna Lee	Ernst, Anneliese	Fluckiger, Louise W.
Davies, E. Jean	Duncan, Mrs. C. S.	Erskine, Kathy	Folsom, Nancy
Davies, Lillian	Duncan, Ione	Esterak, Winnie	Fong, Kim
Davis, Blanche	Duncan, Lewia C.	Ethel, Helberg	Foote, Norma
Davis, Carol	Duncan, Marie	Ethington, Ellen June	Forsman, Olga
Davis, Erma	Duncan, Virginia	Ettrick, Inga R.	Fowler,
Davis, Esther	Duncombe, Leah	Evans, Asenath	Carol Jacobsen
Davis, Hazel	Dunford, Diane	Evans, Bonnie	Fox, Lucy Grant
Davis, Jacoba	Dunford, Dolores	Evans, Carolyn	Fox, Maurya M.
Davis, Lillian	Dunyon, Joleen	Evans, Elva	Foxley, Grace
Davis, Linda	Durrant, Ardelle	Evans, Glenda	Franc, Ida
Davis, Lorraine	Dye, Myrle	Evans, Jerry B.	Franke, Anneliese
Davis, Rosalie Ann	Dyer, Raquel P.	Evans, Jessie	Franke, Anneliese S.
Davis, Valerie	Earl, Annette Garff	Evans, Joyce	Freeman, Dee
Davison, Janet	Earl, Thelma	Evans, Linda M.	Freeman, Elaine
Dawson, Elizabeth	Earnshaw, Elva	Evans, Marilouise	French, Ella
Daynes, Barbara	Earnshaw, Florence	Evans, Ruth Clark	French, Gwen
Dean, Luzzette	Eastwood, Connie	Everett, Blanche	Freund, Patricia
Dean, Sylvia W.	Ebaugh, Mrs. W. C.	Ewig, Kristie M.	Frey, Goldie
Dearden, Joyce	Eborn, Jeannine A.	Faber, Paula	Frost, Cathy
Deardorff, Betty Jean	Eccles, Carolyn	Fail, Mrs. A. K.	Frost, Rosalie R.
DeBoise, Patricia A.	Edgington, Mrs. C. W.	Fail, Margaret	Frye, Korinne K.
DeBry, JoAnn	Edgington, Eleanor	Fairchild, Lee Ann	Fryer, Maisie B.
Decker, Gladys	Edgington, Ellen	Falkner, Connie	Fuller, Lael J.
Decker, Marjorie	Edgington, Isabel	Fall, Mrs. A. K.	Fullmer, Maud S.
Decker, Mary	Edwards, Edna	Fallows, Lorna	Fullmer, Mrs. N. O.
DeJong, Patricia J.	Edwards, Helen	Falsetti, Rose	Fullmer, Pearl
DeLange, Jennie	Edwards, Jean	Fanning, Audrey Ann	Furner, Duffie
Della-Piana, Ilene B.	Edwards, May	Farley, Vivia	Fyfe, Joan
DeLoney, Wilma	Egan, Mrs. A. J.	Farr, Marion Ipson	Gaddis, Irene Covey
Dennison, Sarah T.	Egan, Mrs. A. T.	Farr, Mary Lou	Gail, Mrs. A. K.
Denny, Joyce B.	Egan, Minnie W.	Faulkner, Seena Lee	Gale, Ella
Derrick, Joyce L.	Eggers, Lorraine	Faux, Yvonne	Gale, LuJean
Derricot,	Eggert, Joanne	Fechser, Joan	Gardner, Alaine B.
Carolyn Evans	Ekins, Dana S.	Felt, Marion	Gardner, Annie B.
DeSpain, Lillie	Eliason, Leone H.	Ferguson, Jane	Gardner,
Devey, Dowena	Elkins, Alice Davis	Ferguson, Mary S.	Helen Richards
DeVries, Jeanine	Ellen, June Ethington	Ferrell, Florence	Gardner, J. Alaine
DeVries, Jeannie A.	Ellington, Ellen June	Ferrin, Minnie	Gardner, Mariel Pack
DeWit, Mary	Ellis, Barbara J.	Feser, Bonnie Jean B.	Gardner, Persis
Dewsamp, Maurine	Ellis, Lillian	Fetzer, Carol	Gardner, Rexine
Dewsamp, Millicent	Ellis, LuDean	Fetzer, Leona	Garnett, Mrs.
DeYoung, Ann	Ellis, Vera	Fidon, Virginia	Garrf, Annette
DeYoung, Audrey G.	Ellison,	Field, Harriet	Garrick, Mary Jo
DeYoung, Naomi	Catherine Cone	Field, Helen W.	Gates, Betty E.
Dial, Verna	Ellison, Hazel	Field, Katherine	Gaunt, Edna

Gaylord, Alice
Gee, Beverly C.
Geertsen, Alma J.
Geertsen, Jane
Gehrman, Meta
Geis, Idella
Geis, Mrs. N. E.
Gentry, Colleen
George, Allene
Gerber, Sharilyn
Gerrard, Carol S.
Geving, Sandra M. C.
Gibbons, Mrs. Harvey
Gibbons, Mrs. Mildred S.
Gibbs, Betty
Gilbert, Wendy Annette
Gilchrist, Linda
Giles, Annette
Giles, Genaline
Giles, Miri
Giles, Mirt
Giles, Una
Gillespie, Robin
Gillette, Viola P.
Glad, Laura Bowen
Glade, Florence
Glade, Virginia
Glenn, Mary
Glenn, Thelma
Glochner, Hilda
Glore, Clara
Goates, Leda
Gobie, Jacqueline
Goddard, Alice R.
Goddis, Irene C.
Gold, Cherry
Gold, Edwina
Gotberg, LaVon
Gourley, Alice
Gourley, Suzanne
Graham, Aenon
Graham, Lois
Graham, Sue
Grand-Pre, Jean E.
Granger, Mrs. W. K.
Grant, Mrs. H. J.
Graves, Annetta
Gray, Blossom
Gray, Claudine
Gray, Mary W.
Green, Carol D.
Green, Carolyn B.
Green, Catherine S.
Green, Leesa J.
Green, Marlene
Green, Ruth
Green, Sharon
Greenhalgh, Rita L.
Greenwood, Mae M.
Gregerson, Carol L.
Gregerson, Ethelene
Gregerson, Mrs. Grant
Gregory, Shawnie K.
Griffin, Jeanne
Griggs, LeMat Draper
Griggs, Myrna D.
Grotepas, Lucy
Grover, Justine R.
Grundvig, Sherrie
Guderson, Birdie
Gull, Sally L.
Gundersen, Lou
Gunderson, Carrol A.
Gunn, Dorathea
Gurney, Marie B.
Gutke, Nellie
Guymon, Elva
Gygi, Helen
Gynn, Mrs. Ora
Gyr, Agnes
Haarbosch, Nettie
Haas, Mary J. Lemmon
Hadler, Lily M.
Hadlock, Esther
Hahn, Annette
Hahn, Naomi
Haight, Charlotte
Haight, Mary Jane
Haina, Janet
Haina, Marilyn
Hale, Bessie G.
Hale, Cherie
Hales, Agnes
Hales, Ann
Hales, Shirley
Halgren, Ann
Hall, Beth
Hall, Diane
Hall, Hazel
Hall, Valerie N.
Halliday, Nina
Halloman, Marieta C.
Halsett, Josie
Haltiner, Maurine
Halton, Ethel
Halton, Margaret S.
Hamblin, Emmy A.
Hamilton, Doris W.
Hamilton, Lynda A.
Hammond, Janet Y.
Hammond, Lottie
Han't Hoff, Afitha
Hanks, Merlyn
Hanna, Janet
Hanna, Marilyn
Hanney, Lillian
Hanney, Lillian G.
Hansen, Alta
Hansen, Annie M.
Hansen, Dawn
Hansen, Donna R.
Hansen, Elizabeth
Hansen, Janet
Hansen, K. Janet
Hansen, Mary Alice
Hansen, Mary Barnes
Hansen, Nancy M.
Hansen, Peggy
Hansen, Susan
Hansen, Wilma D.
Hanson, Jerelyn
Harding, Donna
Harding, Evelyn
Harding, Renee
Hardman, Betty J.
Harmon, Gwen
Harmon, Kathryn
Harmon, Lillian E.
Harper, Rozella M.
Harretor, Lucy
Harrington, Ione
Harris, Emily
Harris, Esther
Harris, Joanne
Harris, Mabel E.
Harris, Mary Lou
Harwood, Elise C.
Harwood, Karalee C.
Harwood, Margaret F.
Haschower, Lynn L.
Haslam, Emma
Hatch, Carolyn
Hatch, Ida M.
Hatch, Louise E.
Hatch, Louise K.
Hathaway, Gwenda
Haueter, Lucy
Haueter, Lucy Parkinson
Hawkes, Dorothy
Hawkes, Vera
Hawkins, Charlotte
Hawkins, Marilyn
Hawkins, Sadie
Hawley, Dorothy W.
Hayes, Leah Ann
Haynal, Verle R.
Heath, Beryle
Heath, Brenda
Heath, Luella S.
Heaton, Flora
Heeps, Joyce
Hegessy, Mercedes
Helberg, Ethel
Helbling, Arnelle B.
Henderson, Mrs. A. M.
Henderson, Dorothy
Henderson, Emma
Henderson, Helen
Henderson, Kay
Henry, Medora
Hepler, Mary
Hepworth, Ida
Hermann, Jessie Alice S.
Herrin, Sherry A.
Hess, Suzanne Knight
Heugley, May Russell
Hewes, Mary P.
Hewman, Roselina
Heyman, Barbara Jean
Hiatt, Anita
Hickman, Mavis
Hicks, Kay
Hielkema, Rienkjeboer
Higgins, Elsie
Higgins, Jackie
Higgins, Mildred
Higgs, Afton
Hillenbrand, Nellie
Hillier, Helen
Hills, Mary M.
Hinckley, Donna
Hinckley, Eunice N.
Hinkley, Leonore
Hirschman, Gwen
Hirst, Myrna
Hodson, Jewel Lin
Hoehner, Edna
Hoel, Jennie
Hogan, Laurel
Hoggan, Sarah
Holdaway, Inez
Holland, Sally K.
Hollingshead, Jeanne
Holt, Mabel
Holten, Margaret
Holten, Margory
Holyoak, Millie N.
Hood, Joyce C.
Hopper, Joan
Horman, Birdie
Horn, Annegret E.
Horne, Alice
Hornes, Marie
Hornes, Marie J.
Horrocks, Joan
Horsley, Geraldine
Housecroft, Mary R.
Houston, Dorothy
Houston, Karina
Houston, Karma
Howard, Nancy
Howard, Virginia
Howell, Ann C.
Hoyt, Barbara Frazer
Hubbard, Barbara Anderson
Hubbard, Natalie
Hudson, Gladys
Huff, Loralee
Huggins, Jackie
Hunsaker, Bertha M.
Hunsaker, Jo Ann
Hunter, Ann
Hunter, Chris
Hurst, Viviene

Hurzeler, Janet
Hutchings, Beverly
Hutchings, Carol
Hutchings, Fay
Hutchinson,
Rose Marie
Hyde, Florence Kimball
Ingalls,
Virginia Duncan
Ipson, Marion E.
Ipson, Virginia Glade
Irvine, Esther
Isaacson, Gladys
Isaacson, Virginia
Jack, Mary R.
Jackson, Cecile
Jackson, La Rue
Jackson, Lucile
Jacobsen, Phyllis
Jacobson, Carol B
James, Francis
James, Genevieve
Janks, Sharon Ann
Janson, June
Jardine, Winnifred E.
Jarman, Jay
Jarvis, Rosemary K.
Jenkins, Edna
Jenkins, June
Jenks, Roma J.
Jenks, Sharon Ann
Jensen, Afton E.
Jensen, April
Jensen, Arlene V.
Jensen, Callie
Jensen, Elwayna
Jensen, Margret
Jensen, Marjorie
Jensen, Mary
Jensen, May
Jensen, Ruth
Jeppsen, Maren
Jerrome,
Celia Huffaker
Jirzeler, Janet F.
Johanson, Elsa L.
Johanson, Solveg A.
Johnatakis, Karla L.
Johnson, Betty
Johnson, Beverly
Johnson, Carol
Johnson, Mrs. E. L.
Johnson, Elaine
Johnson, Frieda
Johnson, Janeel
Johnson, Jean W.
Johnson, Jo Beth
Johnson, Jolyn
Johnson, Legia M.
Johnson, Marjorie W.
Johnson, Mary L.
Johnson, Nancy D.

Johnson, Reida
Johnston, Catherine Jill
Jones, Afton
Jones, Agatha
Jones, Ann
Jones, Elma
Jones, Elna C.
Jones, Elsie Nilson
Jones, Hilda M.
Jones, Jean
Jones, Joyce
Jongkee, Jeannette G.
Jonsson, Jolyn
Jorgensen, Carla J.
Josie, E. Gayle
Judd, Gwenyth
Kaar, Margaret
Kagel, Rebecca W.
Kampf, June L.
Kampf, LaVone J.
Kandler, Mary
Kartchner,
Nadine Trumbo
Kaster, Lina
Kavenagh, Claudia
Kawkes, Vera E.
Kay, Joyce Samuelson
Keddington, Verna
Keele, Beth
Keiser, Annette
Kellgreen, Karin Else
Kelly, Joyce
Kelly, Kathleen
Kelly, Marcella
Kelly, Roberta M.
Kelly, Ruth
Kelm, Mrs. A. C.
Kelm, Hettie W.
Kelm, Linda
Kelsey, Ella
Kelson, Ella
Kendrick, Patricia
Kennard, Dorothy
Kennard, Ruth
Kensinger, Ramona
Kent, Shawnie
Kerr, Helene
Kessell, Gwen
Kessler, Viola
Kessler, Violate
Kessler, Vivian
Kevern, Marian J.
Kevern, Marian T.
Keyes, Sharon
Kieseg,
Naomi Burrows
Kilpatrick, Ruby
Kimball, Carolyn
Kimball, Louise T.
King, Jean
King, Jean R.
King, Marjorie

King, Melody
Kingsolver, Catherine
Kirkham, Alice
Kirkham, Mrs. Alva
Kirkham, Carol
Kirkham,
Joan Backman
Kirkham, Virginia
Kirkpatrick, Mrs. G. D.
Kirkpatrick, Grace
Kissell, Bonnie B.
Klinger, Sherrie
Kloock, Lois G.
Knaus, Frances
Knight, Minnie M.
Knighton, Ruth
Knott, Martha Rae
Knowles, Eleanor
Knowles, Kathryn
Knowlton, Agnes B.
Knowlton, Agnes S.
Koch, Barbara
Koch, Mrs. H. Walter
Koelliker, Carol L.
Kofford, Kirsten
Kofford, Shanna R.
Koning, Janette
Koons, Evelyn
Koop, Ramona Leah
Kooy, Annette Marie
Krafft, Katherine
Kreek, Barbara
Kretchman, Sally
Kretchman, Susan K.
Kritzer, Judith
Kritzer, Ruth
Krock, Mrs. H. Walter
Kroker, Emily
Kruger, Hilda K.
Kruger, Martha
Kruger, Ruth
Kruse, Lucretia
Kynaston, Audrey
Lach, Bonnie H.
Lach, Helen
Lafferty, Kathleen
Lambert, Kathleen
Lamoreaux, Lerue
Lamoreaux,
Lota Paxman
Lamoreaux, Verne
Landward, Monica
Lane, Jane C.
Larkin, Florence
Larsen, Ethel
Larsen, Virginia
Larson, Marjorie
Last, R. Lee
Latimer, Beulah
Latimer, Estill
Latimer, Leslie
Latimer, Ruth

Laughlin, Linda
Law, Ethel M.
Lawson, Betty Jo.
Lay, Hazel
Leaming, Laura
Leavitt, Lynn H.
Lee, Carol
Lee, Golda
Lee, Gwendolyn H.
Lefebre, Joan
LeFevre, Maris C.
Leisher, Rosalind
Leishman, Karla
Leitz, Verna M.
LeMelle, Margie D.
Lemmon, Mary Janine
Leonard, Valena
Leonudakis, Athena
Leonudakis, Connie
Lewis, Erma Sewell
Lewis, Laree M.
Liance, Sarah E.
Liddell, Julia A.
Lieber, Miriam
Liechty, Arlene
Lietz, Verna
Light, Mrs. G. A.
Light, Gwen
Limburg, Beverly S.
Limburg, Carol Lee
Limburg, Suzanne
Lind, Marian
Linde, Erna
Lindell, Molly
Lindman, Carol Ann
Lindsay, Carrol
Lindsay, Emma E.
Lindsay, Helen
Lindsay, Neva
Lines, Nancy
Link, Hilda
Linn, Agnes M.
Linton, Jean
Lish, Janet
Liston, Marilyn
Lloyd, Charlene
Lloyd, Gayle A.
Lloyd, Melba
Lloyd, Naomi DeYoung
Lloyd, Mrs. Norman
Loasli, Darlene
Long, Phyllis W.
Longee, Genevieve
Loosli, Darlene
Loria, Marilyn
Lougee, Genevieve
Love, Marguerite
Lovelace, Linda L.
Loveless, Gladys
Low, Colleen
Low, Myrle
Lowden, Anne B.

Lowe, Marguerite
Lowell, Nada P.
Lower, Deborah S.
Loy, Hazel
Lublin, Murl
Lukow, Paula A.
Luna, Shelley
Lund, Lottie
Lund, Toni
Lundquist, Donna
Luresden, Ada
Lustig, Sylvia
Lusty, Lucy
Lyance, Sarah E.
Lyance, Sarali B.
Lyman, Esther
Lyman, Yvonne
Lym-Druce, Linda
Lyon, Adele
Lyon, Juanita
McAfee, Lillian
McAllister, Kate P.
McCullough, Jackine S.
McDonald, Donna
McDonald, Janet
McDonald, Kathleen
Mace, Mary Lynn
McFarlane, Lois
McFarlane, Susan
MacFarlane, Susan
MacGrady, JohanneE.
McGregor, Mrs. F. A.
McGregor, Mrs. H. C.
McGuire, Florence
McHugh, Donna Hauck
McHugh, Donna L.
McInttyre, Ruth
McIntyre, Shirlene
Mackay, Dixie
McKay, Genevieve Cherry
McKay, Joyce
McKay, Kidone
McKay, Marilyn
Mackay, Mavis
McKay, Midene
McKay, Teddy
McKendrick, Rose
McKendrick, Mrs. W.
McKenna, Margaret
McKensie, Dorothy
McLachlen, Grace
McMahon, Tress
McNitt, Helen
McPhail, Violet
McSharry, Mrs. G. T.
McSharry, Helen
McWilliams, Anita
Madden, Merna Anne
Madsen, Beverly A.
Madsen, Donna
Madsen, Mary Lou
Madsen, Rosalie
Malcolm, Priscilla
Malcolm, Rose
Malcolm, Winifred
Maly, Karla
Mangelson, Ruby
Mangum, La Veta
Mangum, Lena
Mann, Betty D.
Mann, Mrs. J. W.
Mann, Ramona R.
Marble, Maurine
Marchant, Karen
Marchant, Marva
Marchant, Nancy Hansen
Marcusen, Linda
Marcusen, Nanci
Margetts, Jean R.
Maringer, Aurora
Marks, LuAnn
Marler, Margot
Marley, Bessie
Marsh, Carolyn
Marshall, Alta
Marshall, Ida
Marshall, Mary
Marshall, Ruth
Marston, Annette L.
Martin, Mrs. J. J.
Martin, Minnie
Marvin, Miriam
Marx, Marva N.
Mason, Camille
Mason, Clo Ann
Matheson, Sharilyn G.
Mathews, Wanda
Matthews, Cherie W.
Matthews, Sharon K.
Maughan, Patricia
Maughan, Sarah Roberts
Maughn, Mary Ann
Maughn, Patrticia
Maw, LaRue
May, Georgiana T.
Mayhew, Aenona
Meline, Roberta E.
Mendenhall, Carol
Mercer, Mimi I.
Merrill, Ione C.
Metzlaar, Lora Leeh.
Meyer, Barbara Brutt
Meyers, Dorothy
Michels, Mrs. Sylvia G.
Michi, Helen S.
Mickel, Sylvia G.
Middaugh, Cherie
Midgley, Dot
Midgley, Lucile V.
Miller, Ann C.
Miller, Emmelin
Miller, Fonda
Miller, Jan P.
Miller, Joan Van Hemingen
Miller, Linda Rae
Miller, Lynette A.
Miller, Minnie
Miller, Myrna
Miller, Nancy
Miller, Shirley J.
Miller, Stella F.
Miller, Susan
Millerberg, Joan
Millerberg, Lorna J.
Mills, Iryntha
Mills, Lynette
Mills, Tryntha
Mills, Mrs. W. C.
Minardi, Elaine
Miner, Ethel B.
Miner, Ruth
Minson, Carol Ann
Mitchel, Kay
Mitchel, Sylvia G.
Mitoray, Linda
Mixter, Mrs. C. T.
Moffit, Alta
Moffitt, Joy Olsen
Monson, Janene
Monson, Lorna F.
Monson, Lynne L.
Monson, Marian H.
Monson, Mary
Montague, Ann Parkinson
Montague, Tris
Montgomery, Beverly
Moore, B. Diane
Moore, Donna
Moore, Janice D.
Moore, Marilyn
Moray, Evelyn
Morgan, Audrey D.
Morgan, Audrey K.
Morgan, Gladys E.
Morgan, Laura
Morgan, LuJean
Morgan, Mildred
Morley, Bessie
Morley, Nancy
Morley, Sue
Morley, Vallerie
Morrey, Reno
Morris, Evelyn
Morris, Joyce L.
Morris, Mavis
Morris, Mrs. William N.
Morrison, LoisGraham
Mortensen, Winnie
Moss, Bessie
Moss, Carol B.
Mottes, Pia
Moulton, Fern
Moulton, Sena
Muchow, Catherine
Muelleck, Renate
Munk, Kathryn
Murdock, Bonnie
Murdock, Claire
Murdock, Elva B.
Murdock, Joyce
Murk, Bessie
Myers, Dorothy
Myers, Jackie
Nansen, Mabel L.
Narramore, Lois
Nasfell, Gail Patricia
Nasuer, Lydia
Naylor, Elaine
Nebeker, France
Neeley, Joanne
Neff, Jean R.
Nelson, Adelaide B.
Nelson, Barbara
Nelson, Betsy
Nelson, Helen Sheya
Nelson, K. Ruth
Nelson, Linda
Nelson, Marie
Nelson, Mary
Nelson, Myrtle
Nelson, Niena S.
Nelson, Patricia
Nelson, Rebecca D.
Nelson, Ruth
Neslen, Nila
Nester, Virginia
Newman, Colleen E.
Newman, Connie M.
Newman, Ione
Newman, Jone
Newman, Rosalind P.Walton
Newren, Louise
Nicholls, Ann
Nichols, Jeannette H.
Nichols, Patricia
Nicholsen, Betty Sue
Nielsen, Elrena
Nielsen, Elrona E.
Nielsen, Ida Merle
Nielsen, Karen J.
Nielsen, Mary S.
Nielsen, Patricia S.
Nielson, Mrs. A. H.
Nielson, Mrs. A. W.
Nielson, Carol
Nielson, Donna
Nielson, Eunice
Nielson, Lorna
Nielson, Mary
Nielson, Mayre Beth
Nielson, Patricia Ann

Nielson, Ragna
Nielson, Ruth M.
Nielson, Vera R.
Nielson, Virginia
Niesen, Eva
Nilson, Elsie
Nixon, Myrene K.
Noall, Elizabeth
Noall, Evalyn
Noble, Betty
Noorda, Janet
Nordberg, Jo Lynn
Norris, Janet
Nunley, Sandra
Nuttall, Barbara
Nylander, Ruth
Nypower, Helen
Oberg, Janet
Oborn, Annie M.
O'Farrell, Winnie
Ofgreen, Pearl
Og, Norma Mason
Ohlson, Barbara
Olander, Sharlene
Oleson, Lois
Oliphant, Ida
Olpin, Audrey
Olsen, Christy
Olsen, Edith W.
Olsen, Gayle
Olsen, LuAnn
Olsen, Nancy D.
Olsen, Thera Lou
Olsen, Ziona Dawn
Olson, Doral
Olson, Iris
Olson, Lettie
Olson, Marjorie
Olson, Melody
Olson, Nancy
Omer, Dorothy M.
Omer, Josephine
Omer, Pauline
Orschard, Jeanne C.
Osborne, Hazel
Osgathorpe, Carlene
Oslen, Joy
Osmond, Eileen
Oswald, Mavis Elizabeth
Ottesen, Mary
Ottosen, Ellen
Overdick, Annie
Overduyn, Marie
Owen, Lois
Owen, Mrs. R. M.
Owen, Virginia
Pack, Mariel
Pack, Rosalind
Packard, Jan
Palmer, Ethel
Palmer, Evelyn
Papworth, Ruth W.
Park, Chloe M.
Parker, Cleone
Parker, Grace
Parker, Jean
Parker, Wendy
Parker, Mrs. Will C.
Parkinson, Ann
Parkinson, Carol
Parkinson, Lucy
Parry, Connie
Parry, Donna Neilson
Parry, Georgia
Parry, Nola
Parry, Viola
Parsons, Mary Helen
Partner, Margaret
Partridge, Beth
Partridge, Corine Rae
Patterson, Ruth
Payne, Nancy
Peach, Evelyn R.
Peacock, Kaye M.
Pearce, Janet
Pearson, Anne
Pearson, Dorothy
Pearson, Elizabeth Anne
Pearson, Mrs. John
Pearson, Nancy R.
Peck, Hanne Jane
Peck, Marylyn Moore
Peirce, Marillyn
Pendleton, Erma
Pendleton, Sylvia
Penrose, Fay
Pepper, Lorraine S.
Perkins, Josephine
Perner, Mildred Jane
Perry, Georgia R.
Perschon, Elvira
Perschon, June
Peters, Mrs. A. S.
Petersen, Elna D.
Peterson, Audrey
Peterson, Bonnie Mae
Peterson, DeVota M.
Peterson, Elna D.
Peterson, Ida
Peterson, LaVerne
Peterson, Marian
Peterson, Peggy
Peterson, Raquel
Peterson, Sherie L.
Peterson, Shirley C.
Peterson, Shirly
Peterson, Theone
Petruzzelli, Ann E.
Petry, Louise
Phillips, Lois D.
Pinegar, Frances Marlene
Pinegard, Frances
Pingree, Donna
Pinney, Mary K.
Pitthan, Elizabeth
Pitts, Florence T.
Pixton, Cleone
Platt, Gayle
Platt, Kay
Platt, Patricia
Player, Mabel
Player, Nora
Ploeger, Annarae
Plonzek, Lorella J.
Plum, Betty Sue
Poelman, Carol
Poll, Judith M.
Ponkamen, Luisa
Pope, Carol Trumbo
Pope, Gloria E.
Pope, Gloria P.
Porter, Elizabeth
Porter, Gloria
Porter, La Rae
Porter, Sam
Porter, Sandra
Porter, Saundra
Potter, Jennie
Preece, Ruth
Price, Elaine
Price, Pat
Price, Rene U.
Price, Ruth Urry
Prince, Mayna
Prouty, Almira
Pugh, Beatrice
Pursley, Tanya
Pyper, Joan
Quigley, Glennis
Quist, Edna
Rachell, Rosella
Raddatz, Joanne
Ralston, Miss O. C.
Randall, Shirley
Randle, Ruth Willis
Rasmussen, Lara E.
Rasmussen, Laurel Hogan
Rawlings, Ramona
Ray, Bonnie L.
Ray, Lisa Joan
Ray, Ruth Velene
Read, Etta
Read, Maxine
Record, Linda H.
Redfored, Marilyn
Reed, Barbara D.
Reed, Carol Burns
Reeder, Emeren J.
Rees, Ruth
Reeves, Marie G.
Reeves, Marie Y.
Regan, Mrs. S. A.
Reicker, Jerrie
Reid, Ann Rotzler
Reiley, Mildred
Reinicke, Inge Erna
Reitz, Nancy M.
Rencher, Agnes
Reschke, Ione
Reynolds, Frances Catherine
Reynolds,Jacquelyn J.
Rich, Mayme S.
Rich, Nina Jean
Richards, DeEtte
Richards, Dianne A.
Richards, Helen
Richards, Mary
Richards, Mrs. H.T.C.
Richards, Patricia
Richards, Rosalie
Richards, Vera
Richards, Vicky
Richardson, Annette
Richardson, Bonnie
Richardson, Debra L.
Richardson, Ellen B.
Richardson, Hope
Richardson, Hortense
Richardson, Nora
Richardson, Verla
Rickards, Lee Anne
Ricketts, Ruth
Rickey, Kathleen
Ridd, Joan Broman
Ridges, Ella
Rieske, Marti B.
Rigby, Joyce
Rigby, Lauralee W.
Rigby, Leah
Riley, Kathleen Anne
Rimli, France
Ririe, Edna
Riswald, Anna
Riswald, Mrs. Gilbert
Robbins, Edith C.
Roberts, Kizette
Roberts, Sarah
Robertson, Ednalene
Robertson,FrancesC.
Robertson, Ruth
Robinson, Barbara
Robinson, Dorothy
Robinson, Jackie
Robinson, Kaye Gertrude
Robinson, Laura
Robinson, Louise
Robinson, Melba
Robinson, Venice
Rockwell, Bonnie
Rodeback, Cheryl
Roden, Janet
Roden, Joyce

Rogers, Aura
Rogers, ConnieCollard
Rogers, Lillif
Rogers, Lucile
Rogers, Venice M.
Rollins, Joan
Romney, Ardelle
Romney, Bertha
Romney, Beverly
Romney, Emma Lou
Romney, Karen L.
Romney, Marcia Lois
Roothoff, Maria E.
Roothoff, Mrs. M. E.
Roothoff, Mrs. R. K.
Roozemond, Nantje
Rose, Dorette C.
Rose, Miriam
Rose, Virginia
Rosebrangh, Dorothy C.
Rosenberg, Eleanore
Rosenberg, Ruth
Rosendahl, Renatte S.
Rosenham, Ida
Ross, Mrs. Don
Rosser, Nellie
Rosvall, Cecil
Rothoff, Mrs. M. E.
Rotzler, Ann
Roundy, Marilyn
Rowley, Gwen
Rucker, H. Jerrie
Rumel, Alice Thomas
Rumel, Gloria C.
Russel, Caroline
Russel, Carolyn F.
Russell, Ellen
Russell, Evelyn
Russell, Mary
Russell, May
Russon, Diane
Rustad, Lottie
Rydman, Karen N.
Rytting, Gloria
Sadler, Lilie M.
Sadlier, Mrs. W. G.
Sagers, Jessie Alice
Sain, Myrtle
Salmond, Janeel J.
Samuelson, Clara
Samuelson, Janet A.
Samuelson, Joyce
Samuelson, Marie
Sandberg, Esther
Sandburg, Colleen Cleo
Sanders, Carolyn
Sanders, Judy
Sanders, Margaret
Savage, Barbara
Savage, Gladys
Saville, Betty Gene
Saville, Pat M.
Saxter, Annamae
Schade, JoAnne
Schaifermeyer, Jane
Schamel, Gwendolyn
Schepman, Grace
Schetselaar, Sheri
Schierendregt, Annie
Schlosser, Carolyn
Schmidt, Mary
Schoenfeld, Sue
Schoenhals, Mrs. J. A.
Schofield, Norma
Schofield, Susie
Schow, Alceodene H.
Schrader, Helen
Schrader, Ray Ann
Schramm, Margaret
Schreiner, Norma
Schreiter, Norma E.
Schriveberger, Johanna
Schroder, Ray Ann
Schuette, Renate
Schulze, Jane Reed
Schumann, Allie
Schumann, Alma
Schwan, Eva
Schylzke, Astrid M.
Sconberg, Ida
Scorup, Jean
Scott, Aimee
Scott, Diane
Scott, Joan Cottrell
Scott, Mae G.
Searle, Cleo L.
Searle, Grace
Seeley, Drucilla Bott
Seeley, Ethel
Seelig, True Ree
Seely, Karen
Seidl, Jean
Sequin, Josephine
Servoss, Dorothy
Severinsen, Cheryl
Shaffer, Laura C.
Shaffer, LuAnn B.
Shand, Laura
Sharp, Joy F.
Sharp, Pat L.
Shaw, Charlene
Shaw, Vivian M.
Shea, Mary
Sheilds, Mrs. Claude
Sheldon, Dorothy
Shelley, Janette L.
Shenon, Patricia
Shepherd, Berl
Shepherd, Bertha
Sherman, Mary Alice
Sherriff, Mary
Sheya, Helen
Shields, Mildred
Shields, Mrs. Claude
Shierendregt, Annie Murray
Shindler, Leah
Shindler, Mary
Shipman, Grace J.
Shopman, Grace
Short, Judy
Shrack, Leola
Shumate, Sara L.
Shumway, Carolyn
Shurtleff, Leone
Shurtliff, Helen
Shurtliff, Leona
Shurtliff, Ruth
Shutt, Doris
Siciliano, Susan B.
Siddoway, Barbara
Siegmann, Ella
Silva, Nancy N.
Simister, Carol D.
Simmonds, Mildred
Simons, Marjorie
Simper, Beatrice
Simpson, Sylvia J.
Sitterud, Velda
Slachura, Hildegard
Slade, Mrs. F. J.
Slade, June
Slater, Gertrude
Slater, Lu Lani
Slingerland, Suzanne Hess
Slock, Anna Marie
Slone, Irene
Slotbloom, Caroleen
Sluder, Corinne
Smart, Carol B.
Smedley, Sylvia
Smith, Mrs. A. L.
Smith, Adelaide
Smith, Arlene R.
Smith, Betty
Smith, Carol
Smith, Darlene S.
Smith, Dorothy
Smith, Edith B.
Smith, Fawn B.
Smith, Frances
Smith, Gertrude
Smith, Helen Kerr
Smith, Jesse E.
Smith, Kathryn
Smith, Laura Lee
Smith, Laurel
Smith, Lony
Smith, Loraine
Smith, Lory
Smith, Mabel
Smith, Margaret
Smith, Martha
Smith, Mattie G.
Smith, Maude M.
Smith, Pauline
Smith, Relia
Smith, Ruby
Smith, Yvonne
Smoot, Laura
Smurthwaite, Florence
Snow, Charlene
Snow, Villette E.
Snyder, Barbara
Snyder, Fredna
Snydergaard, Myrtle
Softley, Margaret
Sohn, Cordelia
Sohn, Ziona Dawn
Solomon, Rosetta
Sorensen, Joan P.
Sorensen, Mariel
Sowby, Laurie W.
Sowerwine, Joyce
Spandre, Joan Fyfe
Speaks, Leslie A.
Spencer, Bertha C.
Spencer, Ione
Spencer, Joan Blackhurst
Spencer, Ruth
Spencer, Sherryl Marie
Sperry, Annarae
Sperry, Anne P.
Sperry, Kathleen
Spilsbury, Jewel
Spjut, Abbie Burrows
Spjut, Norma E.
Springer, Dianne E.
Staal, Hilda
Stachura, Hilda
Stafford, Iris
Stahl, Margaret
Standing, Joleen Dunyon
Standings, Norma
Stanfield, Joan
Stanford, Linda B.
Stanton, Mary B.
Starr, Barbara
Staten, Diane
Stauffer, Joyce
Steed, Della M.
Steenblik, Lois N.
Steinaker, Ruth V.
Stephens, Peggy Peterson
Stephens, Sherine E.
Stevanson, Marietta
Stevens, Erma
Stevens, Mildred
Stevenson, Ann R.
Stevenson, Hilda C.
Stevenson, Marietta

Stewart, Irene
Stewart, Martha
Stewart, Pamela
Stewart, Pat Nielson
Stewart, Patricia
Stewart, Shauna Lee
Stine, Diana Marie
Stobbe, Marie Haymond
Stockman, Dorothy
Stoker, Mary
Stoker, Mrs. May
Stoler, Harriet H.
Stoneman, Wilhelmina
Stoudt, Doris G.
Stout, Lorraine
Stout, Shirley
Stowell, Patricia
Stratford, Ella
Straup, Mary
Streadbeck, Carol
Stringham, Emma
Strong, Sharon A.
Stucki, Bonnie
Stucki, Margaret
Stucki, Olive
Suess, Esther
Summerhayes, Beth
Summerhayes, Mary
Summerhays, Carol Jean
Summerhays, Lillian
Summerhays, Ruth
Sutherland, Leona
Swan, Emma
Swanger, Lou Ann
Swensen, Alice
Swensen, Elaine
Swensen, Shirley S.
Swenson, Alice F.
Swenson, Ann S.
Swenson, Ann W.
Swenson, Dorthea
Swenson, Merla
Symons, Arzella
Syndergaard, Myrtle
Tadje, Frieda
Taft, Vera
Takahashi, Margaret
Talbot, Kathleen
Talbot, Merna Anne
Talles, Harriet
Tanner, Alfreda
Tanner, Helen J.
Tanner, Jennie
Taylor, Carolyn
Taylor, Donna
Taylor, Esther V.
Taylor, Ethelyn P.
Taylor, Eunice
Taylor, Jacqueline
Taylor, Julie
Taylor, June Burns
Taylor, Lyle
Taylor, Marie
Taylor, Vicky
Teach, Daryl Jean
Teerlink, Evelyn
Teerlink, Marie
Terrell, Karen
Terry, Iris
Terry, Pat J.
Terry, Sally
Tesch, Daryl
Tew, Susie S.
Thacker, Susanne
Thatcher, Carole
Thelin, Mildred V.
Thiriot, Rhea
Thomas, Agnes
Thomas, Alice
Thomas, Ann Davies
Thomas, Emma Lindsey
Thomas, Evangeline
Thomas, Joan
Thomas, Lyle
Thomas, Marie J.
Thomas, Muriel
Thompson, Barbara
Thompson, Beverly
Thompson, Elma J.
Thompson, Evelyn
Thompson, Marie Samuelson
Thomson, Elizabeth
Thorn, Imogene
Thornell, Sally
Thornton, Pearl
Thorpe, Annetta
Thorup, Karen
Thurgood, Patsy Ann
Tipton, Aurelia D.
Tipton, Marie D.
Todd, Patricia
Tolman, Odessa
Tomas, Mrs. Julian M.
Tonge, Betty Jo
Tongee, Genevieve F.
Torgersen, Ruth
Torgerson, Marylin
Toronto, Norma
Torres, Marie
Tovey, Fern
Towsley, Miriam
Tracy, Violet H.
Tranter, Joene
Trottier, Dorothy
Truman, Jill
Trumbo, Carol
Trumbo, Nadine
Tsukamoto, Maryetta
Tucker, Lois
Tucker, Patricia
Tuckett, Ethel
Turman, Sharon J.
Turner, Annette
Turner, Mary Lou
Tweedie, Mary Helen
Twitchell, Ardythe
Ulmer, Mildred
Urke, Brenda K.
Urquhart, Barbara L.
Valdri, Mrs. B.
Van de Mere, Lena
Van Dorn, Carol F.
Van Gelderen, Louise
Van Heiningen, Joan
Van Oostendorp, Lulu
Van Voorhies, Marilyn
Van Wagoner, Carol Ann
van't Hoff, Afitha
Vance, Barbara
Vance, Carol
Vander Knaap, Antonia J.
Vander Toolen, Joan
Vander Werff, Dowena Joan
Vander Werff, Sandra J.
Vanderhooft, Louise H.
Vane, Frances
Veenstra, Nantje
Venema, Patricia Marie
Verde, Joy
Vernon, Marlene
Vicklund, Hannah
Vincent, Beth
Vincent, Ina R.
Vincent, Lynne
Vincent, Wyonna
Visser, Minke
Vogel, Colleen B.
Vogeler, Mrs. A.
Voorhees, Thelma
Voyles, Mildred
Wagner, Elaine
Wagner, Olive
Wagoner, Margie Angell
Wahlen, Sandra M.
Waite, Betty Gates
Wakefield, Pat
Waldron, Enid W.
Waldron, Frances
Walker, CoDele
Walker, Doris
Walker, Emma
Walker, Mary Lou
Walker, Willa Rae
Walkingshaw, Jane
Wall, Lola B.
Wallberg, Cherie
Wallborg, Helen
Walton, Margaret
Wardle, Rela
Ware, Eleanor
Ware, Mildred
Waring, Barbara
Warren, Mrs. O. P.
Watkins, LaRue
Watson, Dorothy
Watson, Ina R.
Watson, Marjorie
Wayner, Olive E.
Weaver, Lillian
Weaver, Sylvia
Webb, Carolann
Weigel, Hendrika
Weigel, Marie
Weille, Elvisa E.
Wells, Ingeborg
Wenzel, Alma F.
Wernick, Hildegard
Weseman, Irene
West, Beverly
West, Louise
Westman, Ruth P.
Wheeler, Valane
Wheelwright, Sylvia L.
Whinston, Marsha
Whitbeck, Vera
White, Carol
White, Deleen
White, Georgianna
White, Suzanne
Whitehead, Betty
Whitehead, Gertrude
Whitehead, Ruth
Whitelock, Susan
Whitely, Marjorie
Whitney, Joyce
Whitney, Wilberta
Whitton, Eluned
Wiegel, Hendrika
Wiegel, Marie
Wight, Marjorie
Wignall, Jeanne
Wilbert, Myrna Hurst
Wilcox, Blanche
Wilcox, Madeline
Wilcox, Ruth
Wilde, Rosemary T.
Wilkes, Jeanne C.
Wilkes, Jeanne M.
Wilkins, Mrs. R. A.
Wilkins, Sandra
Wilkins, Vera H.
Wille, Elvira E.
Wille, Klara
Willes, Adrianne
Williams, Bessie
Williams, Betty
Williams, Donna
Williams, Gladys
Williams, Helen J. C.

Williams, Julie L.
Williams, Marilyn Covey
Williams, Natalie
Williams, Pat
Williams, Sandra
Williams, Sarah
Williams, Saundra F.
Williams, Thais
Williamsen, April J.
Willis, Ruth
Willy, Adrienne
Wilson, Delayne
Wilson, LaRae E.
Wilson, Lauralee
Wilson, Stephanie F.
Wilson, Stephanie W.
Wims, Dorothy
Winburn, Betty
Winegar, Carol
Winters, Jane
Wiscomb, Bette
Wiscomb, Thora
Wise, Diane
Wissmar, Fay
Wolstenholme, Melissa
Wonnacott, N. Joy
Wood, Dolores Dunford
Wood, Dorothy
Wood, Hazel
Wood, May
Woodbury, Ann M.
Woodhouse, Sytske S.
Woods, Darlene A.
Woods, Emily S.
Wooley, Dorene
Woolley, Alida
Woolley, Minerva
Woolsey, Enid
Woolstenholm, Melissa
Woolstenholm, Mrs. M.
Workman, Shirley
Wouden, Carolina L.
Wouden, Kathryn Dana
Wright, Connie Manwaring
Wright, Dale Ann
Wright, Elva
Wright, Mrs. E. S.
Wright, Margaret
Wright, Sandra Fletcher
Wright, Thelma
Wronski, Patricia T.
Wuerch, Stephanie F.
Wustrack, Dorothy
Wuthrick, Deena D.
Wybrow, Renee
Wynn, Sylvia
Yancey, Elinor M.
Yearout, Cliphane
Yearsley, Karen A
Yeates, Irene S.
Young, Bernice
Young, Elma
Young, Frances H.
Young, Janet
Young, Kathy O.
Young, Laurel
Young, Mary Lou
Young, Norma Rae
Young, Renee
Zabriskie, Janet Larson
Zeeman, Joyce
Zupan, Gayle C.

Tenors

Abbott, S. A.
Abrams, Howard
Acomb, L. I.
Aiono, Fotu
Aldous, John
Allen, Arthur A.
Allen, Frank J.
Allen, Franklin
Allen, Jack R.
Allen, Jerry
Allen, Maryon L.
Allred, Allan
Allred, Larry Allen
Amundsen, Eugene K.
Anderegg, Thomas Henry
Anderson, Alex P.
Anderson, Dorrell L.
Anderson, Gerald E.
Anderson, James Wayne
Anderson, Nephi
Anderson, Phil M.
Andrus, James R.
Andrus, Jay O.
Andrus, Neil
Andrus, Willis
Angel, Arthur
Archibald, LeRoy A.
Archibald, Ronald S.
Arnold, Dwight
Arntz, Mark
Asay, Robert
Astin, J. A.
Astin, J. N.
Atkin, Sidney
Atkinson, Marc
Austin, Gordon
Aydelotte, John E.
Backer, Richard
Badger, David R.
Bailey, John A.
Bakels, Gerry
Baker, John W.
Baker, Richard E.
Bales, O. T.
Ballif, Lyman
Barber, Harold J.
Barker, Richard
Barlow, Richard W.
Barr, Goerge E.
Barton, John
Bates, Edward
Bates, Max L.
Baugh, George T.
Bauman, Thomas D.
Bauman, William W.
Beatie, N. Ross
Beers, Norman L.
Behunin, George F.
Belgique, Daniel
Bell, Donald L.
Bell, Lee
Bell, Richard
Belnap, Charles
Bennett, Fred
Bennett, Jeff
Bennett, Jeffrey Alan
Bennion, Don B.
Bennion, Donald
Bennion, John W.
Bennion, K. H.
Bentley, Frank
Best, Alfred
Betenson, Blaine
Bettridge, James
Bettridge, Kendall
Beyer, Ralph W.
Biggs, Dr. Melvin C.
Biggs, Melvin C., Jr.
Bigler, L. B.
Billings, George
Bingham, Budd
Bird, Dennis
Bird, Louis
Birdge, S. Elliott
Biship, Lynn
Bishop, Marvin J.
Bishop, Max M.
Bitter, Charles
Black, Roger
Blackburn, O. Dale
Blackhurst, Richard
Blackner, Arnold
Blackwell, Leland
Blair, Bill
Blair, Kenneth
Blair, Victor
Blanchard, Rod Nelson
Bluck, H. R.
Bock, Claus D.
Boden, J. Freeman
Bogarth, Marguirite
Bollschweiler, Robert P.
Boner, Wayne G.
Booth, Kaye
Borden, J. Freeman
Bordeux, Freeman
Bottom, Edward D.
Bough, George T.
Boughton, Bob
Bowen, J. H.
Bowers, J. D.
Boyer, Joe H.
Brackett, Thomas E.
Bradford, Bill
Bradford, Ted
Bradley, James E.
Brady, E. Lionel
Brain, A. G.
Brain, E. J.
Bretzing, Walter
Brimhall, James
Bringhurst, George
Broadbent, David
Broadhead, J. Paul
Broadhead, Paul
Brooks, Nyman C.
Broome, Guenter E.
Brown, David A.
Brown, David L.
Brown, Elbert H.
Brown, Garth
Brown, George
Brown, J. D.
Brown, J. Garth
Brown, S. B.
Brown, Steven J.
Brown, Steven Kent
Brown, Teleni
Bryden, Elmer L.
Buckley, Jeffrey R.
Buiengo, O. O.
Bumett, A.
Bunker, Ted
Burkhart, Bruce E.
Burnett, A. J.
Burt, Leon
Burt, Neil
Burton, J. L.
Busby, Harley
Bush, Sterling
Butterworth, Ed
Cahill, Jerry P.
Calder, Mac
Calder, Robert M.
Caldwell, A. E.
Call, Evan L.

Call, O. Jay	Condie, Richard P.	Dudley, Joseph S.	Garrett, Joseph B.
Call, R. L.	Cone, William L.	Duke, Leslie	Garrett, Lewis
Call, Richard	Cooke, William	Duncan, Earl	Gartrell, Alan D.
Call, William	Coombs, Ernest E., Jr.	DuQuesne, A. J.	Gastleton,
Campbell, James	Cornwall, Claude C.	Durham, Alfred	Leonard Gerald
Campbell, Jared Alan	Cornwall, Douglas J.	Durham, L. Marsden	Geertson, Richard M.
Cannon, Elias M.	Cornwall, M. C.	Dyer, Calvin O.	Geis, Gustave
Cannon, George	Cosgrove, William	Eberly, Lawrence	Geis, N. E.
Cannon,	Costa, Dim	Edmunds, Clyde	Geis, Nephi E.
George M., Jr.	Cottrell, Lloyd B.	Edwards, Alan	Gergory, Harry
Cannon,	Cowburn, R. H.	Edwards, Lee	Germain, George D.
George Nibley	Cowles, Harper B.	Egan, W. Gerald	Giaugue, A. G.
Cardwell, Gaylen K.	Cox, Lamoine	Eliason, Dr. Richard J.	Giauque, A. G., Jr.
Carlisle, Marvin	Crane, Ian Howard	Elihm, Burril	Gibbons, E. A.
Carlston, Bill	Critchlow, Robert K.	Elsberry, Thomas B.	Gilgen, James K.
Carlston, L. R.	Crocheron, Ken	Engh, Henry	Gillespie, William
Carrier, Edward W.	Crotch, W. C.	Erekson, Reid	Gillette, David L.
Case, S. W.	Crotch, William	Ericksen, Gerald	Gillette, Eugene
Castle, Louis A.	Crotch, William Edward	Erickson, E. Edwin	Gillette, Eugene E., Jr.
Castleton, Jerry	Cummings, Charles	Erickson, Dr. Rex	Gillings, John
Castleton,	Curtis, Harold	Eschler, Harold	Giner, Allen
Leonard Gerald	Curtis, Steven E.	Evensen, Scott D.	Goff, Harold
Castleton, Robert D.	Curtis, Ted	Evertsen, D.	Gorter, Jan
Chadwick, Lynn	Cushing, James	Exchler, Harold	Gout, John
Charles, J. Stanley	Cutler, Raul W.	Faber, Michael	Graham, Douglas
Chase, R. T.	Davenport, E.	Fairbanks, C. L.	Graham, Fred
Chesley, Evan	Davenport, Thomas	Fallows, Albert	Granger, William
Chesley, Evan G.	Davies, John	Farr, Coridan (Ted)	Grant, Richard
Chesley, William L.	Davis, Doug	Farr, Lewis L.	Graves, Charles
Christensen,	Davis, Jay	Fawson, H. L.	Gray, Howard M., Jr.
Charles Curtis	Davis, John	Felt, Owen L.	Green, Blaine F.
Christensen, Grant	Day, Daniel	Fericks, Franklin	Green, C. G.
Christensen, J. F.	Dearden, Conway	Ferre, Loren W.	Green, R. W.
Christensen, Jensen	Decker, Larry A.	Ferrell, A. M.	Greenwell, Edward
Christensen, Peter D.	Decker, Larry Lee	Ferrell, Munroe	Gregory, Harry
Christensen, Ronald	Degin, Erwin	Ferricks, Frank	Gregory, Keith
Christensen, William L.	Degles, Thomas	Fetzer, Clark B.	Griffin, Marcus
Christiansen, H. J.	DeHaan, John E.	Fields, Zane Craig	Griffiths, Sheldon
Christianson, Hyrum J.	DeHaan, Paul	Fisher, Alexander	Grundman, Albert
Clapham, Charles E.	DeHaas, John	Fisher, Lon	Gunderson, Had
Clapham, G. H.	Dekker, Roger	Fleming, M.	Gurney, Brent
Clapham, George	Denke, Wilford	Flemming, W. H.	Gushee, Oliver
Clark, Dennis R.	Denos, George	Flink, Hans A.	Gushee, Oliver W., Jr.
Clark, James Alan	DeRyke, Harry	Flink, Hendrik	Hagger, Clifford J. A.
Clark, Osborn P.	Despain, Douglas	Flores, Ricardo T.	Hales, Dr. Bernell
Clark, P. G.	Despain, Noel D.	Fluckiger, J. DeOrr	Halliday, David
Clark, Percy	DeSpain, Robert	Fong, Bryan	Halliday, David M., Sr.
Clauss, Curt A.	DeYoung, Lewis H.	Fortie, J. A.	Halverson, Ray
Clawson, Douglas A.	Dickey, Mark	Foster, Frank	Hammond, West
Clawson, Lawrence	Dock, Roger	Foulger, Paul A.	Hand, John T.
Clawson, Orin	Dolato, Dennison D.	Francis, Allen A.	Hanks, Merlyn
Clayton, Lawrence	Done, Arthur	Fraser, E. W.	Hansen, J. Peter
Clayton, Robert	Doris, Klaas	Frazee, Howard N.	Hansen, Roger L.
Clayton, Weath	Dorrell, Roger	Frazer, E.	Hardy, Crawford R.
Cleary, James	Doty, Claudius	Freese, Samuel	Harris, LeRoy M.
Clemens, J. David	Doubleday, Henry	Fry, David	Harrison, Conrad B.
Cobb, Kent	Dowse, William	Fuller, Marvin O.	Harrison, James
Collett, Dean	Drews, Arnold	Gaige, E. W.	Harrison, Karl
Collingwood,	Drier, John	Gainey, Frank	Haslam, James E.
George R.	Druce, John L.	Gale, LeRoy	Hathaway, Clark P.
Combs, Barry	Duckworth, James	Gamble, James J.	Hawkins, Merrill
Combs, David Alonzo	Dudley, Joseph H.	Garn, Phil	Hayward, W. C.

Headman, Melvin
Heilkema, Henry H.
Helmes, William
Henderson, M. J.
Herman, Gideon
Hermance, Jon S.
Hermance, Jonathan S.
Herramann, Arthur
Hesla, Bret I.
Hewes, Gerald
Hewes, Robert
Hicken, Dale
Hicks, Dennis L.
Hill, Marlin
Hille, John
Hinchcliff, C.
Hinchcliff, Lester
Hinckley, Richard A.
Hircher, Fred, Jr.
Hogan, Rulon
Hogge, Elmer
Holbrook, Keith
Holdaway, DeMar
Hollingshead, K. G.
Holmes, Wendell
Holmes, William
Homer, Raymond
Horman, Theodore
Horsley, Richard
Huff, Jake D.
Hultquist, Arnold
Humphrey, Bill
Hurzeler, Arthur
Hurzeler, Arthur, Jr.
Hurzeler, Fred J.
Hurzley, Fred G.
Hyder, Virgil L.
Iba, Gerald
Ipson, George V.
Ipson, Jared
Isaacs, Bruce E.
Ison, Ben R.
Jacobsen, Cecil
Jacobsen, T. E.
James, Jay
James, Jay R.
Jarvis, Thomas
Jeffs, Louis
Jenks, Jack
Jensen, Charles G.
Jensen, David
Jensen, Gaylen
Jensen, Graydon
Jensen, James M.
Jensen, John
Jensen, Robert W.
Jessop, Donald
Johansen, Francis
Johnson, Bill
Johnson, Elbert
Johnson, Ernest H.
Johnson, Glenn H.
Johnson, Maurice R.
Johnson, Norman O.
Johnson, Ray P.
Johnson, Reid
Johnson, Richard
Johnson, Rick
Johnson, Stanley
Johnson, Wallace
Johnston, Edgar
Jolley, Layne
Jolley, Wayne
Jones, A. B.
Jones, Jack
Jones, Kenneth P.
Jones, Leslie A.
Jones, Raymond
Jonsen, Elmer
Jurzeler, Arthur, Jr.
Kartchner, Jerry D.
Katz, Mr.
Keller, Eugene
Kelley, Stephen H.
Kemp, Jess
Kennard, James B.
Kent, Jack
Key, Thomas
Kilpatrick, David
King, Karl
Kirby, Gerald
Kjar, Joseph E.
Kleingeld, John
Knight, Frank W.
Koldewyn, William J.
Krier, John
Kuepper, Rolf K.
Lach, John E.
Lake, Larry
Lake, Lawrence P.
Lamoreaux, Warwick E.
Lample, R.
Larsen, Alwyn B.
Larson, Arvid
Larson, Donovan
Laycock, Fred
Lee, Frank
Lee, Homer Franklin
Lee, Morris
Leota, Telani L.
Lester, William I.
Lindsay, Kenneth A.
Littlewood, Bryan D.
Lloyd, Jonathan
Lloyd, Leanord
Lloyd, Lewis
Lloyd, William
Loetmulder, A.
Logan, M. B.
Lukenbach, Leonard
Lukow, Thomas J.
Lund, John R.
Lund, N. O.
Lund, Norman
Lundberg, Eldo
Lundberg, Wallace E.
Lyon, Jack
McDaniel, John
McDonald, Kenneth
McDonald, LeGrand
McFarlane, Raymond R.
McGregegor, Douglas
McGregor, H. C.
McKenna, E. G.
McKenna, Edward
McKinney, Don E.
McMillan, Michael D.
McMurray, James A.
McMurrin, Harold
McNeill, Frank
Malcolm, A. C.
Mammott, Terry
Marr, Donald P.
Marshall, Richard
Marti, Lynn A.
Marti, Ray
Marti, Ray K.
Martin, C. C.
Martin, Earl
Martin, Frank
Martin, Lloyd R.
Martin, Norman
Martin, Raymond
Martin, Reed H.
Martinez, Nester L.
Mason, Clarence
Mason, Wesley L.
Masters, Raymond R.
Mathews, Robert
Meibos, O. R.
Memmott, Terry
Mendenhall, T. H.
Mendenhall, Thomas
Metcalf, Robert Lamar
Michaelis, Clayton
Michaelis, Otto
Michell, Bart
Miller, J. Dale
Miller, Walter
Millett, Denton
Mitchell, Bartlett C.
Mixter, C. T.
Moncarr, James
Montague, Edward F.
Morgan, John A.
Morgan, Robert H.
Morman, James E.
Morrell, Grant B.
Morrison, C. Grant
Morrison, John
Morton, W. P.
Mugleston, David Louis
Murray, Gerald R.
Murray, Jerry
Musig, Elwood
Musig, Elwood O.
Naisbitt, Gilbert A.
Nak, Charles
Naylor, Garth L.
Naylor, Raymond T.
Naylor, Rolland
Nederhand, Frank
Neilson, James H.
Nelson, Larry A.
Nelson, Dale
Nelson, Osborne
Nerderhaus, Frank
Nibley, William
Nichols, Dr. Paul
Nielson, David S.
Nielson, John Marlowe
Nielson, Nephi
Nilson, Lynn
Nilsson, Sven O.
Nordberg, J. C.
Norman, James
North, Donald
Nuttall, Will
Nuttall, William T.
Ogden, A. Roland
Olpin, Howard R.
Olsen, J. N.
Olsen, J. V.
Olsen, Vern
Olsen, Vern W.
Olson, Alvin E.
Ottley, Earl H.
Packard, Bennett D.
Packard, C. F.
Packard, Clarence
Packard, Robert C.
Papworth, W. G.
Pardoe, Frank
Parker, Virgil J.
Parry, David
Parry, J. H.
Pass, Dale
Pater, Dick G.
Pater, Richard
Paul, Fred W.
Paulos, Steven T.
Paxman, Craig W.
Paxton, Douglas
Paxton, Robert Eugene
Pearce, E. Jay
Pearce, Jay
Pearce, Richard B.
Pearson, Paul
Peck, Dale L.
Peck, Mark
Peck, William
Peirce, Earle, Jr.
Pennock, J. E.
Penrose, Wallace
Peters, A. S.

Peterson, Brad
Peterson, Bradley
Peterson, Erv
Peterson, Ervin M.
Peterson, Jay J.
Peterson, Lowell
Pexton, Milton
Pexton, Ronald
Phillips, Ray
Pidd, Harry B.
Pike, Charles R.
Pike, E. E.
Pike, Malcolm, Sr.
Platt, Paul
Pollard, Alfred G.
Pollard, Frank
Pollard, Theron
Pollei, C. W.
Poole, Stanley S.
Porter, Lyman
Postma, James
Powers, Kim A.
Prather, John L.
Prather, Loren J.
Pratt, Erving
Pratt, I. T.
Pratt, Orson M.
Price, Richard R.
Prows, Joseph
Purrington, Gordon S.
Putnam, Ralph D.
Pyper, George D.
Quarnberg, David E.
Quayle, J. W.
Quilter, Charles
Randall, Kurt D.
Rasmussen, Allen
Rasmussen, Christian S.
Rasmussen, Everett
Read, Arnold
Reed, Byron
Reeder, Clyde B.
Reese, F. E.
Reese, Fred
Reherd, Hal
Reynolds, Douglas
Rice, Leslie
Rich, Lothaire
Richards, Daniel B.
Richards, Gomer M.
Richards, H. J.
Richards, H. V.
Richards, Joe
Richards, Joseph E.
Richards, Robert
Ridges, Alvin
Rigby, Larry
Rigby, Lester
Rigby, Thomas C.
Rippon, C. S.
Robanz, Sam
Roberts, Don Elmer
Roberts, Shane L.
Robinson, Fred
Robinson, William
Robison, Samuel P.
Roden, George B.
Roden, George E.
Rodrigues, Malacki
Rokes, Willis
Rollins, McKay
Romney, George R.
Romney, Richard Paul
Ross, Jewell
Rowley, Hugh B.
Ruckenbrod, W. G.
Rumel, Herbert E.
Russell, Frank
Russell, John S.
Rutler, Thomas
Sacco, Craig
Salmon, Kay H.
Salter, Joseph
Salter, Joseph W.
Samuelson, A. K.
Samuelson, Anton K.
Samuelson, C.
Samuelson, Carl
Sanders, J. I.
Saunders, A.
Saville, Robert
Saville, Spencer E.
Schaefermeyer, David
Schipaanbrood, J.
Schloss, Fred W.
Schmidt, Glen
Schmidt, Joseph
Scofield, Paul A.
Scott, J. Russell
Scoville, Paul
Seare, B. A.
Sedgwick, Garrett L.
Seegmiller, David
Seifridge, S. W.
Sharp, Robert
Sharp, W. R.
Shepherd, Septimus
Sherrick, Paul
Shewell, Harry
Shockley, Preston
Shurtliff, W. H.
Simpson, James B.
Sirstins, Fritz
Sisam, Dick
Skidmore, Larry
Skidmore, L. R.
Slighting, Adrian
Slok, Hendrick O.
Smart, Elden
Smith, A. T.
Smith, Alma
Smith, Clarence L.
Smith, Dr. David E.
Smith, Hyrum Joseph
Smith, Richard
Smith, Robert
Sorensen, Dale M.
Sorenson, M. A.
Southerland, John
Spencer, Dr. Maitland
Sperry, Florence
Springer, Gordon
Spry, Sam
Standing, Vaughn
Stark, M.
Stark, Mamie
Steadman, Calvin
Stephens, Clifford
Stolar, Philip
Storrs, Richard
Strand, LeRoy M.
Streadbeck, Brian
Stringham, C. J.
Summerhayes, C. E.
Summerhayes, J. B.
Summerhayes, J. J.
Summerhays, George
Summerhays, Paul
Summerhays, Roger
Swenson, H. W.
Swenson, Hyrum
Swenson, Milton O.
Taggart, Bruce
Taggart, Richard L.
Taggart, Scott
Talbot, Gary F.
Taylor, Gary
Taylor, Grant Paul
Taylor, LaVell
Terry, Michael
Thidell, Aaron
Thomas, Edward
Thomas, Haynes
Thomas, Kendall R.
Thomas, Kent R.
Thomas, R. Ken
Thomas, Stiles
Thomas, W. C.
Thomas, W. J.
Thompson, Herbert
Thornton, John R.
Thornton, Richard G.
Thorton, G. O.
Thurman, D. J.
Tischner, Gerald
Tisdel, K. M.
Tisdel, Ken
Titze, Ango R.
Todd, Ira H.
Toronto, Paul
Tucker, David G.
Tullar, Coyle Crosby
Turley, Fred J.
Turner, David
Turner, Frank
Twitchell, LaMar
Udell, George A.
Utley, Roy
Vaeninga, A. C.
Valentine, Dale M.
Van Den Akker, M. C.
Van der Wiel, A.
Van Duren, J. A.
Van Dyke, A. G.
Van Gelderen, Rene
Van Norman, Richard W.
Van Slooten, Harold
Van Tussenbrook, G.
Van Wagoner, Mark
Van Weezep, John
Van Zelm, Bram
Verhaaren, Carl
Vernon, W. M.
Vincent, Ben W.
Visser, John
Voelker, A. H.
Vogel, Mark
Waddell, D. K.
Wagner, Harry H.
Waite, T. H.
Wakefield, D. G.
Waldrop, Bruce Taylor
Walker, A. C.
Walker, Dr. Glen H.
Walker, Milton H.
Walker, W. N.
Wallace, Scott P.
Walton, David
Ward, Moroni W.
Wastell, Richard
Watson, Herman
Weaver, Larry
Weber, Alan
Weber, Ray
Weddington, Robert
Weight, Gary H.
Wells, Jerry D.
Welsh, Charles
Welter, W. J.
Welti, C. J.
Wendel, Douglas J.
Wendell, Norman
Wernick, Frederich
West, Earl
Whitaker, Russel O.
White, Donald
White, Geoff
White, Mondell
White, Verdi
White, Verdi Ray, Jr.
Whitelock, Kenly
Whiting, Doug
Whitlock, Bob
Whitney, R. E.
Widdison, Howard
Wilcox, Frank

Wilde, Jesse E.
Wilkens, Robert A.
Wilkin, Frank
Wilkins, J. L.
Wilkins, R. A.
Willey, Dr. R. T.
Williams, Alfred
Williams, Bob
Williams, David G.
Williams, J. T. II
Williams, James
Williams, Jeff
Williams, Jeffrey H.
Williams, John
Williams, R. C.
Willis, Bertram
Wilson, Bruce
Wilson, Hamilton F.
Winder, Dick
Winegar, Keith
Winn, Frank
Winter, S. D.
Winterton, James C.
Wise, George C.
Wixom, Joe S.
Wojtowicz, John Paul
Woltgen, John W.
Wood, Allan
Wood, David
Wood, Douglas
Wood, George
Wood, M. Douglas
Wood, Marvin H.
Wood, Richard
Woodbury, George
Woodruff, Serge
Woods, Stephen G.
Woolf, J. Preston
Woolley, A. M.
Woolsey, K. P.
Wooten, James H.
Worley, Dr. N. R.
Wouden, George
Wouden, J. W.
Wouden, Jacobus
Wouden, Marinus
Wright, David
Wright, Melbourne
Wright, R. M.
Wunder, Richard
Yearout, Paul
Yeates, Dennis
Young, A. P.
Young, Dick
Young, L. S.
Zachreson, Martia K.
Zito, Michael
Zoetmulder, Albertus
Zorneren, William

Basses

Ackroyd, W. H.
Ackroyd, William
Adams, John A.
Adams, Samuel S.
Aird, Jack
Albiston, Thomas
Alder, Michael Dean
Aldous, H. K.
Aldous, Heber
Aldous, Ralph
Allart, David D.
Allart, Dirk
Allart, Jack C.
Alleman, John C.
Allison, Carl
Alsop, Hugh
Amott, Don R.
Amundson, O. A.
Andelin, Willard
Anderegg, Henry E.
Anderegg, Thomas H.
Anderson, Andrew M.
Anderson, Clyde
Anderson, Dick
Anderson, Doyle
Anderson, Hagbert
Anderson, Dr. Howard T.
Anderson, Kim
Anderson, Lawrence
Anderson, Le Grande
Anderson, Ted
Andrus, Douglas
Andrus, Paul C.
Anthon, Jack Ronald
Arbon, Lloyd E.
Arm, Walter
Arnberg, Bertel
Arnesen, Brian L.
Arnold, George W.
Arnold, Ted
Arthur, Even
Ashby, Wayne E.
Ashton, Donald
Ashton, Homer
Astin, John
Athay, Donald B.
Athay, Donald R.
Aydelotte, Jeffrey T.
Ayres, Merl
Bacon, Vincent H.
Baer, Dr. Robert D.
Bailey, Ferrell G.
Bailey, William C.
Baily, Richard P.
Baird, James
Baird, Robert
Baird, W. E.
Baird, W. H.
Baker, Howard
Baker, William L.
Ball, Robert
Ballard, Seth
Banachaugh, Roy
Barber, H. E.
Bardwell, A. F.
Barg, Don C.
Barker, Allan
Barlow, Joseph
Barlow, Rampton
Barnes, Thomas E.
Barrett, William A.
Barry, Kent M.
Baskin, Sid
Bateman, Keith G.
Bates, Daniel Fetzer
Bates, Fay
Bates, John F.
Bates, Ralph
Baughman, Frank F., Jr.
Bauman, Richard W.
Beales, G. Landon
Bean, Richard
Beckstead, J. R.
Beckstead, Lee A.
Beer, Ted
Beesley, Fred
Behunin, Roy Alan
Bellamy, John R.
Belnap, Dayne R.
Belnap, Hal R.
Belnap, Dr. W. Dean
Belt, Jacob
Belt, Jacobus A.
Belt, James A.
Bennett, Fred L. W.
Bennett, Harold H.
Bennett, R.
Bennett, Reed H.
Bennett, W. P.
Bennett, Wallace F.
Bennion, Ken
Bennion, Merrill
Bennion, Owen
Benson, R.
Benson, Ralph C.
Bergslagle, Daniel
Berhman, Glen D.
Bernards, William
Berndt, N.
Berndt, Norman G.
Bernhisel, D. M.
Bernstrom, Harry A.
Berrett, A. G.
Berry, Steve C.
Betts, John F.
Biesinger, Thomas
Bingham, Budd
Binnie, Robert
Birch, Larry B.
Birchell, Thomas
Bird, C. W.
Bird, Charles R.
Bird, Denny
Bird, Gale
Bird, H. C.
Bird, Heber S.
Bird, W. G.
Birk, William A.
Birrell, Phillip
Bishop, Russell
Bitton, Lou S.
Black, Joseph E.
Blackhurst, Richard
Blackhurst, Roy
Blamires, Kent C.
Blankenship, Jack E.
Blatter, Layne
Blinco, Eugene L.
Blindauer, Harlan H.
Blomquist, W. H.
Bolto, George F.
Bond, Richard
Bons, P.
Booth, L. H.
Bowen, Culbert
Bowers, Alfred
Bowers, Dennis
Bowers, Levi
Bowring, John B.
Bowring, W. D.
Boyd, Lynn A.
Bradford, Charles
Bradford, Chick
Bradford, Robert
Bradshaw, Dennis
Brady, Ted
Bretzing, Mr.
Bretzing, Vernon
Brey, Steven
Brinkman, Donald
Brinton, Eric
Brinton, Roy J.
Britton, Norman A.
Brooks, William R.
Brough, Eugene
Brown, Donald
Brown, George C.
Brown, J. Steven
Brown, Joseph S.
Brown, Kay
Brown, Lee A.
Brown, Nephi
Brown, Richard R.
Browning, J. L.

Brubaker, John H.
Bruce, Robert
Budge, S. Elliot
Bullock, Gerald I.
Burgin, Dave R.
Burgon, Horace E.
Burgoyne, Dale H.
Burk, William O.
Burkhardt, R. O.
Burnham, Wendell
Burrows, Marvin
Burt, D. G.
Burt, D. M.
Burt, Neil
Burton, Melvin P.
Burton, Nelson A.
Burton, Richard Ross
Busby, Harley M.
Bush, Barrie L.
Butler, G. J.
Butters, James
Bywater, Murray A.
Caldwell, W. Jay
Call, Don R.
Call, Everett H.
Call, Schuiler
Cameron, John
Cameron, Robert L.
Campbell, Gene
Campbell, Serge
Cannon, Ralph
Capson, Albert
Capson, Maurice
Card, Clinton S.
Carey, Allen H.
Carlisle, Richard W.
Carpenter, Douglas B.
Carter, Greg L.
Case, Lee
Castleton, Robert H.
Chapman, Dr. Eugene H.
Chapman, H. L.
Chapman, James H.
Chapman, Robert E.
Chapman, Vernon J.
Chapman, Vernon L.
Chapman, Vernon T.
Chappuis, Marcel
Cheney, Richard
Chipman, D. L.
Christensen, Bjorne
Christensen, David G.
Christensen, Gary
Christensen, H. W.
Christensen, Dr. Hugh B.
Christensen, J. D.
Christensen, Jay
Christensen, O. D.
Christensen, Peter D.
Christensen, Ray S.
Christensen, Richard P.
Christopher, Dr. J. R.
Christopher, John
Christopher, Raymond
Christopherson, Grant
Christopherson, M. E.
Christopherson, Victor
Chryst, Robert
Church, Lewis R.
Churchill, W. J.
Churchward, Phil
Clark, Dwight P.
Clark, Howard D.
Clark, Owen
Clarke, Robert
Clarkson, F.
Claus, John J.
Clay, Ross
Claypool, Lee E.
Clayton, Weatherford T.
Clements, Earl
Coates, Jerry
Cobb, J. K.
Cobb, Kent
Coles, LeRoy
Collard, Romny J.
Collett, Dick
Collier, Douglas
Collier, Douglas O.
Collier, Robert
Colyar, Richard R.
Colyar, Robert
Combs, Ernest E.
Comstock, Robert J.
Connariato, Joseph J.
Cook, John
Cook, Dr. John, Jr.
Cook, Dr. John H.
Cook, Robert W.
Coolbear, D. W.
Coombs, Alan H.
Coombs, Ernest, Jr.
Coombs, Ernest E., Sr.
Coombs, Robert E.
Coon, Clifford A., Jr.
Corbett, Walter J.
Cornwall, Dr. R. C.
Cornwall, S.
Cornwall, Spencer
Cottrell, Lloyd
Covey, Stephen
Cowles, Harper B.
Cowles, LeRoy
Cowsert, William F.
Cox, Victor
Cox, William M.
Coy, Victor
Craven, Frank L.
Craven, Melford
Craven, Norville
Creek, Justin
Crist, Robert
Crockett, Justice J. Allan
Curtis, LeRoy H.
Cutler, Halden
Cutler, Joseph T.
Dame, John L.
Damon, George N.
Danzig, Peter A.
Dauler, Dr. Thomas P.
Davidson, James
Davis, Clifton
Davis, Lynn H.
Davis, W. D.
Davis, W. H.
Davis, William
Dawson, J. Terence
Dawson, Lerton
Daynes, Robert F.
Daynes, Royal W.
Dean, Jasper H.
Debendiner, Frank
DeGooyer, C.
Deiu Onden, C.
Demars, Steve
Demke, Otto
Demke, Wilford
Den, Orden C.
Denison, Ronald H.
DenOwden, C.
Derrick, Gary
de St. Aubin, Mark David
Despain, N. Douglas
Despain, Noal
Deters, Ernest G.
Dewsnup, H. C.
Dewsnup, H. E.
DeYoung, Lewis H.
Dick, Richard S.
Dimond, C. Lloyd
Dobson, Dick
Dolley, Wallace
Donaldson, Kent
Donelson, Richard
Donkin, Bob
Doran, Ray L.
Doris, G. R.
Dorius, R. Joel
Dorius, Ray E.
Dorzie, Jacob
Doxie, Paul G.
Doxey, T. G.
Drake, David
Drake, Elvin
Drake, Lewis E.
Duffy, James V.
Duffy, John L.
Duncan, A. M.
Duncan, G. C.
Duncan, Homer B.
Duncan, LaMar
Duncan, Louis C.
Duncan, Mickey
Duncanson, Don D.
Duncanson, DormanD.
Dunn, Phillip B.
Dunn, Ronald L.
Durham, Alfred
Durham, George H.
Durrant, Gary C.
Durrant, Michael W.
Dyer, Calvin
Dyer, Kenneth
Dyer, Richard
Eastman, Elvin J.
Ebaugh, W. C.
Eberhardt, Alex E.
Eberhardt, Alexander
Eberhardt, F. J.
Eberhardt, John E.
Eccles, Albert, Sr.
Eccles, Albert, Jr.
Edison, Goerge
Edmondson, RobertC.
Eldridge, Fred
Eleason, H. L.
Ellis, Richard G.
Ely, Dr. Robert Stewart
Emric, Douglas
Ensign, A. L.
Ensign, Albert
Ensign, Horace
Ensign, Hugh S.
Epperson, L. T.
Epperson, Lawrence
Ericksen, David G.
Ericksen, Eric R.
Ericksen, F. H.
Ericksen, Harlan
Erickson, Calvin
Erickson, Dr. Rex
Eriksson, H. Rick
Eriksson, Herbert
Ernst, Justus
Ertel, Robert B.
Eschler, Harold
Eskelson, La Mar
Evans, Fred
Evans, Gordon
Evans, J. M.
Ewig, Mark Gerard
Faber, Clinton
Faber, Stanley
Fagergren, Mark A.
Fairbanks, Artho
Falk, Werner
Fanning, John W.
Farley, Greg D.
Farley, Gregory
Farnsworth, Karl
Fenton, Neal LeRoy
Ferguson, J. Stephen

Ferguson, James S.	Glauser, Werner	Harris, David	Hunt, D. G.
Fernel, O.	Glissmeyer, A. H.	Harris, Joseph C.	Hunt, D., Jr.
Ferrell, Howard	Glissmeyer, August	Harris, Kenneth	Hunter, Bill
Ferrell, Willard	Goates, Brent L.	Harris, Richard	Hurzeler, Art
Ferro, A. M.	Goates, Delbert	Harrison, Ben	Hurzeler, Arthur
Feruley, Edgar	Goates, Les	Harrison, Karl	Hurzeler, R. W.
Fetzer, Paul B.	Godard, F.	Harrison, Thomas G.	Hutchingson, Ray
Fetzer, Richard	Gold, Nicholas B.	Harrison, W. J.	Hyder, Virgil L.
Fetzer, Wallace S.	Goodwin, R.	Harward, Thomas	Inch, S. R.
Findlay, Richard B.	Goris, George Brian	Harward, Thomas Kendall	Jack, Calvin O.
Fisher, Alexander A.	Gould, Bryan K.	Hatch, Barry C.	Jackman, Victor A.
Fisher, L.	Graham, Wesley O.	Hatch, C. Bradford	Jackson, Richard W.
Fitt, Paul B.	Granque, Gerald S.	Hayes, Robert	Jackson, William H.
Fitzen, Frank	Grant, Richard G.	Head, Grant	Jacobsen, Mark K.
Flandro, Dayle	Graves, F. Charles	Head, N. L.	Jacobson, David W.
Flandro, Royce	Gray, Howard M., Jr.	Heath, David	Jaensch, Melvin
Flandro, Scott C.	Green, James	Heder, Lloyd E.	Jaloszynski, John
Flegal, Douglas C.	Green, Jefferson I.	Helbling, David L.	James, F. W.
Fluckiger, Lyman	Greenwood, Marion J.	Henderson, Mark Artie	James, Glen F.
Fluckinger, W. Lynn	Gregerson, Craig	Henderson, Milton J.	James, John
Folsom, Maurine	Gregerson, Dr. Grant	Henderson, Robin G.	James, Robert F.
Folsom, Theron	Gregerson, Welch F.	Hendricksen, Oscar J.	Janke, Lane E.
Ford, Hugh J.	Gremlich, Kurt F.	Heppley, A. J.	Janke, Mark L.
Fowler, W. R.	Griffin, John	Heppley, Albert L.	Jellison, Harry
Fox, Richard L.	Griffiths, John	Herrmann, Don	Jensen, Grant E.
Foxley, W. L.	Griggs, James	Hess, Bill	Jensen, Harold
Francom, William	Grover, Gary M.	Hesse, Hyrum	Jensen, Jay E.
Freed, Richard O.	Grover, Robert W.	Hey, Nigel S.	Jensen, Louis
Freeman, Dale L.	Guertler, Klaus	Heywood, John Lane	Jensen, Niels
Freeman, Dean L.	Gunderson, Dale	Hicken, Ward	Jensen, P. J.
Freeze, Wallace	Gunnell, W. Wayne	Higgins, Raymond C.	Jensen, Robert
French, Darrell L.	Gutke, Gordon	Higgins, Rowland C.	Jentzsch, Heber C.
French, Gary	Guyman, Max R.	Hilton, Raymond S.	Jeppson, Saylor C.
Frisby, H. L.	Hale, Gerald S.	Hinckley, Ira	Johansen, Bob
Fry, W. Harry	Hales, Dr. Bernell	Hodson, Grant B.	Johanson, Robyn M.
Fuller, Dennis C.	Hales, Monte	Holbrook, Robert B.	Johansson, Claus
Fuller, F. C.	Hales, W. M.	Holdaway, W. S.	Johnson, Bill
Fullmer, Willard V.	Halgren, Joseph	Hollands, J. Val	Johnson, Dale
Gaar, Blanchard	Halverson, Ray	Hollbrook, Bob	Johnson, E. L.
Gabriel, Martin	Hamilton, James	Hollingshead, Richard	Johnson, Frank C.
Gahansson, Claus	Hammond, West	Holmes, John	Johnson, Fred
Gallagher, Terance	Hampton, W. M.	Home, G. N.	Johnson, James H.
Gardner, Kent	Hancock, Charles H.	Honell, Carroll L.	Johnson, Kenneth C.
Gardner, Richard K.	Hancock, Hal	Hook, Ernest E.	Johnson, Larry
Garff, Hershal V.	Hanks, Merlyn	Hook, Jim	Johnson, Leon
Garff, R. DeVal	Hansen, Golden K.	Hooper, Henry	Johnson, Leonard
Garff, Robert	Hansen, Reed L.	Horn, L. N.	Johnson, Mace
Garr, Blanchard	Hansen, Walter H.	Horne, Grant	Johnson, Mahlon
Geertsen, Eugene C.	Hansen, Wayne	Horrocks, B.	Johnson, William R.
Germain, George	Hansen, Wiley F.	Horrocks, Rulen	Johnston, Joshua
Gerstner, Marvin	Hanson, W. H.	Houtz, Evans B.	Johnston, Robert K.
Geving, John D.	Harding, Phillip A.	Howard, W. Allen	Jolley, Wayne L.
Gibson, James A.	Hardy, Grant	Howell, Carol L.	Jones, James W.
Gieke, Gordon	Hardy, Jim	Howell, Dr. E. Virgil	Jones, Leslie A.
Gilbert, James W.	Hardy, Ray	Howes, William	Jones, Raymond
Gilchrist, Donald B.	Hargrove, Robert J.	Huff, William F.	Jones, Reed
Gilchrist, Kent	Harline, H. L.	Huff, William L.	Jones, Ronald L.
Giles, H. E.	Harman, Frank G.	Humphries, Lee	Jongkees, Aries
Gill, Gordon	Harmon, H. Craig	Hunsaker, A. Irwin	Jonsen, Harold H.,
Gillespie, John	Harper, Coles	Hunsaker, E. P.	Jonson, Frank C.
Glade, Melvin	Harriman, R. D.	Hunsaker, Elmer	Jordan, James A.
Glauser, Rudolph	Harris, Clinton		Judd, T. Conrad

Kanon, Roelof
Keddington, Alvin
Keddington, Arthur
Keddington, Blaine
Keddington, Dick
Keddington, Harold
Keddington, John K.
Keddington, Richard
Keiser, James D.
Kelly, T. R.
Kelm, A. C.
Kelm, Robert G.
Kemp, Jessie
Kendall, Jackson W.
Kent, C. B.
Kent, Charles
Kimball, Edward L.
Kimball, James Arno
Kimble, Glenn E.
Kingdon, John
Kirby, Gerald B.
Kirk, A. J.
Kirkham, Dale
Kirkham, El Moine
Kirkham, James Arno
Kirkham, Rick M.
Klomp, Gerard
Kloock, Arnold G.
Knight, LeVoy
Knighton, Morris
Knighton, Norris
Knighton, William M.
Koew, William J.
Korstad, H. M.
Kragh, Borge
Kreek, Justin
Kunewa, Jesse K.
Kunkel, Raymond
Kunz, Calvin S.
Kynaston, Don
Lake, John E.
LaLonde, Paul A.
Lambert, George H.
Lambert, George K.
Lambert, Richard D.
Lambert, Richard N.
Lambert, William P.
Lamborn, Richard D.
Lambrick, Edward J.
Lamoreaux, Walter
Lamoreaux, W. S.
Lamoreaux, Warwick
Landvatter, Harry L.
Langdon, W. M.
Larson, Mark
Latimer, Lon
Law, A. W.
Lawrence, George
Laycock, Fred
Laykness, Leslie A.
Layton, Lawrence M.
Lee, Benjamin
Lee, Jon P.
Leeman, Theodore
LeeMaster, Vernon J.
Lemmon, Clyde
Lewis, Benjamin H.
Lewis, John C.
Light, Skipper
Lillewick, O. K.
Limburg, David
Limburg, Stephen W.
Linday, Dean
Lindsay, O. S.
Lindsley, James Russell
Livingston, Blayne
Lloyd, George C.
Lloyd, Jon
Lloyd, Layton
Loofbourow, Graham
Loofbourow, Wada
Lord, Walter
Love, Eugene L.
Loveless, Bill, Jr.
Lovendahl, Norman
Lowden, David P.
Lower, William F.
Lower, William F., Jr.
Lubbers, Joseph
Ludwig, P. J.
Luke, William S.
Lund, Anton
Lund, Ross
Lund, Weber
Lund, Whitney D.
Lunt, A. H.
Luts, Clarence O.
Lyman, J. A., Jr.
McAllister, LaVar J.
McAllister, Richard B.
McAllister, Wells A.
McBride, Kevin P.
McCartney, S. A.
McClellen, Richard
McConkie, James
McCoun, J. Gene
McCune, Craig S.
McDaniel, Stanley K.
McDonald, Edward
McDonnell, Edward I.
McEntire, James E.
McIntyre, Clyde
Mackay, W.
McKay, W. M.
McKendrick, John
McLaughlin, Howard B.
McMahon, Deane F.
McMullin, J. Herry
McMullin, Jerry
McRae, Marion
Madrian, Jost E.
Madsen, Andrew J.
Madsen, Andy
Madsen, Franklin
Magee, Maurice
Magginetti, William
Maher, Jim
Mangelson, Ronald C.
Mangum, Earl Marvin
Mangum, M. Eccles
Manookin, K. M.
Manookin, Robert P.
Mansen, Thorn J.
Manwill, Lee S.
Marble, Jack L.
Marchant, Richard
Marchant, Robert
Marindale, Edgar E.
Marsden, Rodger
Marti, Ray
Martindale, Edgar E.
Marvin, George E.
Mathews, H. C.
Mattill, Dr. F. A.
Maxwell, C. H.
Maxwell, Morris
Maxwell, W. LeGrande
Maycock, Clyde
Mendenhall, Spence
Mendoza, Aaron
Mensel, Robert J.
Meredith, Steven E.
Merrill, Rex W.
Mes, Gabriel
Mettz, Sidney
Meux, Milton O.
Miles, Morris
Miller, Adelbert H.
Miller, Byron
Miller, Gordon L.
Miller, Leigh
Millett, Novarre
Mills, Norman
Milne, Spencer
Minen, Richard Maxwell
Miner, R. Eddington
Miner, Ralph E.
Miner, Reed
Mitchell, Byron
Moffatt, Gerald
Monson, Earl
Monson, Gene P.
Montague, David O.
Moore, Garth R.
Moray, John
Moray, Richard
Morgan, Blain R.
Morgan, Donald
Morgan, Vernon R.
Morley, Clarence
Morrell, E.
Morrell, Grant B.
Morris, Jade Lynn
Morris, Miles
Mortensen, A. M.
Mortensen, David
Mortensen, Hyrum
Mortimer, A. M.
Moser, W. A.
Mower, David W.
Muchow, Ronald D.
Mueller, Richard J.
Murphy, Warren
Musig, C. Ronald
Musser, Wayne
Myers, Horace C.
Namauu, Gladiol
Neal, Lloyd William
Nebeker, John
Neilson, A. W.
Neilson, Don
Neilson, Kirk
Neilson, Kirk Merrill
Neilson, Quinton
Nelson, Charles R.
Nelson, Greg
Nelson, J. Fielding
Nelson, John
Nelson, Leon A.
Nelson, Michael D.
Nelson, Monte N.
Nelson, Ralph
Nelson, Val Rene
Nelson, Victor
Nelson, William J.
Nessa, Raynor
Neumann, Reinhard
Newren, Leslie
Newren, Loey Y.
Nicholes, David S.
Nicholes, E. H.
Nicholes, Dr. Paul S.
Nichols, Elmarion
Nichols, R.
Nielsen, A. W.
Nielson, Don
Nielson, Kirk M.
Nielson, Larry N.
Nielson, Leonard C.
Nielson, Quinton
Niesen, Hans
Nims, J. P.
Noall, L. Brooke
Norman, James
Norman, Keith E.
Norris, Stephen
North, Donald T.
North, G. W.
Noyes, Lucian
Noyes, Lyman W.
Nylander, Axel A.
Nypower, Louis
Obaugh, William R.
Oblad, Otto O.
Ofgreen, Adolph S.
Ofgreen, John
Ogden, David H.
Ogden, John W.
Ogden, Robert
Oldroyd, Stephen
O'Larry, Stanley B.
Olsen, Emmett K.
Olsen, Keith B.
Olsen, Ray
Olsen, Willis
Olson, Keith B.
Olson, Larry F.
Omer, Gerald
Omer, John S.
Omer, Wayne
Ostermiller, Dirk
Ovard, Martin S.

Overduyn, John
Overly, John W.
Owen, Gordon
Owen, John D.
Owen, John L.
Pack, Wallace
Palmer, Charles W.
Papenfuss, H. C.
Papworth, Wesley G.
Parkes, Dick
Parr, Reed
Parrish, C. R.
Paxton, Charles E.
Payne, Mike
Peabody, A. H.
Pearce, Kelly
Pearson, Edward
Pearson, Owen B.
Pedersen, H. Robert
Pedersen, Lyman
Pedersen, Robert
Pederson, Robert
Penny, William H.
Penrose, Charles W.
Perkins, Waldo
Peterborg, Jo Lee
Peterson, A. F.
Peterson, Edwin O.
Peterson, F.
Peterson, Ferdinand
Peterson, Gerald H.
Peterson, Glen H.
Peterson, Jared H.
Peterson, Lowell S.
Peterson, M.
Peterson, Melvin
Peterson, N. Harols
Peterson, P. Melvin
Petts, Doyle
Phelon, Richard J.
Pierce, Earle, Jr.
Piercey, C. J.
Pike, Charles R.
Pike, Douglas C.
Pike, Douglas E.
Pike, E. E.
Pike, Edward
Pinkerman, Joseph K.
Pipes, Vaughn L.
Pitts, Mark
Pixton, Charles
Pixton, Richard
Platt, Edward O.
Platt, F. B.
Platt, Frank G.
Poch, Spencer Eugene
Poll, Steve V.
Pollard, A. George
Pollman, Lloyd
Porter, David K.
Porter, J. E.
Porter, J. L.
Post, William
Postma, Wilbur
Poulson, David G.
Pratt, George W.
Prettyman, Duane C.
Price, Joseph P.
Price, Joseph R.
Price, Walter Gary
Provost, Sterling
Putman, Gerald
Quillian, Joseph
Rabiger, David E.
Ralston, O. C.
Ramsey, Gordon
Rasmussen, C. V.
Rasmussen, Everett
Ray, Byron A.
Read, Earl
Read, Earl, Jr.
Read, William Earl
Record, Stephen C.
Redman, Ben M.
Reed, Byron G.
Reed, I. E.
Reed, Parr
Reeve, Reed L.
Regnier, Gerard
Reichter, Horst H.
Reid, James Michael
Reynolds, C.
Reynolds, Clifford M.
Reynolds, Dale
Rhoades, David G.
Rich, A. J.
Richards, D. B.
Richards, David
Richards, Earl
Richards, Earl H.
Richards, Howell V.
Richards, Oliver C.
Richardson, Harold B.
Richardson, Justin V.
Richardson, Ron
Ridd, Gordon L.
Ridges, Douglas
Ridges, W. Lance
Ridous, Ralph
Rigby, Jerry A.
Rigby, Lester
Rigby, Robert
Rigby, Thomas C.
Robbins, Phil
Robertson, David F.
Robinson, David L.
Robinson, Don
Robinson, John
Robinson, L. E.
Robinson, Richard L.
Robinson, W. F.
Robinson, W. J.
Robison, James B.
Roden, Steven
Rogers, Vere
Rogers, Wayne
Rogerson, K. M.
Rogerson, Ken
Rokes, Willis P.
Romney, Bruce
Romney, Keith B.
Romney, O. D., Jr.
Ronneburg, E. V.
Rosendahl, Jerry
Ross, Lowell R.
Ross, W. Harvey
Rossiter, Stanford
Roswell, Neal N.
Roth, Oscar A.
Rowland, Stephen
Rowsell, Neal M.
Ruefenacht, Russel
Rumel, Herbert
Rumel, John
Rumel, Ronald
Russel, Jay
Russell, Boyd
Russell, Earl
Russell, F. C.
Russell, Frank
Russell, Galen E. III
Russell, J. N.
Russell, Jay M.
Russell, John S.
Russell, Laird
Russell, V. A.
Russell, Valoran
Russon, John K.
Russon, Robert S.
Rytting, Bryce W.
Rytting, Lorry E.
Rytting, Marlow
Salberg, John
Salvati, Phillip
Sams, Robert B.
Samuel, Charles
Samuelson, Wendell
Sandberg, H. C.
Sandberg, Reinhold
Sandberge, Dewey
Sanders, Dr. John M.
Sanderwall, Nelson
Sands, Fred R.
Sargent, Morris
Saville, Bob
Saville, Leslie H.
Saville, Lester H.
Sawyer, Clayton A.
Schaeffer, Don
Schaeffer, Donald
Schelin, Evan
Schetselaar, Gordon
Schipaanboord, Jack
Schmidt, Alfred B.
Schmidt, Charles L.
Schmidt, Rainer
Schneider, David A.
Schoenhals, Alvin J.
Schow, Andrew
Schreiner, John
Schreiner, William L.
Schreyer, Franz
Schwartz, John D.
Schwartz, Walter J.
Scopes, R. O.
Scott, James M.
Scotton, Rick
Scoville, Joel
Scoville, Paul A.
Scown, Paul D.
Scrow, Andrew
Severinsen, Mark
Shaffer, M. Ralph
Shand, David
Shaw, Coad
Sheche, James B.
Shedd, Robert Lyle
Sheehe, James B.
Sheets, Ed
Sheldon, William
Shepherd, Nat
Shepherd, R. L.
Shewell, Maximus
Shewmake, Walter
Shields, Jed
Shingleton,
Willard E., Jr.
Shirts, Jed R.
Show, Philip K.
Shrader, Rodney P.
Shurtliff, Dr. John W.
Simpson, Jonathan
Sirstens, Walter
Skidmore, A. J.
Skidmore, Allen
Slagowski, D. E.
Slagowski, Roger
Slagowski, Ronald E.
Sloan, Brent
Smith, A. L.
Smith, Bob J.
Smith, Bradley R.
Smith, Cary L.
Smith, Cornelius
Smith, Dr. David E., Jr.
Smith, E. T.
Smith, Earl
Smith, Fred E.
Smith, Gary L.
Smith, George H.
Smith, Jerry L.
Smith, Ken
Smith, Kenneth G.
Smith, LeeRoy
Smith, Leon G.
Smith, Mansel
Smith, Richard
Smith, Robert
Smith, Thomas
Smurthwaite, H. G.
Smurthwaite,
Michael B.
Snow, Philip K.
Snow, Philip R.
Snow, Stephen M.
Snyder, Clyde R.
Snyder, Ronald H.
Sondeno, Milton J.
Sorenson, J. Leon
Southwick, A. J., Jr.
Spence, Lynn
Spencer, Robert L.
Spendlove, Joseph
Sperry, Joseph W.

Spilker, Melvin F.
Springer, Gordon
Stallings, Rex
Stam, James
Standing, Earl L.
Standing, Vaughn L.
Stanford, Melvin J.
Stanger, Marrill
Steenblik, Paul K.
Steorts, Jerry
Stephens, Paul
Stevens, Bob
Stevens, Paul
Stevens, Walter L.
Stewart, John F.
Stirk, Reginald D.
Stirk, Reginald K.
Stoker, C. L. Kenny
Storrs, N. L.
Story, Lance O.
Stout, Richard O.
Straup, Fred
Streadbeck, Arval L.
Stringfellow, Burton R.
Strong, Fred
Stroud, C. H.
Stroud, Caswell
Stucki, Herman W.
Summerhayes, Joseph L.
Summerhays, Joseph R.
Summerhays, Mr.
Sundberg, D. F.
Sundstrom, Dale
Swenson, Roy A.
Swenson, S. H.
Swenson, Vernie C.
Sykes, Robb
Sylvester, James F.
Syme, Gordon
Tak, Hendrik W.
Takasaki, Roman Y.
Talmage, Sterling B.
Tame, Eldon F.
Tanner, Phil
Tarbox, Lewis R.
Tarbox, Russell
Taylor, Bayard
Taylor, Jon M.
Taylor, Norman
Taylor, Ralph
Teegarden, Byron L.
Teerlink, Leland J.
Tegge, Lothar W.
Tellefsen, Leo
Tellefsen, Ted
Tensmeyer, Lowell
Terry, Michael
Terry, Philip
Thatcher, Carvel K.
Thaxton, Theodore J., Sr.
Thaxton, Theodore J., Jr.
Thomas, Boyd J.
Thomas, John A.
Thomas, Julian
Thomas, M. F.
Thomas, M. J.
Thomas, Maroni
Thomas, Moroni, Jr.
Thomas, Paul
Thomas, Ray
Thomas, Robert D.
Thomas, William J.
Thompson, Cannon
Thompson, Darrell
Thompson, Douglas
Thompson, Orson A.
Thorn, Brent
Thorson, Arthur
Thorson, Karl Alvin
Thurgood, Robert
Tisdel, K. M.
Tompson, Lou B.
Topham, Barry
Topham, Daniel P.
Torgerson, E. Carl
Torgerson, Earl
Torgerson, Norman
Towsend, R. Brad
Tracy, Oman M.
Tranter, David
Trapp, Jerry
Trehwine, J. H.
Trimble, Ray
Tucker, John
Tueller, Arch
Turner, Fred S.
Urry, Francis
Van Der Plas, Herman H.
Van Gelderen, Ronald
Van Noy, Ray
Van Os, C. G.
VanRoosendaal,Arien
Van Slooten, John Richard
VanTussenbrock, Bert
Van Tussenbrook, A.
Van Wagoner, Gary
Vance, Wallace R.
Vande Mere, Jan W.
Vander Werff, Dowie
Vanderwerff, Glen B.
VanNoy, Ray
VanTussenbroek, Gerrit
Veekers, Boyd
Vernieu, John T.
Vernon, Robert
Vickers, Boyd
Vickers, DeForest
Vincent, Robert
Voelker, Arthur H.
Von Behren, James Arnold
Vonk, William J., Jr.
Vote, N. R.
Waite, J. W.
Waite, R. L.
Waite, Robert S.
Walkley, J. B.
Wallace, Walter
Ward, Melvin L.
Ware, Henry
Watkiss, H.
Watson, Richard A.
Weaver, Don M.
Weaver, Ted L.
Webb, Walter L.
Weber, George
Weech, Merrill R.
Weeks, Wilfred H.
Weenig, Carl
Wegeland, Dan B.
Wegener, Karl
Weight, Gary H.
Weight, Wilford
Weinegar, Kent
Weinsinger, Kurt
Weiser, Jim
Weiss, Max
Welch, Art
Welling, H. S.
Wells, Maurice
Welsh, Benton D.
Welsh, John
Welsh, Ronald E.
Welte, Conrad
Welti, Walter
Weshe, Walter
West, James David
West, Lawerence
West, William K.
Wetherell, F.
Wetherell, Fred R.
Wettstein, Daniel
Whalley, W. D.
Wheadon, Peter K.
Wheeler, Don
Wherland, E.
White, Farnum E.
White, Robert G.
Whitehead, Carvel
Whitney, R. E.
Wiglama, Arie W.
Wilde, L. Clair
Wilkin, G. R.
Wilkins, David H.
Williams, Clayton R.
Williams, Nelson
Williams, Russell
Williams, Scott
Williams, Tom
Wilson, A. F.
Wilson, Merrill L.
Wilton, C. M.
Wims, James C.
Wingert, William L., Jr.
Winn, Frank
Winsor, Rulon S.
Wintch, Clair
Wiscomb, A. I.
Wolfgram, Harold
Wood, David R.
Wood, G. C.
Wood, John H.
Wood, Joseph H.
Woodbury, W. H.
Woodhouse, Stephen K.
Woodworth, Mark
Wooley, David R.
Woolley, E. Richard
Woolley, Edwin R., Jr.
Worden, Dale S.
Worley, W. J., Jr.
Wright, Amos L.
Wright, Bruce
Wright, Dr. E. S.
Wright, Gary H.
Wright, Ronald A., Jr.
Wright, Wesley Dean
Wright, Willard S.
Wynne, Sam
Yohansen, Klas
Young, Lorenzo S.
Young, McCready
Zancanella, Robert C.
Zerull, Dietmar
Zervill, A. O. J.
Zimmer, Markus B.
Zimmer, Marvin A.
Zimmer, Marvin R.
Zimmer, Max
Zinn, George
Zueger, Elden W.
Zupan, Terry
Zurligen, Leland S.

Unclassified by Voice

Billings, Anna Wilcox
Burton,Janene Monson
Christensen, Elizabeth Hansen
Christensen, Paul E.
Cook, Carolee
Cook, Elaine
Haker, Pamela Fetzer
Jorgensen, Lynone
Layton, Beverly
Neville, Kerol
Pingree, John
Richins, Fay
Smith, Kristie
Sorenson, Gustav
Young, Effay Van Cott

Notes

Chapter One: The First Musicians

1. Thomas L. Kane, *The Mormons, A Discourse Delivered Before The Historical Society of Pennsylvania: March 26, 1850* (Philadelphia: King and Baird, Printers, Sansom Street. 1850), 32–33.
2. "Concert," *Deseret News*, 22 June 1850.
3. "Deseret Philharmonic Society," *Deseret News*, 1 March 1855.
4. "Musical Tour," *The Deseret News*, 29 August 1855.
5. Edward W. Tullidge, *History of Salt Lake City* (Salt Lake City: Star Printing Company, 1886), 771.
6. Tullidge, 771.
7. Tullidge, 772.

Chapter Two: George and Lavinia Careless

1. Tullidge, 773.
2. "Veteran Musician Tells Of Step From London's Opera Houses To First Orchestra In Salt Lake," *The Salt Lake Tribune* (hereafter cited as *Tribune*), 20 May 1928, Society Section.
3. George D. Pyper, "In Intimate Touch with Professor George Careless I," *The Juvenile Instructor*, March 1924, 173.
4. "The Singing During Conference," *Deseret Evening News*, 9 May 1870.
5. George D. Pyper, *Romance of an Old Playhouse*, rev. ed. (Salt Lake City: The Deseret Press, 1937), 307.

6. Bruce David Maxwell, "George Careless, Pioneer Musician," *Utah Historical Quarterly*, Fall 1985, 134.
7. In the LDS Church a ward is an ecclesiastical unit. Each corresponds to a geographical area and in early Salt Lake many wards supported a school.
8. "The Concerts," *The Deseret News*, 5 January 1871.
9. "The Concert Last Night," *The Deseret News*, 8 March 1871.
10. "Deseret Philharmonic Society," *The Deseret News*, 26 April 1871.
11. "Formation Of A Choral Society," *Tribune*, 7 January 1871.
12. "Grand Concert," *Tribune*, 31 March 1873.
13. Pyper, "In Intimate Touch with Professor George Careless III," *The Juvenile Instructor*, May 1924, 235.
14. Tullidge, 774.
15. "The Messiah," *The Salt Lake Daily Herald*, 4 May 1875.
16. Tullidge, 777.
17. "First Grand Orchestral Concert," *The Salt Lake Daily Herald*, 22 March 1879.
18. Pyper, *Playhouse*, 310.
19. *Salt Lake Daily Herald*, 22 May 1883.
20. Tullidge, 779.
21. "The Creation," *The Salt Lake Daily Herald*, 11 May 1881.
22. "Mammoth Orchestra," *Salt Lake Daily Herald*, 22 March 1885.
23. "Professor Careless' Society," *Salt Lake Daily Herald*, 24 October 1886.
24. "Belshazzar," *Salt Lake Daily Herald*, 8 June 1887.
25. "Utah's Most Famous Singer," *Deseret Evening News*, 31 August 1901.
26. Tullidge, 778.

Chapter Three: Evan Stephens, Choirs and Operas

1. "Music Chants," *Tribune*, 11 October 1891.
2. "The Music Festival," *Tribune*, 31 May 1890.
3. "Stephens Quits The Choral Society," *Tribune*, 20 March 1894.
4. Charles Jeffrey Calman, *The Mormon Tabernacle Choir* (New York: Harper & Row, 1979), 57.
5. *Deseret Evening News*, 21 November 1903.

Chapter Four: Early Symphonic Music

1. "Our Orchestral Possibilities," *Salt Lake Daily Herald*, 27April 1884.
2. "Our Chances For The Formation Of A Good Orchestra," *Salt Lake Daily Herald*, 11 January 1886.
3. *Deseret Evening News*, 15 March 1888.
4. "Tonight's Concert," *The Salt Lake Herald*, 17 April 1892.
5. "Music Chants," *Tribune*, 22 May 1892.
6. *Deseret Evening News*, 24 November 1902.

7. Ibid., 29 November 1902.
8. The new Orpheum on Second South between Main and State Streets, which is now the Capitol Theater and the home of Salt Lake City dance and opera, was built in 1912.
9. This Church of Jesus Christ of Latter-day Saints institution, though it was variously known as LDS University, LDS College, and LDS High School, "never rose above the commercial college, and junior college grade" (B. H. Roberts, *A Comprehensive History of the Church of Jesus Christ of Latter-day Saints: Century I*. Vol. 6. Brigham Young University Press: Provo, Utah. 1965. 518).
10. "Philharmonic Next Sunday," *Tribune*, 30 March 1913.
11. "Anton Pedersen," *Musical America*, 30 May 1913, 37.

Chapter Five: A New Century

1. "Music Festival a Great Success," *Tribune*, 9 April 1907.

Chapter Six: Professor Squire Coop

1. "Funeral Of Mrs. M. H. Coop," *Deseret Evening News*, 13 January 1902.
2. "Music Notes," *Deseret Evening News*, 13 April 1901.
3. Ralph V. Chamberlin, *The University of Utah, A History Of Its First Hundred Years, 1850 to 1950* (Salt Lake City: University of Utah Press, 1960), 295.
4. "Music Notes," *Tribune*, 25 September 1904.
5. "Working To Raise Standard Of Music," *Tribune*, 19 November 1905.
6. Letter, D. R. Allen, Secretary, Board of Regents of the University of Utah, To Coop, 26 April 1910, included in Dr. Howard T. Anderson, "Professors I Have Known" (unpublished television script), The Oratorio Society of Utah Collection, Accession Number 738, Box 1, Folder 3, Special Collections Department, University of Utah Library, Salt Lake City (hereafter cited as U of U Society Collection).
7. "Planning Consolidation," *Tribune*, 26 February 1911.
8. "Professor Squire Coop To Be Displaced," *Deseret Evening News*, 15 April 1913.
9. "Squire Coop To Leave University," *Tribune*, 15 April 1913.
10. "Will Carry Out Plans," *Tribune*, 20 April 1913.
11. "Music And Musicians," *Deseret Evening News*, 19 April 1913, sec. VI.
12. "Musical Society Pass Resolutions," *The Utah Chronicle*, 21 April 1913.
13. "Concerning Professor Squire Coop," *The Utah Chronicle*, 21 April 1913.
14. In 1915 University of Utah President Joseph T. Kingsbury and the board of regents demoted the popular non-LDS head of the English depart-

ment and dismissed four non-LDS professors and instructors. The head of the Latter Day Saints High School, a prominent Mormon with no previous university teaching or administrative experience, was appointed the new head of the English department and the faculty dismissals partially explained as necessary to give this new man a free hand in choosing his own staff. Student, faculty, alumni, and several downtown groups called without success for investigations of the matter; sixteen faculty members resigned in protest; lawsuits were threatened; and ultimately the American Association of University Professors conducted an investigation which, among other conclusions, determined that of the charges leading to the dismissal of the four faculty members in 1915, "three specify no proper grounds for such action, and the fourth is without basis in fact;" that "The President of the University and the Chairman of the Board of Regents by their recent action virtually gave notice that the expression by a professor, in private conversation, of an unfavorable opinion of their [i.e., of the president's or chairman of the board of regents'] qualifications for office would be a ground for dismissal;" and that "under the present administration, unverified gossip, coming from persons unwilling to assume public responsibility for their statements, has played an unfortunate part in the affairs of the University of Utah...." (*The American Association of University Professors, Report of the Committee of Inquiry on Conditions at the University of Utah*, July 1915, 40–41.)

The investigation also found that Osborne J. P. Widtsoe, the man appointed by the regents to succeed as head of the English department, who had, as already mentioned, been connected with Latter Day Saints High School, and who was a bishop in the LDS Church and a former editor of the *Juvenile Instructor*, a Church publication, did not have the academic preparation "usually expected in those appointed to headship of important departments in either colleges or universities in good standing (ibid., 80)."

Dean Frank E. Holman, one of the staff members who resigned in protest over Kingsbury's actions (in a speech reprinted in *The Chronicle*, the university's student newspaper) made what is very likely a reference to Professor Coop's plight of two years' earlier, when he said: "But the suspicion that is most unworthy is the suspicion of the administration as to men's characters. I have come in contact with this directly and I know exactly what I am talking about. There have been instances previous to the present difficulty in which men have been dropped from the faculty on account of petty gossip with regard to their characters. In those instances it was gravely whispered to us— 'Don't ask questions; you will harm the men involved.' The administration put it upon the magnanimous ground of shielding this or that person's reputation (see the 25 March 1915 issue, p. 3)."

As a result of these difficulties reforms were instituted in the relationship between faculty and administration that, had they been in place earlier, would have made impossible such dismissals without formal charges or hearings as those of Professor Coop or the victims of the 1915 episode.

15. "Squire Coop," *The Morning Examiner* (Ogden), 20 April 1913.
16. "Squire Coop Returns; Was Ill In New York," *Tribune*, 14 September 1913.

Chapter Seven: The Salt Lake Oratorio Society

1. "'Oratorio Society' Can Accomplish Much," *Tribune*, 17 May 1914.
2. "Musicians Form An Oratorio Society," *Tribune*, 18 May 1914.
3. *The Salt Lake Herald-Republican*, 17 May 1914.
4. "Oratorio Society To Hold Meeting Today," *Tribune*, 15 November 1914.
5. "Oratorio Society Is Busy Rehearsing," *Tribune*, 22 November 1914.
6. Articles of Incorporation of Salt Lake Oratorio Society, 14 January 1915, Utah Business regulations Department, Division of Corporation and Commercial Codes.
7. "Will Sing 'Messiah' Oratorio On New Year's," *Tribune*, 20 December 1914.
8. "The 'Messiah' Presentation Scores A Surprise," *Deseret Evening News*, 2 January 1915.
9. "Greatest Oratorio For New Year's Day," *Tribune*, 27 December 1914.
10. "Oratorio Society," *The Salt Lake Herald-Republican*, 2 January 1915.
11. "Oratorio Society Scores A Triumph," *Tribune*, 2 January 1915.
12. "The 'Messiah' Presentation Scores A Surprise," *Deseret Evening News*, 2 January 1915.
13. "Oratorio Society's Work Well Begun," *Tribune*, 3 January 1915.

Chapter Eight: The Tabernacle Debut

1. "Music," *Deseret Evening News*, 9 January 1915.
2. "Cash Receipts & Disbursements Of The Messiah, 1 January 1916," Minutes of the Salt Lake Oratorio Society (hereafter cited as Minutes), 20A, U of U Society Collection, 3:2.
3. "Oratorio Society To Be Heard Saturday," *Tribune*, 26 December 1915.
4. "'Messiah' Finely Rendered," *Deseret Evening News*, 3 January 1916.
5. *The Salt Lake Herald-Republican*, 9 January 1916.
6. "Cash Receipts & Disbursements Of The Messiah, 1 January 1916," Minutes, 20A, U of U Society Collection, 3:2. The relative value of the 1916 dollar is evident from the following, which was taken from the 1 and 2 January 1916 editions of *The Herald-Republican*. Wages: government, $75 monthly; railroad breakmen, $120 monthly; day laborers, $2.50 per eight hour shift. Rents: three to five room apartments, $9 to $32.50 monthly. Prices: men's suits, $10; seven-passenger Studebaker touring car, $845; new bungalow, $2,350.
7. *The Salt Lake Herald-Republican*, 17 December 1916.
8. *Deseret Evening News*, 23 December 1916, sec. 2.

9. "A Notable Musical Event," *Deseret Evening News*, 2 January 1917.
10. "Messiah Production Interest Is Marked," *Tribune*, 24 December 1916.
11. "'Messiah' Production To Open New Year," *Tribune*, 31 December 1916.
12. "Great Composition Arouses Thousands," *Tribune*, 2 January 1917.
13. *The Salt Lake Herald-Republican*, 7 May 1916.
14. "A Notable Musical Event," *Deseret Evening News*, 2 January 1917.
15. Ibid.
16. Ibid.
17. "Incomplete Report Of Receipts And Disbursements Of The Messiah Performance, 1 January 1917," Minutes, 26–7, U of U Society Collection, 3:2.
18. "Great Composition Arouses Thousands," *Tribune*, 2 January 1917.

Chapter Nine: The First Creation

1. Minutes, 21 January 1915, 15. U of U Society Collection, 1:2.
2. "Thousands Hear Rendition Of 'The Creation,'" *Deseret Evening News*, 14 May 1917.
3. For an early example of the consideration the Society has always shown other musical organizations in the community, see "'Messiah' Rehearsal Hour Moved Forward," *Tribune*, 13 December 1914, in which it is announced that Messiah rehearsals have been rescheduled to accommodate chorus members attending a Salt Lake Philharmonic concert.
4. "Dedicate New Capitol Monday," *The Salt Lake Herald-Republican*, 8 October 1916.
5. "State Capitol Is Dedicated," *Deseret Evening News*, 10 October 1916.
6. "New Capitol Dedicated To Public Use," *The Salt Lake Herald-Republican*, 10 October 1916.
7. "Great Throng At Opening Of State Capitol," *Tribune*, 10 October 1916.
8. *Deseret Evening News*, 13 January 1917, sec. 2.
9. "Prompt Response For Community Music," *Tribune*, 18 March 1917.
10. "Opportunity Is Here To Show Appreciation," *Tribune*, 15 April 1917.
11. "Oratorio Society To Sing 'Creation' May 6," *Tribune*, 22 April 1917.
12. Minutes, 2 May 1917, 35. U of U Society Collection, 3:2.
13. Ibid., 10 May 1917, 38.
14. *Deseret Evening News*, May 1917, sec. 2.
15. *Deseret Evening News*, 12 May 1917, sec. 2.
16. "Thousands Hear Rendition Of 'The Creation,'" *Deseret Evening News*, 14 May 1917.
17. "'Creation' Carries Community Lesson," *Tribune*, 20 May 1917.
18. "Vast Throng Thrilled By Music Feast," *The Salt Lake Herald Republican*, 14 May 1917.
19. As with several early *Messiah* renditions, no 1917 *Creation* program is

available. It is certain, however, that the rendition was somewhat abbreviated. We know this because, starting at 4:45 and concluding at 6:00 P.M., it was only an hour and a quarter long. By comparison, the 1921 *Creation* (for which a program is available) began at 7:15 P.M. and ended virtually in the dark. As this was in June, and assuming mountain standard time, it could have done little less than approach two hours in length; but even the 1921 version omitted several numbers in the first and second parts, and included none of the third.

Chapter Ten: Judas Maccabaeus

1. "Squire Coop Is Orchestra Leader," *Tribune*, 19 October 1917.
2. Deseret Evening News, 10 November 1917, sec. 2.
3. "'Messiah' Embodies Highest Of Music," *Tribune*, 23 December 1917, Society Section.
4. Letter, John Daniel Spencer to Mrs. Kate B. Carter, President of the Daughters of the Utah Pioneers, 4 September 1941, 12. Utah State Historical Society.
5. "Community Service Of 'The Messiah' A Huge Success," *Deseret Evening News*, 2 January 1918.
6. Ibid.
7. *Deseret Evening News*, 19 January 1918, sec. 2.
8. *Deseret Evening News*, 2 February 1918, sec. 2.
9. *Deseret Evening News*, 30 March 1918, sec. 3.
10. "Tabernacle Choir Gives Fine Rendition Of 'Elijah,'" *Deseret Evening News*, 6 April 1918.
11. "Oratorio Society Will Hold Rehearsal Today," *Tribune*, 22 December 1918, Society Section.
12. "Prof. Coop Drops In During Oratorio," *Deseret Evening News*, 2 January 1919, sec. 2.
13. "Oratorio Society Is Abreast Of The Times," *Tribune*, 30 March 1919, Society Section.
14. *Tribune*, 8 June 1919, Society Section.
15. "Tabernacle Choir Renders 'St. Paul,'" *Deseret Evening News*, 7 June 1919.
16. *Deseret Evening News*, 6 September 1919, sec. 2.
17. "Victory Oratorio Will Be Given Wednesday," *Tribune*, 5 October 1919, Society Section.
18. "Tribute Is Paid To Utah's Heroes Living And Dead," *Deseret Evening News*, 9 October 1919.
19. "Oratorio Given For Servicemen," *Tribune*, 9 October 1919.
20. "Tribute Is Paid To Utah's Heroes Living And Dead," *Deseret Evening News*, 9 October 1919.
21. *Deseret Evening News*, 18 October 1919, sec. 3.
22. "Communication By Squire Coop," *Tribune*, 14 December 1919, Society Section.

23. *Deseret Evening News*, 8 November 1919, sec. 3.
24. *Deseret Evening News*, 3 January 1919.
25. "Oratorio Society Pays Tribute To A. H. Peabody," *Tribune*, 29 February 1920, Society Section.

Chapter Eleven: Wandering Minstrel

1. "Great Throng Hears Oratorio," *Tribune*, 10 July 1920.
2. "Messiah Stirs Great Audience," *Tribune*, 2 January 1921.
3. "City Should Preserve Oratorio As Institution," *Tribune*, 9 January 1921, Society Section.
4. Ibid. To this time only the 1919 *Judas Maccabaeus* and the 1920 *Creation* had received significant support.
5. "Community Music Needs Real, Organized Support," *Tribune*, 16 January 1921, Society Section.
6. "Authors' Club Honors Director Squire Coop," *Tribune*, 30 January 1921, Society Section.
7. "Oratorio Stirs Vast Audience," *Tribune*, 17 June 1921.
8. "Thousands Are Delighted With Great Oratorio," *Tribune*, 21 June 1922.
9. *The Deseret Evening News*, 1 July 1922, sec. 3.
10. Telegram, Mayor C. Clarence Neslen to Dr. Ernest C. Moore, director of the University of California, Los Angeles, 1 December 1922, Archives of the University of California at Los Angeles (UCLA).
11. Night Letter, Dr. Moore to Mayor Neslen, 2 December 1922, UCLA Archives.
12. "Oratorio Gains Sublime Plane," *Tribune*, 2 January 1923.

Chapter Twelve: Home-Talent Conductors

1. "The Messiah Huge Success," *Tribune*, 2 January 1924.
2. "Sustained Interest In Oratorio Is Essential," *Tribune*, 6 July 1924.
3. "Singers Voice Glory To God," *Tribune*, 1 July 1925.
4. "Oratorio Chorus Needs To Work Year Round," *Tribune*, 3 January 1926.
5. "Oratorio Rated As One Of Best," *Tribune*, 2 January 1926.
6. "Many Charmed With Oratorio," *Tribune*, 2 January 1927.
7. "Oratorio 'Elijah' To Be Presented By Choir In Dramatized Form," *The Deseret News*, 5 November 1927, sec. 3.
8. "Tabernacle Choir To Present 'Elijah' On Pretentious Scale," *The Deseret News*, 12 November 1927, sec. 3.
9. "Oratorio 'Creation' Given Competent Presentation," *Tribune*, 18 July 1928.
10. "Efforts Of Local Artists Call For Better Attitude From Public; Student Orchestra Scores Success," *Tribune*, 22 July 1928, Society Section.
11. "'Creation' Produced With Great Success," *Evening Herald* (Provo), 18 July 1929.
12. Messiah Program, 1 January 1929, Oratorio Society Memorabilia

Collection of Mrs. Edith S. Anderson (hereafter cited as the Anderson Collection).

13. Gail Martin, "In The Major Key," *The Deseret News*, 16 December 1933, Society Section, The Christmas News edition.
14. "Oratorio Presented To Big Crowd At Tabernacle," *The Deseret News*, 2 January 1935.
15. "Majestic Messiah To Be Rendered Sunday Morning," *The Deseret News*, 27 December 1930, sec. 3.
16. J. Spencer Cornwall, *A Century Of Singing, The Salt Lake Mormon Tabernacle Choir* (Salt Lake City: Deseret Book Company, 1958), 225.
17. Letter, Horace H. Shrader of New Albany, Indiana, to Annette Richardson Dinwoodey, 21 December 1931, U of U Society Collection, 1:2.
18. "'Messiah' Held Best Musical Here During '33," *The Deseret News*, 1 January 1934.

Chapter Thirteen: The Minstrel Comes Home

1. "'Messiah' Thrills 10,000 Persons In Presentation At Salt Lake Tabernacle," *Tribune*, 30 December 1935.
2. Martin, "'Messiah' Rendition Marks Advance In S. L. Cultural, Civic Progress," *The Deseret News*, 30 December 1935.
3. Martin, "Oratorio Presented To Big Crowd At Tabernacle," *The Deseret News*, 2 January 1935.
4. Minutes, 18 November 1936, 30, U of U Society Collection, 1:4.
5. Martin, "In The Major Key," *The Deseret News*, 16 December 1933, Society section, The Christmas News edition.
6. Letter, Coop to Oratorio Society Board, 1 July 1939, U of U Society Collection, 1:2.
7. Undated letter, Coop to Dr. Bennion, U of U Society Collection, 2:34
8. Lesley Goates, "Capacity Audience Hears 'The Messiah,'" *The Deseret News*, 30 December 1940.
9. Ibid.
10. Typed copy of letter, Coop to Dr. Bennion, 23 October 1941, U of U Society Collection, 3:2.
11. Letter, Dr. Bennion to Coop, 8 December 1942, U of U Society Collection, 3:2.
12. Dr. Bennion's Typed notes for the December 27, 1942, KSL Messiah selections broadcast, U of U Society Collection, 2:10.
13. Letter, Coop to Dr. Bennion, 7 October 1942, U of U Society Collection, 3:2.

Chapter Fourteen: The Postwar Messiah

1. Letter, J. Spencer Cornwall to Dr. Bennion, 2 January 1947, U of U Society Collection, 4:3. The reference to cigarettes evidently alludes to the tobacco addiction of Otto Klemperer, the Society's first postwar guest conductor. Judge J. Allan Crockett (in personal conversation) relates that Klemperer committed the indiscretion of lighting a cigarette in the Tabernacle.

2. Letter, Mrs. Squire Coop and Sheila to Dr. Bennion, 26 November 1945, U of U Society Collection, 3:11.
3. Con (more often Conrad B.) Harrison, "Messiah Gains High Praise Of Record Crowd," *The Deseret News*, 31 December 1945.
4. Dr. Lowell M. Durham, "Music Lovers Pleased By '47 Oratorio," *Tribune*, 29 December 1947, sec. 2.
5. "Dr. Greenfield Snaps A Finger At Handel 'Messiah' Tradition," *Ogden Standard Examiner*, 25 December 1949, sec. A.
6. Letter, Dr. Thompson Stone to W. J. Thomas, 11 November 1949, U of U Society Collection, 5:2.
7. "'Messiah' Wins High Praise For Artistry," *Deseret News*, 2 January 1950, sec. B.
8. Durham, "'The Messiah' Caps City's Musical Year," *Tribune*, 1 January 1951.
9. Harrison, "Inspired 'Messiah' Rendition Thrills Packed Salt Lake Tabernacle Crowd," *Deseret News and Salt Lake Telegram*, 3 January 1955, sec. B.
10. Durham, "'The Messiah' Exalts Big S. L. Audience," *Tribune*, 3 January 1955.

Chapter Fifteen: The Thor Johnson Era

1. "Messiah Conducting—A Unique Experience," *Tribune*, 27 December 1963.
2. Harrison, "10,000 Hear 'The Messiah' Performed In S. L. Tabernacle," *Deseret News*, 31 December 1950.
3. Sir Ernest MacMillan, "Handel Expert Scans Past, Tidies Work," *Tribune*, 21 December 1952, sec. B.
4. Harrison, "Yuletide Message Voiced In 'Messiah'," *Deseret News and Salt Lake Telegram*, 19 December 1955, sec. B.
5. Durham, "Utahn's Thrill To 40th 'Messiah,'" *Tribune*, 19 December 1955.
6. Copy of letter, Mrs. M. Woolsey to KSL Radio, 19 December 1955, Anderson Collection.
7. Copy of undated letter, Hope LaRue Swengel to KSL Radio, Anderson Collection.
8. Unsigned copy of letter, The Salt Lake Oratorio Society to The Presiding Bishopric c/o Bishop Isaacson, 21 April 1950, U of U Society Collection, 5:22.
9. Letter, Bishop Thorpe B. Isaacson to Jack Thomas, 12 June 1951, U of U Society Collection, 6:6.
10. Letter, Herold L. Gregory to President Henry D. Moyle, 16 April 1960, U of U Society Collection, 7:5.
11. Harrison, "'Messiah' Emphasizes Christmas Meaning," *Deseret News and Salt Lake Telegram*, 23 December 1957, sec. B.
12. Harold Lundstrom, "S. L. Oratorio—Triumph Of Moving Drama," *Deseret News and Salt Lake Telegram*, 21 December 1959, sec. B.

13. Letter, William D. Sullivan, President, Local 104, A. F. of M., to Dr. Howard T. Anderson, 16 November 1967, Anderson Collection.
14. Draft of letter, Dr. Howard T. Anderson to Dr. Thor Johnson, 5 August 1973, Anderson Collection.
15. Minutes, 11 September 1973, Anderson Collection. They read in part: "Edith Anderson read a letter from Dr. Thor Johnson saying he would conduct our next Messiah performance only if we accept the program exactly as he recommended."
16. Lundstrom, "'Messiah'—A Gold Mine," *Deseret News*, 17 December 1973, sec. A.

Chapter Sixteen: The Nielson Chorus

1. These remarks by John Marlowe Nielson were taken from an introductory passage to his Society scrapbook for the years 1962 through 1977, which he kindly made available to the author.
2. Lundstrom, "'Messiah' Oratorio Attracts Throng," *Deseret News and Salt Lake Telegram*, 31 December 1962, sec. B.
3. Janet Young Hammond and Valena M. Berntson, Responses to questionnaire, 22 February and 2 February, 1986.
4. Michael Fox, "Maestro Interprets Original 'Messiah,'" *Tribune*, December 1968. Other commentators put the attendance at the first Messiah in Dublin at nearer seven hundred persons.
5. Lundstrom, "Crowd Praises 'Messiah'," *Deseret News*, 28 December 1964, sec. B.
6. Jim Fitzpatrick, "50th 'Messiah' Rendition Awes Tabernacle Crowd," *Tribune*, 20 December 1965.
7. Lundstrom, "An Exciting Music Treat," *Deseret News*, 20 December 1965, sec. B.
8. Lundstrom, "Oratorio Society's 'Messiah'—That 'Hallelujah!' Says All," *Deseret News*, 20 December 1971, sec. B.
9. Fitzpatrick, "Conductor Catches Handel's Lyricism," *Tribune*, 19 December 1964.
10. Lundstrom, "Handel's Genius Illuminated," *Deseret News*, 16 December 1974, sec. B.
11. Lundstrom, "His Influence Will Be Felt And Missed," *Deseret News*, 13 December 1974, sec. D.

Chapter Seventeen: Contemporary Messiah

1. Letter, F. Michael Watson to Mrs. Annette R. Dinwoodey, 30 July 1976, Anderson Collection.
2. Lundstrom, "Romantic 'Messiah' Brings Ovation," *Deseret News*, 20 December 1976, sec. C.
3. William S. Goodfellow, "Hendl At Helm Again," *Deseret News*, 14 December 1978, sec. C.
4. Wetzel, "Conductor Places His Mark Upon Handel's 'Messiah,'" *Tribune*, 18 December 1978, sec. B.

5. Wetzel, "Televising Handel's 'Messiah,'" *Tribune*, 7 December, 1980, sec. E.
6. Dorothy Stowe, "'Messiah' Set For TV," *Deseret News*, 15 December 1980.
7. Wetzel, "A Long Time From Prophecy to Resurrection," *Tribune*, 15 December 1980, sec. C.

Chapter Eighteen: Expanding Horizons

1. Fitzpatrick, "S. L. Oratorio's Concert: Earnestness, Sincerity," *Tribune*, 17 April 1965.
2. W. H. Hadow, "The Viennese Period," *The Oxford History of Music*, Vol. V (Oxford: Clarendon Press, 1904), p. 151.
3. Keith Burris, "S. L. Oratorio 'Pleasing,'" *Deseret News*, 17 April 1965.
4. Lenore Sagon, "S. L. Oratorio In Aspen Triumph," *Deseret News*, 24 July 1967, sec. C.
5. Letter, James N. Cain, Executive Director of the Aspen Music Festival, to Dr. Howard T. Anderson, 31 July 1967, U of U Society Collection, 7:25.
6. Wetzel, "Grant Johannesen Shines In All-Beethoven Concert," *Tribune*, 10 May 1981, sec. E.
7. Stowe, "Unfamiliar Works, Same Spirit," *Deseret News*, 11–12 May 1981, sec. C.
8. Lundstrom, "Singing Was Full-bodied," *Deseret News*, 28 June 1976, sec. B.
9. Stowe, "Performers Peak For S. L. 'Elijah,'" *Deseret News*, 24 June 1978.
10. Wetzel, "Performance Of 'Elijah' A Disappointment," *Tribune*, 24 June 1978.
11. David L. Beck, "Elijah Was A Strong Performance," *Tribune*, 6 June 1977.
12. Anne Mathews, "In 70th Year Oratorio Society Gives Triumphant 'Elijah,'" *Tribune*, 18 June 1985, sec. A.
13. John Charles, "Elijah Infused With Life," T*he Edmonton Sun*, 16 September 1985.
14. Lundstrom, "Oratorio, Haydn Delight Tabernacle Audience," *Deseret News*, 12 June 1972, sec. A.
15. Associated Press dispatch, Jerusalem, 6 June 1983 1725 MDT, Anderson Collection.
16. Stowe, "Jewish Zealots Disrupt Utah Oratorio Concert," *Deseret News*, 10 June 1983, sec. B.
17. Judy Siegel, "Chief Rabbi Gave Okay To 'Messiah' Protest," *The Jerusalem Post*, 11 June 1983.
18. Lee Case, response to questionnaire, 3 March 1986.
19. Stowe, "Jewish Zealots Disrupt Utah Oratorio Concert."
20. Siegel, "Chief Rabbi Gave Okay To 'Messiah' Protest."

21. Stowe, "Jewish Zealots Disrupt Utah Oratorio Concert."
22. Stowe, "Utah Choir Reassured By Israelis," *Deseret News*, 11 June 1983, sec. A.

Chapter Nineteen: The Heart of the Society

1. Laurie Williams Sowby, response to questionnaire, 10 February 1986.
2. Barbara J. Alvey, response to questionnaire, 15 February 1986.
3. Fay S. Patrick, response to questionnaire, 9 December 1986.
4. Loretta Henderson, response to questionnaire, 27 February 1986.
5. Kent M. Barry, response to questionnaire, 19 February 1986.
6. Joyce Orlob Evans, response to questionnaire, 10 January 1986.
7. Jane P. Brown, response to questionnaire, 30 January 1986.
8. A. Ray Trimble, response to questionnaire, 14 February 1986.
9. Elrena Nielson, response to questionnaire, 3 February 1986.
10. Jayna Friberg, response to questionnaire, 15 March 1986.
11. Julie L. Williams, response to questionnaire, 25 February 1986.
12. Minutes, 27 January 1975, Anderson Collection.
13. Oratorio Society of Utah Messiah Performance 1986 Vs. 1985, Anderson Collection.
14. Wetzel, "Economic Hard Times Hit Salt Lake's Arts Institutions," *Tribune*, 5 April 1987, sec. E.
15. "Thousands Hear Splendid Rendition Of Haydn's Masterpiece 'The Creation' On University Campus At Sunset Hour," *The Deseret News*, 21 June 1922.

Bibliography

Alexander, Thomas G. and James B. Allen. *Mormons & Gentiles, A History of Salt Lake City*. Boulder, Colorado: Pruett Publishing Company, 1984.

American Association of University Professors, *Report of the Committee of Inquiry on Conditions at the University of Utah*. 1915.

Ames, Jeanne Wignall. Private papers and documents concerning the Oratorio Society of Utah for the period 1949–1969.

Anderson, Edith Smith. Private papers and documents concerning the Oratorio Society of Utah for the period 1915–1987.

"Articles of Incorporation of the Salt Lake Oratorio Society." These and other official Society documents are on file with the Utah Business Regulations Department, Division of Corporations and Commercial Codes, Salt Lake City.

Brown, Deane Wakley. *Growth and Development of Utah Professional Symphonic Orchestras Prior to 1940*. Master's thesis. Brigham Young University, 1959.

Calman, Charles Jeffrey. *The Mormon Tabernacle Choir*. New York: Harper & Row, 1979.

Catalogue of the University of Utah and Announcements for 1906–1907. University of Utah, 1906.

Chamberlin, Ralph V. *The University of Utah, A History of its First Hundred Years, 1850 to 1950*. Salt Lake City: University of Utah Press, 1960.

Cornwall, J. Spencer. *A Century of Singing, The Salt Lake Mormon Tabernacle Choir.* Salt Lake City: Deseret Book Company, 1958.

—*Stories of our Mormon Hymns.* Salt Lake City: Deseret Book Company, 1961.

Deseret News. Newspaper. Name varies. Salt Lake City: 1850–1986.

Durham, Lowell M. "On Mormon Music and Musicians," *Dialogue, A Journal of Mormon Thought* (Summer 1968), 19–32.

Edmonton Journal, The. Newspaper. Edmonton, Alberta: 1984.

Edmonton Sun, The. Newspaper. Edmonton, Alberta: 1984.

Evening Herald. Newspaper. Provo, Utah: 1929.

Ewen, David. *The New Encyclopedia of the Opera.* New York: Hill and Wang, 1971.

Geiringer, Karle. *Haydn, A Creative Life In Music.* 3rd ed. Berkeley: University of California Press, 1982.

Hadow, W. H. *The Oxford History of Music.* Oxford: Clarendon Press, 1904.

Harrison, Conrad B. "The Utah Symphony Story." An essay on the Utah Symphony published in nine installments in the Utah Symphony programs from 24 October 1959 through 16 March 1960.

—*Five Thousand Concerts, A Commemorative History of the Utah Symphony.* Salt Lake City: Utah Symphony Society, 1986.

Jacobi, Peter. *The Messiah Book: The Life & Times of G. F. Handel's Greatest Hit.* New York: St. Martin's Press, 1982.

Jenson, Andrew. *Latter-Day Saint Biographical Encyclopedia.* 4 vols. Salt Lake City: Western Epics, 1971.

Jerusalem Post, The. Newspaper. Jerusalem: 1983.

Kane, Thomas L. *The Mormons, a Discourse Delivered Before The Historical Society of Pennsylvania: March 26, 1850.* Philadelphia: King and Baird, Printers, Sansom Street, 1850.

Kennedy, Michael. *The Oxford Dictionary of Music.* Oxford: Oxford University Press, 1985.

Maxwell, Bruce David. "George Careless, Pioneer Musician," *Utah Historical Quarterly* (Fall 1985), 132–142.

Minutes of the Board of Regents of the University of Utah. University Archives, University of Utah, Salt Lake City, Utah, 1904–1913.

Muir, Leo J. *A Century of Mormon Activities in California.* Salt Lake City: Deseret News Press, 1955.

Nielson, John Marlowe. Private papers and documents concerning the Oratorio Society of Utah for the period 1962–1986.

Ogden Standard Examiner. Newspaper. Name varies. Ogden, Utah: 1913, 1949.

Poll, Richard D., Thomas G. Alexander, Eugene E. Campbell, and David E. Miller, eds. *Utah's History.* Provo, Utah: Brigham Young University Press, 1978.

Price, Ray. "Utah's Leading Lady Artists," *Utah Historical Quarterly* (Winter 1970), 65–85.

Pyper, George D. "In Intimate Touch With George Careless I, II, III, and IV," *The Juvenile Instructor* (March, April, May, June 1924).
—*Romance of an Old Playhouse*. Revised edition. Salt Lake City: The Deseret Press, 1937.
Roberts, B. H., *A Comprehensive History of the Church of Jesus Christ of Latter-day Saints: Century I*. 6 Vols. Provo, Utah: Brigham Young University Press, 1965.
Salt Lake Herald. Newspaper. Name varies. Salt Lake City: 1870–1920.
Salt Lake Tribune, The. Newspaper. Salt Lake City: 1871–1986.
Schonberg, Harold C. *The Great Conductors*. New York: Simon and Schuster, 1967.
Spencer, John Daniel. Letter to Mrs. Kate B. Carter, President of the Daughters of the Utah Pioneers (4 September 1941). Utah State Historical Society, Salt Lake City, Utah.
Tullidge, Edward W. *History of Salt Lake City*. Salt Lake City: Star Printing Company, 1886.
University of California at Los Angeles (UCLA) Archives. C. Clarence Neslen, telegram to Dr. Ernest C. Moore (1 December 1922).
—Dr. Ernest C. Moore, night letter to C. Clarence Neslen (2 December 1922)
University of Utah Special Collections, Manuscripts Department. Arthur Pedersen Freber Collection. MS 234.
—Oratorio Society of Utah Collection. Accession No. 738.
—Robertson, Leroy J., Collection. MS 38.
—Shepherd, Arthur, Collection. MS 103.
—Summerhays, John W., Collection. Accession No. 845.
Upton, George P. *The Standard Oratorios, Their Stories, Their Music, and Their Composers*. Chicago: A. C. McClurg and Company, 1891.
Utah Chronicle, The. Newspaper. University of Utah: 1913.
Utah Writers' Project. *Origins of Utah Place Names*. 3rd ed. Salt Lake City: Utah State Department of Public Instruction, 1941.

Throughout the index Oratorio Society of Utah is abbreviated as OSU. Photographs are indicated by boldfaced numbers. Entries for Appendix A, the only appendix indexed, include A and B column designators. Endnotes are designated by chapter and note number separated by a colon, and follow all other references. Where one or more subheadings make reference to musical compositions, these precede other subheads as a separately alphabetized unit.

Index